T0356065

Contemporary Black History

Series Editors
Peniel E. Joseph
Department of History
Tufts University Department of History
Medford, MA, USA

Yohuru Williams
Department of History
Fairfield University Department of History
Fairfield, CT, USA

Maintaining the guiding vision of founding editor Manning Marable, this series features cutting-edge scholarship in Contemporary Black History since 1945, underlining the importance of the study of history as a form of public advocacy and political activism. It focuses on the postwar period, but it also includes international black history, bringing in high-quality scholarship from around the globe. Series books incorporate varied methodologies that lend themselves to narrative richness, such as oral history and ethnography, and include high-quality interdisciplinary scholarship combining disciplines such as African-American Studies, Political Science, Sociology, Ethnic and Women's Studies, Cultural Studies, Anthropology, and Criminal Justice.

Ibram X. Kendi

The Black Campus Movement

A History of Black Student Activism

Second Edition 2025

Ibram X. Kendi
Boston University
Boston, MA, USA

Contemporary Black History
ISBN 978-3-031-37393-0   ISBN 978-3-031-37394-7   (eBook)
https://doi.org/10.1007/978-3-031-37394-7

Cover illustration: © Associated Press / Alamy Stock Photo

This Palgrave Macmillan imprint is published by the registered company Springer Nature Switzerland AG.
The registered company address is: Gewerbestrasse 11, 6330 Cham, Switzerland

If disposing of this product, please recycle the paper.

In memory of the youth who died during the Black Campus Movement.
Benjamin Brown, 22, community activist, Jackson State, May 12, 1967
Leonard D. Brown Jr., 20, Southern University, November 16, 1972
Rick "Tiger" Dowdell, 19, University of Kansas, July 16, 1970
Phillip Gibbs, 21, Jackson State, May 14, 1970
James Earl Green, 17, high school student, Jackson State, May 14, 1970
Willie E. Grimes, 20, North Carolina A&T, May 22, 1969
Samuel Hammond Jr., 18, South Carolina State, February 8, 1968
Larry D. Kimmons, 15, high school student, Pepperdine, March 12, 1969
Delano Middleton, 17, high school student, South Carolina State,
February 8, 1968
Harry Nicholas "Nick" Rice, 18, University of Kansas, July 20, 1970
Denver A. Smith, 20, Southern University, November 16, 1972
Henry E. Smith, 19, South Carolina State, February 8, 1968
Samuel "Sammy" Younge Jr., 21, Tuskegee, January 3, 1966

Preface to the Second Edition

It was the early summer of 2010. I had just finished my first academic year as a college professor. It was ten years before the police murders of George Floyd and Breonna Taylor led to the largest series of demonstrations in American history, catapulting the antiracist movement onto the international stage. All these demonstrations against racism, demonstrations for antiracism, in turn, led to a withering effort to crush this budding movement by framing antiracist work as "critical race theory" (CRT) and then "wokeism" and then diversity, equity, and inclusion (DEI) by misrepresenting CRT and wokeism and DEI as anti-White; by banning antiracist books, African American Studies, and diversity offices; by banning antiracist policies that promote racial equity, like affirmative action; and by calling for race neutrality, when race has never been neutral.

With this all happening, the fall of 2010 seems such a long time ago. It is when I went on leave from my college and began a year-long postdoctoral fellowship. I secured a reprieve from teaching and found myself in an intellectual community conducive to writing my first book—this book. Little did I know I would be researching a generation of Black students who had built an antiracist educational movement that racist Americans attacked in much the same way that racist Americans attacked the antiracist educational movement fifty years later. The roots of today's racist attacks on antiracist education can be found in the racist reaction to the Black Campus Movement (BCM). Little did I know.

My focus that summer of 2010 was on the lens of the future: the past. I had already secured research grants to visit archives in North Carolina,

Texas, Kentucky, and Missouri. I planned a month-long research drive that summer. I wanted to go where the BCM began—the South.

I rented a car. I departed from my parents' home in Northern Virginia. I headed south on Interstate 95. I visited college and university archives in southern Virginia and then headed to North and South Carolina. After some research in the Carolinas, I drove to college and university towns in Georgia, Alabama, and Mississippi. On this cross-South road trip, I'd wake up in a motel, check out, spend business hours in the town's college archive(s), drive about three or four hours to the next town, check into a motel, eat, sleep, and wake up the next day, and do it over again. I mostly visited historically Black colleges and universities (HBCUs) and little known historically White colleges and universities (HWCUs).

In Mississippi, I had to pick up a new rental car. My first rental broke down in Greenwood. After hundreds of miles each day for weeks, the car was finished with me. But I was just beginning. From western Mississippi I headed south to hit archives in Louisiana and then drove west on Interstate 10 into Texas, where I eventually conducted research at the Lyndon Baines Johnson Presidential Library in Austin. I headed north to Dallas where I visited extended family. It proved to be a pit stop in the research journey. Fueled up socially, I headed north through Oklahoma and east to college towns in Missouri, Kentucky, and West Virginia and made my way back to my parents' home in Manassas, Virginia.

I cannot recall how many college archives I visited that summer. Perhaps forty or fifty? After the summer, over the 2010–2011 academic year, I scoured hundreds of college archives and corresponded with countless archivists and librarians. I learned how vital librarians were to society, as the keepers of humanity's greatest treasure—knowledge. I also met my future partner, Sadiqa, in April of 2011, as I finished researching for this book. When we wed two years later, instead of changing her last name to mine, we decided to change both of our last names to one we chose together. The byline of the first edition of this book in 2012 was in my former surname, Rogers. The byline of this second edition, which has been made more readable and accessible and features a new chapter structure and additional concepts, is in our married surname, Kendi. I changed my middle name to what these students wanted: *Xolani*, which means "peace" in Zulu.

At the time, I did not know that my new personal relationship with this charming woman, and my older professional relationship studying these student activists, would shape much of my life over the next decade—both hidden from public view. In 2010, I was passionate about researching and chronicling African American history, in this case the story of this influential generation of antiracist Black students. Passion carried me through that solitary cross-South drive. Passion carried me through the daunting task of researching, collecting, studying, and organizing primary and secondary sources that documented Black student activism at the more than 1,000 colleges and universities in the late 1960s and early 1970s.

But I could not pinpoint, back then, the source of my passion. I can now. My passion came from how much I learned *from* these students. I learned from these students that in order to create justice and equity, colleges could not take a passive approach of merely taking down "Whites only" policies. Colleges need to aggressively and affirmatively take action against injustice and inequity. That is why these students called for what became affirmative action in college admissions and beyond. I learned from these students how it wasn't just segregationist ideas of biological racial hierarchy that were racist. Assimilationist ideas of cultural or behavioral racial hierarchy were racist ideas, too. These assimilationist ideas dominated academic disciplines in the late 1960s—a domination cloaked in the fantasy of race neutrality. That is why these students called for a new discipline, an antiracist discipline, which they called Black Studies. That is why these students called for a new HBCU, an antiracist HBCU, which they called a Black University.

I learned their antiracist vision for higher education through how these students envisioned Black Studies and the Black University. They rejected the tradition of the removed university in an ivory tower, housing the indifferent scholar who pursues knowledge for knowledge's sake and who supports the student advancing herself up the socioeconomic ladder of success. These students envisioned the university coming down from the tower, working with communities, organizing interdisciplinary research projects and service-oriented learning courses in the community, housing the scholar who is pursuing knowledge for change's sake, and supporting the student as she acquires the tools to advance her community. These students rejected higher education for assimilation and accumulation. They envisioned higher education for liberation.

I learned from these students that it is no longer enough to be "not racist" when the status quo represents widespread racial inequity and injustice. I learned from these students that people must activate themselves or remain complicit in the maintenance of the status quo. People must actively play a small or large part in dismantling the power and policy structure of racism. People must be antiracist. These students were not a monolith. I disagreed with some students on some matters. They disagreed with each other constantly on ideology, on strategy, on theories of change, on nonviolence, on goals. But they commonly agreed that they needed to look in the mirror when looking for the drivers of antiracist change. As I studied their stares into the mirror, I could not help but look in the mirror myself.

I had plenty of time to look in the summer of 2010. When I was not going through boxes and folders in college archives, I was thinking in solitude on long drives, on campus walks, at meals, in motels. The students who changed higher education changed me, fifty years later. These students set my scholarship on the path to exploring the history of racism and exploring what it means to be antiracist. This is not merely my first book; it is foundational.

Boston, MA, USA   Ibram X. Kendi

Author's Note

There are hundreds of colleges and universities named in this history book. To make the book more concise, the full name of the college or university is usually mentioned only on the first reference, particularly when "college" or "university" comes at the end of the name. For example, after the first reference to "Howard University," all subsequent references will state "Howard." Also, when colleges have well known abbreviations (NYU for New York University) or well-known shorter nicknames (UPENN for University of Pennsylvania) the full name will be spelled out upon first reference with the abbreviation or nickname in parentheses. All subsequent references will use the known abbreviation or nickname. Upon first reference, when the college or university has its location within its name (University of Kansas), the institution's location will not be noted. Upon first reference, when the college or university does not have its location within its name (Colgate University), the state or known city where it is located will be referenced. In all subsequent references, the location of the college or university will not be listed. Many of the colleges and universities have different names today than when the events described in this book happened. For example, many of the institutions now named universities used to be named colleges. For clarity of the reader, the current name of the college or university is used in this book.

Contents

LIST OF PHOTOS

INTRODUCTION

Fists balled and raised, black berets, head wraps, swaying Afros, sunglasses, black leather jackets, army fatigue coats, dashikis, African garb, Curtis Mayfield singing "We're a Winner" in the background, shouting from fuming lips and posters in the foreground: "Black Power, racism, relevancy, Black pride, revolution, equality, nonnegotiable demands, student control, Black Studies, Black University"—higher education was under siege. The academic status quo had been destabilized.

On February 13, 1969, Black student activism soared to its highest level. Nine hundred National Guard members strolled onto a University of Wisconsin campus with fixed bayonets that Thursday. Some rode on jeeps decked with machine guns. Helicopters surveyed the thousands of protesters in Madison. If the presence of city police had stirred campus activism a few days earlier when Black students kicked off their strike, then the National Guard whipped students into a frenzy. After picketing and obstructing traffic during the day, about ten thousand students, with Black torchbearers leading the way, walked in the cold from the university to the Wisconsin capitol building in the largest student march of the Black Campus Movement. Their bodies may have been freezing that night, but their mouths were on fire: "On strike, shut it down!" "Support the black demands!"[1]

Meanwhile that day, the nationally renowned San Francisco State University strike—a protest that popularized the mantra "On strike, shut it down!"—entered its third month. At University of California, Berkeley (UC Berkeley), police brutality caused the two-week-old boycott of classes to escalate. Black Student Alliance (BSA) members at Roosevelt University in Chicago continued their week of disrupting classes to teach Black Studies. The night before, BSA members rejected a deal offered by Dean of Students Lawrence Silverman that included amnesty and written responses to their demands for a Black Studies Department under their control. In a statement, the BSA yelled, "We will continue our program, BY ANY MEANS NECESSARY!!!" Black students at the flagship campus of the University of Illinois delivered a list of demands to administrators on February 13. They called for the establishment of a Black Cultural Center and a Black Studies Department and the hiring of fifty Black residence hall counselors and 500 Black professors.[2]

At Duke University in North Carolina, forty-eight Black collegians entered the administration building in the early morning, walked to the central records section, and told the clerical workers they had to leave. They nailed the doors shut, threatened to burn university records if the police were called, and renamed the space "Malcolm X Liberation School." They issued thirteen demands, including the creation of a Black Studies Department controlled by students, money for a Black Student Union (BSU) building, a Black dorm, and an end to "racist policies."[3]

At City College of New York, also on February 13, President Buell Gallagher stood on a snow-covered lawn in front of the administration building and delivered a speech that swirled coldly around affirming the five demands issued a week earlier. Livid, since they wanted a firm commitment that day, 300 Black and Puerto Rican students swarmed into the administration building and ejected its workers. They plastered their demands on walls and ceilings, and one student waved a sign that read, "Free Huey: Che Guevara, Malcolm X University."[4]

While City College students occupied the building for three and half hours, more than 90 percent of students at Mississippi Valley State University avoided classroom buildings. Stokely Carmichael had launched "Black Power" into America's political atmosphere in 1966, in Greenwood, ten miles from Mississippi Valley State. Wilhelm Joseph Jr., of Trinidad, like Carmichael, had been radically moved by Carmichael's call for Black power. Joseph successfully ran for student body president on a ticket that boasted, "We are going to move this place! This is a black college." Under his leadership, Mississippi Valley State students pressed for the ability to don African garb and Afros, to study people of African descent in their courses, and to terminate campus paternalism, student powerlessness, and the poor quality of faculty and facilities. In total, they presented twenty-six demands leading to the boycott. State police and campus security officers swooped in and transported 196 strikers to Jackson, imprisoned a dozen others, and put out a warrant on four leaders (including Joseph). Close to 200 protesters were expelled.[5]

February 13, 1969, looms as the most impactful day of the Black Campus Movement. If there was a day, or *the* day, that Black campus activists forced the racial reconstitution of higher education, it was February 13, 1969. Black students disrupted higher education in almost every area of the nation—the Midwest in Illinois and Wisconsin, the Northeast in New York, the Upper South in North Carolina, the Deep South in Mississippi, the West Coast in the Bay Area. It was a day that emitted the anger, determination, and agency of a generation that stood on the cutting edge of antiracist change. It was like no other day in the history of Black higher education—a history of racism and antiracism, accommodation and advancement, isolation and community. Like the Black Campus Movement it highlighted, this day had been in the making for more than a hundred years and changed the course of higher education for decades to come.

February 13, 1969, stands at the apex of the Black Campus Movement, the subject of this book. During this movement, which emerged in 1965 and petered out by 1972, hundreds of thousands of Black campus activists (and sympathizers), aided on some campuses by White, Latino, Native, and Asian students, requested, demanded, demonstrated, and protested for an antiracist learning experience. Activist ideologies ranged from reformist to revolutionary. In most cases, students considered an antiracist education one that engaged Black literature from the perspective of Black people and gave students the intellectual tools to fix a society broken by racism. Black students organized at over a thousand colleges and universities, in every state except Alaska. When they principally utilized *campus activism* against higher education during this eight-year social movement, they were *Black campus activists*, distinct from both the many Black students who chose not to participate and students engaged off campus in the myriad Black power groups in the late 1960s and early 1970s.[6]

To disentangle this social movement from other threads of activism during the Black Power Movement (BPM), from the campus movements waged by other racial groups at the time, and from Black student off-campus activism during the classical civil rights period (1954–1965), this struggle among antiracist Black students at historically White and Black institutions to reconstitute higher education from 1965 to 1972 has been termed the *Black Campus Movement*. Even though they both tend to be conceptually located in what is widely known as the Black Student Movement, this late 1960s Black power campus struggle represented a profound ideological, tactical, and spatial shift from early 1960s off-campus civil rights student confrontations. They were not merely different phases of the Black Student Movement. They were unique social movements or, more precisely, separate but interlocking tussles in the *Long Black Student Movement* from 1919 to 1972.[7]

Akin to the Black Arts Movement, Black Theology Movement, and Black Feminist Movement, to name a few of the Black power social movements scholars have distinguished, this period of Black student activism should be understood as a social movement in its own right. In addition, even though Black students battled the same structure in the same space with similarities in their ideas and tactics and were sometimes allies, their struggle must be conceptualized as being independent of White campus activism. *The New York Times* published a story on May 12, 1969, with the headline, "The Campus Revolutions: One Is Black, One White." The BCM was a part of and apart from three larger social movements: the multidecade-long Black Student Movement, which began after World War I; the multiracial student movement of the Long Sixties; and the multiobjective Black Power Movement of the late 1960s and early 1970s.[8]

At HBCUs and HWCUs, Black campus activists formed the nation's first chain of politically and culturally antiracist BSUs, under various names, and gained control of many student government associations (SGAs). They utilized these BSUs and student government associations as pressure groups to pursue a range of campus alterations, including an end to paternalism and racist policy and the addition of more Black students, faculty, administrators, and Black Studies courses, programs, and departments. They fought at almost every HBCU for a Black-controlled, oriented, and radical Black University to replace what they theorized as the White-controlled, assimilationist, bourgeoisie, accommodationist Negro university. Their ultimate aim was to revolutionize higher education.

Black campus activists did not succeed in revolutionizing higher education. However, they did succeed in centering a series of historically marginalized academic ideas, questions, frames, methods, perspectives, subjects, and pursuits. They were able to succeed in pushing into higher education a profusion of antiracist reforms—in the form of people, programs, and literature. Most decisively, but least chronicled, Black campus activists succeeded in challenging the academy's century-old racist ideals. The 1954 *Brown v. Board of Education of Topeka* decision, which deemed segregationist policy in public education to be unconstitutional, did not do this. Neither did the Civil Rights Act of 1964, which outlawed overtly discriminatory employment practices and segregation in public accommodations. The BCM forced the rewriting of the racist constitution of higher education, the central finding of this historical text.[9]

In 1965, there existed at least four entrenched racist elements that had long undergirded the racist constitution of higher education: the *moralized contraption, standardization of exclusion, assimilationist curricula*, and *ladder altruism*. The moralized contraption was a system of rules, in place at practically all HBCUs, that regulated student freedom and agency. HBCU students were told when to eat, sleep, study, and socialize. Chapel, convocation, and class attendance were mandatory, and women faced additional restrictions at HBCUs. These rules, injected by White and Black assimilationists, were meant to Christianize and civilize and, ultimately, to induce submission to the racist, capitalist, patriarchal American order. The ideas that justified these rules were deeply colonialist, racist, and sexist, and the moralized contraption resembled the off-campus segregationist directives that continuously kept African Americans a step away from enslavement for a century after the Civil War. In place of the contraption, Black campus activists demanded moral freedom.

Moreover, the exclusion of Black people from faculties, student bodies, administrations, coaching staffs—from every facet of the communities at HWCUs—was standardized because the exclusion was not by happenstance. Inequity is never a coincidence. The exclusion stemmed from longstanding racist policies and practices. The prohibition or marginalization of Black scholarship from curricula was standardized by academics at both HWCUs and HBCUs. Black people were customarily excluded from many (usually private) HBCU professorial bodies and presidencies into the 1920s and from boards of trustees into the 1960s. There were instances in which Black concepts and people found their way into these terrains, but these were the exceptions to the rule, to the standard. The desegregation movement created many of these exceptions, as did the small postwar flow of Black students into HWCUs. Black students demanded more than exceptions; they desired the standardization of inclusion.

Exclusion was not merely standardized in 1965. White people and their cultures were standardized in scholarship and, thereby, in curricula. The histories and cultures of White people, the literature produced by White people, scholarship on White people, and courses focusing on White people were all standardized. European history and literature, for example, were not presented as such. They were presented as world history and literature that everyone in the world should learn, while not learning African and Asian and Native history and literature. Whatever ends up being the standard ends up being believed to be superior. And this purportedly superior European (and Euro-American) way of knowing and being was systematically imparted to students of all races in courses. This *assimilationist curricula* ended up educating generations of Black students to be White, to assimilate into the cultures of White people. But in the late 1960s, inspired by Black power ideas of cultural pride and Black solidarity, these Black campus activists rejected assimilationist curricula; they demanded antiracist curricula.

When they were not imparting assimilationist curricula academics and higher education officials were instituting and encouraging ladder altruism. They taught altruistic Black college students to believe that their personal advancement up the American ladder of success advanced Black America as a whole through the societal doors they opened and through their function as role models. Meanwhile, academics, politicians, and capital allowed colleges and universities to serve as ladders, lifting Black students up politically, economically, and culturally from the Black masses. In contrast to ladder altruism, Black campus activists demolished the personal and institutional ladders and demanded an ideological and tactical reconnection to their communities through grassroots activism.

In the end, Black campus activists during the BCM challenged the rules and regulations (moralized contraption), Black marginalization from practically all facets of higher education (standardization of exclusion), Eurocentric courses (assimilationist curricula), and an academia that encouraged and facilitated their removal from the masses (ladder altruism).

Literature on the BCM has been largely subsumed under the historiographies of the Student Movement, Black Student Movement, and Black Power Movement, with White students, early 1960s civil rights protests, and off-campus activism, respectively, receiving most of the attention. The Black campus struggle has been largely relegated to and scattered among these three areas of inquiry. When the BCM has been studied, the treatments have almost always been campus specific, as historians have detailed the struggle at the University of Illinois, University of Pennsylvania (UPENN), Columbia University, Rutgers University, Cornell University, New York University (NYU), and San Francisco State—to name the most expansive and prominent campus studies. The South Carolina State University (1968) and Jackson State University (1970) massacres of Black students have also been examined. *The Black Campus Movement* provides the first comprehensive national examination of Black campus activism at historically Black and White four-year colleges and universities in the late 1960s and early 1970s. It situates each campus struggle in the national movement and delivers a national purview for future campus studies.[10]

The Black Campus Movement not only centers the combating of the racist constitution of higher education at the locus of this history. It connects the activism at HWCUs and HBCUs. It continues the recent scholarly revelation of the array of radicalism at HBCUs in the late 1960s and early 1970s, the multitude of women activists, Black power organizing with White people, and Black student activism prior to 1960.[11]

At the same time, *The Black Campus Movement* presents the range and attainments of Black power, negotiating local with national activism, connecting and disconnecting Black power to and from civil rights, elaborating on the most recent golden stretch of Black educational antiracism, providing the movement a context for the rise of Black Studies, and showing the vicious backlash to the BCM. It identifies 1969 (as opposed to 1968) as the peak of Black student activism, at both HWCUs and HBCUs, and the national clamor for relevancy, including Black Studies. It pulls the origin of the movement back from 1967 or 1968 to 1965, while demonstrating that the Orangeburg Massacre (February 8, 1968) and the assassination of Martin Luther King Jr. (April 4, 1968) did not spark the struggle, as some scholars have claimed. Those societal tragedies only accelerated it. This book proves that the movement did not start at HWCUs, nor did the most "militant" protests disrupt those institutions. It complicates the more celebrated story of campus activism at HWCUs and expounds on this emergent literature by illuminating the largely unknown struggle at rural liberal arts colleges, remote institutions in the Great Plains, Northwest, and New England, and recently desegregated southern HWCUs.[12]

The study enters the discourse at the time of an evolving battle among the increasingly powerful "race-neutrality" and "colorblind" advocates, who oppose multiculturalism and antiracism and are reinscribing the pre-1965 racist constitution of higher education. At the same time, the vines of diversity continue to ensnare the halls of the academy and grow further away from their roots of resistance—systematically unearthed and revealed at a national level for the first time in this book.

Neither the cultural nor political-economic features of the movement—their cause and effect—are shortchanged during this historical analysis. The words, deeds, and perspectives of Black campus activists reside at the center of this investigation. The documents they produced and their voices, presented in publications during the movement, provided the bulk of the evidence. Oral history interviews of activists conducted after the struggle, secondary campus-specific studies, and documents produced by the marginal actors of the movement—administrators, professors, and Black political leaders, for instance—enhanced this story. Campus-specific ideas, outlooks, reactions, requests, demands, protests, and implementations were synthesized into a national depiction of the movement.

The first two chapters provide an introduction to the history of Black higher education in the United States before the emergence of the BCM in 1965. Chapters 3, 4, 5, and 6 discuss the activist response to racism and segregation on and off campus by chronicling the Long Black Student Movement from 1919 to 1962. More than thirty years of mass Black student activism set the stage for the movement. In particular, the successes, failures, repression, and ideological and tactical lessons emanating from the civil rights movement (and early Black power) in the first half of the 1960s provided the immediate social conditions that spawned the BCM. Chapter 7 presents this making of the movement from 1963 to 1965, and Chap. 8 identifies the factors that refined and circulated Black student ideology during the BCM. Since they on occasion reference the BCM and the 1960s, these eight chapters are not traditional historical narratives but rather provide the historical context for the emergence of the BCM.

Chapters 9 and 10 provide a narrative historical overview of the BCM. Chapters 11 and 12 delve deeper into the movement by examining the disposition of Black student organizers—their demands, protests, and support—while Chaps. 13 and 14 disclose the forms of opposition and repression students faced. The final chapter lays out the new ideals (and reforms) their struggle brought to life or, rather, forced to the center. An epilogue providing a posthistory of Black campus activism and the revitalization of the racist constitution through "egalitarian exclusion" concludes *The Black Campus Movement*.

CHAPTER 1

An "Island Within": Black Students in the Nineteenth Century

People of African descent educated themselves for thousands of years in scholastic centers across Africa. They learned about and analyzed the social, physical, and spiritual world of antiquity in renowned universities in Egypt that taught legendary Greek philosophers and, later, in the bustling West African cities of Timbuktu and Jenne. When hundreds of thousands of Africans were snatched from their communities and enslaved in the United States, they were shut out of colleges and universities for two centuries, as were most Americans.[1]

Outside of the formal academy, African people maintained their storied tradition of higher learning by informal means and in clandestine schools. Eighteenth-century poet Phillis Wheatley and the multitalented Benjamin Banneker both received a home-schooled higher education. Princeton president John Witherspoon secretly tutored John Chavis, who went on to study at Washington and Lee University in Virginia in the late 1790s. (His great-great-grandson Ben Chavis later powered the Black Campus Movement at the University of North Carolina at Charlotte.) Sent out to a religious family as a teenager, Maria Stewart found refuge in the family library and took advantage of religious teaching to become an intrepid nineteenth-century public speaker for women's rights and abolition. Jemmy, Gabriel Prosser, and Nat Turner are a few of the innumerable enslaved and free Africans who employed their higher learning in the planning and execution of revolts of the enslaved, which invariably led to revolts of enslavers against Black learning.[2]

© The Author(s), under exclusive license to Springer Nature Switzerland AG 2025
I. X. Kendi, *The Black Campus Movement*, Contemporary Black History, https://doi.org/10.1007/978-3-031-37394-7_1

Alexander Twilight, who graduated from Vermont's Middlebury College in 1823, became the first known person of African descent to earn a bachelor's degree in the United States. Likely the son of biracial parents, he probably passed for White. He parlayed his education into positions in the pulpit and the Vermont General Assembly in 1836, becoming the earliest known state legislator with African ancestry. Edward A. Jones (Amherst College) and John Russwurm (Bowdoin College) became the second and third graduates in 1826. As Russwurm established the nation's first Black newspaper, *Freedom's Journal*, Jones attended Trinity College in Connecticut, securing Black America's first M.A. degree in 1830.[3]

Promoters of free Black removal from the United States to Africa (or what they termed "colonization") welcomed the emigration of Jones, who helped found Sierra Leone's first Western colonial college, and Russwurm, who became a school superintendent in Liberia. Quite a few of the early Black graduates and educators bowed to the relatively conservative dictates of the day that posed Black emigration to Africa as the solution to the enslaving society's racial quandary: what to do with free Black people. These pioneers were imbued with an assimilationist Pan-Africanism, a belief that African Americans should impart their "superior"

Photo 1.1 Alexander Twilight (Supplied by staff, Special Collections, Middlebury College, Middlebury, Vermont)

civilization to "backward" Africans. Their educational benefactors were often the American Colonization Society (ACS). Enslavers desiring the ejection of free Black people, Christians distressed by Africa's "pagans," and those who believed emigration must follow Black emancipation—the "colonizationists," as Carter G. Woodson termed them—were an antebellum force.[4]

These White colonizationists held assimilationist ideas, meaning they expressed that Black people can be civilized in the mores of White people. They promoted education for colonization, or educating African Americans to go back to Africa and advance an "inferior" race. Colonizationists tried to inaugurate schools in the 1820s in Newark, New Jersey, and Hartford, Connecticut, but their schemes were sometimes foiled by Black assimilationists guided by ladder altruism. These Black thinkers asserted that both races were capable of receiving the same education for the same purpose—training a talented few to lead and provide a model for the many in the United States. Joining these Black assimilationists in opposition to the colonizationists were some White abolitionists, who also held assimilationist ideas. These White abolitionists believed they were endowed with a civil or Christian mission to educate African American leaders to uplift and civilize their communities in the United States. This relatively unknown ideological dispute *between* assimilationists who supported education for Americanization and education for colonization was the first great debate over the function of Black higher education.

Assembling in Philadelphia in 1830 and 1831, the First Annual Convention of the People of Color went on record as opposing the ACS's colonization rationale for the higher education of "African youth." The delegates proposed the establishment of a Black college in New Haven, Connecticut, so Black Americans could receive "classical knowledge which ... causes man to soar up to those high intellectual enjoyments ... and drowns in oblivion's cup their moral degradation." But New Haven residents voted against it. Unyielding, the convention delegates, with the support of the New England Anti-Slavery Society, struck a deal with Noyes Academy in Canaan, New Hampshire. They would build an interracial, manual labor school.[5]

As quickly as the daylight of upper learning beamed for New England Black people, night fell. In 1835, 300 White Canaan residents, with a hundred oxen, dragged the schoolhouse a mile down the road into a nearby swamp, where they set it on fire. "No sable son of Africa remains to darken our horizon," a speaker proclaimed after the institutional lynching.[6]

Despite the resistance, the HBCU idea gained traction, particularly since new pages were needed for the list of talented Black Americans turned away from HWCUs. No more than fifteen were admitted before 1840. Even though they warmed to the Black college idea, Black and White abolitionists stalled the growth of HBCUs for colonization, compelling colonizationists to focus collegiate funding on aspiring Black emigrants. Black Americans' own stirring to create a Black college for Americanization was likewise halted, until Richard Humphreys, a Philadelphia Quaker, bequeathed $10,000 to educate people of African descent. In 1837, his money gave birth to what is now Cheyney University outside of Philadelphia.[7]

Twelve years later, in 1849, Charles Avery founded Pennsylvania's Allegheny Institute. In 1851, New York abolitionist Myrtilla Miner founded the University of the District of Columbia (UDC) amid a groundswell of antagonism in the enslaving city. The Presbytery of New Castle in Pennsylvania garnered funds to build Lincoln University in 1854. Two years later, Cincinnati Methodists founded Wilberforce University, which served the mulatto children of enslavers until the Civil War. Deep in in debt, school officials appealed to the African Methodist Episcopal Church. With Bishop Daniel A. Payne leading the way as the nation's earliest Black president of a U.S. college, in 1863 Wilberforce became the first college controlled by Black Americans.[8]

Like many HWCUs at the time, these initial HBCUs primarily provided preparatory programs—special high schools and sometimes junior colleges—for students aiming to teach, preach, embark on a mission, or attend a university. Lincoln (PA) became the first bachelor's-degree-granting HBCU in 1865.[9]

As antiracist change flung open the doors of HBCUs, racist tradition kept the revolving doors of HWCUs closing in Black faces. In 1845, Dartmouth College president Nathan Lord refused to "have a flood of blacks" at his New Hampshire college because he doubted "the fitness of Africans," a rare *doubt* in the age of outright dismissals. "They will need cultivation as a people, for centuries, before many of them will hold their way with long civilized and Christian Saxons, if, indeed, that is ever to be expected, which I doubt." Nonetheless, unlike many, President Lord kept his college open to "help a struggling people," revealing his assimilationist ideas.[10]

In 1847, David John Peck, the first Black American admitted to medical practice, graduated from Chicago's Rush Medical College. The college was named after one of the early abolitionists and scientific racists, Benjamin Rush, who claimed African phenotypic features verified leprosy in a 1799 academic talk. Founded to accept all students, regardless of race or gender, New York Central College allowed Black students to enroll upon its opening in 1849 in upstate New York. Charles L. Reason, an abolitionist, suffragist, and son of Haitian immigrants, joined its faculty as a professor of belles lettres (Greek, Latin, French) and an adjunct professor of mathematics. As two other Black scholars accompanied the nation's first known Black professor at an interracial college in 1850, Lucy Stanton, the daughter of Cleveland abolitionists, became the first Black woman to graduate from a U.S. college. She completed the "ladies course" of study at Oberlin College in Ohio.[11]

Meanwhile, that fall in 1850, Martin Delany entered Harvard University's medical school along with Daniel Laing and Isaac Snowden. When the three Black students entered the lecture hall for their first class, the noisy room of 113 White students fell into a loud silence. Harvard's White male students "endured" the three Black pariahs. But when the faculty voted to admit a White woman in December 1850, within days the White males met and passed a resolution barring both White women and Black men. Concerning the latter, the resolution stated, "We cannot consent to be identified as fellow students with blacks." The faculty upheld the racist (and sexist) policy. Snowden and Laing finished at Dartmouth with the help of the ACS, setting out for Liberia in 1854.[12]

But Delany, intending to practice in the States, was crushed when Boston abolitionists did not press for his readmission. The ordeal led Delany to later write of his "sad, sad disappointment" with White abolitionists, hastening his ideological journey to Pan-Africanism, Black colonization, and antiracism. Even as he advised emigration, unlike assimilationists, Delany demanded education for self-determination and self-respect at home, the final thrust of Black thought that birthed Black higher education.[13]

As enslaved Black people emancipated themselves and in turn dictated the course of the war in 1862, Mary Jane Patterson, the daughter of fugitives from Raleigh, North Carolina, became the nation's first known Black woman to receive a B.A. degree. Fanny M. Jackson and Frances J. Norris were next in line at Oberlin, finishing in 1865, the year before Sarah Jane Woodson accepted a professorship—the first black woman to do so—in

English and Latin at Wilberforce. In total, twenty-seven Black Americans, all of whom could fit in a single classroom, had received bachelor's degrees prior to the passage of the Emancipation Proclamation in 1863.[14]

When the Civil War drew to a close, aside from family and land, the newly freed searched for knowledge. Northern White missionaries descended on the South to douse the "downtrodden." They found legions of antiracist Black educators creating their own schools to obtain what had been kept from them—self-determination, self-respect, equality, power, and civil rights. "They have a natural praiseworthy pride in keeping their educational institutions in their own hands," reported William Channing Grant, a White American Missionary Association teacher from New England. "What they desire is assistance without control." Black educators and White missionaries launched a cause for organized education between 1861 and 1871, which W.E.B. Du Bois described as "one of the marvelous occurrences of the modern world; almost without parallel in the history of civilization."[15]

They started building schools as early as 1861 in territories occupied by Union forces, which was the origin, in 1862, of Western University in Kansas and LeMoyne-Owen College in Memphis. The movement reached its peak as the battle cries ceased. From 1865 to 1867, a staggering minimum of seventeen HBCUs were established. Five states founded institutions, along with the American Missionary Association, Presbyterians, Methodists, Baptists, Episcopalians, United Church of Christ, and African Methodist Episcopal (AME) Church. The formerly enslaved Rev. Richard C. Coulter, from Augusta, Georgia, aided in the birth of Morehouse College in 1867, the same year Congress chartered Howard University in Washington, DC. As many as two hundred private HBCUs opened in the 1870s and 1880s, but most closed not long after due to constraints related to finances, racism, and clientele.[16]

The antebellum debate over education for colonization or Americanization was eclipsed by a relative Reconstruction consensus on the mission of Black higher education, forged by progressive assimilationists. Black higher education would utilize European classical curricula to school intellect, self-reliance, moral regeneration, Christian orthodoxy, and the tools for American citizenship. HBCUs were to raise an army of teachers and preachers (and to a lesser extent professionals, politicians, and entrepreneurs) to guide the race out of their hundreds of years of political captivity, forced illiteracy, and supposed moral degradation.

Assimilationists who desired a higher education that trained Black students to accomodate to political and economic captivity had to sit on the sidelines of history. However, they bided their time and planned. The most prominent postbellum accommodating assimilationist, General S.C. Armstrong, founded Hampton University in Southern Virginia in 1868. Compared to White people, who had three centuries of "experience in organizing the forces about him," African Americans "had three centuries of experience in general demoralization and behind that, paganism," he once wrote. At Hampton, Armstrong created a model of education for accommodating assimilationists that would take hold of Black higher education with the support of Southern segregationists and Northern capital when they deconstructed the gains of Reconstruction.[17]

Armstrong endeavored to mold teachers who would go out and fashion a submissive, stationary, easily exploitable Black laboring class through the language of morals, Christianity, virtue, thrift, and freedom. "The Hampton-Tuskegee curriculum was not centered on trade or agricultural training; it was centered on the training of teachers," according to James D. Anderson. Of the 723 Hampton graduates in its first twenty classes, 84 percent became teachers. The habitually exaggerated manual-industrial component to the Hampton curriculum was to "work the prospective teachers long and hard so that they would embody, accept, and preach an ethic of hard toil or the 'dignity of labor,'" Anderson explained. Armstrong's new solution to the old problem (what to do with free Black people) resembled the model of education for colonization. Instead of training teachers for the maintenance of colonialism and White supremacy in Africa, Armstrong trained teachers for the maintenance of exploitative labor relations and White supremacy in the American South.[18]

Still, Armstrong failed to convince people like Virginian Better Puryear, that higher education for control was possible. Education "instills in his mind that he is competent to share in the higher walks of life, prompts him to despise those menial pursuits to which his race has been doomed, and invites him to enter into competition with the white man," which he is destined to lose due to his inferiority, Puryear stated in 1877.[19]

At the dawn of Black higher education in the mid-nineteenth century, White presidents, administrators, and professors were the norm at HWCUs and HBCUs, with credentialed Black Americans excluded, unavailable, or unrecognized. At every HBCU, students were imprisoned with bars of regulations by means of the widespread institutionalization of the moralized contraption. HBCUs emerged as moralizing plantations. This contraption was politically configured to teach subordination. It was philosophically roused by religious affiliations, the presence of women (who purportedly needed an additional set of patriarchal rules), the racist ideas of the nineteenth century (such as the hypersexuality, immaturity, intellectual inferiority, and laziness of African Americans), the concomitant desire among ladder altruists to nurture or demonstrate racial equality and Black civilization to White Americans, and the fact that initially many colleges were only colleges in name, having mostly boarding students of elementary, junior, and high school age.

Replicating the White New England schools and colleges, educators wrote assimilationist ideas into the original HBCU curricula. Just as these lily-white New England institutions did not label themselves Euro-American or White institutions, they did not brand their literature and scholarship and curricula as such, either. It was "classical" education, teaching "high culture." Latin and Greek erudition were placed on a pedagogical pedestal at HBCUs. To gain admission to the 1868–1869 freshman class at Howard, students needed to read "two books of Caesar, six orations of Cicero, the *Bucolics*, the *Georgics*, six books of Virgil's *Aeneid*, Sallust's *Cataline*, two books of Xenophon's *Anabasis*, and the first two books of Homer's *Iliad*," according to graduate school dean Dwight Oliver Wendell Holmes.[20]

Amid the European topics, courses and content specializing in Africa were practically nonexistent. But few objected. Some Black Americans had internalized the racist ideas that Africa was figuratively the "dark continent," shaded from the sun of progress, civilization, and history. Many believed that people of African descent were innately inferior or that slavery or colonialism made them inferior. Academics accentuated cultural assimilation along with Black civic grooming for lifelong swimming in the White American mainstream.

Initially, the standardization of exclusion of Black literature did not seem to unnerve many Black students. If anything, many were motivated to demonstrate that they could learn anything White people could. Others were like Richard Wright, who shortly after graduating from Clark Atlanta University in 1876 used the classics, through words from Humboldt and Herodotus, to assert that "these differences of race, so called, are a mere matter of color and not of brain."[21]

With more than 90 percent of Black Americans in the South in the decades after the Civil War, HBCUs were effectively the only option for most aspiring collegians, unless they wanted to trek up North to the meager number of desegregated HWCUs. Discouragement, custom, and then laws preserved the standardization of exclusion of Black Americans from HWCUs in the South. One of the few exceptions was Maryville College in Tennessee, which boasted thirteen African Americans among its 137 students in 1876. Kentucky's Berea College, a liberal arts institution that admitted its first Black student in 1866, stood as the foremost exception. Thereafter, twenty-seven White students left the school "in a disgraceful manner." Undaunted and committed to principle, school officials kept the admission gates open, and Black Americans were enrolled at Berea during the next few decades—96 during the 1866–1867 school year (with 91 White students) and 129 (with 144 White students) in 1877–1878. Berea alone prevailed as the only truly integrated college in the nineteenth century.[22]

Formerly enslaved people of varying ages attended HBCUs in large numbers during the Reconstruction Era. In the fall of 1872, a 16-year-old coal miner from West Virginia, with a small satchel containing all his possessions, made the five-hundred-mile trek to Southern Virginia, begging and working for travel money along the way. Up from slavery, with fifty cents in his dirty pocket and starving for food and admission to the school of his dreams, Booker T. Washington secured a position as a janitor and enrolled at Hampton. An astute 10-year-old Anna "Annie" Julia Haywood (later known as Anna Julia Cooper) entered Saint Augustine's University in 1868. Over the next nearly fourteen years in Raleigh, she distinguished herself academically, honing her pioneering voice from the South. She followed the footsteps of Mary Jane Patterson, a fellow native of Raleigh, and enrolled at Oberlin in 1881. During that historic year, the AME Church founded Morris Brown College (Georgia), Southern University (Louisiana) was established, Booker T. Washington created Tuskegee University (Alabama), and Spelman College opened its doors in Atlanta as the only institution for Black women offering college courses. Cooper pursued the classical academic track typically restricted to men at Oberlin, as did Ida Gibbs (Hunt) and Mary Church (Terrell), who graduated with her in 1884. Oberlin alumni made up an estimated 75 of the 194 Black graduates from northern colleges between 1865 and 1895.[23]

The year after this dynamic, soon-to-be activist trio finished, a brilliant and confident 17-year-old from Western Massachusetts walked onto the grounds of Fisk University in the fall of 1885, "thrilled to be for the first time among so many people of my own color." However, in W.E.B. Du Bois's three years in Nashville, there persisted "an abyss between my education and the truth of the world." Exemplifying the abyss, Du Bois selected for his commencement speech in 1888 German Chancellor Otto von Bismarck, who had just hosted a conference of European colonizers of Africa in Berlin. Like most HBCU faculty, Fisk professors did not discuss the imperial rivalry to exploit foreign materials, markets, and labor. "I was blithely European and imperialist in outlook; democratic as democracy was conceived in America," Du Bois later lamented.[24]

On the other hand, Du Bois displayed his "two-ness," his conscious Blackness, by seeking out his racial peers at nearby institutions when he enrolled at Harvard in the fall of 1888. Thus the indignities he encountered on campus—being mistaken as a waiter or rejections from student organizations—were alleviated by his small support system and maturing sense of self. He had his Black "island within," he said. He did not try to venture into the sea of Whiteness. He knew he "was in Harvard but not of it."[25]

As the federal government withdrew from the South in the 1870s and the movement to disenfranchise southern Black Americans and separate public space gained momentum at the turn of the century, segregationists carved up the South based on the color line. Clark Atlanta had its state appropriations cut off by Georgia lawmen in 1888. In 1890, the University of Maryland law school ejected its "two intelligent young negroes." Tennessee legislators compelled Maryville College to segregate in 1901. The Kentucky state legislature passed the Day Law in 1904 barring interracial schools, extinguishing America's brightest beacon of educational integration, the year after Carter G. Woodson, the father of Black history, earned his Berea degree. Berea did not resume admitting Black Americans until the 1950s.[26]

Meanwhile, segregationists substantially reduced the funding of public HBCUs and eradicated anyone and anything at these colleges that undermined Southern White political supremacy and capital accumulation. For instance, in 1878 Mississippi segregationists reduced Alcorn State University's annual appropriation, ended state scholarships, reduced classical offerings, and gave the HBCU a new focus: "scientific and practical knowledge of agriculture, horticulture, and the mechanical arts." Accommodating assimilationists bent to their will. Writing a benefactor in 1894, Alabama A&M University principal W. H. Councill coolly asserted, "The south has done more for the negro than any other section of the globe." Antiracists and progressive assimilationists stood their ground. Thomas DeSaille Tucker, a graduate of Oberlin and the founding president of Florida A&M University in 1887, emphasized liberal arts in his teacher training program until state officials forced his resignation in 1901.[27]

Southern segregationists were supported by Northern bankers, merchants, railroad tycoons, and other corporate principals, including John F. Slater and John D. Rockefeller Sr. The power of Southern politicians,

Northern corporate philanthropists, and accommodating assimilationists fractured the Reconstruction consensus of Black higher education for advancement. Then the second dispute on the function of Black higher education unfolded. Should Black higher education teach African Americans to accommodate to disenfranchised, separate, second-class citizenship as semiskilled agricultural, mechanical, and manual laborers controlled by White capital? Or should Black higher education provide (White) liberal arts training in order to equalize the races and give Black Americans the intellectual means to fight for civil rights and for the radicals—power? Accommodation or power—that was higher education's demarcating line, crisscrossing the deepening color line.

Tuskegee president Booker T. Washington emerged as the chief Black proponent of the accommodating assimilationists (even as he secretly supported civil rights causes). "The wisest among my race understand that the agitation of questions of social equality is the extremest folly," Washington stated at the 1895 Atlanta Exposition. Du Bois led the charge for the progressive assimilationists, crystallizing their philosophy when he declared the need for a college-trained "Talented Tenth," because "the Negro race, like all races, is going to be saved by its exceptional men."[28]

This Washington/Du Bois debate has been overplayed in the history of Black higher education. Downplayed has been the pervasive sway of White capitalists and assimilationists—those whom William H. Watkins termed the "white architects of black education." They used their power and capital to build a system with assimilationist curricula, the moralized contraption, and ladder altruism, an educational system that buttressed the exploitation of Black labor, an educational system purposely designed for control. By 1900, capitalists and Christian missionaries marched in unison, like European colonialists around the globe, financing HBCUs in the name of civilization, progress, and moral growth, when their real aim was to establish White political supremacy and capitalist growth from cheap and accommodating Black labor.[29]

By the outbreak of the First World War, the vast majority of Black students attended HBCUs affiliated with missionary societies and churches supported primarily by corporate philanthropies like the Slater Fund, Rosenwald Fund, Jeannes Foundation, Peabody Education Fund, and Carnegie Corporation. Grants were steeped in accommodationism *and* concepts of evolution. "Race relations would gradually change, presumably for the better, if Blacks were willing to remain within the boundaries of 'acceptable' behavior," read the evolutionary offer, Watkins, explained.[30]

CHAPTER 2

"We Were Invisible": Black Students in the Twentieth Century

At the turn of the century, HBCUs increasingly laid out the red carpet for trustees, state and federal politicians, and philanthropists to court their political and economic favor in grand spectacles that bordered on minstrelsy. The artistic, moral, aesthetic, and manual talents of the students and the college were displayed with more pomp than intellectual substance. Usually, African American students were ordered by HBCU presidents to sing spirituals, which to the benefactors harkened back to the good ole days of slavery. Some singers of spirituals resented the ritual but went along out of adoration for the president or the benefactors' money or fear of punishment. In the 1920s, some students refused to demean themselves and sing, including Howard students and future civil rights organizer Ella Baker of Shaw University in North Carolina. But the slavery shows went on and the money poured in to pacify the Talented Tenth. Many HBCUs resembled plantations, with White and Black overseers for presidents, enslaved faculty and staff, students as the cotton, and racist power as the enslavers. In April 1906, Booker T. Washington welcomed a host of powerful figures, from Secretary of War William H. Taft to steel mogul Andrew Carnegie to Harvard president Charles William Eliot. They were celebrating Tuskegee's four-day "silver jubilee," which intermixed speeches with spirituals sung by a student choir and flowing donations.[1]

At the same time, though, during the early years of the twentieth century, HBCUs not following the Hampton-Tuskegee model, namely,

I. X. Kendi, *The Black Campus Movement*, Contemporary Black History, https://doi.org/10.1007/978-3-031-37394-7_2

Clark Atlanta, Fisk, Howard, and Talladega College in Alabama, started to become cradles of Black scholarship, which blossomed after World War I. To Allen Ballard, these Black scholars "provided the basic intellectual antidote to the venom of racism pouring forth from both Northern and Southern holders of white professorial chairs."[2] Despite the venom, with the reformation and deterioration of HBCUs and the South, more Black students started looking North for college. At some institutions, White students prevented their admission, while at others, absolute exclusion in admissions was maintained, as at George Washington University in Washington, DC. Not surprisingly, then, fewer than seven hundred Black students had graduated from HWCUs by 1910. In 1912, the University of Michigan had the third largest enrollment (thirty-nine) behind Oberlin and the University of Kansas. Brown University in Rhode Island trained five Black men from 1877 to 1912 who became college presidents, including John Hope of Morehouse. Gertrude Amelia Mahorney graduated from Butler University in 1887, presumably the first Black woman to earn a degree from an Indiana college. George Washington Carver earned bachelor's (1894) and master's (1896) degrees from Iowa State University and became the school's first Black professor, before Washington managed to lure the scientist to Tuskegee.[3]

Like Carver in the 1890s, Black students were locked out of dormitories at Iowa State well into the twentieth century. The problem grew to such a magnitude that, in 1919, a recently relocated Black couple had to provide a rooming house for students. An untold number of families opened homes to students excluded from dorms at HWCUs, and some were vocal *supporters* of this racist policy, which provided them with customers. Black students at Iowa State, like others around the nation, would not be permitted to live in dorms until after World War II. Nor would they all be permitted to attend school in peace.[4]

Black students were victims of the surge of violence that terrorized Black Americans during the era of lynching. In 1914, for example, White men brutally struck Augustus Granger, a dental student at the University of Pennsylvania (UPENN), with stones, until he fought back with a knife, stabbing an assailant. HBCU students reportedly also carried weapons for protection during this period.[5]

In athletics, during the early twentieth century, some teams refused to play those with Black Americans, and sometimes hotels and other businesses declined interracial squads, a situation that continued into the 1960s. The College of William & Mary in Virginia and Georgia Tech

University chose not to play Rutgers, which in the late 1910s had on its football roster All-American Paul Robeson, the future world-renowned singer, actor, and antiracist. West Virginia University also insisted it could not play with Robeson on the field, but ultimately Robeson did line up. At six feet two inches and 190 pounds, he stood four inches taller and weighed twenty pounds more than most football players at the time. On the first play of the game, the West Virginia player facing him on the other side of the line of scrimmage leaned forward. "Don't you so much as touch me, you black dog, or I'll cut your heart out," he threatened Robeson. When the whistle blew, Robeson dashed at the player and slammed him to the ground. "I touched you that time," Robeson whispered. "How did you like it?"[6]

In the first few decades of the twentieth century, the stifling sense of isolation and segregation at HWCUs and the moralized contraption at HBCUs contributed to a low retention rate of Black students, as it would for decades. At Cornell, none of the six students in the 1904 cohort returned the next year. Alarmed, the remaining Black students formed a support group. It was popular. On December 4, 1906, seven male students refashioned the group into Alpha Phi Alpha, the nation's first Black American intercollegiate Greek-letter fraternal organization. It was the sunrise of Black student organizing—not to change the racist constitution, but to endure it.[7]

The racist restrictions those seven men faced resembled the patriarchal restrictions women were subjected to at Howard. By 1910, Howard had graduated a mere twenty-three women, compared to fifty-eight at Fisk and eighty-two at Shaw.[8] Incoming and outgoing mail passed through the matron, who sometimes acted as a censor. Going off campus alone in Washington, DC, without a chaperone was out of the question. Expulsions were a fact of life for any woman daring to smoke, drink, entertain men in an unapproved manner, or escape the socially fortified campus. As late as 1913, Howard's board of directors decreed that any woman teacher who married "would be considered as having resigned her position." All these restrictions, policies, and judgments estranged junior Ethel Hedgeman. She was encouraged to form a sisterhood by Professor Ethel Robinson, a Brown alumna who shared her sorority experiences. The St. Louis native, along with eight other liberal arts students, formed Alpha Kappa Alpha at Howard on January 15, 1908—the nation's first Black sorority. It was "no accident," historian and civil rights activist Paula Giddings observed, "that the first Black fraternity was established at a predominantly White university," where Black men were socially ostracized, "or that the first Black sorority emerged at a coeducational one like Howard," where Black women were socially hampered.[9]

In 1910, Indiana University (IU) seemed eerily like Cornell in 1906 (and appeared to be like Butler, where Sigma Gamma Rho was chartered in 1922). The ten Black male IU students were disallowed from using recreational or entertainment facilities on campus. They could take up space on campus, but there was no place for them. They were socially homeless, invisible to the majority, with no virtual or physical dwelling. Elder Diggs had had enough. He brought the ten scattered men together to establish Alpha Omega. Eventually, the men gave their organization permanence by founding Kappa Alpha Nu on January 5, 1911. Soon, their house parties attracted isolated Black American students from across the state who were in search of a community, even if for one joyous night. Three years later, presumably in reaction to a White IU student who nick-named the new fraternity "Kappa Alpha Nig," the fraternity changed its name to Kappa Alpha Psi. By the time the Kappas took on their new moniker, three more Greek-letter organizations had formed at Howard—Omega Psi Phi (1911), Delta Sigma Theta (1913), and Phi Beta Sigma (1914)—and Zeta Phi Beta was established there in 1920 (Iota Phi Theta was founded in 1963 at Morgan State University in Baltimore).[10]

Only three of the nine Black fraternities and sororities were established at HWCUs. But most of their early growth could be found at White colleges, where the need for social refuges and campus housing became vital in the early twentieth century. Like their White counterparts, Black fraternities and sororities utilized Greek names and symbols, maintained an exclusive membership, and performed rituals. They were "not conceived to transform society but to transform the individual," explained Paula Giddings—a reflection of higher education's imparting of ladder altruism.[11]

Stalled and in some cases retreating for almost three decades, Black higher education surged forward during and after World War I. The push came from the Great Migration, wartime chaos, and the *New* Negro, filled with a newfound race pride. A growing force of antiracist scholarship engaged in revisionist and inventive literature on people of African descent, such as W.E.B. Du Bois's studies of southern Black Americans and Carter G. Woodson's Association for the Study of Negro Life and History in 1915 and Negro History Week in 1926. These educators introduced Black history, sociology, and literature courses at HBCUs, and they founded Black literary groups. Tougaloo College in Mississippi, hired faculty who introduced the school's first courses in Negro history and literature. Two new electives were inserted at Howard in 1918—"Race Problems" and "The Negro in American History." Several HBCUs hired Black presidents and professors.[12]

Some Black students in the early twentieth century did not welcome these developments. Poet Langston Hughes surveyed his fellow students on the matter at Lincoln (PA) in the late 1920s. He found that only a few Black students at this HBCU objected to the absence of a Black history or literature course, and two-thirds of the 127 juniors and seniors did not want Black professors. "The reasons given were various: that Lincoln was supported by 'white' philanthropy, therefore whites should run the college; that favoritism and unfairness would result on the part of Negro teachers toward the students; that there were not enough Negro teachers available; and that things were all right as they were, so why change? Three students even said they just didn't like Negroes. Two said they did not believe Negro teachers had the interest of students at heart. Another said members of his own race were not morally capable!" These Black students had internalized racist ideas, angering the antiracist Hughes. The college had "failed in instilling in these students the very quality of self-reliance and self-respect," he wrote, "which any capable American leader should have."[13]

At the same time, the first Black student social movement, powered by students like Hughes, emerged during a drastic postwar modification of the collegiate composition. Public high schools were being opened around the country, yielding more students. Many HBCUs that had served as more or less boarding high schools for decades started granting bachelor's degrees—colleges such as Prairie View A&M University (1919) outside of Houston, Spelman (1924), and Mississippi's Jackson State University (1927). Talladega's ratio of non-college students to college students in 1907 was 180 to 1. The ratio at Alabama's oldest HBCU tightened to three to one by 1927—five years later it was one to one. Tuskegee, Saint Augustine's, Hampton, Voorhees College (South Carolina), Saint Paul's College (Virginia), Oakwood University (Alabama), and Stillman College (Alabama) were also part of the surge in degree-granting HBCUs, whose number increased from thirty-one in 1915 to fifty-four in 1954.[14]

Before the 1920s, Black higher education was primarily a male phenomenon at private HBCUs. In 1914, for every public HBCU student, there were forty private HBCU students. But by 1926, the ratio had dropped to three to one. In 1935, it was 1.5 to 1. More were attending public HBCUs in the 1950s. A mere two out of every ten graduates were women in 1920. This number doubled by 1930, and in 1940, more Black women were graduating from HBCUs than Black men.[15]

In addition to demographic factors and first-wave feminism, the National Association of College Women (NACW) played an important role in this upsurge. NACW president Lucy Slowe, who in 1922 became the first HBCU dean of women at Howard, impressed upon presidents the need to create similar positions. They did so when the population of women students skyrocketed in the 1930s and 1940s. The NACW joined students in challenging aspects of the moralized contraption. "When a college woman cannot be trusted to go shopping without a chaperone she is not likely to develop powers of leadership," Slowe wrote in 1931.[16]

During and after World War I, the Black collegiate student population grew tremendously. From 1914 to 1925, the number of HBCUs increased 81 percent and their populations skyrocketed 533 percent. There was a massive upsurge of Black college graduates—more than ten times more from HBCUs in 1936 (2,130) compared with 1914 (180) and about a fivefold increase at Northern White colleges. More Black students in the country graduated from college between 1926 and 1936 than in the previous 300 years combined. Changes to the institutional, gender, and numerical configuration of HBCUs sometimes led to enhancing the moralized contraption. At Jackson State, for instance, a series of regulations came into effect in 1924 related to women's chaperonage, curfew, required attendance, and shopping days and stated that "vulgar language and bad habits will be sufficient for exclusion from the school."[17]

To curb the surge of Black students and meet the rising tide of post–World War I White racism, Northern and border HWCUs maintained or instituted official and unofficial segregationist policies and retained, with few exceptions, only White faculty, administrators, and staff in their ranks. Catholic University in Washington, DC, put in place a color bar in 1919, and it remained in place for almost two decades. At UPENN, Black students could not enter the cafeteria and were required to eat their lunch under the stairs of the library. Frederick W. Wells, a Columbia law student, received at least two death threats from the Ku Klux Klan. He also witnessed a burning cross on campus in 1914. In the late 1920s, Adam Clayton Powell Jr. tried to pass for white at New York's Colgate University, where there were about five Black men out of about one thousand males. When Powell pledged an all-White fraternity, members discovered his African ancestry and publicly rejected him. His White roommate, who had befriended Powell, demanded his removal from their room. University officials backed the removal. The future Harlem preacher and congress-man never again tried to pass on the White side of the racial line.[18]

In 1927, Butler officials issued a quota. No more than ten Black stu-dents were to be admitted per year, and each had to have three letters of recommendation from "substantial," presumably White, citizens. African Americans were forced to take an extra history course to make up for the gym class they were forbidden from taking. "Nobody said anything ugly to us," said Mildred Marshall Hall, who arrived at the Indianapolis institu-tion in 1929. "They just didn't see you—we were invisible." The quota was not lifted until 1948.[19]

Harvard accepted Ewart Guinier but denied him a scholarship because it had already fulfilled its reported quota of one funded Black student per class. Unlike other Harvard freshmen, who were required to live in the campus dormitories, Guinier was granted permission to live at home. "Men of white and colored races shall not be compelled to live and eat together," stated the *Harvard Alumni Bulletin* of 1923. At a freshman assembly in 1929, with over a thousand people in attendance, Guinier, the only Black American, stuck out, or, more precisely, disappeared. As stu-dents exited the hall, conversations sprang up all around him like sprin-klers, but he stayed dry. "No one looked me in the eye: no one spoke to me," he said. "As I walked towards a group, they would move away." Not one Harvard professor ever called on him in class. Not one White student ever initiated a conversation with him. The first person to acknowledge his humanity, to render him visible, happened to be a Black graduate student he met at the campus bookstore. "Welcome to Harvard!" shouted Ralph Bunche, the future educator, diplomat, and civil rights power broker.[20]

The Ohio State University, the University of Michigan, and the University of Iowa also sanctioned residential segregation in the 1930s. Several Northern HWCUs excluded Black students, claiming they did not want them "subjected to discrimination," as Williams College (Massachusetts) president Tyler Dennett put it in 1935. Racist restrictions and social isolation, coupled with the rising Black enrollment, led to the founding of sociocultural groups. The Negro Students Club at UC Berkeley hosted dances in the mid-1930s and complained in 1935 when a Black student was denied service at a student-run barber shop. The Negro Student's Club at San Francisco State held "social meetings" in 1937. The University of Chicago had a Negro Student Club, criticized as being seg-regationist by a writer in *The Chicago Defender*. "The aim of the 'Negro Student Club' is to immediately alleviate and ultimately to abolish ...

lamentable" campus conditions, explained John H. Johnson, future head of the Johnson Publishing Company, in defense of his organization in 1937. The club organized balls, participated in Negro History Week activities, hosted a lecture by Howard's William Leo Hansberry on ancient Ethiopia, and hosted dancer Katherine Dunham and her cast, which performed *Tropical Revue* in 1945.[21]

As Black students steered through racist waters at Northern HWCUs, the racist waters sometimes became more perilous for HBCU students in violently segregated areas. To White Southerners clinging to a strict racial hierarchy between the world wars, Black college students, in the vein of free Black people during slavery, embodied present displacement and future reordering. For racist White Southerners who did not attend college, and most did not, the presence of knowledgeable and confident Black students often undermined their sense of superiority and, thus, their sense of self. Nowhere was this situation as galling as in Atlanta—one of the prime centers of Black higher education *and* the Southern White supremacist order.

The swelling of Black students at its HBCUs in 1920s swelled the tensions in the city. In 1928, when a Morehouse student named Barnes entered a café to request payment for an overdue bill on papers he had delivered, the proprietor shot him in the head to "teach him how to act when talking to a white man." A grand jury "justified" the murder. Two years later, White men shot and killed Dennis Hubert, a Morehouse sophomore and son of a local Baptist pastor, claiming he "insulted a white woman" at a public park on June 30, 1930. Morehouse secured the state's most successful White criminal lawyer, William Schley Howard, and these six men became the first White people to be convicted of the murder of a Black person in Georgia.[22]

On campus, Black students still faced restrictive rules at segregationist White and assimilationist Black colleges in the 1930s, and most curricula remained culturally assimilationist. Few sets of coursework and even fewer courses discussed the Black experience at HWCUs. HBCU curricula, aside from perhaps one course on Negro history and another on Negro literature, were at times barely distinguishable from those at HWCUs. According to Horace Mann Bond, Fisk professor and later dean at Dillard University in New Orleans, during that decade "Cicero, Livy, Horace, Quintilian, Tacitus, and Prose Composition afforded a rather full fare in Latin, while Greek could hardly be said to suffer neglect when every student was expected to read Xenophon's *Memorabilia*, Homer's *Iliad*,

Sophocles' *Antigone* and other Greek tragedies, the New Testament in Greek, Thucydides, Plato's *Apology* and the *Crito*, and Demosthenes' *On the Crown.*[23]

The Great Depression of the 1930s proved a Greek tragedy for many HBCUs, replaying the dismal days during the panic of 1873. Some folded; most weathered the economic tornado by cutting back and raising tuition—pricing out families held afloat by Black farmers and domestics, who were not benefactors of the New Deal. Those HBCUs that survived saw a somewhat brighter day. Educators had finally convinced the Southern Association of Colleges and Secondary Schools to consider accrediting HBCUs in 1930. In 1933, the Association of Colleges and Secondary Schools for Negroes formed to promote the advancement of HBCUs. The critical mass of Black students, aided by the National Association for the Advancement of Colored People (NAACP), started challenging the separate-but-equal doctrine in the 1930s, pointing to their inability to attend graduate school in the South. Refusing to desegregate, state legislatures and philanthropists appropriated funds to found new HBCUs, beefed up existing ones, and established graduate and professional programs at HBCUs over the next few decades.[24]

As the Depression ebbed in 1939, Congress instructed the Office of Education to study the state of Black higher education. The agency reported in the 1942 *National Survey of the Higher Education of Negroes* that Black K–12 students were allocated one-third the amount of funding that White students received and that the school years of Black Americans tended to be one to three months shorter, resulting in many students' being poorly prepared for college. During World War II, HBCUs could do little about this predicament, as the male presence on Black campuses fell by half. Along with this population reduction, certain funds customarily earmarked for HBCUs were diverted to the war effort. Together, they were a "double assault" on the livelihood of HBCUs, wrote Tuskegee president Frederick D. Patterson in 1943. As a result, Patterson appealed that year to his fellow presidents of private Black colleges to kick off a "unified financial campaign." His peers obliged, and the next year twenty-seven member colleges founded the United Negro College Fund to raise funds for private HBCUs and provide scholarships for aspiring students. Four years later, another group of college presidents formed the National Scholarship Service and Fund for Negro Students to "increase and broaden opportunities for Negro students at interracial colleges."[25]

Black World War II veterans returned to the states with GI Bill (Servicemen's Readjustment Act) benefits in hand, looking to earn a college degree. Often their knocks on the doors of institutes of higher learning only led to more knocks. Black colleges experienced a roughly 25 percent increase in the fall of 1944, maxing out their space, and many White colleges refused to admit Black people or increase their quotas. It was a travesty for Black veterans to face this reality after having put their life on the line for their country in the war.[26]

During the war, a partnership emerged between the federal government and higher education. It morphed into a postwar partnership in which federal dollars poured into collegiate research coffers, producing scientific and technological knowledge that augmented the nation's imperial endeavors, industrial engine, and domestic patriotism. This fresh pool of funds allowed colleges and universities, mostly HWCUs, to expand rapidly over the next few decades. Meanwhile, the marginal manual-industrial versus intellectual debate achieved a postwar consensus of classical liberal arts curricula *and* business, technology, or science courses that assuaged both accommodating and progressive assimilationists.[27]

W.E.B. Du Bois emerged as an antiracist opponent of this postwar consensus, which the Black Campus Movement would soon challenge. In fact, while the Pepsi-Cola Scholarship Board circulated a College Primer for Negro Students in 1948, Du Bois circulated his "memorial address" to the forty-five-year-old notion of the "Talented Tenth" and ladder altruism. "I assumed that with knowledge, sacrifice would automatically follow," he explained. "In my youth and idealism, I did not realize that selfishness is even more natural than sacrifice." As an alternative, he offered the "doctrine" of the "Guiding Hundredth," whose "passport to leadership" would be "expert knowledge of modern economics as it affected American Negroes" and the "willingness to sacrifice," imploring students to jump off ladders, unveiling grassroots altruism.[28]

"The object of the world is not profit but service and happiness," said Du Bois speaking to the postwar generation of Black students, who entered an almost wholly segregated academy. The days of Jim Crow flying over higher education were numbered, though, with Black students and NAACP lawyers on the hunt and the U.S. Supreme Court increasingly siding with them. The 1940s and 1950s saw some Northern HWCUs drop (or increase) their quotas, and border-state HWCUs were voluntarily, court ordered, or community pressured to desegregate. As *The New York Times* reported in 1950, "greater progress has been made in the last two years toward breaking down segregation in higher education than at any time since the Civil War." The walls continued to come down in the South throughout the 1950s, with the bulk of Black Americans desegregating graduate programs. A few Northern HWCUs had even hired Black faculty. The Julius Rosenwald Fund subsidized the appointment of Allison Davis, a sociologist and anthropologist, at the University of Chicago in 1941. In the 1940s, the NAACP disseminated a list of qualified Black professors to HWCUs. A mere sixty Black professors taught at White institutions in 1948.[29]

Racist White students, faculty, and alumni urged their Deep South college administrators to stick to tradition when the U.S. Supreme Court ruled as unconstitutional the separate-but-equal doctrine in its *Brown v. Board of Education of Topeka, Kansas* decision in 1954. The Universities of Mississippi, South Carolina, Alabama, and Georgia listened to students, rabid segregationist public opinion, and politicians, defiantly deepening the color line. For example, the University of Alabama publicly demonstrated its insolence by admitting, mobbing, and then expelling Autherine Lucy in 1956. Despite segregationist recalcitrance, collegiate desegregation carried on with a trickle of Black students. Clennon King was not one of them. For requesting admission to the University of Mississippi in 1958, he was temporarily confined to a state mental hospital for an evaluation of his sanity. Ironically, the year before, Black students thought King, then an Alcorn State history instructor, needed to be excluded from their campus after he published articles disparaging Black Americans.[30]

Many desegregated colleges and universities took down their "Whites only" signs only at the admissions offices. They remained posted on dorms, either excluding the few Black students outright, as at the University of Texas at Austin in 1956, or segregating the students, such as at Northwestern University and the University of Illinois in the late 1940s. Or, as at Earlham College in Indiana, the fresh handful of Black students were forced to live alone until they found a roommate on their own. Then, when they found a place to live, some Black students were terrorized, as at Harvard in 1952 (cross burning) and Louisiana State University in 1953 (rocks thrown in their rooms). Black students at HWCUs far from Black population centers complained about the lack of Black barbers and beauticians. They also encountered long-standing racist rituals. Those admitted to Missouri State University in the fall of 1954 likely came across Delta Sigma Epsilon sorority's Delta Darkey Minstrel show, billed "as one of the biggest events of the year."[31]

Meanwhile, Black students witnessed the attacks on their HBCUs by the federal government in the late 1940s and 1950s. McCarthyism and the frenzied search for communists had zeroed in on Fisk—one of the citadels of Black intellectualism. In 1949, Fisk president Charles Johnson testified that communists had not infiltrated HBCUs before the House Un-American Activities Committee (HUAC). Two years later, another Congressional committee held hearings in Memphis, claiming that Fisk had formerly had two communist teachers and a communist student (Du Bois in the 1880s). Before the committee, Johnson calmly addressed the meaninglessness of former affiliates and assured the committee that there were no communists at the Nashville college. In 1954, HUAC traveled back to the area—this time in Dayton, Ohio—and summoned Fisk Mathematics Department Chair Lee Lorch to testify. Like other antiracist White professors in the 1950s, Lorch had been deemed too controversial to hire by HWCUs and welcomed by an HBCU willing to take the risk with his impressive credentials. Lorch refused to discuss previous affiliations. The next day, Johnson announced that his contract would not be renewed.[32]

While HBCU presidents were fighting off the anticommunist fervor in the 1950s, they were acquiring their accreditation and removing the last of their elementary and secondary students. HBCUs were shedding their industrial veil and asserting a liberal arts identity in the 1950s. HBCU presidents were also preparing for their annual "shows" for visiting White trustees and philanthropists, which still occurred into the 1950s. These shows dwindled in the 1950s though, as the United Negro College Fund increasingly aided private colleges, and Southern states increasingly funded their public HBCUs to stave off the march of desegregation. HBCUs lost potential students as Black Americans continued their twentieth-century mass migration to the North and West and migrated in meager numbers to newly desegregated HWCUs. Civil rights student activists in the early 1960s used Black colleges as bases. Thus, the contradictions of the racist constitution at HBCUs were exposed when some college officials expelled or restricted protesters.[33]

In 1961, Georgia Tech peacefully desegregated—the first Deep South school to do so without a court order. Yet peace did not reign at the University of Georgia (1961), University of Mississippi (1962), or University of Alabama (1963), where federal troops were needed to protect newly admitted Black students from White mobs. However, these violent desegregation sagas were the exception. Desegregation picked up steam in 1962 and only increased as civil rights activism peaked in 1963. Most institutions admitted students during summer sessions to lessen the racist reaction, yet they only allowed in a few, with student bodies in the South resembling faculties in the North and West in 1963. Massachusetts Institute of Technology (MIT) and NYU had two Black professors, Princeton University and Notre Dame University had one, Harvard had no tenured Black professors, Columbia had no Black full professors, and Yale University and Stanford University had no Black professors. Among prestigious institutions, two of the "sanctuaries" for Black professors were the University of Chicago and the University of California at Los Angeles (UCLA), with no more than six.[34]

Congress augmented the stream of Black students by passing the Civil Rights Act of 1964 and the Higher Education Act of 1965, which provided financial assistance for students and increased federal funding. The Civil Rights Act gave government agencies the power to withhold federal money from racist programs or institutions. In fear of this loss, many of the remaining holdouts cracked opened their doors. In April 1965, 1,830 colleges and universities out of around 2,100 had submitted signed assurances of compliance with the Civil Rights Act.[35]

Inspired and pressured by the civil rights movement or campus activists, some institutions, such as Wesleyan University in Connecticut, Los Angeles's Occidental College, UCLA, and Rutgers, initiated programs to recruit a small contingent of Black students as early as 1963.[36] Meanwhile, throughout the 1960s, private Northern and Western HWCUs and Southern HBCUs toyed with desegregating their student bodies by launching student exchange programs, often through denominational ties. By 1967, Southern HWCUs were not just desegregating but had also joined what became a recruiting rush, primarily for the brightest Black Americans, offering four-year scholarships at colleges such as Wake Forest University in North Carolina. NYU and Roosevelt also established scholarship programs, and corporations and foundations such as the National Distillers and Chemical Corporation, Ford Foundation, and Rockefeller Foundation did the same. Because of the movement pressure, recruiting efforts, and scholarship offers, the number of Black students attending HWCUs shot up by 70 percent in 1965. There were about 200,000 Black students in higher education that fall, about 4.5 percent of the total enrollment of 4.5 million. By 1967, the enrollment had increased to 5.15 percent.[37]

The history of Black higher education prior to the BCM is a story of debate and consensus among assimilationists, segregationists, and antiracists. Black students resided on an island at the center *and* periphery of this narrative of hugs and tugs. They were at the center, since the dominant position at sea changed and dictated the nature of their island, their lives, more profoundly than any other group, and they were on the periphery—displaced from the sea—with nonstudents giving them little influence on the dictates and restructuring. Thus, Du Bois's island within was forced—serving as both the students' political position and their sociocultural place of refuge. Only through the Long Black Student Movement did they endeavor to leave the island. Only through the BCM did they finally center themselves in the discourse of Black higher education.

CHAPTER 3

"Fighting Back!": The Making of the New Negro 1828–1919

Black student activists started to leave their politically, socially, and culturally isolated "islands within" decades before the 1960s. In a larger sense, Black activism did not abruptly burst onto the scene in the mid-twentieth century. In recent years, historians have provided new frameworks within which to chronicle this extended story, pulling the origin of the twentieth century Black freedom struggle back to the 1920s and extending the purview of activism to the North and West. In 2005, historian Jacquelyn Dowd Hall termed this new historiography the "Long Civil Rights Movement," exposing the sea of activism throughout the country in the late 1930s, 1940s, and early 1950s. In Hall's conception, the Long Civil Rights Movement encompasses not only these formative struggles but also the classical civil rights period (1954–1965) and the Black Power Movement.[1]

Scholar Peniel Joseph challenged this "master narrative," contending that Black power should not be subsumed "under the all-powerful rubric of civil rights." In fact, Joseph introduced the concept of the "Long Black Power Movement" with roots in the New Negro Movement and the politics of Marcus Garvey in the 1920s. In sum, historians have elongated the two most storied Black social movements of the twentieth century—stretching, complicating, and adding fresh voices, themes, and events to these stories.[2]

Weaving in and out of both the elongated civil rights and Black power movements with roots in the 1920s strolled the Long Black Student Movement. Just as the traffic for civil rights and Black power did not begin

© The Author(s), under exclusive license to Springer Nature Switzerland AG 2025
I. X. Kendi, *The Black Campus Movement*, Contemporary Black History, https://doi.org/10.1007/978-3-031-37394-7_3

in the 1960s, neither did the mass, concerted activism of Black collegians. After almost a century of scattered, disconnected protest events during the antebellum era, the post-Reconstruction period, and the early twentieth century, the Long Black Student Movement began after World War I in the New Negro Campus Movement (NNCM) in the 1920s and early 1930s. The Long Black Student Movement focused increasingly (though not entirely) on acquiring off-campus civil rights from the mid-1930s to the early 1960s and then ventured into Black power, reaching its pinnacle in the late 1960s and early 1970s during the Black Campus Movement. The Long Black Student Movement built on previous gains and recycled and erected ideologies, tactics, and aims.

Black student demonstrations and activism had surfaced almost a century before the Long Black Student Movement. John Newton Templeton, a formerly enslaved South Carolinian, spoke at the 1828 commencement of Ohio University on the topic "The Claims of Liberia." The fifth Black graduate in the United States called for the "gradual" decline of "one of the greatest evils in our day," which had hindered "hapless Africa … in order that its total overthrow be permanent." He made the case that continental African people were capable of "intellectual improvement and self-government," as shown by the success of missionaries in teaching "multitudes" to read and write. Seeking donations for colonization, Templeton charged, "If there is then a true philanthropist or patriot in the house … let him evince it by his liberality and bounty, by undertaking the cause of the oppressed."[3]

When the abolitionist movement gained traction in the 1830s, galvanized by freedom revolts and given voice in booming antislavery speeches and periodicals, students lent their crusading voices to this struggle. Templeton actually reversed his pro-colonization stance in 1834.[4] Seven years later, on January 27, 1841, Thomas Paul of Dartmouth delivered a forceful speech in Boston before the Massachusetts Anti-Slavery Society. The preacher's son had been schooled as an apprentice at abolitionist William Lloyd Garrison's *The Liberator* and had studied at Noyes Academy before its institutional lynching. The antislavery society formed "to stay this torrent of vice that is rushing over us," Paul hammered home at the speech's height. "It is to lift up our perishing countrymen … It is to give opportunity for the development of the moral and intellectual powers of man … It is to save our churches and ministers … It is to wipe a foul blot from our country." But abolition was dying away, said the upholders of slavery, he recanted. "Dying away? Impossible! *Truth* never dies. Her course is always onward.

Though obstacles may present themselves before her, she rides triumphantly over them; and the more formidable the enemy, the more terrible the encounter, and the more glorious the victory."[5]

Almost a decade after Paul's words electrified abolitionists, Lucy Stanton gave "A Plea for the Oppressed" at Oberlin's commencement exercises on August 27, 1850. The first Black American to complete the "ladies course" presided over the Oberlin Ladies Literary Society. The brave Stanton ridiculed slavery in Ohio, which bordered an enslaving state, in the midst of an unprecedented amount of abolitionist persecution, two weeks before the enactment of the chilling Fugitive Slave Act. "The Anti-Slavery pulse beats faintly," Stanton began. But "ye that advocate the great principles of Temperance, Peace, and Moral Reform … will you not plead the cause of the Slave?" She paused, then stoutly declared, "Slavery is the combination of all crime. It is War. Those who rob their fellow-men of home, of liberty, of education, of life, are really at war against them as though they cleft them down upon the bloody field." Stanton closed with words of hope and, from history's standpoint, words of prophecy. "Truth and right must prevail. The bondman shall go free. Look to the future! Hark! The shout of joy gushes from the heart of earth's freed millions!"[6]

Enslaved Black people did go free a decade later, as Stanton engaged in her itinerant teaching career. Some Black students may have left their colleges to join the Union Army, just as John Copeland left Oberlin in 1859

Photo 3.1 Lucy Stanton (Courtesy of the Oberlin College Archives)

to join John Brown's raid on the federal armory at Harpers Ferry, West Virginia, that failed in its attempt to spark a mass rebellion of enslaved people. Before facing death at the gallows, Copeland dispatched a letter to his family in Ohio: "I am not terrified by the gallows, which I see staring me in the face, and upon which I am soon to stand and suffer death for doing what George Washington was made a hero for doing." Heroic Black student voices continued to be heard when the Civil War ended, as they filled the refrain of the Reconstruction consensus on Black higher education. And their sorrowful songs were heard when the segregationists disenfranchised their fathers and brothers and violently exchanged America's nascent interracial democracy for renewed White supremacy. Like their racial brethren in the community, Black students were not immobilized by the fall of HBCUs from 1880s to the first decade of the twentieth century. From the nadir sprung the first Black student protests.[7]

Hiram Revels, the first Black U.S. senator, resigned his post to become Alcorn State's inaugural president in 1871. He established a classical curriculum at the public HBCU, supported by a generous appropriation, like most HBCUs manifesting the Reconstruction consensus of education for advancement. By 1874, with White segregationists, Revels intoned reverence for racist White people, infuriating students. They organized a crushing boycott of classes, filed complaints with officials, and triggered a mass exodus from the school and a short vacation for Revels.[8]

At Nashville's Roger Williams University, later incorporated into LeMoyne-Owen, the assimilationist ideas and strict financial maneuvers of the White president and treasurer were "obnoxious" to the vast majority of the one hundred HBCU students. In 1887, the students threatened to strike. They were likely led by Frank Levi Trimble, who in the early 1890s roomed at Brown with Morehouse's future president, John Hope. An indignant President William Stifler told reporters, "It is simply a war of the races, as there will always be when the negroes have a chance, but I tell you they have to submit this time." In the end, with local Black community support, students did not submit.[9] Stifler and the treasurer were dismissed.

That summer of 1887, students at Hampton petitioned the faculty "as a discontented working class," historian James Anderson explained. The resentment and resistance had been building for years. According to students Perry Shields and W.H. Scott, "every apprentice of the school signed his name," denouncing the menial level of training, hard labor, and meager wages and working conditions. "Four years at a trade like ours, working from 7 a.m. to 5:50 p.m., is enough to break down the constitu-tion of a man, much less boys in the bloom of youth," Scott said. The protest petition and other forms of passive resistance were ignored or dele-gitimized during those years of student strife at Hampton. Meanwhile, Armstrong publicly boasted that at his model institution, "there was no begging except for more work."[10]

In the fall of 1887, a daughter of formerly enslaved people in South Carolina enrolled at Barber-Scotia College in North Carolina. Soon, Mary Jane McLeod (Bethune), the future founder of Florida's Bethune-Cookman University in 1904, became the "unacknowledged leader" of her peers and convinced the administration to give senior women the abil-ity to serve as chaperones in place of teachers when students left campus.[11] Black student activism continued into the first decade of the twentieth century, although it remained sporadic. Just as students did not idly take the excessive maneuvers of assimilationists or paternalists on their cam-puses, some did not accept the regressive transformation occurring in their communities, either. After the Arkansas legislature segregated street cars in 1903, students at Shorter College, an HBCU in Little Rock, released a protest publication, *The Voice of the Twentieth Century*. "The law was intended to humiliate negroes and every time a negro man, woman, or child goes to the back seat or sits on the cars while this iniquitous law is in force, the negro is humiliated. Simply stay off the cars. Stay off the cars." Riders heeded the students' call, and ridership plunged 90 percent in Little Rock and other cities and remained at that level for weeks. But Black communities could not sustain the boycott.[12]

What appears to be the first nationally known Black student protest occurred two years later at Howard. Students demanded the removal of their "prejudiced" White president, John Gordon, who restricted the power of Howard's Black deans. On December 8, 1905, four hundred students assembled in the chapel at noon for the regular service. When Gordon appeared, a student near the front stood and yelled, "Down with Gordon!" In unison, students rose to their feet, waved their hats and coats in the air, and hissed and applauded as they marched out of the church and went on strike. By the end of the month, Gordon had resigned, becoming the first of more than a hundred college presidents over the course of the twentieth century to be forced out of their offices by Black student activ-ists. The students demanded a Black president, but the trustees selected another White minister, Wilbur Thirkield. Not even two months after the Howard strike, about two hundred Talladega undergraduates vacated their Alabama HBCU over the appointment of L.O. Parks, a "Southern white man," as assistant farm superintendent. It "was a blow at their manhood," the students said.[13]

That September of 1906, some Talladega students may have crossed paths with people fleeing the Atlanta Race Riot. White fury toward Black Americans had been inflamed by racist articles and politics and by job competition. It exploded into a five-day-long White invasion of Black Atlanta on September 22. Dozens of Black Americans and two White Americans were killed. During the White riot, most Black Americans stayed to defend their communities, including those in Brownsville, which adjoined Gammon Theological Seminary and Clark Atlanta. Armed Clark Atlanta students reportedly defended their campus, too. Learning of the riot in Alabama, W.E.B. Du Bois rushed to his home on the Clark Atlanta campus. He had never handled a weapon before this, but he immediately bought a shotgun and two dozen rounds to patrol the campus, in wait for a mob that never came. "I would without hesitation have sprayed their guts over the grass," the cofounder of the NAACP later said.[14]

Two years after the NAACP was founded, on October 21, 1911, none of the two hundred students reported for class after the faculty of North Carolina A&T State University hung another rule on them: mandatory Saturday courses. The senior and junior classes of the HBCU were perceived to be the leaders of the strike and were expelled. Up North that year at Cornell, Pauline Ray and Rosa Vassar had been denied dormitory rooms. Traveling a mile and a half from campus, these Black women had "grown tired of climbing the hill or getting half frozen waiting for street cars." Learning of their predicament and that of others before them, in 1911 sophomore St. Lucia native James B. Clark pleaded passionately for justice in the *Cornell Era*, the student weekly. "Is that the way Mr. Cornell's ideals are being carried?" he asked. Gertrude Martin, advisor to Cornell's women, announced that the university did not have a racist ban. "I advised them to go somewhere else, as they would not find it pleasant for them living at Sage College," she said. It was a common justification at the time for campus segregation. The majority of Cornell's White women students (269 in total) petitioned the trustees in late March 1911 to officially bar Black Americans. Within days, Ray and Vassar, still desiring campus rooms, issued the following statement: "We don't seek social equality. If we could live at Sage College, as far as convenience and comfort goes, we would be as one with the rest of the girls, but in all things social we would be as separate as two fingers on one hand," they declared, echoing Booker T. Washington. A week later, Cornell president Jacob G. Schurman publicly unlocked the women's dorm for Black students.[15]

In 1912, thirty-three Howard women, restless from the patriarchal campus rules and inspired by the advancing women's suffrage movement, requested the appointment of a dean of women to "direct them in all womanly activities." The request was not granted for a decade. In 1913, two months after Delta Sigma Theta was founded at Howard, Osceola Adams rallied her Delta sisters to participate in a suffrage march in Washington, DC, on March 3. They accompanied Ida B. Wells-Barnett and upwards of ten thousand women who marched down Pennsylvania Avenue, unfazed by the horror-inducing walls of male police officers halting their progress at times or by the male onlookers throwing items or slurs. Back on campus, these Deltas were subjected to criticism for their engagement. "But we expected that," said Madree White. "Those were the days when women were seen and not heard. However we marched that day in order that women might come into their own … In those years Delta took a stand."[16]

In January 1914, students at Shaw and Clark Atlanta took a protest stand when one of their own was punished for defying a college rule. Shaw activists also demanded a Black president. Seven hundred Howard students boycotted classes for a few days in April 1916 following the suspension of the senior class for unlawfully using the gym for a dance. In 1917, Morehouse men staged a four-day strike to annul required attendance at study hall.[17]

The eyes of Black America were transfixed on East St. Louis, Illinois, the year Morehouse men eyed the end of compulsory study hall. White residents launched a vicious riot in 1917. They were incensed at the job competition in aluminum factories posed by southern Black migrants and incited by racist businessmen, union organizers, journalists, and politicians. Dozens of Black people were killed and thousands were driven from their homes by arsonists. Three weeks later, ten thousand protesters marched from Harlem to midtown Manhattan, blaring their resentment with their silence.

The East St. Louis riot and aftermath loomed as a dress rehearsal for what James Weldon Johnson termed the "Red Summer" of 1919. During a six-month period, northern White people in twenty-five cities and towns violently tried to assert their supremacy over the emboldened Black residents, proud returning veterans, and the newly arrived southern migrants.

Black Americans stridently defended their humanity, urged on by Claude McKay's poem "If We Must Die," published in 1919. "Like men we'll face the murderous, cowardly pack/ Pressed to the wall, dying, but fighting back!"[18]

A new mood stirred in the political and cultural pot of Black America in the late 1910s and early 1920s—a mood that had grown into a conviction by the mid-1920s. Resentment lingered from the stingingly racist 1915 film *The Birth of a Nation*. During the Great Migration up North and out West, more than a million Black Southerners tossed hope, ambition, impatience, heightened expectations, and the tangible and symbolic notion of travel to a better life into the pot. Many of the 400,000 or more Black men who served in World War I injected into the pot their fighting spirit, a sense of urgency, a taste of interracial activity, and the seasoning of change, as did untold numbers of first-wave feminists and clubwomen. The self-determination slogans of President Woodrow Wilson were thrust into the pot, along with parallel ideas emerging from the Russian Revolution in 1917. Scholars and artists accelerated their striving in Black American self-discovery, self-examination, and self-inventiveness. Some Black Americans downgraded political accommodation, cultural assimilation, and reverence of White people and cultures, allowing another ideology to rise in its place. The mood, then conviction, became encapsulated in two words: New Negro.[19]

"Old Negro" students largely submitted to what Claude McKay, speaking of his Tuskegee experience in the early 1910s, called "the semi-military, machine-like existence."[20] But those were the Old Negro students. New Negro campus activists were a fresh breed—older and more diverse. They were ideologically driven by New Negro literature and leaders. They were inspired by internationally circulating notions of passive resistance, the burgeoning African colonial civil rights struggle, and the domestic strike-laden union movement. New Negro campus activists were shielded by their snowballing numbers and moved by the atmosphere of post-war change.

Antiracist leaders, such as the venerable Pan-Africanist organizer Marcus Garvey, built organizations harnessing the newness, as did a young NAACP. Renaissance poets, novelists, musicians, and essayists, such as Langston Hughes, Zora Neale Hurston, Jessie Fauset, and Countee Cullen, gave African American culture a sweeping artistic and philosophical visibility. Some of these artists received their literary debuts as students at HBCUs in the 1910s or the formative period of the movement. Hurston, for

Photo 3.2   Zora Neale
Hurston at Howard
(Courtesy of Prints &
Photographs
Department, Moorland-
Spingarn
Research Center)

example, worked on the staff of Howard's literary journal, *The Stylus*,
where she published her first short story in 1921.[21] Antiracist intellectuals,
many of whom attended and often taught at HBCUs, gave the New Negro
meaning in books, journals, and newspapers in the earliest concerted out-
pouring of scholarly literature on the Black American experience. Shaw
professor Benjamin Brawley, for instance, published his 1921 social history
of African America a year before Carter G. Woodson published his own.
"The Negro now loves his own, cherishes his own, teaching his boys about
black heroes, and honors and glorifies his own black women," Brawley
wrote. "A whole people has been reborn; a whole race has found its soul."
E. Franklin Frazier discussed "New Currents of Thought Among the
Colored People of America" in his 1920 master's thesis at Clark University
in Massachusetts. Frazier had an essay in the New Negro Movement's
prime anthology, *The New Negro*, edited in December 1925 by Howard
philosopher Alain Locke.[22]

Many Black students enrolled in colleges imbued with the novel mood.
With high schools finally planted widely across the American landscape,
the Black collegiate population jumped by 50,000 each year during the
1920s, quintupling over the entire decade. The number of women at
HBCUs also doubled. The members of this Great Migration to mostly

HBCUs did not form an ideological monolith, just as students throughout the Long Black Student Movement thought in their own, individualized ways. Assertiveness and racial pride swept up many New Negro youth minds. These independent, antiracist inclinations collided with a moralized contraption and assimilationist curricula. It all generated the first social movement waged by Black students.

CHAPTER 4

"God Speed the Breed": The New Negro Campus 1919–1936 Movement

As White students enjoyed their "age of flappers and bootleggers, coon-skin and bathtub gin, hot jazz and new dance crazes," the New Negro Campus Movement propagated slowly and steadily in 1919 and the early 1920s. In the spring of 1920, Wilberforce students learned that their Monday date time between the genders had been eliminated, and they had to walk along gendered pathways to their classes. Soon after, a short-lived rebellion gripped the campus until President William Scarborough relented. The suspension of seniors for insubordination prompted a strike in March 1921 at Johnson C. Smith University in North Carolina.[1]

Most HWCUs overtly barred Black students or urged them to stay away from the dormitories "for their own sake" to maintain the standardization of exclusion. This happened at even the most diverse HWCU in the nation, Oberlin. In 1919, Beulah Terrell decided to rally her peers. She was the daughter of Mary Church Terrell, who in 1923 urged college students to "eradicate prejudice by starting a crusade" against racism and sexism. As would become standard operating procedure for HWCU activists in the New Negro Campus Movement, Beulah Terrell solicited the help of the NAACP, and together they forced the ban's removal. This aiding of Black campus activists at HWCUs in the 1920s is one of the more notable, but unrecognized, feats of the teenaged NAACP.[2]

© The Author(s), under exclusive license to Springer Nature Switzerland AG 2025
I. X. Kendi, *The Black Campus Movement*, Contemporary Black History, https://doi.org/10.1007/978-3-031-37394-7_4

The NAACP assisted students when Harvard president A. Lawrence Lowell declined to desegregate freshman dormitories. "We do not owe it to him to force him and the white into social relations that are not, or may not be mutually congenial," Lowell rationalized. In the spring of 1922, upperclassman Edwin B. Jourdain Jr., the world's best broad jumper, called for an end to segregation on campus. President Lowell did not budge. But in a year, NAACP officials, students, professors, alumni, and prominent newspapers had joined the cause. The campaign touched W.E.B. Du Bois, a Harvard alumnus, who proclaimed it as "perhaps the most heartening sign of sanity on the race problem that has happened in fifty years. Not a single person of importance has yet dared to defend Lowell." In April 1923, Harvard's board of overseers stopped defending Lowell as well, unanimously repudiating his segregationist policy.[3]

As the press zeroed in on Harvard, in November 1922, a group of students at Storer College in West Virginia got into a fight with local White youth. Utilizing the quick trigger of HBCU presidents to punish "insubordination," President Henry T. McDonald expelled the three students—and along with it the calm that existed on campus. Students briefly boycotted classes, and some withdrew from college.[4]

In 1923, the calm had receded at HBCUs more generally, as the New Negro Campus Movement agitated toward its climax. In May, students boycotted, and some withdrew from the AME Zion's Livingston College in North Carolina, while Ella Baker, the future civil rights organizing stalwart, petitioned nearby Shaw to allow women to wear the latest fashion trend—silk stockings. In 1918, the year Baker enrolled just short of her fifteenth birthday, Shaw applicants needed an "unblemished moral character" and willingness to "comply cheerfully with reasonable rules and regulations." By her senior year in Shaw's high school, around 1923, her willingness and cheerfulness in facing the rules had subsided, if they were ever there. Grasping this, a group of women, mostly older and in college, who Baker said "didn't have guts enough," requested she lead the petition. Aghast, the dean of women not only denied the request but also gave the students extra chapel time to pray for forgiveness. She called Baker into her office. Expecting to see a remorseful girl after issuing a threat of expulsion, the dean was startled by Baker's resolve and fainted at one point. "But it didn't bother me," Baker said, "because I felt I was correct."[5]

Countee Cullen, a NYU student already attracting attention for his poetry, spoke in the summer of 1922 in New York City during an event hosted by the League of Youth. "The young American Negro is going in strong for education; he realizes its potentialities for combating bigotry and blindness," and it is "working a powerful group effect." The group effect exhibited itself that summer at a Black student conference down the Eastern Seaboard in Atlantic City, New Jersey. Students from this conference and possibly the League of Young continued to hold discussions into the fall of 1922 and the winter of 1923. Ultimately, they decided to found the first national Black student organization in American history—the American Federation of Negro Students (AFNS). Its founding conference convened at Howard in April 1923, attracting delegates from Oberlin, Yale, Cornell, Lincoln (PA), Tuskegee, Howard, and a few high schools. Students installed an executive committee composed of seven students, with I.J.K. Wells of Lincoln (PA) presiding. The AFNS selected as its slogan "A more progressive people." The students were addressed by Howard faculty members and administrators, including philosopher Alain Locke. AFNS resolved for the institutionalization of antiracist and Black history courses in the college curriculum and pledged to launch three drives: "business co-operation," "the stimulation of Race pride," and "the encouragement of education." One of the organizers published a piece in *The New Student* entitled "The Negro Youth Awakening." The AFNS "seeks the fundamental weakness of the situation and proposes to work from the bottom up—a method which appears to be the reverse of that used by the present leaders," Howard's J. Alpheus Butler wrote, theorizing an early grassroots altruism.[6]

AFNS leaders thought that Black higher education had historically overemphasized manual, professional, and classical education. They contended that business education had been neglected, and so in December 1923, the AFNS launched its first initiative: "Bigger and Better Negro Business." Its aim was to encourage business education and inspire students to become entrepreneurs, like Garvey at the time and Booker T. Washington before them. AFNS President I.J.K. Wells mailed out a torrent of folders outlining AFNS ideas to HBCUs and large HWCUs in the winter of 1923–1924, urging students to read them and pass them along. By March 1924, the AFNS had chapters at fourteen institutions, including Howard, Virginia Union, Morehouse, Clark Atlanta, and West Virginia State University, with a reported membership of six thousand, which, if true, made this mobilization of Black students the largest in

American history up to that point. In April 1924, the AFNS gathered for its second national conference in Nashville, welcoming students from the University of Chicago, Northwestern, Meharry Medical College, West Virginia State, Clark Atlanta, and Lincoln (PA). The students elected officers from eight Black fraternities and sororities. They decided to focus all of their efforts in 1924 "upon the economic development of the Race," Wells said.[7]

In addition to a letter Wells sent in June to the editors of several newspapers challenging students to start "selling goods instead of labor," the AFNS spearheaded a campaign in 1924 to name and honor the "ten greatest Negroes America has produced." The "mythical ten," as Black newspapers termed them, were George Washington Carver, Frederick Douglass, Madam C.J. Walker, James Weldon Johnson, *The Chicago Defender* publisher Robert S. Abbott, painter Henry O. Tanner, W.E.B. Du Bois, Booker T. Washington, Paul Laurence Dunbar, and Colonel Charles Young. The naming of the ten, which glaringly omitted quite a few great women, seemed to be the last major campaign of the AFNS. After a failed attempt at fundraising for scholarships and a conference in August 1925, the AFNS declined to relative obscurity by 1926.[8]

While the AFNS provided a deviation for off-campus activism in 1923, segregationists drove the Florida A&M president of twenty-two years, Nathan B. Young, out of his position. Young had refused to place more emphasis on subordinating agriculture and manual learning. The trustees then selected W.H.A. Howard, dean of vocational studies, to take Young's place, against the wishes of alumni and students, who circulated petitions asserting he was "not qualified to be head of a college since he … held no degree." To segregationists, however, his racist ideology qualified him for the position.[9]

On October 8, 1923, Florida A&M students boycotted their classes. A third of the college's 325 students returned home. Three days into the strike, campus activists firebombed Duval Hall, and over the next three months they burned the despised Mechanical Arts Building, Gibbs Hall, and three other buildings. Assigning White guards to restore order by enforcing an evening curfew and patrolling the main men's dormitory only led to more resistance. To the students, there hung a "reign of terror on the campus with white men standing over us with guns at their sides." Eleven young men were expelled during the uprising, but no one ever apprehended the arsonists. Order did not return until the trustees replaced

Howard, in May 1924, with J.R.E. Lee, a former Tuskegee instructor, who presided over Florida A&M for two decades.[10]

Another year-long campaign to push out Fisk president Fayette McKenzie followed the year-long struggle at Florida A&M. McKenzie had just landed the famed Nashville HBCU a $1 million endowment, unprecedented for a Black college. But the money came with strings that interlaced Fisk with the conservative leanings of the donors. McKenzie terminated the Student Government Association, along with the oldest HBCU student publication, *The Fisk Herald*. He rejected a campus charter of the NAACP and tossed NAACP literature out of the library, while inviting Jim Crow entertainment and arrangements for benefactors. McKenzie forbade Fisk women from wearing silk or satin dresses, which were popular at that time. They were required to wear high necks, long sleeves, black hats, and cotton stockings. Officials had to be present for any meeting between the genders. Male and female students were often sent home for walking together in broad daylight. Regulations mandated when students ate, slept, and studied. Students were summarily dismissed for any opposition to Fisk's moralized contraption. President McKenzie's favorite saying resounded: "If you don't like Fisk, then get out!"[11]

W.E.B. Du Bois muted his thunderous voice when he heard criticisms of his alma mater in the early 1920s. He came for his daughter Yolanda's graduation in June 1924 and had the opportunity to speak to the alumni in conjunction with the festivities. With McKenzie and the trustees sitting nearby, undergraduates peering down from the gallery, and alumni sitting in the rows in front of him, the estimated hour-long speech remains one of the most searing face-to-face attacks on a president in American higher education history. "I maintain that the place to criticize Fisk University is at Fisk University and not elsewhere," he said early in the speech. "Fisk is choking freedom. Self-knowledge is being hindered by refusal of all initiative to the students." He fearlessly urged students to boycott the institution. "Fisk will and must survive," he said in closing. "The spirit of its great founders will renew itself, and it is that Spirit alone, reborn, which calls us tonight."[12]

When Du Bois ended his speech, it was only the beginning of his writing and speaking that summer and fall of 1924 to serve "an example either for the Power that furnish the Cash or for the awakening youth and their supporters." One of his more influential articles appeared in *The American Mercury* in October 1924. "It has gradually become a rule of philanthropy that no Negro higher school can survive unless it pleases the white South." To please the White South, HBCUs had to "train servants and docile cheap labor," Du Bois charged in the widely discussed essay.[13]

Fisk youth, like their peers around the nation, followed the example of Du Bois. He became to New Negro campus activists what Stokely Carmichael became four decades later to Black campus activists—a guiding light of resistance. When trustees traveled to Fisk in November 1924, they were greeted by grievances voiced everywhere and a hundred students chanting "Away with the czar!" and "Down with the tyrant!" Seven students met with the trustees and demanded, among other things, a student newspaper, a student council, and an honor system to replace the dreaded Fisk Code of Discipline. In December 1924, students defied curfew and protested on two occasions. On February 4, 1925, more than a hundred male students again ignored curfew and stormed through campus—singing, yelling, smashing windows, and overturning chapel seats to the tune of "Du Bois! Du Bois!" and "Before I'll be a slave, I'll be buried in my grave." At midnight, McKenzie allowed fifty White Nashville officers from a force complicit in a recent lynching to quell the rebellion, enraging Black people in Nashville and throughout the nation. Seven students were arrested—the same students who had met with the trustees in November—even though McKenzie had no proof of their involvement. "McKenzie, You're Through," *The Chicago Defender* shouted from its editorial page.[14]

Nobody was more enraged than Fisk students, who launched a strike the following day that lasted ten tumultuous weeks. Many students withdrew. A large number tried to transfer to Howard. Nashville's White community rallied behind McKenzie, while Nashville's Black community and Fisk alumni stridently supported the strikers. Five weeks into the strike, student leader George Streator proudly proclaimed, "We don't need to do anything except tell the students: 'Boycott this, or boycott that,' and believe me they do it to a finish!" Sensing his firing was imminent, McKenzie resigned on April 16, 1925. His resignation brought to a close the most influential protest of the New Negro Campus Movement. Many of the proposals were thereafter instituted by a temporary leadership committee and the next president, Thomas Elsa Jones. In addition, Jones, a White Quaker, added courses in Black history and literature and sponsored an annual conference with Black scholars. Du Bois, in probably one of his happiest times in almost a century of living, hailed the successful Fisk student "who hits power in high places, white power, power backed by unlimited wealth; hits it openly and between the eyes; talks face to face and not down 'at the big gate.' God speed the breed!"[15]

In the midst of the Fisk strike, Baltimore's *Afro-American* took a panoramic look at the movement and its implications. "Student disturbances ... may be traced to efforts ... to win a larger measure of participation in college control," the editors noted on February 28, 1925. Two decades ago, a "strict military discipline" could be insisted upon, since "education came largely thru philanthropy," with many teachers providing their services free of charge. But today's college student "has grown to the stature where he knows the blessings of self-government and academic freedom and demands them. If rebuffed, he resorts to the strike method. The very appearance of a student strike in an American college may be taken as evidence of growth in intelligence and independence."[16]

Presumably inspired by their Fisk fellows, Howard students started a strike shortly after McKenzie resigned. On May 7, 1925, two days after the university suspended five students for skipping compulsory ROTC—another facet of the moralized contraption that bred docile discipline—Howard students voted to strike. With posters screaming "Don't Be an Uncle Tom" or asking "What Is This Going To Be—An Army or a University?" picketers lined the campus, sometimes blocking classroom buildings. After four days of bitter debate, the faculty issued threats of suspensions and failures. "Are we scared?" some students chanted in defiance. "No!" Fearing Congressional retaliation and facing the unlikelihood of an accord, local alumni convinced students to return to classes on May 14 with the five reinstated, amnesty, and the ROTC requirement suspended while a special committee studied the issue. After the summer vacation, the special committee abolished compulsory ROTC.[17]

However, some students and professors and many alumni were far from pleased with J. Stanley Durkee's presidency and sought to remove him and compel trustees to hire Howard's first Black president. With pressure swelling in that summer of 1925 and into the next academic year, the trustees finally granted students, faculty, and alumni their wish. In 1926, they hired Mordecai Johnson, a 36-year-old Black Baptist preacher.[18]

With the protest activity mounting, a few Black newspapers published scathing editorials in May 1925. Black editors were particularly unnerved by the Howard protest. After interrogating their growing list of grievances, *The Chicago Defender* mocked, "next we shall hear of students striking because they are asked to attend classes; they will insist on writing their own examination questions; they will demand free movies on the campus." Undeterred, New Negro campus activism hovered like a storm cloud above higher education. Amid the storms of the Fisk and Howard protests in 1925, Simmons College students disrupted their Kentucky Baptist HBCU, and forty students, about half of the student body at Lincoln Institute, east of Louisville, vacated the school Berea officials created when forced to segregate. In December, students struck against their "prejudiced" president at Knoxville College in Tennessee.[19]

On December 7, 1925, a group of Black and White students gathered in Lane Hall at the University of Michigan to organize the Negro-Caucasian Club (NCC). Spearheaded by Mississippi native Lenoir Beatrice Smith, the NCC became one of the first, if not the first, interracial civil rights student associations in American history. Smith became the first president of this group, which aimed for the "abolition of discrimination against Negroes." After a clerk at a lunch counter just off campus refused to serve Smith, she went with a sympathetic professor to visit Dean John R. Eiffinger. "My grandfather owned slaves in Virginia, but you mustn't think I'm prejudiced," the dean said. "I would do something for you if I could." It was the first of many grievances the club brought before the dean. Other grievances included Black exclusion from college dances and the college swimming pool. HWCUs tended to bar Black students from every venue, activity, or course that involved physical contact.[20]

NCC members also implored area eateries to desegregate, but they were told White customers would walk out if Black students were served. On a few occasions after the group formed in December 1925, a small set of Black and White NCC members tested this line of reasoning, sitting in at eateries despite not receiving service. Reportedly, White customers did not walk out during perhaps the nation's first student sit-ins.[21]

NCC members (and New Negro campus activists more generally) also began to challenge the assimilationist curricula and the racist ideas that had poured out of the academy since its founding. In the 1920s, academics tended to rationalize American and European colonization of peoples of color and the political-economic plight of the African world as reflecting the natural order of racial hierarchy. Lothrop Stoddard's *The Rising Tide of Color Against White World-Supremacy* had just been published in 1920, and it dominated the mainstream. On the University of Michigan's campus, NCC members were outraged at the racist lectures of zoologist A. Franklin Shull and historian Ulrich B. Phillips, who classified slavery as paternal and humane. To challenge racist ideas and engage in their own study suggestions on Black life, Black students formed literary societies and clubs in the 1920s at schools such as Colgate, City College, Harvard, and Howard.[22]

In 1925, Prairie View A&M students near Houston resisted the inappropriate sexual advances of professors, which led to the termination of President J.G. Osborne. He was replaced by W.R. Banks. Serving in that capacity for two decades, Banks "never forgot that the students were his 'children,' and that he must save them from themselves," according to a college biographer. Thus, as an alternative to giving them the freedom to mature, Banks regulated dress, kept the genders separated, increased the number of religious gatherings, and, when students objected, ordered them to head to the highway and "grab the first thing that went by smoking."[23]

Students involved in a hazing incident at Johnson C. Smith were also told to grab the first thing smoking. It all spawned protests in 1926 that led to the suspension of seventy-five students, mostly first-year students. Nonetheless, with all the activism in the previous few years, the New Negro Campus Movement had new heights to reach. In her commencement address at Shaw as valedictorian of her college graduating class in April 1927, Ella Baker emboldened her peers. "Awake youth of the land and accept this noble challenge of salvaging the strong ship of civilization, by the anchors of rights, justice and love." Students awoke later that year at nearby Saint Augustine's in a weeklong protest for a relaxation of rules.[24]

Presumably the first Black collegiate athletic protest occurred that fall of 1927. At Howard, officials resolved a shortfall in athletic funding by eliminating free housing and food for its football team. Demoralized and underfed, the team suffered a heart-wrenching defeat to Bluefield State University in West Virginia. The loss ended Howard's three-year undefeated streak. The defeat started a weeklong strike in October 1927. It ended with students and alumni pledging to fund sports program amenities.[25]

As Howard players boycotted practices that month, students at Lincoln University of Missouri fumed over the recent firing of their beloved president Nathan B. Young—just as Florida A&M students did in 1923. State authorities were hostile to Young's vision of an academically upgraded, accredited HBCU that did not teach meekness. Young was replaced by Clement Richardson, well known for favoring submissive vocational education. "We are not interested in our lessons any more," one student announced. "We know that they are not running it for our benefit, but for their own." Lincoln's student council called a boycott, and roaming bands of strikers damaged property. Many left "in disgust, never to return again." Disruptions were quelled only when Governor Sam Baker sent armed prison guards to police the campus.[26]

The protests at Howard and Lincoln (MO) in 1927 paled in comparison to what occurred at Booker T. Washington's alma mater. On October 8, 1927, Hampton students assembled in Ogden Hall to view their Saturday evening movie. An administrator made a startling announcement: the lights were going to stay on at the rear of the auditorium above the seats of students with escort privileges. "Lights out," the students began to shout, stomping their feet, perplexed at the latest rule. "The matter of the lights was unusually small" to the students—no more than "the accidental puff of wind that touched off an already smoldering fire." After refusing to sing "plantation songs" for White visitors on Sunday evening, on Monday, what one student said "has been trying to happen for the last ten years" happened. A protest fire smoldered at Hampton. Twenty-one men (and no women on the sexist campus) were elected to serve on the Student Protest Committee. It delivered seventeen requests to the office of Principal James Gregg on Tuesday evening, including a student council composed exclusively of students, resignation of trade teachers without high school degrees, and weighting academic preparation above religiosity in selecting instructors.[27]

Using the same draconian but effective tactic that HBCU administrators used forty years later during the Black Campus Movement when faced with a student-body-wide rebellion, Gregg shut down the campus, expelled all of the students, and told them that to regain readmission they had to sign a "loyalty, obedience and cooperation" pledge. Twenty members of the Student Protest Committee—all of whom were some of Hampton's most promising male students—were suspended for the remainder of the 1927–1928 academic year. Hundreds were placed on probation. The only committee member not to be suspended was an informer. But the New Negroes wrecked his room.[28]

Parents, alumni, and newspapers largely did not come to the aid of the Hampton strikers, no doubt influenced by Gregg's public relations machine, which he kept operating efficiently during the strike. Hampton reopened on October 25, 1927. No strikes were in the offing, but a protracted spontaneous, leaderless campaign of passive resistance against Gregg engulfed the campus, gaining momentum with each passing semester. Anarchy seemed to be on the horizon in 1929. Before catastrophe came, Gregg resigned in May 1929. He was replaced by George P. Phenix, a White New Englander, who steered Hampton away from its vocational past.[29]

"An epidemic of student strikes has been sweeping over the country of late," wrote the editors of the *Pittsburgh Courier* on October 29, 1927. One of the few editorials endorsing the Hampton strike, it demonstrated the pulse of the New Negro Campus Movement. "Many of the rules and regulations in force in colleges and schools are archaic and should be scrapped. Often there is entirely too much restriction," and faculty supervision "too often borders on espionage." Morality "should be taught at home." Many HBCUs "are still run more like disciplinary barracks or reform schools than" colleges and universities attended by free people. "It is quite natural, then, that students should occasionally revolt."[30]

Students denied admission to dormitories and the physical education course protested at NYU in 1927. Freshman Thomas W. Young insisted, in a letter to the NAACP's head Walter White, that his brethren must "keep striking back at every injustice and mistreatment." And further: "If New York University knows that for every offense there is a strong organization ready to 'strike back' she will not be so inconsiderate in her actions." Student pressure and the NAACP's publicity campaign and legal threat prompted NYU to change its official rhetoric, but the segregation continued.[31]

The NAACP also involved itself in a struggle, spearheaded by Loren Miller in the 1920s and Wray Choat in the 1930s, "looking to the wiping out of the various discriminations in Kansas University." They persuaded the legislature to investigate the matter, but Chancellor Ernest Lindley defiantly insisted he was "not afraid of the courts or of publicity." Lindley exclaimed that the "University is a white school, built by white money for white students. If we want to get tough about it the Board of Regents could meet tomorrow and pass a ruling to exclude all out-of-state Negroes." In a rare occurrence, an HWCU chancellor took off the mask and exposed the historically *White* university, despite (or rather due to) having one of the largest Black student populations in the nation.[32]

The climax of the New Negro Campus Movement spanned the period from 1923 to 1927. Yet activism against tyrannical rules did not stop until it linked to the early Civil Rights Movement in the mid-1930s. In 1928, student strikers disrupted two AME Church–affiliated institutions (Kansas's Western and Kittrell College in North Carolina). Before

Langston University students went on strike, they presented to their president ten resolutions in November 1928, including the right to form a
student council at the lone HBCU in Oklahoma.[33]

Writing in the January 1929 issue of *The New Student*, John P. Davis
explained that protests had gripped "nearly every" HBCU in recent years.
Students were rebelling against the "benevolent despotism" of White college presidents or trustee boards indoctrinating "pacifism and servility"
through student codes that prescribed every moment of students' lives
and regulated practically all of their social interactions. "Imagine putting
such a rule into effect at Dartmouth or Smith!" Furthermore, Davis, a
Harvard graduate student, reasoned that the gargantuan number of regulations had been bred on "two fallacies": that Black students are "not
prepared for the exercise of free will" and that "the white trustee and
executive knows unerringly the best method of Negro education." These
White trustees and executives view "Negro students as members of a child
race, thinking they know just the kind of soothing syrup they need." Then
again, the HBCUs headed by Black Americans "suffer from the same fate"
due to their dependence on racist White capital. "It is the old story of
'whose bread I eat his song I sing.'"[34]

Davis failed to add that some Black educators imposed these rules not
just because of the sway of racist White capital. Some Black educators
expressed some of the same assimilationist ideas as their White peers.
Usually conceptualizing themselves as extraordinary, a number of Black
educators believed Black Americans were inferior to White Americans
morally or academically, and it was their duty, as extraordinary Black
Americans, to lift them up—the crudest form of ladder altruism.
Furthermore, to ensure that students were morally up to the task of prov-
ing racial equality and Black humanity to White humanity, these Black
educators maintained the moralized contraption.

Students at Howard rallied and broke up a basketball game when Dean
of Women Lucy Stowe expelled a woman for kissing her boyfriend in
February 1929. "As women we should stand for our rights and if necessary go to the limit so as to protect the integrity of Negro womanhood,"
one unnamed Black woman leader told reporters. That month, as Langston
students staged another protest, *The Chicago Defender*, citing the Howard
"kissing" controversy, suggested that HBCU presidents and deans need to
"hold a stock-taking conference" to "cure" the "problem" of "our college
unrest." When a federal report revealed that a White dean at Benedict
College in South Carolina had lied about his doctoral degree, boycotters

ordered his firing in March 1929. Two months later, a student at North Carolina's Brick Junior College hurried home without notice at the urgent request of his father. Another refused to take part in a college play. Both were expelled. The students were reinstated "after the most riotous week in the history of this institution." The suspension of two students also launched a strike at Alcorn State in 1929.[35]

Even though HBCUs experienced profound hardships during the years of the Great Depression, which began in 1929, the economic downturn did not depress student activism. President J.L. Peacock's barring of Black newspapers from the library and halting of the showing of *The Millionaire*, a Black motion picture, provoked an eight-hour strike at Shaw in early 1930. "He is a Northerner who has gone South and embedded himself in all the 'isms' of the South," wrote alumnus C.D. Jacobs. Students boycotted Georgia's Paine College in April 1930, and the *Pittsburgh Courier* proclaimed, "The day of white presidents of negro colleges is far spent." "The strike fever spread" to North Carolina A&T with a three-day walkout.[36]

The fever subsided in 1931, but it increased the following year. In January 1932, Virginia Union fired a young Rayford Logan who was finishing his doctorate at Harvard. His offense: advocating for a Black president and encouraging his students to think critically. In response to the firing, students protested. A mere 10 of the 316 Knoxville students did not strike that month when 40 students were punished for attending an off-campus dance. Striking Gammon Theological seminarians demanded the firing of a racist professor in March 1932; Langston students demanded the firing of their president in May; and Storer students demanded, along with the NAACP, the erection of a memorial tablet to John Brown on their Harpers Ferry campus.[37]

In 1933, students staged strikes to protest restrictions on class choice at Howard and poor food at Saint Augustine's, against the Virginia University of Lynchburg president (leading to his resignation), and to force the creation of a student council at Lincoln (MO). Bayard Rustin led a strike against the dorm's "bad" food—the only academic year the music major and future organizer of the March on Washington attended Wilberforce. In May 1934, the demotion of a popular school official, Howard Gregg, triggered a march of eight hundred Wilberforce students around their campus, shouting, "We want Gregg!" That year, Howard law students boycotted classes for a week to push out a professor. And a detail of "rough, brutal, and disrespectful" county police and the dismissal of twenty-eight students ended a four-day strike at Virginia State University that decried, among other things, the separate gendered entrances to the library, dining hall, and chapel and the annual "show" of spirituals performed for the governor.[38] Thirty-one striking students were terminated at Alcorn State in 1935, a year that probably saw the lowest number of protests since the beginning of the New Negro Campus Movement. In contrast, at least eight demonstrations rocked HBCUs in 1936. Howard students protested in January and November. A White Morgan State professor's telling of "Mammy" stories sparked a class walkout. In November, food strikes gripped North Carolina A&T, Shaw, and Saint Augustine's. In addition to demanding better food, strikers at Langston demanded a student council, more guidance and fewer threats from administrators, and for women "to be treated as women and not as wards." "The wave of [New Negro campus activism] … sweeping the country," declared the *Pittsburgh Courier*, hit Prairie View A&M and West Kentucky Community & Technical College in 1936.[39]

The New Negro Campus Movement had battered the moralized contraption, which had been utterly fundamental to the racist constitution of higher education from the Civil War to World War I. As wardens of the academy, HBCU officials tended to seek to control every aspect of the lives of their students. The students' crimes were their Blackness, their youth, their gender, their being born in a segregated society, and their being bred within a political economy that primarily wanted them to teach or preach subordination or docile, manual labor. Their moral performance had to be pristine. Their moral "beasts" had to be restrained to attract White benefactors, to mold laborers for White capital, to live in a segregated society, and to demonstrate Black civilization.

Sometimes these justifications of the moralized contraption emerged from the mouths of White presidents and led to demands for the replacement of those presidents with Black presidents. But these justifications were no less racist, no less demeaning, no less dehumanizing coming from Black HBCU presidents. In the racist imaginary, HBCU students needed more policing than the morally and academically superior White college students. Black HWCU students detected a penitentiary too—from the standardization of exclusion, particularly in dormitories.

In effect, the New Negro Campus Movement was a fight for *basic* social and academic freedoms for Black students in higher education, which White students by the 1920s took for granted. The stress of *basic* cannot be understated. Without gaining—or placing themselves on the road to gaining—these basic freedoms to live on campus, eat tasty food, dictate their campus life schedules, socialize, publish student newspapers, organize student governments, not face expulsion for breaking a rule, and file a grievance, the Black Campus Movement would not have been possible, nor would the prime role of Black students in the Civil Rights Movement.

CHAPTER 5

"Strike While the Iron Is Hot": Early Civil Rights Student Activism

The New Negro Campus Movement ebbed in the late 1920s and ended by the mid-1930s. Black student activism changed course, latching onto the nascent Long Civil Rights Movement. And yet, in the growing historiography of the formative years of the Civil Rights Movement, Black students are rarely examined. Instead, New Dealers, community activists, populist politicians, Communists, unionists, anticolonialists, NAACP and New Negro Congress members, and labor organizers are some of the groups often situated at the starting line in the late 1930s. Although some mention has been made of Black student activism of the 1920s, the traditional historical narrative asserts that Black student protesters were marginal actors until the sit-in wave of the spring of 1960.[1]

In actuality, the Long Black Student Movement included the lost years of the late 1930s, 1940s, and early 1950s. As participants of the civil rights struggle, Black students began a concerted battle to bring down Jim Crow in the late 1930s while also campaigning against war, fascism, capitalism, and the racist constitution on their campuses. Thus, after engaging mainly in campus activism in the 1920s and early 1930s, they developed a binary activist focus (campus and community) until the late 1950s, when they were swept up in the off-campus civil rights crusade until the rise of the Black Campus Movement in 1965. Black student sit-ins in 1960 were not the *beginning* of any movement. They were the *crowning event* of mounting civil rights student protest waves coming from the sea of American

© The Author(s), under exclusive license to Springer Nature Switzerland AG 2025
I. X. Kendi, *The Black Campus Movement*, Contemporary Black History, https://doi.org/10.1007/978-3-031-37394-7_5

colleges and universities that slammed into the shores of Dixie throughout the 1930s, 1940s, and 1950s.

The three-decade civil rights student struggle started to lay its roots in the early 1930s. As a Virginia Union University student, James Jackson helped establish the Cooperative Independent Movement (CIM) to "train leaders for the deliverance of our people, through militant action, from every semblance of racial and class oppression." The CIM joined White students at the University of Virginia and presented their grievances to the Virginia legislature concerning fascism, war preparations, racist employment policies, and educational retrenchment. At Fisk, a Denmark Vesey Forum stimulated discussions about racism, where protesters picketed a local Jim Crow theater in the early 1930s, led mainly by graduate student Ishmael Flory. In response to White supremacists lynching Cordie Cheek, a Black teenager living on the edge of campus, the Forum organized a rally on December 15, 1933. Meanwhile, Fisk student council president John Hope Franklin decided to hand President Franklin D. Roosevelt an anti-lynching petition when he visited the campus in November 1934. However, Fisk president Thomas E. Jones cleverly convinced the future historian to refrain from doing so by deceiving Franklin about arranging a personal meeting with FDR. "I took from my disappointment one lesson: Jim Crow America was skilled at deflecting or ignoring appeals to justice and equity," Franklin later wrote.[2]

In 1934, the lone Black congressman, Chicago representative Oscar De Priest, petitioned to abolish the unwritten rule barring Black patrons from the House of Representatives' public dining room. After officials dismissed a waiter who was attending Howard for violating the rule, his peers joined the struggle. On March 17, 1934, about thirty students marched into the Capitol but were prevented from entering the dining room "to test the legality" of the rule. "We are citizens and we can go wherever we want in the Capitol of the United States," the unnamed Howard leader insisted. Unmoved, the Capitol police ejected the students, who returned only to be repulsed again and again. De Priest called their attempted direct-action protest "a serious mistake," since it "would do no good and only causes trouble."[3]

While some people are not aware of the array of student protest activities prior to 1960, historians of student activism tend to locate America's first student movement in the 1930s—concealing the New Negro Campus Movement in the so-called "moribund" 1920s.[4] This 1930s student social movement was not America's first student movement, nor was it wholly White. The American Youth Congress, a prominent organization during that period, had a sprinkling of Black members and sometimes spoke out and campaigned against racism.[5] As an executive in the National Youth Administration, Mary McLeod Bethune founded the National Conference of Negro Youth in 1937, which took a conciliatory approach to civil rights until 1942. Spurred by wartime radicalization, it changed its name to the National Council of Negro Youth, compared fascism to racism, attacked the racist judiciary and segregation in the armed forces, and lobbied for antilynching and anti–poll tax legislation. "We must strike while the iron is hot to end the poll tax once [and] for all, now," said Winifred Norman, the group's chair.[6]

The American Student Union (ASU), the main majority-White student organization of the decade, formed in 1935. It merged the socialist Student League for Industrial Democracy and the Communist National Student League, which had James Jackson of Virginia Union on its national executive committee. The ASU mobilized hundreds of thousands of antiwar students to boycott classes for one hour annually from 1936 to 1939. Although rarely explicitly discussed, the ASU mobilized Black student antiwar activists, too, who often connected militaristic fascism in Germany, Japan, Spain, and Italy (particularly after its invasion of Ethiopia) with militaristic fascism in Georgia, Mississippi, Louisiana, and Alabama. Students at Howard and Virginia Union participated in antiwar conferences. Howard had the sole ASU-initiated strike in Washington, DC, in 1936, with nearly two hundred students attending a parade and mass meeting. Shortly after the ASU strike in 1937, a young John H. Johnson, future founder of *Ebony* and *Jet* magazines, declared, "Yes, students should strike for peace."[7]

"To speak of a powerful student movement without speaking of the Negro student is impossible," wrote Maurice Gates, challenging the ASU the year of its inauguration in 1935. The ASU did in fact speak to the Negro student, due to the Communist Party's directive in the 1930s to attack racism and due to the influence of Black ASU members and chapters at universities such as Virginia Union and Howard. At its national gatherings, ASU delegates resolved to fight lynchings and "discrimination against Negroes" and objected to segregated amenities. "The very foundation of democracy cannot be made stable unless we root out minority discrimination," Bill Davis, a Howard delegate, told the fourth annual

ASU convention in 1939. The ASU demonstrated against racism when Black students at Columbia (1936), the University of Illinois (1938), and Philadelphia's Temple University (1940) were refused service at area businesses. In possibly the ASU's largest rooting-out operation, the Bennett College chapter boycotted nearby theaters in North Carolina with all White films in early 1938, mobilizing more than a thousand college students. With the Nazi-Soviet Pact of 1939, the refusal of some ASU Communists to criticize Soviet imperialism, pre-McCarthy efforts to "clean out communism" on campus, and the United States' entry into World War II, the ASU collapsed by 1941.[8]

The year after the ASU disbanded, in 1942, the Congress of Racial Equality (CORE) was formed by White University of Chicago students, such as George Houser, along with James Farmer, a recent Howard law school graduate. Many of the founders were members of the Fellowship of Reconciliation (FOR), a pacifist civil rights organization inspired by Mahatma Gandhi's philosophy of nonviolence. White middle-class college students almost entirely made up the initial growth of the organization. Nathan Wright Jr., a student at Episcopal Theological School in Massachusetts, was one of CORE's few Black student staffers. He served as the New England field representative in the late 1940s. Wright, who chaired the Black Power conferences of 1967 and 1968, traveled on the Journey of Reconciliation in 1947 along with eight White Americans and seven other Black Americans, including Andrew Johnson, a Black student from Cincinnati. They tested the recent Supreme Court ruling declaring segregation in interstate travel unconstitutional. CORE declined after its famous Journey but revitalized itself during the classical civil rights period (1954–1965).[9]

Black students were part of the unprecedented impetus for what Jacquelyn Dowd Hall termed "civil rights unionism," which rose to prominence in the seminal years of the civil rights struggle in the late 1930s.[10] Yet, as usual, their brand of civil rights unionism or, more accurately, labor politics looked to the left. More than four hundred Black youth, including students from Virginia Union, Howard, Clark Atlanta, Fisk, Spelman, Morehouse, and Morgan State, convened in February 1937 in Richmond under the auspices of the youth section of the National Negro Congress (NNC). They established the Southern Negro Youth Congress (SNYC). "We are here to save ourselves and our people!" declared Edward Strong. As the NNC's national youth chairman, Strong did much of the early planning for the SNYC.[11]

Conditions of Black life are not caused by "the majority of white Southerners …but the few, those who profit by pitting white labor against black labor to the harm of both," the inaugural conference proclaimed. "We have a right to" free and equal schools, homes without poverty, recreational facilities, jobs, the right to organize with White people, suffrage, and the eradication of lynching. Delegates also resolved that "Negro history be added to history books," the establishment of world peace, the freedom of the politically imprisoned Angelo Herndon and the Scottsboro Boys, and the support of the ASU and the NAACP. According to historian Robin D.G. Kelley, SNYC members articulated a "complex radical consciousness that simultaneously advocated interracial unity and black nationalism" or a "politics of inclusion *and* self-determination."[12]

At its peak, the SNYC reportedly claimed a membership of 11,000 in ten southern states. For about a decade beginning in 1937, the group organized annual All-Southern Negro Youth Congresses, often at HBCUs. Paul Robeson gave his first Deep South singing performance in 1942 at the Fifth Congress, held at Tuskegee. In 1944, Mary McLeod Bethune told SNYC delegates to "get ready in heart, in head and in hand, for the new world order which is coming." Honored as "the senior statesman of the American Negro's liberation struggle," W.E.B. Du Bois challenged the 1946 congress to stop "running away from the battle here in" the South and instead "grit their teeth and fight it out right here" using "white slaves of modern capitalist industry" as allies.[13]

In one of its initial campaigns, through the efforts of the hardened Virginia Union activist James E. Jackson, the SNYC helped unionize Richmond's five thousand tobacco stemmers. In 1938, they successfully struck for better working conditions. However, most of the Congress's activism emerged around Birmingham, Alabama, which had become SNYC headquarters by 1940 after its largest conference to date was held there—650 delegates, including students from Alabama HBCUs. Esther Cooper, an Oberlin (1938) and Fisk (1940) graduate who had participated in the ASU, politically tussled with Birmingham City Council members and Public Safety Commissioner "Bull" Connor in petitioning for the desegregation of a local park and playground. She kept the organization alive while her husband, James Jackson, fought in World War II. The group engaged in quite a few civil liberties cases concerning segregation and police and mob brutality in the 1940s. It launched a Free Nora Wilson campaign in Alabama that succeeded in stopping the railroading of this teenager, who sternly defended her sister, accused of stealing, to a White woman. (The SNYC was notified of the case by Caravan Puppeteers, a group consisting mostly of Black college students who in 1940 used puppets to amuse and clandestinely educate rural Black folk about the poll tax, disenfranchisement, and labor disunity.) Like other groups with Black students, the SNYC lobbied the government to investigate the revitalized KKK and to coerce defense contractors to hire Black workers during World War II. The Congress also powered anti–poll tax and anti-Hitler campaigns, as well as efforts toward voter education and registration. By 1949, like countless other antiracist groups, SNYC had been red scared into oblivion.[14]

Unlike many civil rights organizations, the NAACP survived late-1940s and early-1950s McCarthyism. Black students gradually entered the NAACP in the late 1930s, along with or aside from the ASU, SNYC, the Communist Party, church youth organizations, and other campus, local, and national groups. Sensing the strengthening activist impulse of students, the NAACP wisely established the Youth and College Division in March 1936, appointing Juanita Jackson national director. Jackson, who earned a master's degree from UPENN in 1935, had a storied past of youth organizing in Baltimore, having served as vice president of the National Council of Methodist Youth. "Discrimination and segregation are on the increase," Jackson told NAACP youth in 1936. "We cannot lose a moment. We must not falter a step. We must march forward!"[15]

Jackson terminated the "junior branches," reorganizing the youth division into junior youth councils (for those aged 12 to 15), youth councils (for those aged 16 to 25), and college chapters with new guidelines. In her first mobilization campaign, she hurried youth into the antilynching legislation struggle galvanized by a Senate bill first introduced in 1934 (and blocked every year by segregationists). In February 1937, working closely with the SNYC, NAACP college chapters held a series of antilynching radio broadcasts, demonstrations, and programs around the nation, wearing black armbands at events to symbolize their mourning. Each November during "American Education Week" in the late 1930s, Jackson encouraged protests against educational injustices. NAACP youngsters and students also raised money for Black labor struggles and initiated a few "Buy Where You Can Work" campaigns in states such as New Jersey and Indiana. They demonstrated against police brutality and set up "citizenship training schools" to ready Black southerners to register and vote in the late 1930s. In 1938, Jackson resigned her post in order to marry. James

H. Robinson replaced the venerable Jackson, one of the unsung giants of the Long Black Student Movement whom the NAACP's Walter White unsuccessfully tried to retain.[16]

Still, the youth division continued to grow, and students unremittingly formed college chapters, even at Hampton in 1940. Some studied "Negro" history, such as the chapter at LeMoyne-Owen. In March of that year, the NAACP convened the First Annual Student Conference at Virginia Union. At this conference, students condemned the Roosevelt administration's expansion of the military budget at the expense of social programs, thereby opposing foreign war without domestic civil rights.[17]

The NAACP as a whole claimed record membership, stepping up its fight over the color line. For instance, in 1943, Howard's NAACP chapter picketed and desegregated a cafeteria near the college. One of the leaders of the mostly undergraduate group of activists was law student Pauli Murray, the future cofounder of the National Organization of Women (NOW). Howard president Mordecai Johnson squashed another demonstration the next year, on the grounds that it threatened Howard's federal appropriation. At that point, according to Murray, students turned their "reform energies upon the administration of the school and called for a whole review and revamping of administrative procedure ... so that students would have more say," similar to what would happen two decades later.[18]

When World War II ended in 1945, many Black American soldiers and migrants became students. And they gave birth over the next few years to baby boomers, groomed for two decades on far-reaching civil rights and Black power activism before enrolling in higher education in the late 1960s. The mothers and fathers of Black Campus Movement activists were dynamic, and they imparted their dynamism to their children. Fascism had been defeated. Now it was racism's turn. With many veterans joining and starting chapters at colleges such as Cornell, Long Island University in New York, and Columbia, it is not surprising that in the years after the war, NAACP college chapters and youth councils created veterans' committees. Aside from veteran matters, such as securing the GI Bill and ending segregation in the military, which President Harry Truman did in 1948, voter registration appealed to postwar civil rights workers after the White primaries were deemed unconstitutional in 1944.

Georgia students were particularly active in this arena. Arthur Johnson, who became a prominent Detroit NAACP leader in the 1950s and early

1960s, organized Morehouse's NAACP chapter as a freshman in the mid-1940s. The group attracted a membership of fifty, holding meetings every month that drew a teenaged Martin Luther King Jr., whose father was active in the Atlanta chapter. Under Johnson's leadership and at the urging of "Daddy King," the Morehouse NAACP launched a voter registration drive among Black college students across the state in 1946. At around the same time, Coretta Scott joined the Antioch College NAACP chapter after being blocked from honing her teaching skills in the schools of segregated Yellow Springs, Ohio.[19]

NAACP college chapters (and campus-based, usually interracial, organizations, such as the Council of Minority Equality at Indiana's DePauw University) also launched direct-action protests in Northern, Midwestern, and Western states in the late 1940s and 1950s. These protests were against area establishments that excluded Black students. The Pennsylvania State University NAACP chapter staged a demonstration against six segregated campus barber shops, a segregation that resulted in Black students having to travel twenty-eight miles for a haircut. But NAACP youth councils and college chapters hit their lowest point in the early 1950s. They were pulled down by external and internal red purges, the Korean War, and the national office's discouraging of direct action protests where Jim Crow flew legally. All these challenges contributed to the NAACP's declining membership and financial crisis.[20]

NAACP youth councils and college chapters were, on occasion, cradles for antiracist student activists whom civil rights historians have largely sidelined. One of the pivotal, protracted skirmishes of the Long Civil Rights Movement between the 1930s and the mid-1960s was the desegregation of higher education, especially in the South—first graduate and professional schools, later undergraduate programs. The NAACP Legal Defense Fund, led by the likes of Charles Hamilton Houston and Thurgood Marshall, has been placed at the axis of this history. Black student plaintiffs have been relegated to the margins in this story, not often identified as key activists.

In reality, aspiring students thrust themselves into the center of the desegregation of Southern higher education. They applied in droves to segregated schools from the late 1930s to the 1960s, agreed to file lawsuits, served as the vulnerable center of the NAACP's cases, and, if they won, stridently and *crucially* held open doors while weathering social seclusion, separate classrooms, hostile students and faculty, and White mobs. The NAACP Legal Defense Fund brilliantly tried and won these cases, and history has praised their endeavors. However, lawyers can do nothing without clients. Hence, just as significantly, aspiring Black students of varying ages handed the NAACP its cases and implemented the rulings by walking fearlessly into the fog of segregation. Black student activists, supported by NAACP lawyers, desegregated higher education.[21]

The first joint affair between hopeful students and the NAACP tried to cut the color line at the University of North Carolina at Chapel Hill (UNC Chapel Hill) in 1933. *The New York Times* categorized this university that year as "the most liberal State institution in the South in its attitude toward the Negro race." The *Times* added, "There is no likelihood that any other Southern college or university for whites will acquiesce in the admission of Negroes." Thomas Hocutt, a 24-year-old graduate of present-day North Carolina Central University and a hotel waiter at Duke, applied for admission to the state's only school of pharmacy at UNC Chapel Hill in March 1933. Denied on Jim Crow grounds, Hocutt solicited the assistance of local lawyers, who in turn contacted the NAACP. Eager to demonstrate the superiority of legal activism and curb the growing influence of the Communist Party among Black Americans in the 1930s, prompted by the Communist Party's widely touted defense of the nine Scottsboro Boys charged with rape in Alabama, NAACP executive secretary Walter White grabbed the case. James Shepard, the accommodating head of North Carolina Central, fearing White retaliation or out of respect for White propriety, refused to release Hocutt's transcript, dooming the case from the start. Yet, in throwing out the case, the judge also tossed in some hope. Judge M.V. Barnhill stated that the denial was due to Hocutt's race and that he could have ordered the university to review the application fairly. The NAACP proclaimed a moral victory for a new program. Aspiring Black students gazed at the closed door.[22]

In 1935, two aspiring students visibly attempted to pry open Dixie doors in neighboring states. Alice C. Jackson, a graduate of Virginia Union, sought admission to her state's lone graduate program in French at the University of Virginia. Officials denied Jackson's application because of the racist bar and "other good and sufficient reasons." Advised by the NAACP, she mailed a letter to the rector and the Board of Visitors, asking them "to specify the 'other good and sufficient reasons' why you rejected my application." Sensing legal redress, they did not specify. But to hold off desegregation's advance, the Virginia legislature established a graduate school at Virginia State and provided scholarships for Black students to attend out-of-state graduate schools.[23]

The NAACP did not take the University of Virginia to court. However, in 1935, it did defend Donald Murray, an Amherst graduate, whom the University of Maryland law school told it "does not accept Negro students." The Baltimore City Court ordered the University of Maryland to admit Murray, and an appeals court agreed with that ruling the following year. NAACP executive secretary Walter White encouraged the newly enrolled Murray to "work hard" because "by your very manner you will create …a new concept of the Negro." Based on ladder altruism, Black students were supposed to endure the burden of demonstrating the humanity of Black people.[24]

These three Black applicants cracked the dam. Prospective Black students started submitting applications to Southern White admissions offices in the late 1930s. Then the student–NAACP coalition raised the stakes, taking to the U.S. Supreme Court the case of Lloyd Gaines, who had been denied admission to the University of Missouri. In 1938, the Court ruled in *Missouri ex. rel. Gaines v. Canada* that Missouri had violated the equal protection clause of the Fourteenth Amendment of the recent Lincoln (MO) graduate since it did not have a separate but equal law school for Black Americans, thus mandating Gaines's admission. The Court's foray into the "separate but equal" clause vitalized the civil rights community to launch an all-out legal attack on Jim Crow.

Before that assault took shape, tragedy tempered this first victory. In 1939, the Missouri legislature created a law school at Gaines's alma mater. However, Gaines was not one of the thirty enrollees that year at Lincoln (MO). In the meantime, Charles Hamilton Houston and NAACP lawyers had managed to initiate a second case to argue that Lincoln's law school hardly resembled the flagship school, ultimately exposing the fallacy of the "separate but equal" policy. The NAACP had moved Gaines to Chicago after he received death threats. When he needed to be deposed for the second case, he could not be found. Without a plaintiff, the court dismissed the case. Gaines had reportedly been saddened by Missouri's building of a law school at Lincoln, thus prolonging his already three-year wait at the state's flagship law school. He was last seen in Chicago in March 1939. His actual fate remains unknown, but speculation pointed to suicide, self-exile, assassination, or a retreat into hiding, having been bribed or bullied by White supremacists.[25] Still, hopeful Black students constantly applied and stood up as plaintiffs in the 1940s, and by the end of the decade they had fissured a few nearly century-old walls. Silas Hunt decided to forgo his plans to attend the University of Indiana and instead struggled to gain admission to the University of Arkansas. Unexpectedly, the World War II veteran and graduate of the University of Arkansas at Pine Bluff managed to get around the snail-like pace of the court. Seeking to dodge the negative publicity they saw trouble other Southern institutions, the University of Arkansas announced on January 30, 1948, that they would admit qualified Black graduate students, starting with Hunt. He enrolled in law school days later as the first Black American to be admitted to a White public university in the Deep South since the handful admitted during Reconstruction. Hunt attended segregated classes in the law school basement, some of which were attended by a few sympathetic White students, until tuberculosis cut his life short on April 22, 1949.[26]

The well-publicized trial of Ada Lois Sipuel (Fisher), who was attempting to enter the University of Oklahoma law school, inspired Hunt's activism. Following its *Gaines v. Canada* decision, in *Sipuel v. Board of Regents*, in 1948, the U.S. Supreme Court finally ordered her admission. When the daughter of a minister and Langston graduate enrolled in 1949, the university assigned her to a restricted classroom area with a chair marked "colored." George McLaurin, a Black doctoral education student pushing 70 years old, suffered a similar fate when University of Oklahoma admitted him in response to the High Court's order in 1950. The university sat him at a classroom desk in a row reserved for Black people, created a designated space in the library, and made him eat at a different time than White students at a table with a sign overhead that read "Reserved for Colored Only" until compassionate White students ripped it down. McLaurin and the NAACP challenged the legality of campus segregation, and the Supreme Court in *McLaurin v. Oklahoma State Regents* ruled in the coalition's favor. This latest ruling in 1950, along with *Sweatt v. Painter*, which required Black admission to the University of Texas at Austin law school, hampered the attempts of colleges forced to desegregate to insert mechanisms perpetuating the standardization of exclusion.[27]

The energy behind the student–NAACP coalition for the desegregation of higher education received a jolt from these rulings. The endorsement of the ban on educational segregation from the President's Commission on Higher Education in 1947 also vitalized the coalition. Students were encouraged by their younger brothers and sisters who were desegregating high schools in the 1950s. It is not known how many Black

Americans applied to break down higher education's barriers. It is quite possible that thousands of aspiring Black students stared the Jim Crow admissions policies in the face, including several prominent leaders of the 1960s, such as Pauli Murray of NOW and CORE Black Power director Floyd McKissick Sr. To be sure, Ada Sipuel and George McLaurin inspired and invigorated many hopeful Black Americans across the South who were engaged in multiyear battles to attend graduate school in their states.

CHAPTER 6

"Justice Is All We Want": Black Students and Desegregation

The agency of students involved in desegregation court cases has been marginalized in pre-1960s civil rights historiography, but not nearly as much as the Black campus activism that snatched headlines almost every year during the late 1930s, 1940s, and early 1950s. A three-year battle for the first Black professor at City College resulted in the hiring of Max Yergan to teach "Negro History and Culture" in the fall of 1937. Upon the imposition of an earlier curfew for women students at Wilberforce in 1938, several hundred mostly male students boycotted classes and rampaged through campus, hurling rocks at windows and lights until sheriffs arrived and the nine "ringleaders" were expelled. In 1939, Allen University students struck for two weeks, demanding the resignation of the "illegally" installed new president of the AME Church college in South Carolina; a violent strike at North Carolina A&T followed the dismissal of the football coach; and Hampton students vacated classes for five days, angered by the White president and English department chair's unexplained firing of a Black professor.[1]

In 1941, activists at NYU and Harvard protested when Black athletes were benched against Jim Crow institutions, and Howard women showed their discontent with the recently installed dean of women, whom they labeled Hitler, for her "walk-the-chalk-line" rules. However, the major campus protest in 1941 disrupted Tuskegee, where nearly half of the 1,400 students went on strike. Dozens were arrested, suspended, expelled,

© The Author(s), under exclusive license to Springer Nature Switzerland AG 2025
I. X. Kendi, *The Black Campus Movement*, Contemporary Black History, https://doi.org/10.1007/978-3-031-37394-7_6

or battered by police officers in remonstration of "despicable" food sometimes seasoned with flies, ants, roaches, and tacks. In the 1940s, large, spirited food strikes also unsettled Spelman (1942), North Carolina's Livingston College (1946), Alabama A&M (1947), Alabama State University (1948), Benedict (1944 and 1947), and Clark Atlanta (1944), where students complained that the food was "not fit for pigs." Students protested for the reinstatement of suspended and expelled students and for a greater voice in college and disciplinary affairs at Johnson C. Smith and Morgan State in 1943, North Carolina A&T (1945), Lincoln (MO) (1948), Georgia's Fort Valley State University (1949), Elizabeth City State University in North Carolina (1953), and Kentucky State University (1953). Strikes to run off or reduce the power of presidents, who usually prevented student movement, fraternization, and organization, battered Maryland's Bowie State University in 1941, Delaware State University in 1942 and 1949, and Saint Augustine's and Morris College in South Carolina in 1943. Stringent regulations for women prompted strikes at North Carolina Central in 1942 and Virginia Union two years later.[2]

In 1944, the Baltimore *Afro-American* asked some HBCU presidents: "Should college students have the right to strike?" A few said no outright. Most were like Kentucky State's R.B. Atwood, who said, "Students have the right to strike although in my twenty years of experience with students I have known of very few strikes which I have felt were justified." Up North, feeling their causes justified, seventeen student waiters boycotted the segregated faculty club at the University of Chicago in 1945, and public campaigns pushed the nearby University of Illinois into granting dormitory space to Black women.[3]

Mid-1940s campus activism, just like civil rights struggles more generally, were often waged by veterans aghast at the rules and restrictions that mirrored their military lives. In 1946, Charles Evers and his younger brother Medgar, fresh from fighting in World War II, which according to Charles Evers "woke up a lot of Negro GIs," enrolled at Alcorn State (and later registered and tried to vote). The 23-year-old Charles became class president and led a food strike and a campaign "to get the deans to stop treating us like babies." A "bunch of Uncle Toms installed by the white power structure" ran Alcorn State at the time, Charles Evers recalled, and they allowed the use of "the same old white racist textbooks that described us as savages and Reconstruction as a terrible evil."[4]

A similar state of affairs prompted a four-day strike in 1947 at Wiley College in Texas, with some picketers holding signs that read "Down with Dictatorship." Wiley students forced amnesty, the resignation of a dean and two professors, the right to establish a student council, and the elimination of campus separation between men and women.

While students coerced professors, antiracist, activist, and outspoken professors were terrorized by HBCU administrators seeking to prevent faculty radicalism, disloyalty, or clout. Student strikes followed the "unjust" firings of popular professors at Johnson C. Smith in 1942 and Knoxville and Langston in 1949.[5]

Black and Jewish students conducted a strike at the City College in 1949, demanding the ouster of an antisemitic professor and a racist residential hall director, while administrators tried to discredit the students by framing them as communists. NAACP chapters at the University of New Mexico and Columbia protested against exclusionary clauses in campus clubs in 1949 and 1953, respectively. In addition, Black students, sometimes through newly organized NAACP chapters, continued their multi-decade struggle against segregated housing and faculty at institutions such as the University of Wisconsin-Madison and Cornell. With McCarthyism breeding conservatism, campus activism slowed in the early 1950s.[6]

On May 17, 1954, the US Supreme Court ruled in *Brown v. Board of Education* that "separate educational facilities are inherently unequal," rolling back the "separate but equal" doctrine that had been the law of the land for roughly six decades. Black students rejoiced on their campuses. Some, in the midst of their elation, immediately realized the historic mandate. "We should not look on this decision as merely something we have to obey," said Duke's Jolee Fritz and David W. Stith, a North Carolina Central law student. The two vice presidents of the North Carolina State Conference of NAACP youth councils and college chapters urged the youth of their state and the nation to look upon the decision as a challenge "to make Democracy work." For southern White supremacists, federal legal cover for segregation in higher education had been removed. States' rights and hawkishness became their last major recourse. As the Long Black Student Movement accelerated away from the political pit stop of *Brown*, violence stayed on its tail.[7]

Emmett Till became Southern aggression's most notorious post-*Brown* victim. For reportedly whistling at a Mississippi White woman, White supremacists tortured and murdered the Chicago teenager. They beat his face so badly he was unrecognizable. His mother, Mamie Till Mobley decided to have an open casket at her son's funeral and allowed the gruesome pictures of her battered son to be seen around the nation on the cover of *Jet* magazine. No Black American was the same after seeing Till's bludgeoned face. If *Brown* gave African Americans hope, the Till lynching stoked them with rage—a hope and rage that fueled the Civil Rights Movement over the next decade. The murder presumably hit Till's Black peers the hardest, and they turned around and kicked off a stretch of seventeen years of fresh, forceful, and often front-page civil rights and Black Power activism on and off campus.

Civil rights activists first tried to rock the "cradle of the confederacy." Although rarely discussed, some of the first arms in Montgomery came from Black students. In October 1954, slightly less than half of the two thousand Alabama State students rallied, boycotted classes, and burned a campus building in an effort to gain a stronger voice in student affairs. The following fall, they directed their activism off campus. Late in the evening of the day Rosa Parks was arrested in Montgomery for refusing to give up her bus seat, Alabama State professor Jo Ann Robinson, a colleague, and two of Robinson's "most trusted senior students" gathered on campus to pull an all-nighter. For four hours, they cut stencils and mimeographed 52,500 leaflets announcing a bus boycott on December 5, 1955. Then, for another four hours, Robinson and the two students mapped out the distribution routes for the notices, arranged bundles in the appropriate sequence, and loaded them into her car before arriving at her morning class. After the 8 a.m. class, in which the two seniors were enrolled, and working on no sleep, the trio circulated the notices to Montgomery's Black community. Black students supported the 381-day Montgomery bus boycott and the women like Robinson who backed the boycott instead of the buses.[8]

However, in 1956, the epicenter of the Long Black Student Movement was located in another Alabama city—Tuscaloosa. A few months into the Montgomery bus boycott, when many Americans did not know the name Martin Luther King Jr., many heard the name of the youngest of ten children born to farmers from Shiloh, Alabama. With the NAACP's help and a court order, on February 1, 1956, Autherine Lucy enrolled at the University of Alabama as a graduate student in library science. Three days of violent demonstrations by White mobs ultimately led to Lucy's suspension because the University of Alabama claimed it could not keep her safe. When she filed a lawsuit to reverse the suspension, university officials cried slander and expelled her—a tragedy that "enlisted world-wide sympathy for a civil rights cause that was yet to be called a movement," wrote historian E. Culpepper Clark. The episode galvanized the American resistance to and for *Brown*.[9]

It also incited Black student activism. In March 1956, food strikes at Cheyney produced a new food facility. Early the next month, five hundred South Carolina State students, encouraged by the local NAACP, declined to eat dinner in the university cafeteria because Jim Crow distributors supplied some of the products. Students at nearby Claflin University, South Carolina's oldest historically black university, joined the boycott. Soon after the strike began, South Carolina State students raised long-standing grievances with President Benner C. Turner, including his selection of student leaders based on loyalty to his administration instead of merit. The failed strike lasted six days, after which the all-White trustee board expelled several students, including Student Council President Fred Moore, a month from graduation.[10]

On a crowded Saturday bus in Tallahassee on May 27, 1956, less than two months later, Wilhelmina Jakes and Carrie Patterson, two Florida A&M students, sat down on a three-person seat next to a White woman they knew. "Get up or get off," ordered the bus driver, who had pulled over to enforce the racist code. "I'd be glad to get off," Jakes retorted, "if you'll give us our money back." The driver spurned the offer and waited for the police to arrive. The police arrested and charged the students with inciting a riot. The next evening, Klansmen burned a cross on the lawn of their apartment. Word of the incidents traveled through the Florida A&M campus like the sound of its marching band. On May 28, students boycotted classes and city buses, boarding every bus at the main bus depot on campus to pressure riders into getting off. Eventually, all the buses were like those in Montgomery—practically empty. Three days into the boycott, Black community leaders created the Tallahassee Inter-Civic Council to facilitate the boycott and organize crucial carpools.[11]

As Tallahassee buses rolled back their segregationist codes in February 1957, 40 percent of the student body walked out of Mississippi Valley State for thirty-six hours, demanding a student government association to replace the faculty-student committee. It ended with an assurance, but the students did not receive the right to organize their own government for four years.[12] In March 1957, student activists were again on the rampage in Mississippi at the Evers brothers' alma mater, Alcorn State. Clennon King, a Black minister and history instructor, published a series of articles with student pictures in a Mississippi newspaper linking the NAACP with communism, criticizing Black leaders, justifying American slavery, and admiring Uncle Tom. On the third installment of his series, students, supported by President Jesse R. Otis, boycotted his classes and demanded his termination. The all-White trustee board, who arrived in Alcorn on March 7, 1957, to address the matter, ordered the students back to their classes, threatening to close the institution. "I don't give a damn if you burn [Alcorn] down!" one student announced. The next day, student body president Ernest McEwan read a statement, supported by 489 of 571 students, on the chapel steps, after students filed out from a rally. "At 11:55 a.m. the oldest land-grant college in America for Negroes, which was founded in 1871, died." The trustees did temporarily close the college, fired President Otis, replaced him with John D. Boyd, whom the students dubbed the "white man's tool," renewed King's contract, and forced all of the students to vow to bury their activism before they reenrolled. It was an indisputable message to Alcorn State students and to students across the state who followed the affair closely. White people and "white tools" still dominated public Black higher education.[13]

This was a contradiction that Black students did not address until the Black Campus Movement because in the late 1950s, Southern desegregation grabbed most activist attention. As *The Chicago Defender* observed in March 1957, "Negro college students are alive to the issues of the day, and feel an identity with the Negro masses off campus who are fighting for equality and recognition in the South." Black students did not merely feel an identity—they were an intricate part of the fighting force. Applications rushed into the last remaining segregated academic holdouts. Eleven Allen University students, for example, sought admission to the University of South Carolina in 1958.[14] Later that year, about five hundred students arrived in the nation's capital for the "March for Integrated Schools." The next year, more than 30,000 Black and White youth—13,000 were members of NAACP youth councils and college chapters—returned to lobby congressmen and were joined by Martin Luther King Jr., A. Phillip Randolph, and Roy Wilkins.[15]

In the fall of 1958, John Lewis, a student at American Baptist College and future Student Nonviolent Coordinating Committee (SNCC) chairman, noticed a "sense of urgency and awareness spreading among ...

black students throughout" Nashville. "There was a growing feeling that this movement for civil rights needed—no, *demanded*—our involvement." Their consciousness of grassroots altruism and sagacity had been fortified with each newsflash of student strikes, bus boycotts, school desegregation struggles, and even decolonization movements in the 1950s. Black students were taught the basics of nonviolent resistance by attending Fellowship of Reconciliation workshops on their campuses and reading the main Fellowship of Reconciliation pamphlet, *Martin Luther King and the Montgomery Story*, and King's *Stride Toward Freedom: The Montgomery Story*. Black students nurtured on profoundly Christian and paternalist HBCU campuses headed by administrators who had been crusading on morals since their arrival were, not surprisingly, enthralled by King's moral philosophy and by the budding moral crusade against segregation.[16]

In the 1950s, African Americans were pressing against the violence of Jim Crow. In 1959, four White youths abducted and raped a 19-year-old Florida A&M student. When Florida A&M students learned that the rapists might escape punishment, a body of angry, armed students started making plans for a massive march. Student government leaders intervened and organized a one-day class boycott of six hundred students. Students sang, prayed, listened to speeches, and picketed with banners loudly proclaiming "Justice is all we want. Silence is not our motto." Possibly trying to defuse the power students displayed three years prior in the bus boycott, county officials announced that a grand jury would be reconvened. The four youths became the first White people to be convicted for raping a Black woman in the Deep South.[17]

The 1959–1960 academic year has been the most celebrated of the Long Black Student Movement due to what occurred in spring semester. Yet students built a base for the spring launch during the previous summer and fall. Student activists attended the Institute of Nonviolent Resistance to Segregation at Spelman in the summer of 1959. There, Bayard Rustin and Ella Baker spoke. More than six hundred students attended CORE's first Southern interracial institute in Miami that summer. Some of the attendees, such as Patricia and Priscilla Stephens, took these ideas back to their HBCUs. The Stephens sisters, who were Florida A&M students, founded a Tallahassee CORE chapter, holding their first meeting in October 1959 with thirty students from Florida A&M and Florida State University. On November 11, the chapter staged its first sit-in at a "Whites only" lunch counter. But members spent most of their time building the small organization, dissecting Tallahassee segregation, and attempting to negotiate.[18]

The late-1950s sit-ins happening in Oklahoma City, Tulsa, and Stillwater, Oklahoma; Wichita and Kansas City, Kansas; Miami, Florida; Durham, North Carolina; and Marion, South Carolina were local affairs, not nationally reported protests quickly inducing activism in other towns.[19] In Nashville, James Lawson, a Vanderbilt University seminarian and FOR veteran, had run weekly justice workshops in a local church since the fall of 1958. The handful of Nashville students had surged to twenty by the fall of 1959. Lawson and John Lewis had been joined by two future SNCC leaders, Marion Barry and Diane Nash. The group staged its first sit-in at a downtown department store on November 28, 1959, as "a test, nothing more." Soon, the prepared team, like others across the South, would find themselves in the struggle of their lives against Dixie.[20]

After being denied service at the bus terminal in Greensboro, North Carolina, Joseph McNeil discussed the incident with his North Carolina A&T roommate, Ezell Blair Jr. Eventually Franklin McCain and David Richmond joined the discussion about the slow pace of desegregation. "We've talked about it long enough, let's do something," McNeil declared, prompting quietness. From the quietness sprang the beginnings of the loudest battering of segregation in American history. The next day, in the late afternoon of February 1, 1960, with the covert blessing of the local NAACP, Richmond and McCain walked into a Woolworths, accompanied by Blair and McNeil, two former NAACP youth council members. The four North Carolina A&T freshmen sat down at its restricted counter, unaffected by the refusal of service, and remained until the store closed. The next day, Billy Smith and Clarence Henderson joined McNeil and McCain in a replay of day one. Spearheaded by the newly organized Student Executive Committee for Justice, within five days hundreds of students from area colleges were "sitting in." News reports of these sit-ins flashed nationally. Television lounges in Black college dorms across the South were so quiet when these reports came up that "you could hear a rat pissing on cotton."[21]

The Greensboro Four rang the liberty bell of protest, and legions of students heard it—in Durham and Winston Salem (North Carolina) on February 8, 1960, Charlotte on February 9, and Southern Virginia two days later. On February 13, the already organized students were demonstrating in Nashville and Tallahassee. By mid-March, student protests

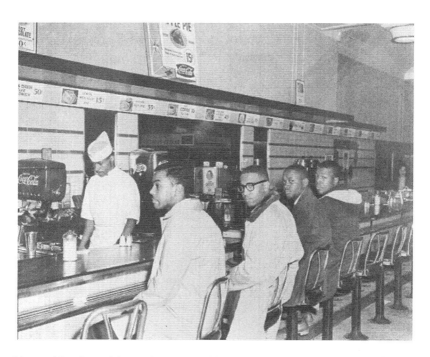

Photo 6.1   Four African American college students sit in protest at a "Whites only" lunch counter during the second day of protest at a Woolworths in Greensboro, North Carolina. From left: Joseph McNeil, Franklin McCain, Billy Smith, and Clarence Henderson (by Jack Moebes, News & Record Staff)

disrupted Atlanta, and by April student protests and demonstrations were rocking seventy-eight southern and border communities. Police tried to stop the surge with thousands of arrests. Parents tried to stop their sons and daughters with threats. Local communities tried to stop them with their violent rigidity. But once these students got going, desegregation became the only brakes that could slow them down.[22]

Some administrators, politicians, and trustees tried to slow them down, which sometimes sparked campus activism at schools such as Jackson State and Voorhees. When Alabama Governor John Patterson ordered the suspension of any Alabama State student who participated in sit-ins, students rallied and were addressed by Martin Luther King Jr. A thousand students threatened to vacate the college if punishments followed their activism in late February. In April 1960, President Atwood at Kentucky State unrecognized the campus CORE chapter and terminated eleven students and two instructors during a week of protests against his administration, which restricted civil rights activism. Soon after, the student gymnasium was firebombed, probably in retaliation.[23]

It became apparent to Ella Baker, former student activist and now first executive secretary of King's Southern Christian Leadership Conference (SCLC), that these lively students were in need of help with coordination. She organized a conference on April 15–17, 1960, at her alma mater, Shaw University, in Raleigh, North Carolina. Nearly two hundred students from more than fifty colleges and high schools from thirteen states heard Baker encourage them in her keynote address to develop their own organization with "group-centered leadership." Not long afterward, the attendees organized SNCC. This new group committed itself to nonviolence and the "politics of direct action."[24]

Deep South desegregation of higher education had barely moved until the court forced the University of Georgia to matriculate Atlantans Charlayne Hunter and Hamilton Holmes. After Georgia Tech narrowly defeated the University of Georgia's basketball team, a crowd of White students mobilized outside of the new students' dorm on the evening of January 11, 1961. With KKK members present and a large banner that read "Nigger go home," the crowd tossed bricks into Hunter's room and set property on fire—violently rebelling at the University of Georgia. White rebels succeeded in replicating the 1956 Autherine Lucy episode. The university withdrew the Black students, and state troopers took them back to Atlanta that night. Their triumph was short-lived, though. Two days later, a federal judge ordered the University of Georgia to readmit the students.[25]

Later that spring semester, CORE repackaged its 1947 Journey of Reconciliation, went freedom riding on buses through the South, and desegregated interstate bus terminals. John Lewis and Howard's Stokely Carmichael were two of the many students on the buses. The widely reported viciousness of the White mobs, who violently obstructed these "Freedom Riders," even destroying a bus in Alabama, riled up Black America. It all led to another wave of students flooding into CORE, NAACP, SNCC, local civil rights associations, and new groups, such as the Northern Student Movement. In the Deep South, students organized clandestine civil rights groups, such as the Mississippi Improvement Association of Students in Jackson.[26]

After hesitating in the summer of 1961, SNCC and CORE joined the NAACP, SCLC, and the National Urban League in the well-financed and Kennedy administration-initiated Voter Education Project in the South. SNCC entered the belly of the beast—rural Mississippi—to register a community of people who had been disenfranchised for nearly a hundred years. In Northern and Western HWCUs, Black students in the political mainstream joined NAACP and CORE chapters, Friends of SNCC groups, and new interracial civil rights campus organizations that raised money for Southern campaigns, staged sympathy demonstrations, welcomed popular activist speakers, such as Malcolm X, rallied against segregationist speakers, and occasionally protested against campus and community racism.[27]

While Black students hacked away at segregation in 1962, sometimes with little success in places such as Albany, Georgia, on September 30, federal officials whisked Air Force veteran James Meredith in an unmarked federal car off to Oxford, Mississippi. Ole Miss had been court ordered to desegregate. Angered by the arriving force of 536 federal officers to protect Meredith, segregationists staged a violent rebellion on campus that night, leaving a French reporter and a maintenance worker dead, 375 people injured, and more than two hundred arrested. The mob defied President John F. Kennedy, who addressed the nation earlier that evening. "In a government of laws, and not of men, no man, however prominent or powerful, and no mob, however unruly or boisterous, is entitled to defy a court order." At the highest count, 20,000 soldiers occupied the campus during Meredith's two semesters, which were filled with unrelenting death threats, hate mail, and taunts. This grandson of an enslaved person graduated in 1963 after existing as "the most segregated Negro in the world," Meredith said.[28]

Since the mid-1930s and the fall of the New Negro Campus Movement, Black students in groups such as the ASU, SNYC, NAACP, CORE, and SNCC waged the Long Black Student Movement. Over the course of the twentieth century, Black students did not stop striking while the iron was hot. As their struggle entered its climax year, 1963, African Americans were on the cusp of acquiring the civil rights they had sought for almost three decades: desegregation and the franchise for Southern African Americans—rights off campus they soon would be demanding on campus.

Higher education seemed headed for complete desegregation. The last three years of the Civil Rights Movement, 1963 to 1965 were crucial in ultimately winning these rights. These years—actually the first half of the 1960s in general—were also critical in nurturing the Black Campus Movement, a struggle several decades in the making.

CHAPTER 7

"March That Won't Turn Around": The Making of the Black Campus Movement

Civil rights and Black Power activists in the 1960s typically sought to raise the consciousness of White and Black Americans, respectively, regarding the debilitating and oppressive effects of mid-twentieth-century racism. Put differently, the Civil Rights Movement whose primary aim was to affect the moral and political conscience of White America to advance Black Americans—or *White suasion*—gave way to *Black suasion* to develop the cultural and political consciousness of Black Americans toward the necessity of Black unity, power, and agency through the Black Power Movement. Guided by the leading youth organization, SNCC, Black students started hastily leaving the civil rights sphere in the mid-1960s, entering the ideological orbit of Black Power. In effect, the failures (and successes) of the Civil Rights Movement set the stage for the Black Power Movement and its arm in higher education, the Black Campus Movement.

After decades of dual activism, the Long Black Student Movement primarily moved off campus from 1959 to 1963. Spurred by African liberation struggles, NAACP outcast Robert F. Williams in North Carolina, Malcolm X, and other radicals and antiracists, some students organized outside of civil rights norms during that period. They created study-turned-protest groups, such as UHURU ("freedom" in Swahili) in Detroit (1962) and the Afro-American Association in the Bay Area (1961)—where early Black Power grew—a "crucial prelude to the better known tale of Black Power after Watts," explains historian Donna Murch. The African American Club formed at NYU and featured a speech by

I. X. Kendi, *The Black Campus Movement*, Contemporary Black History, https://doi.org/10.1007/978-3-031-37394-7_7

Malcolm X in 1962, which stimulated "countless corridor conversations." During the 1961–1962 academic year, Central State University students in Ohio voted into office a slate of officers known as the Reform Action Movement (RAM) wielding an antiracist students' rights platform. Before long, RAM became the Revolutionary Action Movement, relocated to Philadelphia, and, under the stewardship of Max Stanford Jr. (renamed Muhammad Ahmad), provided an organizational base for young revolutionaries in the mid-1960s.[1]

The juniors and seniors who launched the Black Campus Movement in 1965 peopled these revolutionary organizations as well as civil rights outfits in the early 1960s as freshmen and sophomores. Herman Carter, the architect of Southern's 1965 protest, desegregated New Orleans movie houses, traveled on CORE freedom rides, and saw the inside of several Louisiana jails after enrolling in the fall of 1961. Even more future Black Campus Movement leaders first tasted activism in high schools and grade schools in the early 1960s. Edward Whitfield, president of Cornell's Afro-American Society during a building takeover in April 1969, presided over Arkansas' NAACP Youth Council in high school before being estranged from the national office's aversion to SNCC's brand of direct action. A 12-year-old Ben Chavis desegregated his local public library in 1960. In the mid-1960s, Chavis was affiliated with SCLC, SNCC, NAACP, and CORE, keeping his hair short and donning a sport coat, shirt, and tie. By the fall of 1968, the UNC Charlotte student's hair had grown into an Afro, and he wore a field jacket, sunglasses, and black boots, often carrying Mao's *Red Book*, like thousands of Black campus activists. In February 1969, he led his peers in their campaign to transform UNC Charlotte. Chester Grundy desegregated his Louisville high school before becoming a student leader at the University of Kentucky. In 1965, he participated in its Black social club, Orgena ("a Negro" spelled backwards). "We talk about it now, it's like, we were a bunch of backward Negroes," Grundy remembered, "but [laughing] you know that's what we had." By 1968, they had organized a Black Student Union (BSU).[2]

Future Black campus activists participated in the Civil Rights Movement, but even more were aroused by watching the struggle that reached its apex in 1963. The signature protest confronted the South's most lethal center—Birmingham. The ferociousness of Southern segregationists and hesitations and refusals of the federal government to hold them off troubled Black youngsters. That May, they watched on television, like most Americans, as thousands of their peers in Birmingham were clubbed with nightsticks and ripped to pieces by vicious bloodhounds and saw fire hoses breaking limbs, snatching clothes off of bodies, and slamming children and teens against store walls. They heard about the urban rebellion there. "The racists' tactics of using dogs, tanks, and water hoses on women and children was too much for African-Americans to stomach," recalled Stanford, who traveled on weekends that spring building RAM. "Within months mass demonstrations had occurred all over the south. The movement seriously began to gel as the mood of African American people in the North became angry."[3]

They were angry in Birmingham, too. The bombing of the home of A.D. King and the Gaston Motel (SCLC's headquarters) in retaliation for the desegregation accord between SCLC and city leaders unleashed the first major urban rebellion of the decade on May 11, 1963. When King aides tried to disperse the Black rebels, "Tell it to 'Bull' Connor," someone yelled. "This is what nonviolence gets you!"[4]

Like these rebels, some Black youth began to seriously rethink whether the civil rights platform—ostentatious nonviolence, desegregation, uniting with White liberals, and White suasion—was the most effective road to progress. One idea steadily gathered ground—Black solidarity and, in the context of higher education, the need for Black students to band together. In late April, days before the most vicious assaults in Birmingham, thirty-five students at Harvard formed the African and Afro-American Association, inspired by the Southern Movement, Malcolm X, and African independence struggles. Nicknamed Afro, it sought "to promote mutual understanding," to provide "a voice" by publishing their ideas, and to develop leaders to cope "with the various problems of our peoples," the preamble to its constitution expressed. At the study group's founding meeting, students discussed the desirability of desegregation, Black Americans at Harvard, and Black nationalism. Afro's most articulate spokesman, George Armah, championed barring from membership all students not of African descent. During the ensuing controversy over the racial bar, senior John Butler announced, "There is nothing malicious in our desire to be ourselves."[5]

That summer, Alabama segregationists planned a replay of the 1956 Autherine Lucy affair. The Kennedy administration had other plans. Hundreds of National Guard members, state troopers, and city police militarized the University of Alabama when Vivian Malone and James Hood entered on June 11, 1963, on court order. Governor George Wallace, in a televised display of resistance, stood in the doorway of Foster

Auditorium to prevent the duo from registering in segregation's last major public stand in higher education. That evening, after Wallace moved aside and Malone and Hood registered, President Kennedy spoke to the nation. It ought to be possible "for American students of any color to attend any public institution without having to be backed up by troops," he said. "One hundred years of delay have passed since President Lincoln freed the slaves, yet their heirs, their grandsons, are not fully free." Later that night, Byron De La Beckwith, a member of the White Citizens Council, shot and killed NAACP field secretary Medgar Evers in front of his house in Jackson, Mississippi. No, African Americans were not free. "With their mentor now dead, several students started quietly humming a tune laced with contempt for a system that could suddenly and unapologetically snatch Medgar Evers from their midst," historian Jelani Favors noted. In three years, everyone heard the tune's title: Black power.[6]

As the body bags started to pile up, alongside them amassed a number of Black youngsters contemptuous of America and questioning the civil rights program. At least ten civil rights workers were killed during that fateful summer of 1963, and an untold number were injured. Still, the March on Washington in late August provided a boost for civil rights, as did the money from corporate America. Yet on September 15, 1963, a bomb from White supremacists shattered the Sixteenth Street Baptist Church in Birmingham, leaving four girls dead, shattering the civil rights ideological fortress where a declining number of Black youth resided. Three of the girls were 14, one was 11—the age range of the future activists of the Black Campus Movement.[7]

At 7 feet, 2 inches, a skinny and reserved high schooler named "Lew" Alcindor (later renamed Kareem Abdul-Jabbar) attended mass with his mother when the girls were killed. The news of the massacre hit this basketball star in New York City like a bucket of water. It woke him up to be antiracist, as it had other youngsters, through the cold coverage of the White news outlets and the posturing of the Kennedy administration. Alcindor decided that "nobody cared," nor would anybody defend and enrich "black people except black people." He embraced Black suasion. In five years, Alcindor headlined the Black collegiate boycott of the 1968 Olympics.[8]

Ann Beard (Grundy), the future wife of the aforementioned Chester Grundy at the University of Kentucky, already knew that her hometown's moniker was "Bombingham." She heard bomb threats growing up as the pastor's kid in the Sixteenth Street Baptist Church. Her father arrived to pastor the historic church in 1944 (and passed away in 1960). Congregants called Grundy the "Sixteenth Street Baptist Church baby." She was attending high school in New York at the time of the tragedy. One of her teachers handed her *The New York Times* with the news. "I was too shocked to cry. I was just—I didn't know what to feel." The next year, she knew what to feel when she enrolled at Berea. "We had no black faculty and staff. We didn't even have parent figures." She gathered with other Black students who felt the same sense of isolation and formed one of the early BSUs.[9]

Four days after the Birmingham bombing, a group of Black students, "upset going out of their minds" at San Francisco State, petitioned the student government to establish a Negro Students Association (NSA) in 1963. This ended up being the predecessor to the first known BSU, which formed in 1966. According to the NSA's constitution, the study group sought to "engage in the study of Negro history and life; to foster the growth and dissemination of Negro cultural contributions." NSA members agreed on the need for civil rights but were divided over the issue of integration, according to one college official. A group of students organized at the University of Memphis in 1963, and a Black study club materialized at Roosevelt. John Bracey Jr., one of the developers of the Roosevelt group, also participated in the Amistad Society, a Chicago-wide Black history club. (Five years later, Bracey, then a graduate student, was one of the ten student signers of the agreement that ended a thirty-six-hour takeover of Northwestern's bursar's office.)[10]

The year 1963 proved to be the seminal year of Black student organizing at prestigious and urban HWCUs, with moderately large Black populations incited and angered by the Southern civil rights atrocities, colonial struggles, and Northern and Western racism. Meanwhile, HBCU students moved away from off-campus demonstrations and civil rights that year as well. By 1964, they were noticeably headed toward campus activism and Black Power, with protests at Jackson State, Alcorn State, Norfolk State, and Howard. From May 1 to 4, the Afro-American Student Movement, a radical affiliation of SNCC headed by Michele Paul and Betty Rush, convened the first Afro-American Student Conference at Fisk. To RAM's Stanford, who attended and helped plan it, the conference "was the ideological catalyst that eventually shifted the civil rights movement into the Black Power movement."[11]

After a White cop killed a Black teenager and the police department refused to admit guilt in July 1964, a protest turned into an explosive five-night rebellion in Harlem. At the time, Kareem Abdul-Jabbar was participating in a journalism workshop of the Harlem Youth Action Project. Together with the editorial board that produced the workshop's weekly paper, Abdul-Jabbar (and presumably other future college students) interviewed rebels and their supporters. Cries about Harlem's powerlessness in the face of the regular killing of Black people by cops filled these interviews and the special issue his workshop published on the rebellion. Since his youth newspaper was one of the few media voices reviling the police, the fury he felt about the Birmingham blast the year before resurfaced—more robust than ever. Like other Black youngsters across the nation who would soon be rebelling against the racist constitution of higher education, Abdul-Jabbar was radicalized by the underlying causes of the rebellion. A similar cacophony of rebellion eventually spread to Brooklyn and five other cities that summer, including Rochester, Chicago, and Philadelphia. For four straight years, Black urban rebellions cultivated a soil of protest that promoted the necessity of grassroots altruism during the Black Campus Movement. To Black students, grassroots altruism grew into the solution to what became known at the time as the "urban crisis."[12]

Consciousness of racism also grew that summer when three more activists (all college aged) had to be buried in the cemetery of the Civil Rights Movement—Michael Schwerner, Andrew Goodman, and James Chaney. They were SNCC organizers of the Mississippi Freedom Summer of 1964, which, among other things, organized the Mississippi Freedom Democratic Party (MFDP), triggering a wave of violence that compelled many activists to reject nonviolence. The MFDP demanded that its delegation be seated in place of the racist state party at the Democratic National Convention in August 1964. The Johnson administration, not wanting to alienate its fleeing Southern contingent, rejected the MFDP appeal and offered a compromise—two nonvoting seats accompanying the racist Mississippi delegation. "We didn't come all this way for no two seats!" bellowed Fannie Lou Hamer, an MFDP leader from the buckle of Mississippi's Black belt.[13]

Hamer and company defied civil rights leaders, the Johnson administration, and segregationists in Atlantic City in 1964. In a larger sense, the vanguard of the Long Black Student Movement rapidly expanded its distance from the Civil Rights Movement, abandoning White suasion—seemingly as crucial to the Civil Rights Movement as nonviolence. "Things could never be the same," Cleveland Sellers of SNCC recalled. "Never again were we lulled into believing that our task was exposing injustices so that the 'good' people of America could eliminate them. We left Atlantic City with the knowledge that the movement had turned into something else. After Atlantic City, our struggle was not for civil rights, but for liberation." The antiracist wing of the Civil Rights Movement started planting its own Black Power roots.[14]

The women from the MFDP who came to Atlantic City in their natural hair styles enthralled Robin Gregory, a Howard student and SNCC staffer in the Washington, DC, office. "I was really turned on by that statement," she said. When the aspiring painter left Atlantic City that summer, she left the perm on its beaches, along with her civil rights ideology. "I felt it was an affirmation of being who we were," Gregory explained. She did not receive affirmation upon returning to Howard in the fall of 1964, however. Yet, in the fall of 1966, the cultural climate had warmed and Gregory did receive an affirmation. Students elected her the first homecoming queen in Howard's one-hundred-year history as she wore a gleaming Afro, the first (perhaps) of many during the Black Campus Movement.[15]

When Gregory first returned to Howard with her Afro in the fall of 1964, returning White UC Berkeley students who had participated in the Mississippi Freedom Summer wished to radicalize their peers, only to be rebuffed by administrators. Black students carefully scrutinized the widely publicized Free Speech Movement at UC Berkeley that accelerated White campus activism, which by the late 1960s sometimes supported Black campus activism. "It provided watchful black militants with an excellent practical education in the tactics of disruption," explained historian Roger A. Fischer. "They discovered the awesome secret of student power, that the university was pathetically vulnerable to the pressures that could be brought to bear upon it by a relatively small cadre of well organized, deeply dedicated student revolutionaries." Some students, aware of the four decades of debilitating campus protests by Black students since World War I, learned no secrets from UC Berkeley students.[16]

In the meantime, Black students continued to organize. Columbia and Barnard College students, including Hilton Clark, the son of psychologist Kenneth Clark, established the Society of Afro-American Students that fall of 1964. The group formed to serve as a forum for Black students to discuss their problems "and hopefully have the individual come up with some answers for himself." Two years later, a politicized Clark and his fellow society members had come up with answers to the question of whether their college aided them in that process. In their newly issued magazine, *The Black Student*, editors proclaimed that universities do not prepare Black students to cope with their problems "as well as the schools seemingly prepare white students to cope with theirs."[17]

In 1964, societal circumstances ripened for the Black Campus Movement. The "Whites only" signals on campus became more discernible since they were taken down in the federal law books with the summer passage of the Civil Rights Act. Student activists organized groups and steadily accumulated more campus influence with their peers. State authorities and college administrators had become progressively more hostile to progressively more antiracist civil rights activities. The steadily increasing numbers of Black students walking into hostile academic doors at HBCUs and HWCUs were increasingly likely to be veterans of the Civil Rights Movement, having participated in direct-action protests and registration drives in junior high and high schools in the early 1960s. These movement veterans formed a small, highly trained, associated, and politically astute force that gradually considered the college campus the next battleground as the decade reached its midpoint. The victories, tragedies, and outliers of the Civil Rights Movement, which started its decline after its apex in 1963, inspired and alienated this "new generation." The civil rights debacle at the Democratic National Convention in August 1964 and SNCC's subsequent move to Black Power was decisive.

Nevertheless, the Black Campus Movement, like any social movement, needed a societal trigger. It received three in 1965. The assassination of Malcolm X and Bloody Sunday within weeks of each other in early 1965 constituted the first and second triggers, with the Watts rebellion in the summer completing the spawning triad. Malcolm X's death did not impact students like King's murder did in 1968. Student interest in Malcolm X in early 1965 could not compare with the widespread love for the Muslim martyr in 1969 at the acme of the struggle for Black Power, with his autobiography, *Malcolm X Speaks*, iconic posters, and recordings of his speeches in mass circulation. But a rapidly growing loose federation of alienated civil rights veterans and movement outliers had followed Malcolm closely when he lived.

In the late 1950s and early 1960s, as the national spokesman for the Nation of Islam (NOI), Malcolm emerged as a popular leader, particularly after the 1959 CBS documentary *The Hate That Hate Produced*. Black youth were not initially attracted to the breadth of his ideology, since Malcolm wrapped it in NOI theology, which deified Elijah Muhammad, spurned civil rights activism, preached a strict moral code, articulated "traditional" roles for women, taught that White people were inherently evil, and demanded complete separation of the races. As each year passed in the 1960s, Malcolm's rhetoric grew more secular and matured politically.

Consequently, with each year, his appeal to students increased, impressing youth with his booming but clear voice, fiery speeches, quick wit, striking analogies, historical knowledge, glorification of African people and African anticolonial struggles, audacious denigration of White liberals and racism, and down-to-earth yet scholarly rhetoric. In 1964, he left not only the NOI but also its theology, increasingly sharing and refining his ideas of Black national and international unity, self-determination, self-defense, anti-capitalism, cultural pride, and distrust of White liberalism. Other than James Baldwin or Martin Luther King Jr., no Black voice attracted students more than that of Malcolm X in the early 1960s. Malcolm probably lectured to more students in 1963 than in any other year, which presumably influenced the outbreak of antiracist campus organizing that year.[18]

In his most critical speaking engagement affecting Black students, Malcolm faced off with Bayard Rustin on October 31, 1961, at Howard. With the fifteen-hundred-seat Cramton auditorium filled to capacity, sociologist E. Franklin Frazier moderated the debate, titled "Integration or Separation." Howard's student government and the Nonviolent Action Group, a Howard SNCC affiliate, hosted the event. "The black man in America will never be equal to the white man as long as he attempts to force himself into his house," Malcolm argued at one point. "The real problem is that the anemic Negro leader, who survives and sometimes thrives off of gifts from white people, is dependent upon the white man whom he gives false information about the masses of black people." Malcolm's captivating performance deeply impacted many of the attendees, including Stokely Carmichael. At the time, a "European theoretical context" anchored Carmichael's political worldview. But what "Malcolm demonstrated that night ... was the raw power, the visceral potency, of the group our unarticulated collective blackness held over us. I'll never forget it."[19]

It is no wonder that the assassination of Malcolm X on February 21, 1965, devastated thousands of Black youth. Upon hearing the news flash, Merritt College's Bobby Seale, a future founder of the Black Panther Party, went to his mother's house, picked up six loose bricks, walked to the corner, and hurled them at every cop car he saw. Like scores of Black students across the country, Seale's sorrow overwhelmed him, forcing out tears. Black students mourned their fallen icon in services and at rallies at schools such as Southern Illinois and San Francisco State.[20]

Adding fuel to their fire, some Black youth immediately suspected that the US government had a role in the assassination. The American media "right from the beginning have intimated that the Black Muslims killed him, which is so easy to believe because of his rivalry with them," one Black youngster wrote in a statement published in Harvard's student newspaper. "There are several fishy things that make it difficult for any honest person to believe anything." In addition, SNCC circulated an essay two years later on "The Murder of Malcolm X" that questioned the official story of three Nation of Islam assassins.[21]

Malcolm's death motivated a small group of Black students to carry out his mission. Within a few years, a critical mass of Black campus activists would be inspired to actualize Malcolm's teaching, as his name, face, and ideas became the poster elements of the Black Campus Movement. Practically all Black campus activists adored Malcolm X, and one at the University of Texas at Austin apparently renamed himself after his idol.[22]

Still, in 1965, more students were probably stirred to campus activism by what occurred in Selma, Alabama, on March 7 than by the death of Malcolm X two Sundays prior. Since the beginning of the year, SNCC and SCLC had been engaged in a fierce battle for Black suffrage. Martin Luther King Jr. called and then cancelled a march from Selma to Alabama's statehouse in Montgomery. Some SNCC and SCLC members proceeded without King, who believed the march jeopardized the Voting Rights Act that ultimately passed that summer. At 4 p.m. on March 7, the six hundred marchers, many wearing their Sunday best, formed two lines and set out on the roughly fifty-mile trek to Montgomery. They reached the Edmund Pettus Bridge on the outskirts of Selma. When the marchers reached its crest, they saw an army of state troopers and Selma police at the bottom eerily flanked by a hundred White Alabamians waving Confederate flags. They bravely pressed forward.[23]

"Troopers, advance!" Sheriff Jim Clark roared when the marchers did not turn back upon a state trooper's order. With news cameras rolling, the soldiers of segregation slung tear gas and darted forward like a Confederate infantry, pouncing on the six hundred marchers with clubs and whips. The marchers retreated, and the small, mounted army chased them into Selma's Black communities, battering, bruising, and beating them along the way. It was a televised "Bloody Sunday" on March 7, 1965.[24]

Within days, students from Howard delivered a petition with hundreds of signatures to the White House, urging President Johnson "to take any and all necessary measures to stop brutality being done to the Negro people in Selma, Alabama." Nearby Tuskegee students were irate, as almost everyone had viewed the ambush on the bridge. The black-and-white

Photo 7.1 Gwen
Patton as a teenager
(Dr. Gwen Patton
Collection, Trenholm
State Technical College
Archives, Montgomery,
Alabama)

images were like piercing shots of activism. When members of the newly organized Tuskegee Institute Advancement League (TIAL), a SNCC affiliate, rushed into the dorms that Sunday evening to mobilize, just about all the students attended the meetings. TIAL heeded King's directive to join another group of marches in Montgomery on Wednesday, March 10, from a march set to begin in Selma the day before. Three thousand lined up behind King as he left Brown's Chapel on March 9. King halted the march before it reached the valley of the shadow of Bloody Sunday, prayed, and led the singing of "We Shall Overcome." Then King, who had secretly made a deal with federal officials to not force his way through the troopers, turned and walked back to the church, followed by the mystified crowd.[25]

Gwen Patton, like many Tuskegee students, felt outraged and betrayed when she learned of King's about-face. Although she was born into a family of Detroit "race people" in 1943, Patton regularly visited relatives in Montgomery, Alabama, in the 1940s and 1950s. It was during those visits that she began her civil rights work. She served as a teacher in the "citizenship school" held in her paternal grandparents' home, helping ensure that Black people who wanted to vote were prepared to complete the then-required literacy test. At the age of 16, after her mother died, Gwen Patton moved in with her relatives in Montgomery, where she eventually graduated with honors from George Washington Carver High School.[26]

Patton, TIAL's direct-action chair, and her peers resolved to defy King and federal and state officials and showed up the next day in Montgomery anyway. King telegrammed Tuskegee, asking the students to cancel. The Tuskegee administration joined in King's pleas, threatening expulsion and claiming students needed parental permission. As Tuskegee students entered the dining hall for dinner the night before their march, they saw copies of King's telegram on every placemat. "March, March, March!" the students chanted as they banged on their tables and disdainfully read the telegram. That night, they raised more than $1,000 to charter buses to Montgomery, and the next day they waged what they boldly termed "the march that won't turn around."[27]

When Tuskegee students arrived back on their campus, it did not take them long to realize that the same forces they fought in Montgomery dictated to them from the administration building. As SNCC's James Forman attested, Tuskegee students asked themselves, "Is it enough for me just to get an education so that I can join (or remain in) the professional middle class? Does the administration of my school stand for progress or the status quo?" Hundreds of Tuskegee students left civil rights behind to become committed members of the rising Black Power Movement. They wanted their Black college to be just as committed.[28]

"After the march, a lot of people couldn't take Tuskegee any more," Gwen Patton said. Its "contradictions could no longer go unattended." Patton decided to lead her peers in resolving the contradictions, declaring her candidacy for student body president. Against her four male competitors, Patton's platform beckoned "Total Representation for the Total Student Body." When the candidates were ordered to take down campaign signs for a board of trustees meeting, Patton refused and circulated a petition, raising questions about the "great white fathers" on the board. The stand against the administration and her queries about White paternalism and power generated a current of support in April 1965 that carried her into the presidency—the first woman SGA president in the school's history. She was also one of the first (if not the first) students enamored with burgeoning Black power ideas to gain control of an HBCU student government in the mid-1960s with a radical restructuring in mind.[29]

The summer after Patton's election, students were politicized by the thousands of African Americans in Los Angeles who in August 1965 rebelled against police brutality, economic exploitation, dilapidated housing, and poor health care, damaging $200 million worth of property. Police officers killed more than thirty rebels and observers and arrested about four thousand people. Jimmy Garrett, 19, spent most of his time at his parents' home in the middle of the rebellion zone on Vernon between Central and Broadway. He had an impressive resume of activism—sit-ins at 14 in 1960, Freedom Rides in 1961, and work with CORE. He joined SNCC in 1962 and relocated to Los Angeles in 1965 to head SNCC's fundraising efforts.[30]

On Saturday, August 14, 1965, after three nights of rebellion, Garrett interviewed rebels, just as Lew Alcindor did after the Harlem rebellion the year before. "If I put a pillow over your face, and try to smother you and you want to live bad enough you've got to come up breathing quick and fighting hard," one man told Garrett, "that's just what we're doing." That Saturday night was the first of the 8:00 p.m. curfews. Garrett sat on his front porch. He turned his radio down when he noticed a police car. "Get your black ass back into your house!" screamed an officer. He grudgingly and slowly got up. The car circled back around. As he entered the house, he detected the long barrel of a shotgun aimed in his direction. With the door slammed and him scampering up the stairs, he heard three thunderous bursts. "I ran to my parents' empty bedroom and lay shaking on my back for the rest of the night like the spider in Kafka's *Metamorphosis*."[31]

As the smoke cleared from the Watts Rebellion, Garrett climbed out of the puddle of sweat and anxiety on his parents' bedroom floor, dripping with a renewed commitment to the movement. Garrett was one of the SNCC members who that summer after the Watts Rebellion tossed around the idea of the college as a next site for struggle. In the spring of 1966, Garrett enrolled at San Francisco State and in a few months helped build the first organization to use the term "Black Student Union."[32]

CHAPTER 8

"A New Awareness": Movement Speakers, Conferences, and Periodicals

Before Jimmy Garrett enrolled at San Francisco State, one of the major Black Power organizations responsible for the surge of Black consciousness coalesced in the fall of 1965. Out of a study group in Los Angeles led by Maulana Karenga emerged the influential US Organization. "Anywhere we are, US is." The organization pledged to serve the interest of "us"—the Black community. Karenga, the creator of Kwanzaa, served as one of the primary voices that inspired Black campus activists, principally their sense of cultural pride and awareness. While high schooler Robert Lewis labored in the hospital in San Diego recovering from car accident injuries in the fall of 1965, his aunt brought him *The Quotable Karenga*. This book, widely read by Black youth, particularly on the West Coast, "was talking about black," Lewis remembered. "It was talking about Black people, concepts, ideas—like I had never heard it being talked about before." It left such an impression that he became a member of Karenga's US Organization after his recovery and eventually became an activist at California State University, Northridge, receiving one of the nation's stiffest sentences for a building takeover in November 1968.[1]

In addition to his writings and organizing, Karenga impacted the ideology of students through his speaking in the late 1960s. In the fall of 1967, for example, Karenga gave a series of lectures at the University of California at Los Angeles (UCLA) titled "Black Student/Alienation." Karenga suggested a three-point program for survival—self-determination, self-respect, and self-defense—in the initial speech on October 17. It was well

© The Author(s), under exclusive license to Springer Nature Switzerland AG 2025
I. X. Kendi, *The Black Campus Movement*, Contemporary Black History, https://doi.org/10.1007/978-3-031-37394-7_8

received by Harambee, UCLA's Black student group, which in a few months made demands on the administration. Karenga delivered a similar message in February 1968 as the featured speaker at the first annual Oklahoma Conference for Black Collegians at the University of Oklahoma. It was "emotionally engulfing," recalled professor George Henderson. "One minute we were laughing; the next, we were grimacing. The overall effect was consciousness-raising."[2]

After showcasing the lead-up to the Black Campus Movement in the early-1960s civil rights period, this chapter delves into the forces that continuously generated and energized the Black Campus Movement in the late 1960s. Traveling activist-speakers continually praised, motivated, challenged, and developed that energy and antiracist critiques of the academy. Furthermore, through their marathon informal campus discussions, widespread reading, cultural weeks, conferences, and newspapers, Black students profoundly developed their own movement ideology and force. Alongside activist-speakers, Black campus activists circulated Black Power ideas that enhanced their self-determination, self-love, and sense of Black solidarity and raised their consciousness about the irrelevant racist constitution of higher education.

As Karenga fashioned the US Organization, Gwen Patton tried to radicalize Tuskegee during the 1965–1966 academic year. She made headway with campus protests in the fall of 1965, but her spring 1966 administration had to deal with a tragedy. When popular Tuskegee student and Student Nonviolent Coordinating Committee (SNCC) activist Sammy Younge Jr. demanded to use an indoor "Whites only" bathroom, Marvin Segrest, a 67-year-old gas station attendant, shot and killed him on January 3, 1966. His death injected vigor into the already vitalizing campus movement. Students, such as Hampton's Nancy Regina Hooten, dispatched letters to President Johnson. A native of Tuskegee who knew Younge "very well," Hooten wrote: "It hurt me very deeply when I learned of his violent death. Must all people die who are fighting for what rightly belongs to them?"[3]

The murder helped further radicalize SNCC, a group that in turn radicalized campus activists. Soon after Younge's death, SNCC released its first official statement opposing the Vietnam War: "The murder of Samuel Younge in Tuskegee, Alabama, is no different than the murder of Vietnamese peasants, for both Younge and the Vietnamese sought, and are seeking, to secure the rights guaranteed them by law. In each case the United States government bears a part of the responsibility for these deaths." Moreover, SNCC members helped local African Americans in "Bloody Lowndes" County, Alabama, organize the Lowndes County Freedom Organization, choosing the black panther as the mascot of this independent political party. In May 1966, the party had its primary, while SNCC members elected Stokely Carmichael (renamed Kwame Ture), a recent Howard graduate, their new leader. A striking thinker and speaker, the courageous, captivating, and charismatic Carmichael embodied the new defiant young Black generation that Malcolm X had seen approaching around history's corner.[4]

By the summer of 1966, Carmichael had become a national Black power youth icon during the Mississippi March Against Fear, which SNCC used to politicize, organize, and register Mississippi Black people in each town the march entered. During an impassioned speech in Greenwood, Mississippi, on Thursday, June 16, Carmichael hurled the term "Black power" into the American rhetorical mainstream. To Carmichael (and Charles Hamilton), Black power was "a call for black people in this country to unite, to recognize their heritage, to build a sense of community. It is a call for black people to define their own goals, to lead their own organizations. It is a call to reject the racist institutions and values of this society." Blown by the fans of the American media, the call whisked through Black America, among present and future Black campus activists.[5]

Many Black students saw Carmichael in person. He spoke at dozens of community rallies and no less than twenty-five colleges and universities in the late summer of 1966 and the 1966–1967 academic year, while raising much-needed funds for SNCC. Toward the end of August, Carmichael brought his poignant oratory to Boston. "It's time for all black people in Boston to get together and move to gain control over your communities," Carmichael insisted at a rally. In Boston, Carmichael inspired Howard's Adrienne Manns, who was attending a summer school program at Harvard. She had enrolled at Howard in 1964. Coming from a majority-White town and high school, she was struck by its bourgeois, Eurocentric setting. Her roommate needed an extra dorm-room closet. Only opera and (European) classical music boomed from the Fine Arts building. There was one course on Negro History, and only history majors or upperclassmen could take it.[6]

The case of a Howard student being expelled for violating curfew politicized Manns, as did her attending a rally for the Selma protests at the White House in the spring of 1965. But Carmichael's speech in Boston in 1966 proved pivotal in Manns' leap into Black campus activism. Manns thought the Civil Rights Movement had a "passive kind of beggar mentality," and she detested it. "The speech changed me," she said, "because when I realized that what I had been feeling and thinking was not just personal, it wasn't just me—somebody else, in fact someone of prominence and stature, felt the same way and could articulate it. I really felt encouraged."[7]

After speaking at schools such as Princeton, Howard, the University of Michigan, Dartmouth, Hunter College (New York City), and UC Berkeley in the fall of 1966, on January 16, 1967, Carmichael challenged fourteen hundred Morgan State students to adopt grassroots altruism. "Until you begin to help your black brothers in the ghettos, I'll blame you for the rebellions of the past summer and for the ones which will happen this summer." On April 11, 1967, he addressed Tougaloo students for two hours. A student newspaper editor reported "a new awareness in the minds of the students. There has been a lot of thinking going on since he left, and these have been profound thoughts about US Black People." Two days later, Carmichael urged University of Houston students to regain their history from the "cultural terrorism and degradation of self-justifying white guilt." That spring he urged Fisk students to "take over the administration" of their school. And Carmichael spoke to four thousand people at a Seattle high school, urging Black unity. "The way I looked at myself and America changed" during that speech, said Aaron Dixon, who in 1968 led University of Washington's Black Student Union (BSU). With H. Rap Brown assuming the mantel of SNCC chairman in May 1967, law enforcement tailing Carmichael (specifically since campus activism, sometimes violent, followed some of his appearances), and his exile to Guinea, Carmichael's speaking surge slowed during the rest of the decade. However, by the time of his departure from the collegiate speaking scene in 1968, the movement was in full swing.[8]

As Carmichael first started making his college rounds in the fall of 1966, two students at Oakland's Merritt College, dismayed that its Black student group was not acting on Malcolm X's mission, founded the Black Panther Party for Self Defense. Huey P. Newton and Bobby Seale developed a ten-point program of what they wanted and what they believed in October 1966. The fourth point would captivate Black campus activists: "We want education for our people that exposes the true nature of this decadent American society. We want education that teaches us our true history and our role in the present-day society. We believe in an educational system that will give to our people a knowledge of self. If a man does not have knowledge of himself and his position in society and the world, then he has little chance to relate to anything else."[9]

By 1968, particularly through its Free Huey campaign, the Oakland-based Party had become a national sensation, subsuming a groundswell of chapter creations across America, usually with college-aged Black youth. Along with its revolutionary philosophy, assiduously shaped by the contours of antiracist and Marxist ideas, Black students were enthralled by the Party's confrontational posture, actualization of the principle of self-defense, grassroots altruism, cool dress (black berets, pants, and leather jackets), street credibility, community service programs, and charismatic, articulate leaders, including Kathleen and Eldridge Cleaver, Fred Hampton, and Elaine Brown. Some Black students affiliated with both the Black Panther Party and with BSUs or SGAs.

Quite a few BSUs were modeled after the Black Panther Party. In 1969, the Dickinson College Afro-American Organization (AAO) in Pennsylvania changed the title of president to prime minister in order to show support "for the ideals of the Black Panther Party movement," according to AAO Prime Minister Mike Floyd. Black student organizations at both the University of Washington and Duke developed ten-point programs. Moreover, BSUs aided Panthers in their service programs. At Roosevelt, members solicited funds from faculty members and administrators to support a breakfast-for-children program. BSU members held a Free Huey Day at the University of Georgia in May 1969, as Black students around the nation rallied against Panther repression. Yet most profoundly, Panthers inspired (or were involved in) Black campus activism. Panthers in the BSU instigated the renaming of Chicago's Crane Community College to Malcolm X College in 1969. The inspiration was obvious at Franklin & Marshall College in Pennsylvania, where in April 1969 the BSU "proposed EDUCATION, COUNSELING, HOUSING, FINANCE, [and] TEACHERS [to] SUPPORT the FREEDOM AND POWER to determine the destiny" of Black students. Shortly after a delegation of Panthers appeared at Lake Forest College in Illinois that spring, the BSU demanded Black faculty and the right for students to be involved in the interview process. The faculty complied. Ultimately, as historian Jeffrey Ogbar explains, "despite the Panthers' emphasis of organizing the lumpen, the party was incredibly active on college and high school campuses."[10]

A number of Black speakers graced stages at colleges and universities, inspiring Black campus activism and antiracist ideologies. It may be the case that more antiracist speakers and speeches could be heard on college and university campuses in the late 1960s and early 1970s than during any other period in higher education history up to that point. Martin Luther King Jr. occasionally spoke. Days after coming out against the war in Vietnam at Riverside Church on April 4, 1967, King discussed the "illegal and unjust war in Vietnam" at Occidental. H. Rap Brown of the SNCC championed Black Studies at City College in Harlem in October 1967. And then in November at nearby Columbia, Brown criticized American universities as "propaganda mechanisms for white nationalism." He called on Black students to apply their education to changing the world and advancing Black America.[11]

Coretta Scott King replaced her slain husband as Harvard's commencement speaker in June 1968. She encouraged student activists: "In struggling to give meaning to your own lives, you are preserving the best in our traditions and are breaking new ground in your restless search for truth. With this creative force to inspire all of us we may yet not only survive— we may triumph." More than a thousand people jumped up from their seats as she finished.[12]

Shirley Chisholm, the first Black congresswoman and presidential candidate, appeared at more than a half dozen campuses for commencement exercises in the spring of 1969. At Howard, which had been embroiled in protests most of the semester, she gave a ringing endorsement of the Black Campus Movement. Fight the system that "has been denying you the opportunity to be a total man or woman," she proclaimed. Poet Amiri Baraka (previously known as LeRoi Jones) intermittently lectured at institutions. The "black man must finally have the power to govern his life," he said during his forty-five-minute address at Wisconsin's Carthage College in February 1969. Joe Trotter, president of Carthage's AAS, wrote afterwards that "the campus has a Jones hangover."[13]

Fannie Lou Hamer induced at least two hangovers that stimulated protests. "A turning point for all of us was Fannie Lou Hamer being there," said Bertie Howard, who helped take over a Duke building on February 13, 1969. "For a lot of us it caused us to stop and pause and think about what we were going to do." The following February, Hamer spoke closer to her home, at Mississippi Valley State, while students combated their president. At one point, she implored President J.H. White to "go home, and be quiet." "I've seen some of the world's greatest Toms in service," she added, "but this man must be a Nuclear Tom." A few days later, the students marched on campus, still electrified by Hamer's speech.[14]

Muhammad Ali made the rounds during the crucial politicization period. "The truth makes you free—not integration," Ali said in April 1968 to 750 students at Fairleigh Dickinson University in New Jersey. Also formulating Black student ideologies through college speeches were Betty Shabazz, who often spoke at the opening of Black Cultural Centers (BCCs), former National Football League running back Jim Brown, usually pushing Black capitalism, Angela Davis, CORE's Floyd McKissick, Adam Clayton Powell Jr., historian John Hope Franklin, poet Sonia Sanchez, Georgia politician Julian Bond, James Farmer from the US Department of Health, Education, and Welfare, feminist "Flo" Kennedy, author Ralph Ellison, and Black Studies pioneer Nathan Hare, to name a few.[15]

Carmichael's speeches may have been the most important in growing an infant movement, but comedian Dick Gregory gave the most reported speeches during the Black Campus Movement. One report says he spoke at five hundred institutions during the 1967–1968 academic year alone. "I spend about 98 percent of my time today on college campuses—and for a reason," Gregory said at Pittsburg State University in Kansas in September 1968. "I feel that you young folks in America today are probably the most morally committed, ethical group of dedicated young people that have ever lived in the history of this country."[16]

In addition to these national voices, local Black Power leaders often roused students. "We have started to be what we are," declared John Barbour, Hartford's Black Caucus spokesman at Trinity in October 1967. Father James Groppi, a White Catholic priest and one of the leaders of the Milwaukee Black Power Movement, spoke at institutions in the Midwest, including Michigan Tech University. At Iowa's Clarke University in January 1968, Father Groppi said, "Black Power is good, and not anti-Christian." Seemingly the most productive local ideological engineer was Howard Fuller, a community organizer in Durham, North Carolina, and the founding director of Malcolm X Liberation University in 1969. He lectured on Black Power and grassroots altruism at most of the area Black and White institutions, helping to make central North Carolina the hotbed for the Black Campus Movement in the South.[17]

Many of these speakers spoke during Black Cultural Weeks or Weekends (which went by a variety of names), organized annually by BSUs seemingly wherever they existed during the late 1960s and early 1970s. Speeches, films, panel discussions, socials, and artistic events were usually held during these weeks—with an event each night. The week usually gave

Black students and the campus community the first concerted systematic explication of African American history and culture and exposed colleges' assimilationist curricula. Sometimes protests for Black Studies departments and courses were inspired by these weeks. But in most cases, students demonstrated, through these weeks, on the need for Black Studies. These weeks were even observed at Black colleges. From December 10 to 13, 1968, at North Carolina's Fayetteville State, the Black Awareness Week comprised a kickoff speech by Howard Fuller, a play titled *The Word Is Given Black Liberation*, a panel discussion on "The Role of Black Students," a Black cultural program, another panel discussing religion, and a social gathering.[18]

Most profoundly, Black campus activists molded their own ideologies through these weeks. The influence of traveling Black speakers could not compare with the influence Black students had on each other. During these weeks and the movement in general, Black campus activists constantly discussed Black Power, Black nationalism, Pan-Africanism, self-defense, nonviolence, violence, guerilla warfare, racism, Black capitalism, Marxism, Maoism, culture, Africa, Asia, Latin America, Europe, war, poverty, White liberalism, White conservatism, Black conservatism, the Black middle class, segregation, integration, assimilation, colonialism, Third World liberation movements, pedagogy, educational philosophy, the function of education, protest tactics, patriarchy, men's role, women's role, and the role of students in the struggle. They debated the writings of Malcolm X, James Baldwin, Mao Zedong, Ernesto "Che" Guevara, Maya Angelou, Audre Lorde, W.E.B. Du Bois, Booker T. Washington, Frances Beal, and Frantz Fanon, among others. Perhaps no generation of students read more political literature than these Black campus activists; they incessantly deliberated over the function and direction of the campus, local, national, and global movements in their dorm rooms, libraries, social gatherings, Black houses, Greek houses, cafeterias, and, eventually, BSU and Black Studies offices and Black Cultural Centers.

Black campus activists were like their thoughts—constantly on the move to other campuses. They visited other campuses to party, hear Black speakers, attend BSU and SGA meetings, support BSU and SGA events (and protests), give speeches, and organize BSUs and radicalize SGAs. The appearance of Black Oberlin students compelled students at Thiel College in Pennsylvania to organize a BSU in December 1968. Two Texas Southern University students visited St. Andrews Presbyterian College in North Carolina in February 1969 to aid in the establishment of the BSU.[19]

When students at Oklahoma's Creighton University were organizing the Black Coalition in the spring of 1968, they contacted the nationally renowned BSUs at San Francisco State, Stanford, Yale, and Columbia "for information on their constitutions." BSUs also informed their peers about their progress. Shortly after their Black Cultural Center opened in January 1970, Black students at Bowdoin wrote to more than four hundred organizations encouraging them to establish similar centers.[20]

Formally, campus activists connected through a series of conferences they organized during the movement. Aside from the socializing, they proved to be politicizing, motivational, networking, and tactical mini-camps. Groups of students left conferences and soon after organized BSUs, unleashed protests, and intensified their antiracist campus struggles. In late 1966, several groups of college representatives from the Northeast region came to Columbia to hear national leaders speak about Black student empowerment. Several contingents were inspired to organize, including students from Rutgers and Wellesley College in Massachusetts. Crammed in the back seat of a taxi, riding back from the conference, five Wellesley women founded Ethos—a story now fabled at the women's liberal arts college.[21]

"It was very powerful to see the number of black students there and to hear what was happening on other campuses," recalled Elmer Freeman, a Northeastern University activist who attended a conference of Black students in Boston in March 1967. "We came out of that room with a broader agenda because we knew other folks were doing similar kinds of things." On the other side of the country, in Los Angeles, dozens of high school and college activists took part in the West Coast Black Youth Conference during Thanksgiving weekend in 1967. "We must begin to institute programs that speak to the needs of Afroamericans and not programs that are a reaction to white definitions," read the conference's manifesto.[22]

During the weekend of April 13, 1968, about two hundred students, many representing BSUs from forty-two colleges along the eastern seaboard, convened at Princeton for three days. "People don't talk revolution," Charles Hamilton declared in the keynote address. "They make revolution." The next weekend, seventy-eight delegates from thirty-seven HBCUs traveled to Shaw where they had met eight years earlier at the height of the sit-in movement. Shaw president James E. Cheek had issued an announcement to all HBCUs shortly after the death of Martin Luther King Jr. on April 4, 1968.[23]

Quite possibly the most activism-inducing gathering of Black students was the "Towards a Black University" conference at Howard in November 1968. Carmichael said to some two thousand students, "You've got to quit talking and start acting." Karenga suggested that there were eight types of students: the forced student, the integrationist, the political integrationist, the professional student, the athlete, the career student, the intellectual, and the nationalist. The nationalist "is the ideal student," Karenga explained. "He realizes his first commitment is to his people," and a true Black University would produce this type of student. HBCU students left with a clear concept of a "Black University." One Fayetteville State student attendee explained to his campus community that the concept "emerges out of the frustrations of" African Americans "who recognize that the present institutions of higher learning have no relevance to the total Black community." Over the next few years, Black student conferences were held at institutions such as Augustana College in Illinois, Stanford, Jackson State, Princeton, University of Texas at El Paso, and the Universities of Minnesota, Oklahoma, North Dakota, Missouri, and South Carolina.[24]

Photo 8.1   Front cover of *The Harambee* at Tougaloo College (Mississippi) on December 7, 1970 (Courtesy of Tougaloo College)

Finally, Black student newspapers influenced the construction and circulation of their antiracist ideas. Urban rebellions, Black Power, ideas of gender, and the notion of a Black University were a few of the many topics that columnists discussed in HBCU newspapers. Writers also carried stories on the demands and protests at their schools (and other institutions). Sometimes campus newspapers gave voice to the campus struggle at HBCUs, resulting in some administrators clamping down on them with the same ferociousness as they did on protests. In 1971, soon after a story in the *Campus Echo* questioned whether North Carolina Central was "a Black School," President Albert Whiting pulled the newspaper's funding.[25]

At White institutions, BSUs founded, to give a few examples, *NOMMO* at UCLA, *Watani* at University of Montana, *The Black Expression* at Western Carolina University, *Harambee* at New Mexico State University and Duke (after the US Organization's publication title), *Black Explosion* at University of Maryland, *Pamoja* at University of Georgia, *Black Fire* at San Francisco State, *Uhuru* at California State University (CSU) Fresno, and *The Grapevine Journal* at Michigan State University, which reportedly had the largest circulation. Usually funded through their student government allotments, named after African terms, and printed at high quality, these BSU periodicals, which had their HBCU counterparts, like Tougaloo's *Harambee*, publicized the ideas and activities of the Black Campus Movement. BSU journalists reported on their demands and protests (on their campuses and at other schools), challenged the campus community on its racism, and discussed the major Black stories of the day, specifically the repression of Black Power leaders in 1969 and the early 1970s. Poetry, short stories, book reviews, essays, announcements, tributes to Black women and men, and art accompanied the articles. BSU newspapers also provided White students their first lessons on African Americans, attracting new allies. A presumably White Duke student from Washington, DC, wrote the editors of *Harambee* in February 1969. "I have been reading Harambee and have not been able to put it down!" Lynne Anderson expressed. "I have gained a much greater understanding of Blacks. Thank you, Harambee, for one of the most rewarding learning experiences I've had since I've been [at] Duke."[26]

According to surveys in 1968 and 1970, most Black students in college were women, grew up in cities, received little or no financial support from their financially strapped homes, majored in the social sciences, were the sons and daughters of parents who had not graduated from high school, expressed Black pride, were usually older than their White peers, blamed racism for the plight of their people, and were interested in collective Black mobility. Black students were far from monolithic during the Black Campus Movement, though. Black student communities comprised collections of mini-groups ordered by charismatic students, fraternal connections, artistic talents, hometowns, and mutual interests and friendships, to name a few distinguishing factors. A large number of Black students at HWCUs entered so-called remedial programs, such as Educational Opportunity Programs, and joined (or rejected) the movement. Many assimilationist Black students steered clear of the movement—students whom Harry Edwards termed "conforming Negroes." At the same time, on most campuses with large Black populations, it was simply cool to be sporting Black power garb, challenging "the White man" and the institution. At colleges and universities with small Black populations, it was socially, politically, and culturally expedient to be involved in the movement.[27]

It is impossible to pinpoint exactly how many students were involved in the Black Campus Movement. Drawing from empirical and anecdotal data at the time, presumably about a quarter (a conservative estimate) of Black students on college campuses in the late 1960s and early 1970s participated in the movement by speaking out against the racist constitution, regularly attending BSU or radicalized SGA meetings, or participating in a single protest. Roughly another quarter seldom attended meetings and never protested but sympathized with and supported the struggle in their own way. The rest of the "conforming Negroes" (a quarter or potentially one-half) opposed the movement with their silence and sometimes public rebukes.[28]

The movement became the primary aim of many radical students who were often shrewdly loyal to their conception of "Blackness" or Africanity, hated imperial White supremacist capitalism and liberalism, considered African American culture viable in its own right, embraced self-defense or violence, envisioned new Black institutions, were unafraid of protesting and dramatically challenging their colleges and universities, and attempted to fuse their social and academic interests with their political and cultural activities. However, most activists seem to have been more moderate, juggling (and separating) the politico-cultural struggle with their academic and social lives, while also ideologically juggling antiracist and assimilationist thoughts, socialist and capitalist ideas, non-violence and self-defense, protest tactics with negotiations, profound fear and intense courage, higher educational reforms and radical changes, and optimism and pessimism for American institutions. Many Black moderates seemingly flocked to BSUs or activist SGAs (often momentarily, some-times permanently) when they felt personally threatened, a campus or societal issue intrigued them, campus social norms thrust them into a campaign, or due to a community or campus tragedy, such as Bloody Sunday, urban rebellions, assassinations, or an act of harassment on campus, all of which were rampant in the late 1960s.

Black capitalists and Marxists ideologically battled, patriarchs and feminists clashed, cultural nationalists and revolutionary nationalists argued, homophobic students and gays and lesbians were at odds—the ideological divides were endless in this politically and culturally charged movement residing in America's centers of ideas. On many campuses, Black women had to fight sexism in their BSUs and SGAs while they fought racism on their campuses. By the early 1970s, some Black women were participating in the Black Campus Movement and the Black Feminist Movement, organizing panels, festivals, and conferences to discuss Black womanhood and feminism.[29]

Throughout the movement, Black feminist students questioned and rejected sexist sentiments, specifically in the movement. Because numerous men considered the movement male terrain, suggesting women activists were supposed to support men and reproduce and raise the Black nation. In 1971, Gerry Whitted at North Carolina Central wrote, "I (a young, black woman) am told that this man is going to change me from matriarch to woman. In my 'new definition,' I find myself on some African pedestal/stool, bound and gagged (for my protection, they say) ... So I stand there and every now and then my gag is removed so that I can scream 'Black Power! Justice! Freedom! Africa, unite!'" Most women refused the gag and used their resounding voices to demand the racial reconstitution of higher education. In a letter to Wellesley President Ruth Adams in 1969, the Black student group named Ethos attested that "A propensity for forgetting our names has often been demonstrated. For those who have difficulty distinguishing us, we have a suggestion. Call us merely Black Women. For that is basically what we are, that is the basis upon which we operate as a group. That is the basis of our ethos."[30]

The Civil Rights Movement directly and chiefly spawned the Black Power Movement of the 1960s and 1970s and all of its movements, including the Black Campus Movement. Many of the early Black power activists were trained during the civil rights era. Furthermore, desegregation had to precede the striving for diversity. New Negro and civil rights students eliminated most of the segregation and regressive rules at Black and White colleges. In 1965, after protest knocking for half a century, Black students were finally residents in the house of the academy—some measure of freedom at HBCUs, some measure of place at HWCUs. Like any new resident, Black students then began a movement to clean up the vestiges of racism and, just as importantly, move in vestiges of antiracism for Black America. Inside, but on the margins, they placed the entirety of the racist constitution of higher education on their list of renovations: the moralized contraption, assimilationist curricula, the standardization of exclusion, and ladder altruism. Since the New Negro Movement, Black students had pecked away at the moralized contraption and Black exclusion from power at HBCUs. The Civil Rights Movement provided enlightening lectures in the standardization of exclusion at HWCUs after they enrolled. At both, activists began to uncover the assimilationist curriculum. They increasingly grew disturbed by the disproportionately high number of White trustees, presidents, and faculty—and demanded Black people in their stead.

Moreover, during the classical civil rights period (1954–1965), the example of SNCC, CORE, and other groups compelled Black students to marginalize ladder altruism. The old idea that the uplift of Black students away from the masses of Black people uplifted Black America no longer held nearly as much weight. In addition, early-1960s striving for civil rights in the community allowed students to clearly view their unsupportive, often restraining colleges as their longtime ladders, removing them from the masses. Instead, they wanted to break down the ladder and replace it, reforming or revolutionizing their colleges into organs of antiracist change, organs producing antiracist agents. These hacks over multiple decades on the racist constitution of higher education came down on the academy with the most unbridled level of Black student energy and focus in American history during the Black Campus Movement.

CHAPTER 9

"The Black Student Is Demanding":
The Black Campus Movement, 1965–1968

Like the hostility that greeted their racial brethren when they migrated to majority White urban centers throughout the twentieth century, a poisonous racist backlash hit Black students when they entered HWCUs in the mid-1960s. Higher education may have desegregated, but many of the new Black students still felt excluded, removed from the academic, social, and cultural milieu of the campus with few (if any) relevant courses or social and cultural outlets, particularly at non-urban HWCUs. "A solitary man, a foreigner in a strange land" was the language used by Stan Herring, vice president of the Association of Black Collegians at Pennsylvania's Gannon University in November 1968; a student at North Carolina's St. Andrews University used the phrase "a rat in a maze." At Wisconsin's Lawrence University, "you are alone—stranded in the middle of white culture," said an unnamed student. "This university is an oasis in the desert, surrounded by vultures who are only waiting to pick up a crumb, a smell, a taste, and a feel of black nitty-gritty substance," wrote the Afro-American Students Association at the University of Iowa in May 1968. Meanwhile, a few Michigan Tech students in an "alien white atmosphere" felt that the Black student had two choices: "give up his black identity or perish."[1]

At many HWCUs, campus police officers continuously harassed Black students. Some White students demeaned them by using derogatory names and sayings, making insulting phone calls, waving Confederate flags, singing "Dixie," organizing minstrel shows, and defacing their

I. X. Kendi, *The Black Campus Movement*, Contemporary Black History, https://doi.org/10.1007/978-3-031-37394-7_9

flyers, posters, doors, and campus property. On some occasions, they poured lighter fluid under Black students' doors and set it on fire. When walking across campus, Black students were hit with objects or stared at in a hostile manner. Drive-by insults were common, along with offensive bathroom poetry. Black students occasionally found their cars had been vandalized, damaged, or, worse, set ablaze, as occurred at the University of North Dakota in September 1968. Some White trainers and nurses seemed surprised Black students could get hurt. Several White professors notoriously assumed that Black students were unintelligent and spewed racist ideas in the classrooms, such as the Cornell economist who reportedly said in the spring of 1968 that urban African Americans "play sickly and perverted games stressing cunning and survival, as in the jungle." Campus publications proclaimed Black inferiority. In the spring of 1967, Columbia's humor magazine satirized the formation of a Black fraternity as "trying to provide Negro students with a home away from home, a sort of haven for the noble savages in this world of chrome and glass."[2]

Then there was the endless litany of questions. Part of the Black experience at Trinity University in San Antonio, according to Reggie Butler, was "being asked questions like 'why do Blacks want so much and do not want to work?': a question so naïve it is only surpassed by the nerve of the person asking it." Even more naïve were the questions that came after tragedies. "I was terribly sorry to hear about Dr. King," said a White student to a grieving Black student in the Yale cafeteria the morning after King died in 1968. "But I'm interested to know how all this affects a Negro. Would you mind telling me just how you reacted to it?" The Black student just glared at the White student for a few moments. After answering the question silently, he left the dining room, leaving his half-eaten breakfast behind. The questions kept many Black students in a perpetual emotive bind. "Am I here to educate or gain an education?" they would ask themselves. Usually, they tried to do both, while the racist ideas leaking from the questions drove them to fury. Charged a Yale activist, "I came here to be a student not to educate whites about blacks. I'm tired of being an unpaid, untenured professor."[3]

At HBCUs, the conditions were not much better in 1965. At quite a few (usually private) HBCUs, the faculty bodies were mostly White and included some assimilationist Black professors. At Tougaloo in 1968, 60 percent of the professors were still White. "The whole direction of the college is set and controlled by white supremacists," said Political Action Committee leader Howard Spencer that year. Most of the professors at Clark Atlanta were White, and none of the shared art and psychology instructors at the Atlanta University Center were Black in 1968.[4]

The vast majority of HBCU boards of trustees were either all White or majority White, and they employed Black presidents that were often assimilationist and accommodating to racism. Therefore, many HBCUs still had compulsory class, ROTC, and chapel attendance in 1965. They usually prohibited smoking, drinking, cross-gender dorm room visitation, and student franchise on college matters and mandated curfews and dress codes (usually for women). For instance, as late as 1967, officials at Grambling State University, Louisiana, did not allow women to wear pants and locked the dorms at 10 p.m. Grambling students ate breakfast at 6 a.m. in a dining hall with large hanging signs ordering them to "take bite-size mouthfuls" and "break bread before eating." There was not a single Black Studies program or department in 1965, and at both HBCUs and HWCUs, courses focused on Africans Americans were rare. Although weakened by the Long Black Student Movement and recent civil rights measures, the moralized contraption, standardization of exclusion, assimilationist curricula, and ladder altruism still comprised the racist constitution of higher education in 1965.[5]

Like any social movement, the Black Campus Movement did not start all at once. The day after Bloody Sunday, on March 7, 1965, two Black student protests challenged a historic HBCU and a HWCU with a storied history of enrolling a relatively large number of Black students. In late February, saying it would alienate White benefactors, Hampton officials refused to allow students to conduct a sympathy demonstration in town for the ongoing Selma voting rights campaign. On February 25, students called for the freedom to speak, demonstrate, and determine the college's curriculum and student code. In a passionate letter, Hampton student leader Donald Hughes pledged that his peers were no longer "cottoning to the White man" or "eating cheese for the White man's money. Do we need funds that only serve to perpetuate the things that the Negro is trying to get rid of once and for all—non-self-reliance, subordinating due to fear and feelings of inadequacy? No!"

Still reeling over administrators' intransigence and outraged by the carnage on the Selma bridge, about two hundred students rallied outside Hampton's administration building on March 8, 1965, with signs that read "We want freedom" and "Hampton a Reformation or College." Three days later they staged a sit-in, blocking the entrance to administrators' offices. President Jerome Holland met none of the demands and eventually expelled the student leaders. Nevertheless, the Hampton affair became one of the pioneering first calls of the movement for their Negro university controlled by White benefactors to be refashioned into a "Black University," dictated by and for African Americans. Gwen Patton and her comrades at Tuskegee would make a similar call in a few weeks, after their Montgomery "march that won't turn around." Although neither group initially used the term "Black University," the two HBCUs that formed the model for all four elements of the racist constitution over the previous hundred years at HBCUs were among the first to face the Black Campus Movement. It signaled the prospect of a new day for Black higher education, brought about by a new social movement. If the historically conservative Hampton and Tuskegee could be radicalized, anything seemed possible.[6]

The day after Bloody Sunday, students also disrupted the University of Kansas, which had annually amassed one of the largest HWCU Black student populations for more than a half-century. Hundreds of campus activists demonstrated inside and outside of the president's office, demanding the abolition of segregated Greek organizations and housing. About 110 students were arrested, including soon-to-be NFL running back Gayle Sayers, "The Kansas Comet." During the early years of the Black Campus Movement at HWCUs, the removal of the standardization of exclusion in student enrollments, clubs, and housing galvanized activists. In contrast, HBCU activists, during the initial years, sought to complete the removal of the moralized contraption. Actually, that March 1965, campus activists pressed to drive out the contraption, upgrade their facilities and services, and increase student power at Winston-Salem State University and present-day North Carolina Central, where picket signs shouted "Human Rights! Civil Rights! What about Student Rights?"[7]

"You do not take a person who, for years, has been hobbled by chains and liberate him, bring him up to the starting line of a race and then say, 'you are free to compete with all of the others,' and still justly believe that you have been completely fair." Thus declared President Lyndon B. Johnson to Howard's graduating class on June 4, 1965, sounding like a proponent of antiracist affirmative action. Yet, on many campuses, Black students were still hobbled by chains. The racist constitution of higher education stymied academic freedom. Even at Howard, two months before Johnson's commencement address, students protested administrative fetters.[8]

When Black students returned in the fall of 1965, animated by the scorching Watts Rebellion, "symbols of slavery" still adorned newly desegregated Southern campuses, including festivals with racist caricatures, Confederate flags, and the singing of "Dixie" at school events, prompting protests at schools such as University of Texas at Arlington. In November 1965, Herman Carter declared that "Southern University perpetuates academic slavery, not freedom" before leading hundreds of his peers in rallies and marches. At Tuskegee that month, Gwen Patton and fellow activists marched on the president's home, boycotted the vesper service, walked out of a required chapel meeting, and organized a "turn-over-your-plate" protest in the cafeteria—all for more student rights, freedom, and power. Meanwhile, the Ivies made the concept of "diverse campuses" an aspiration that fall. "We don't want the well-rounded boy so much as the well-rounded student body," a Columbia admissions officer announced. Soon, Black students would be requesting an antiracist well-rounded body of scholarship, a well-rounded faculty, a well-rounded curriculum, and a well-rounded offering of services and facilities.[9]

Those well-rounded requests were voiced at quite a few campuses in the spring of 1966. BSUs were established or took on a new political posture. Marianna Waddy assumed the presidency of the nation's first organization that used the term "Black Student Union" at San Francisco State. After asserting that the college had tried to "white-wash them," Waddy declared, "We will now strive to incorporate the eminent and profound concept of blackness into a new and positive image of black students on this campus." SOUL at North Carolina A&T complained about cafeteria food, and the first of several campaigns during the movement to oust a HBCU president reached its zenith at Alcorn State. NAACP state field director Charles Evers, the former student activist, aided the protests for the ouster of President John D. Boyd, whom he described as "only concerned with pleasing white folks."[10]

After students (particularly at HBCUs) engaged in dual, campus and off-campus, activism in 1965, Black student activism started focusing primarily on campus issues in 1966. Marquette University in Milwaukee faced its first protest that fall of 1966, and women in the senior class demonstrated for more rights at Tougaloo. BSU members introduced the Black Studies idea at San Francisco State. The idea of Black Studies to thoroughly examine the experience of people of African ancestry from their perspective and for their benefit emerged logically from the minds of BSU members, brewed with Black power ideas of self-determination, Black pride, and criticism of assimilationist curricula. Additionally, the concept of a Black Studies department surfaced when BSU members realized that students should be receiving credit for courses in their Black Arts and Culture series, which they ran in the fall of 1966 in San Francisco State's Experimental College for student-created, not-for-credit courses. The idea at San Francisco State quickly emerged into a crusade for a new discipline.[11]

Additional BSUs materialized that fall of 1966, such as at NYU, where the organizers pledged to find "ways of making white middle-class NYU more meaningful to the black student." At Wesleyan, collegians founded a study group that read, among other things, Frantz Fanon's *The Wretched of the Earth*, *The Autobiography of Malcolm X*, and *Up From Slavery* by Booker T. Washington.[12] By the spring of 1967, James Baldwin and Richard Wright had become literary saints, and *The Autobiography of Malcolm X* had become required reading for anyone who claimed on campus the new, hip, progressive, and, sometimes, exclusive identity—Black.[13]

The San Francisco State BSU had established and was controlling the first Black Studies Program in American history by the spring of 1967, taking courses out of the Experimental College and convincing departments to sponsor them for credit. But this was not enough for the BSU. They wanted complete control over their courses, organized in a department so students could receive a degree from their Black Studies. On March 1, 1967, BSU president Jimmy Garrett officially presented "A Proposal to Initiate an Institute of Black Studies at San Francisco State College" to the Instructional Policy Committee of the Academic Senate. "There is no such thing as an integrated institution when the educational process is geared towards one group of students," he wrote. For the rest of the spring and summer, San Francisco State faculty nitpicked on minor issues on the proposal, and frustrations mounted among BSU members regarding traditional channels of instituting a new academic unit.[14]

Many of the other BSUs and SGAs around the nation advocated, through traditional channels, a few Black courses. In addition, there were protests in the spring of 1967 to undo the standardization of exclusion in student clubs, athletics, and academics at schools such as Illinois Wesleyan University, Vanderbilt, and Wichita State. The April affair at Wichita State

University in Kansas led to the organizing of a Black student group, which engaged the efforts of many Black campus activists at HWCUs that spring.[15]

Propelled by SNCC organizers who had returned to organize Black colleges, students at quite a few HBCUs, including Texas Southern, Fisk, Lincoln (MO), South Carolina State, and Howard, waged protests and violent rebellions in the spring of 1967. They demonstrated their displeasure with their "Negro" universities (with the first demands for a Black University), student powerlessness, police violence, poor food, assimilationist professors, and administrators who fired popular professors. Shouts of "We are in slavery" echoed during the Howard protests. To sociologist Nathan Hare, who was fired from Howard for his activism, Black students were seeking to overthrow the "plantation milieu" and the "missionary mores" under the "supervision of an outmoded generation of Negro overseers. They are no longer willing to cry 'Uncle' to Uncle Sam or Uncle Tom." Hare urged college administrators to keep pace with and channel "this new student vigor" so that Black colleges could become a "vanguard of a brave new spirit of social change." If they "fail to meet this challenge," then "it is going to be a long, hot fall."[16]

They did fail, and, consequently, students confronted Black and White colleges. A rapidly growing minority of the Black students were becoming more organized, more vocal, more active, more committed, and more determined to transform higher education. Black journalists took notice. "The Black student is demanding ... a shaking, from-the-roots-up overhaul of their colleges," stated a December 1967 report in *The Chicago Defender*. *Look* senior editor Ernest Dunbar reported on the "birth of 'Afro' or all-black clubs and societies" in his magazine, a piece republished in several student newspapers that fall. "Time was when the occasional Negro accepted at an Ivy League school ... worked fanatically to become what he imagined was a proper college gentleman," Dunbar wrote. "Today a new breed of black cat is tearing up white campuses." In the fall of 1967, Black students tore up San Jose State University, Berea, Grambling State, Central State, and San Francisco State—forcing campus closures at the latter two colleges.[17]

In the spring of 1968, BSUs had either heard about the development of Black Studies at San Francisco State or had conceived of a similar need on their own campuses. After the death of three Black students in the Orangeburg Massacre at South Carolina State in February 1968, during a campaign to desegregate a nearby bowling alley, the number of protests increased dramatically. Black Power icon H. Rap Brown demanded revenge. "If it takes twenty to thirty million Blacks to tear up the country, we'll do it," he declared. Most of the campus activists did not tear up the country. However, the Orangeburg Massacre did tear up some passive minds, and activist ones formed in their stead. It was the first of two events that spring that stirred legions of students into campus activism. The major protest in reaction to the massacre occurred at the main incubator of the movement at HBCUs: Howard. Students issued the "Orangeburg Ultimatum," which demanded, among other things, the creation of a radical Black University and took over the administration building for 102 hours in a nationally renowned protest in March 1968 that inspired demonstrations at other HBCUs.[18]

In the first three months of 1968, Black campus activists also met with campus officials and submitted grievances, usually through BSUs recently established at a number of institutions, such as Northeastern, Occidental, Virginia's University of Mary Washington, UCLA, and New Mexico State. If the movement received a nudge from the Orangeburg Massacre, then it received a shove from the murder of Martin Luther King Jr. on April 4, 1968. Once hesitant students volunteered for the antiracist struggle, and campus activism started to become more prominent. Central State student Jaribu Hill in Ohio "got as serious as the time we were living in," he said. "I never looked back on the meaningless life I had lived before. I lived a life of conviction, resistance and protest on my college campus."[19]

As cities burned after King's death, some Black students at Florida A&M, Tennessee State University, Lincoln (MO), and Jackson State joined in the urban rebellions. But most Black students attended and spoke at memorial services held at practically every institute of higher education in the United States. Some boycotted services in protest, such as the eighty Harvard students who stood on church steps holding their own commemoration. "If they come out of there with tears in their eyes," said Jeff Howard, the president of Afro, pointing to the church, "we want it to be plain that we don't want their tears. We want black people to have a place here at Harvard." A few days after King's murder, Vassar's Black women issued a thunderous statement: "White America ... has plainly demonstrated that the only tactics that can move its violent heart is violence. Force only responds to force and power to power. Pretty soon this nation will be shuddering in a paroxysm of Black Power."[20]

Higher education shuddered in a paroxysm of what historian Stefan Bradley termed "black student power" for the rest of the spring 1968 semester. Campus activists usually formed BSUs (or took over SGAs) at schools where Black students were unorganized before King's death. Newly organized BSUs forcefully and often publicly submitted their first formal sets of demands, seemingly the most prevalent occurrence in April and May 1968. Protests were more likely to disrupt the minority of institutions with older BSUs that had demanded racial restructuring for years. Requests for Black Studies courses had been elevated to demands for programs and departments. Entreaties to reduce White racist ideas had expanded to demands for Black Cultural Centers. Pleas for a few more Black students and professors were now demands for dozens of faculty and student quotas. The paroxysm shuddered colleges and universities in almost every state—Iowa, California, Michigan, Connecticut, Wisconsin, Illinois, Massachusetts, Oregon, Alabama, New York—to name just a few.[21]

While Black students crafted their demands, some were mystified as they watched the deluge of Black students enter into higher education. Through his death, King dramatically appealed to the moral conscience of White America, particularly those in the academy, as dozens or, probably, hundreds of institutions succumbed to students' requests or often on their own accord established scholarships, recruiting initiatives, antiracist committees, and other memorials in King's honor. Colorado State University, for example, started a memorial fund "to produce a thousand Martin Luther Kings for the one we lost."[22]

Influential protests hit Tuskegee, where students took trustees and the president hostage in early April, and Northwestern, where in early May activists led by James Turner and Kathryn Ogletree cleverly gained a department and Black dormitory, among other things, by means of a building takeover. Initially demonstrating in opposition to the building of a gymnasium in a nearby Harlem park against the wishes of residents, Black and White students seized five buildings in late April at Columbia. Black students occupied Hamilton Hall, placing a cardboard sign on its door proclaiming "Malcolm X University, Founded 1968 A.D." Students welcomed into the occupied buildings famous journalists, who received lectures on American imperialism and racism before leaving and making this the most publicized campus demonstration of the 1960s student movement.[23]

On April 30, after seven days of negotiations between students and the administration, with the faculty trying to mediate, the administration dispatched the New York City Police Department (NYPD) to end the demonstration. Administrators were likely confident that Harlem would not destroy the campus in an act of vengeance. With no resistance, the Black students quietly walked out of Hamilton Hall and into the police vans. NAACP executive director Roy Wilkins, the movement's major antagonist, even praised these Black students. While the NYPD cleared the four buildings with White students on the South side of campus, about a thousand mostly White students watched, some of them jeering, taunting, and ridiculing the police. When the police finished, they walked back into formation, broke from their line, and flailed away at the students. The clouds of police nightsticks unleashed a rain of student blood. All told, 148 were injured and 707 arrested (charges were later dropped) in the crowd and from the buildings. Enraged, more than five thousand Columbia students spent the rest of the semester protesting for the right to "restructure the university."[24]

After the politically tumultuous summer of 1968, the largest and most radical incoming class of Black students in history walked into the academy in the fall of 1968. Many came from seats of antiracism across Black America. Eight hundred members of Howard's freshman class identified themselves as militants. At White colleges, dozens of groups formed BSUs, including at Catholic and Wake Forest. Black students hardly felt like aliens, needing to recede to islands within as their contemporaries had done. As an unnamed Yale student said, "When there were just a handful of us here, we felt isolated and defenseless in a white world, so we just went along, I guess. But with more black kids coming in each year, we've started getting together and we have a lot more confidence."[25]

Enrollees were able to find comfort in Black Cultural Centers, take the nation's first Black Studies courses, or seek advice from the growing assemblage of Black administrators and professors. An English professor taught a new Black literature course at Northeastern. "I wanted to see the fruits of our labor," said enrollee Jim Alexander. "I've read all the books, long ago. Most black students have." However, Black students were far from satisfied. Several officials forecast an upsurge of Black campus activism. Before classes began in the fall of 1968, some administrators took precautions, while others simply ignored the warnings.[26]

Throughout the duration of the Black Campus Movement, the early fall had the lowest levels of activism, since the influxes of students compelled BSUs and SGAs to reorganize, while leaders and their political ideologies jockeyed for control. Usually after BSUs and SGAs had modified their practices, their new managers began asserting themselves. After controversy rocked California in connection with Black Panther Party member Eldridge Cleaver's teaching a course that fall at UC Berkeley, and following a prominent protest at the University of Illinois, all eyes became fixated on two San Jose State students. Tommie Smith and John Carlos raised their fists in protest at the Olympics in October 1968. "Black America will understand what we did tonight," said Smith at a press conference after the event.[27]

Black America understood, and possibly no segment of it more than the activists' peers. Black students started clenching their fists and lowering their heads during the playing of the national anthem at collegiate events. And they continued protesting. San Francisco State's BSU started the longest student strike in American history on November 6, 1968, for a series of demands, including an autonomous Black Studies department. With most of the school's 18,000 White students behind the BSU in a broad multiracial coalition, the strike lasted almost five months, inspiring Black campus activists around the nation.[28]

Dozens of White colleges were consequently disturbed by Black students demanding an antiracist education in November and December of 1968, colleges such as the University of Massachusetts Amherst, Bluefield State (where students firebombed a building), Fordham University in New York, Brown, and the University of Wisconsin-Oshkosh, where about ninety Black campus activists were arrested and expelled on "Black Thursday." Even more groups of students, at Ohio's Case Western Reserve University and the University of San Francisco, for instance, issued demands and usually engaged in marathon negotiating sessions with administrators. Before 50,000 people at the Houston Astrodome on November 23, 1968, Lynn Eusan, sporting an Afro, put on the crown of homecoming queen at the University of Houston. She emerged as a source of pride for activists on campus and in the city until her tragic murder in 1971. A campus park is now named after Eusan.[29]

CHAPTER 10

"We're Going to Get What We Want Now": The Black Campus Movement, 1969–1972

In December 1968, Robert Smith, the recently fired president of San Francisco State, told *the Chronicle of Higher Education* that higher education "is at a serious and crucial turning-point." Higher education still largely refused to reconstitute itself. The increased demands issued after King's death had been addressed only partially on some campuses and hardly at all on others. Consequently, even though the San Francisco State strike waned in January 1969, the movement as a whole surged, beginning its climactic semester with a rash of protests, usually to force home those post-King-assassination demands. Brandeis University in Massachusetts, Queens College, University of Pittsburgh, Wilberforce, North Carolina's Shaw, Wittenberg University in Ohio, and UC Berkeley were all sites of protest that month. On King's soon-to-be birthday holiday, twenty-five Black campus activists at Swarthmore College outside of Philadelphia were engaged in the seventh day of their siege of the admissions office, demanding the active recruitment of Black students, faculty, and administrators. Like his peers throughout the nation, Swarthmore president Courtney Smith was severely strained those seven days. On the eighth day of the siege, shortly before he was to meet with a faculty committee to consider the demands, Smith suffered a fatal heart attack. Shock and sadness unsettled the campus; in sympathy, the twenty-five students ended their protest.[1]

Death continued to reign the next day. Two UCLA students, John Huggins and Alprentice "Bunchy" Carter, leaders of the Los Angeles

I. X. Kendi, *The Black Campus Movement*, Contemporary Black History, https://doi.org/10.1007/978-3-031-37394-7_10

Black Panther Party, were gunned down by members of Karenga's US Organization at the end of a BSU meeting of 150 students. The students had deliberated over the selection of a director for the recently created Afro-American Studies Center, a selection US members and the Black Panthers had quarreled about since the fall. The divisive work of FBI agents had doggedly intensified their clash.[2]

In early February 1969, academics attended the American Association of Colleges conference, where almost every speech, panel, and discussion started or ended in a debate concerning the movement and its implications. Meanwhile, the movement quickened its activities, appearing at the University of Virginia, North Carolina A&T, University of Dayton, and Huston-Tillotson University in Texas, reaching its pinnacle on February 13, 1969. On February 21, 1969, thousands of students memorialized their fallen leader, Malcolm X, slain four years earlier on that day. During the next month, headlines from Black student protests became an everyday occurrence, with the most notorious demonstrations challenging administrators at the University of Texas at Austin, Mills College in Oakland, Rutgers, Pepperdine University in Southern California (after a White security guard killed Larry Donnell Kimmons, a Black high school student, during a confrontation over Kimmons's desire to play basketball on campus), and students took Morehouse trustees (including Martin Luther King Sr.) hostage to press for their demands for a Black University. In the midst of this turmoil, the *Wall Street Journal* reported that "Black Power is the force causing the greatest schizophrenia on the campus at the moment."[3]

Even though there had been several violent protests, the academy did not totally link the movement with violence, nor did it give the more radical demands legitimacy until Black students strutted out of an occupied Cornell building with guns and Harvard established a Black Studies department within days of each other in late April 1969. Ironically, as their demands were legitimized, the academy grew more insensitive to them, and violence was an ever-present threat. Still, the activism did not abate. In late April and May of 1969, among other protests, Black students took over an entire City College campus for fourteen days, which contributed to the installation of a widely touted (and censured) open admissions policy; twelve hundred students seized a Hampton administration building; students gained control over a Voorhees building with arms, barricaded themselves inside six buildings at Howard, forced the closure of Alabama State for two weeks, and engaged in a shoot-out with police at

North Carolina A&T for three days, an exchange that killed a student. This peak academic year of the movement led to massive repression and substantial reforms.[4]

Gwen Patton, who had joined the staff of the National Students Association since leaving Tuskegee, led around a hundred of her peers out of its convention in El Paso, Texas, in late August 1969. "We no longer can be part of a racist" group, Patton said to the media. The National Students Association leaders used "black problems for their own purposes to gain financial grants from foundations." Encouraged by Nathan Hare and under Patton's leadership, Black collegians formed their own group. The National Association of Black Students (NABS) became the principal national network for campus activists during the final years of the movement.[5] As Patton set up the NABS, Black students and HWCU officials launched the greatest recruitment drive of Black students, faculty, and staff in American higher education history.

Nevertheless, the staffing boom had its downside. HWCUs amplified their raiding of HBCUs for professors, leading to massive turnover. Miles College in Birmingham, for instance, with a faculty of sixty-one in 1969,

Photo 10.1 Howard Fuller talking to a student in front of Malcolm X Liberation University, October 1969 (Photo by Bill Boyarsky)

had to replace forty-five teachers over the course of the previous three years. "Every black Ph.D. who has his name mentioned twice, or has published in the slightest review, is besieged by Northern as well as Southern white institutions—most often in response to militant, urgent and often threatening demands by their black students," Spelman history department chair Vincent Harding explained to *The New York Times* in 1969.[6]

Aside from the new reforms and policing tactics, when higher education opened its doors in the fall of 1969, everything seemed out of whack. Black students, professors, administrators, and government leaders were still at odds over some of the core demands of the movement. There were fierce tugs of war for power over newly established Black Studies programs among African Americans themselves and between them and campus officials. Students and their allies became increasingly divided over ideology, tactics, and goals, marking the beginning of the end of the BCM. Black campus revolutionaries who wanted to escalate the movement to another level were combating activists who wanted to protest for reforms that their colleges had not yet instituted, and both of those groups were confronting students who wanted to nurture the gains won in the spring of 1969 (or off-campus matters). They all scurried around campuses trying to attract the unprecedented numbers of Black students who enrolled in higher education institutions in the fall of 1969.[7]

Hundreds of new initiatives, such as Black Studies programs, diversity offices, and Black Cultural Centers, were unveiled in the fall of 1969. But Black leaders such as the NAACP's Roy Wilkins questioned their efficacy, and many of the progenitors of the reforms faced serious judicial repression, slowing the movement. Yet California's Nairobi College, North Carolina's Malcolm X Liberation University (MXLU), and a few other colleges that students built to provide a relevant and socially responsible education opened their doors. Betty Shabazz spoke at MXLU's opening ceremonies. Painted in black on a peach-colored wall just inside the door of its building was a Malcolm quotation, proclaiming that this was a school for members of "a new generation of black people who have become disenchanted with the entire system and who are ready now and willing to do something about it." Upon its founding, Director Howard Fuller said, "This university will provide a framework within which black education can become relevant to the needs of the black community and the struggle for black liberation."[8]

The revolt of the Black athlete picked up at schools that fall, most prominently in the series of protests and refusals to play in contests against

Mormon-controlled and what the activists deemed theologically racist Brigham Young University (BYU). Although much of the national attention focused on the revolt of the Black student-athlete and on the University of California Regents' second crusade in successive years to oust a radical Black professor (this time Angela Davis of UCLA), Black campus activists made demands and protested at colleges, such as Central Connecticut State University, Marshall University in West Virginia, Iowa's St. Ambrose University, Connecticut's Fairfield University, and Vassar College in New York, where critical masses had just been reached. Protests still occurred at institutions where critical masses had long dotted the landscape, including at Fisk in December 1969, where students called for a Black University "controlled and administered by black people," devoted to their cultural needs, identified "completely with blacks," teaching "skills necessary for black existence," and void of White employees.[9]

Some administrative reactions to protests became more militant that semester. They met threats of demonstrations with counterthreats of prison time and stood up to the force of protests by swiftly using the force of the newfangled campus police state. It was now up to the students to change tactics. Black campus activists largely did not, and the growing ineffectiveness of proven tactics propagated disillusionment. The mounting number of retaliatory demonstrations to decry attacks on their communities also contributed to the decline.

Black students at the UNC Chapel Hill, Tufts University in Massachusetts, and Harvard fought for the rights of Black campus nonacademic workers that fall of 1969. For once, *The New York Times* affirmed their efforts. "Racial discrimination in the building trades must not be allowed to benefit from the vast expansion of construction programs on college campuses all over the country." During the Harvard protest campaign in December 1969, "Masai" Hewitt of the Black Panther Party, the NAACP's Roy Wilkins, SCLC's Ralph Abernathy, and CORE's Roy Innis shared the stage for the first time that decade at Boston College. Wilkins in particular, a major antagonist of the Black Campus Movement, had grown more sympathetic to Black Power and sought to create some "common ground" with the Black Panther Party in 1969, as historian Yohuru Williams documents. Like Black students across America, the speakers were enraged about the recent police onslaught against the Panthers headquarters in Los Angeles and the vicious police murder of Chicago Panthers Fred Hampton and Mark Clark. "The Panthers today, next week CORE or the SCLC, the week after it may be the NAACP," Innis stated. The murders and Panther repression added to a year of political assassinations, harassment, raids, and unjust imprisonments of Black power activists, which increasingly attracted the attention of students—another phenomenon that slowed the campus movement.[10]

"As Lafayette heads into the 1970's, there is a new awareness of the 'black problem' on the campus," wrote *Lafayette Alumnus* editor Ronald R. Parent, to begin the winter 1970 special issue on the movement at Lafayette College in Pennsylvania. It contained an interview with Roland Brown, Lafayette's first Black graduate, who had graduated in 1949. "When I was young we took the view that the white man has that which you want, so you pacify him until you get what you want from him and then you do not have to pacify him any longer. The black student today says, the dickens with pacifying the white man, we're going to get what we want now."[11]

In the spring of 1970, the waning of the movement continued, but there was still a rash of activism against the "white man." New campaigns at suburban and rural White liberal arts colleges with recently enrolled multitudes of Black people were the new sites of activism that spring. Colleges such as Bowdoin and Colby College in Maine, where students occupied a chapel for a week, Mount Holyoke College, Southern Oregon University, Heidelberg University and University of Mount Union in Ohio, and Cedar Crest College, Kutztown University, Elizabethtown College, and Rosemont College in Pennsylvania weathered the movement. Students struck some universities, including the University of Michigan, the University of Toledo, Florida State, Creighton, and the University of Northern Iowa. HBCUs were not exempt—Bishop College in Texas and Mississippi Valley State were disrupted.[12]

That spring of 1970, Black students saw some of their hard-fought gains dismantled, as the defensive struggle to maintain diversity strengthened, which would eventually supersede the movement to gain diversity. San Francisco State president S.I. Hayakawa fired six Black Studies professors on March 2, 1970. It was one of the largest political firings of Black professors at an HWCU in history, until eight of the twelve Black Studies instructors at CSU Fresno received similar notices that spring. Four hundred students discussed the fact that their advances were being rolled back when they attended a "Black Unity Conference" at Stanford in early May 1970.[13]

Days before, on April 30, 1970, President Nixon had announced the escalation of the Vietnam War, ordering troops into Cambodia. His announcement escalated a vanishing anti-war movement. On May 4, during an antiwar protest at Kent State University in Ohio, National Guard members killed four White students. Black students did not enthusiastically join the outbreak of strikes following the Kent State murders, angering some White students. Black Americans did protest against the war and racism at a few institutions.[14]

Not even two weeks after the Kent State tragedy, another tragedy struck Jackson State. After a night of violent disorders, in part stemming from the discovery of a bell in the campus warehouse that used to summon students to class and chapel as if they were slaves, President John Peoples met with student leaders. They discussed the causes of the rebellion the night before, and for nearly two hours on May 14, 1970, they complained about the bell, the lack of a bridge walk over the dangerous Lynch Street, the women's curfew, poor cafeteria food, and the irrelevant, bourgeois "Negro" university. That night, a small group of activists started tossing rocks at automobiles driven by White motorists on Lynch Street, a major Jackson thoroughfare that ran through campus. The disruption intensified. Just as on the night before, the Jackson police and state patrolmen, many of whom were known Klansmen, stormed onto the campus with the order to "go in there and scatter them damn—those Negroes." In addition, a Jackson police lieutenant assembled a group of officers to disperse more than a hundred students in front of a women's dormitory, Alexander Hall, on Lynch Street. It was about midnight, and some of the women students had just entered the dorms before curfew, after being escorted by their male friends, who were still milling around. The lawmen stopped in front of the dorm. "You white pigs!" "White sons-of-bitches!" The students were irate at the police presence. A bottle smashed loudly onto the Lynch Street pavement in front of the officers. "They're gonna shoot!" a student screamed.[15]

Officers then let off round after round at the crowd of students, who quickly fell, tried to take cover, and raced into the dormitory. Officers even shot at the dormitory. Women students scurried about in the dorm to other rooms and under their beds, dodging bullets. Chips of brick, concrete, and glass fell like an avalanche on students taking cover below. Thirty seconds later, the patrolmen stopped shooting, sent for all of the city's ambulances, and approached the dormitories, checking the student bodies that lay sprawled in front of them. Near a small magnolia tree in front of the hall, they discovered the dead bodies of two young men. One was 21-year-old Phillip L. Gibbs, a junior at Jackson State and father of a young son, and the other was James Earl Green, 17, a senior track star at

Photo 10.2 Two
students at Jackson State
peer from a dormitory
window that was shot
out by police on campus,
May 15, 1970 (AP
Photo/Jack Thornell)

a local Jackson high school. The patrolmen spread out and found at least eight students and one community member injured. The next day officials closed the campus for the rest of the semester. Klansmen donning badges instead of sheets had killed Black youth.[16]

An outcry of sadness and fury rose up from Black America when it woke up to the news that morning of May 15, 1970. Investigations and punishments were demanded of these officers, who claimed they were defending themselves against sniper fire. No group was more upset than Black students in Jackson and across the nation. As White colleges had erupted after Kent State, so too did Black colleges after Jackson State. According to Howard president James E. Cheek, the resentment of his students neared the "breaking point." Rallies and demonstrations occurred at HWCUs, too. When several Black students at Ohio State tried to lower the American flag to mourn the deceased, they fought off a group of White students trying to stop them.[17]

Fifteen HBCU presidents met with President Nixon and urged him to recommend that police officers not carry guns on campuses and to make a national televised address to affirm the "government's resolve to protect the lives of black citizens." President Nixon demurred, but as a palliative he did offer more money to HBCUs. Charles Evers, the venerable Mississippi leader, started to reconsider nonviolence. "I've preached non-violence because I don't think blacks can win the other way, but there comes a time when a man doesn't care anymore about winning. The day of killing niggers is gone to hell." Shunning White suasion, CORE's Floyd McKissick observed "the conscience of America was not even pricked" when the two Black students and six Augusta (Georgia) men were killed (in an urban rebellion days before the Jackson massacre). "We must all learn from this. For it is further evidence that there is no way for Black men to reach the conscience of white America." Despite the President's Commission on Campus Unrest finding that bigotry, not self-defense, led to the slaying of the students, in the fall of 1970, a Mississippi grand jury found the police "were justified in discharging their weapons." Further, in April 1972, an all-White Mississippi jury ruled that neither state officials nor police were liable for civil damages. The *New York Amsterdam News* editorialized, "This decision is simply another nail in the coffin of America's system of justice and equal treatment in the courts."[18]

Usually, repression either slows or accelerates a social movement. It sometimes depends on whether the movement is decelerating or quickening before the repression. The Orangeburg Massacre and King's assassination in the spring of 1968 caught the movement when it was accelerating. On the other hand, the Jackson State tragedy occurred when the movement was slowing, and thus it proved to be yet another cause of the demise of the Black Campus Movement.

The level of activism noticeably dipped in the fall of 1970. The calm on "most of the country's campuses" that fall had "been so pervasive as to have been almost unsettling," according to *The New York Times*. Ideological divisions had widened, particularly due to the growing sway of Pan-Africanism, feminism, Black capitalism, cultural nationalism, and Marxism. Black Studies courses had been introduced in colleges across America, which blunted the thorniest issue of their activism. Scores of student leaders had graduated or been removed from campus before the fall of 1970, either voluntarily or involuntarily, and the achievements of the movement were regularly assaulted. "We have to constantly fortify our position," said an Oberlin student.[19]

During the 1970–1971 academic year, protests to keep movement gains became more prominent and the students grew more interested in off-campus issues, specifically political repression, including the Free Angela (Davis) campaign. Yet Black students, who for the first time were more likely to attend college outside the South, still waged offensive protests to demand novel measures—sometimes athletic—that academic year at numerous institutions, including Syracuse University, Fontbonne University in Missouri, Western Connecticut State University, University of South Alabama, Norfolk State University, St. Mary's University in Texas, Prairie View A&M, Bluffton University in Ohio, Texas Christian University, Colorado State University Pueblo, Providence College, the University of Georgia, and the University of Florida ("Black Thursday").[20]

As the movement decelerated in 1971, Black students did not have the living voices that galvanized their activism, as most of the Black power leaders had been killed, jailed, or exiled. The pendulum continued to shift among Black students during the 1971–1972 academic year from offensive to defensive protests and from on-campus to off-campus concerns, such as the Attica Prison massacre in New York in September 1971. Officers killed and injured unarmed prisoners when they took back the upstate New York penitentiary from prisoners who had seized it to demand better conditions. But offensive protests for new demands still prevailed, manifesting once again at HBCUs and institutions with new critical masses, such as Indiana University—Purdue University Indianapolis (IUPUI), Tougaloo, Wartburg College in Iowa, Eckerd College, Wilberforce, University of Hartford, University of Nevada, and Murray State University.[21]

Benjamin E. Mays, the former Morehouse president, noticed in his travels in the spring of 1972 that the "campuses—on the whole—are much calmer." The assessment did not stem from the fact that higher education had responded to the needs of Black students. The racial constitution had almost completely changed on the surface, in the public academic rhetoric, but that does not mean the new creeds—moral freedom, standardization of inclusion, antiracist curricula, and grassroots altruism—were totally implemented. "Much is said" about aiding Black students, but "little is being done," found a researcher who surveyed more than a thousand colleges. *The Chronicle of Higher Education*'s report in the spring of 1972 on "Higher Education and Black America" further determined that "the black studies programs … now fill a standard, if insecure, niche in the curriculum." But the struggle still had one more semester.[22]

In the fall of 1972, the declining specter of Black campus activism affected higher education, including negotiations at Franklin College in Indiana, Angelo State University in Texas, and University of North Alabama and an almost total boycott at the University of Arkansas at Pine Bluff. The last major demonstration of the Black Campus Movement occurred at the university with the largest collection of Black students in the nation—Southern University in Louisiana. In the fall of 1972, President G. Leon Netterville ran the university like a feudal lord. Nothing of significance happened without his approval, which was why Psychology Department Chair Charles M. Waddell resigned in mid-October 1972 when the president did not allow him to fire a professor who had sexually harassed women. Disturbed, students formed a coalition of groups, Students United, and drew up a list of demands for more student and faculty power.[23]

In a gathering with more than five thousand students, on October 24, President Netterville rejected the students' demands. Shock quickly transformed into fury. The five thousand students rushed out of the gymnasium like a battalion and trudged five miles to the state board of education's office to see State Superintendent Louis Michot. But Michot was away in Atlanta, and when one of his subordinates came out to speak with the students, they called for the resignations of President Netterville and two other administrators. They were not finished marching that day. Numbering a reported seven thousand, they walked over to the state capitol in one of the largest Black student marches in American history to meet with Governor Edwin Edwards. He told the students he would be willing to help. Activists returned to campus and arranged for 80 percent of roughly eight thousand students to boycott classes. On October 31, President Netterville shut down the Baton Rouge campus, while activists at the New Orleans campus had initiated their own boycott and eight-day building takeover the day before. On November 6, the Baton Rouge campus reopened with more than three hundred heavily armed sheriff's deputies and city police ready to stamp out the class strike. It persisted.[24]

On the morning of November 16, in an attempt to put an end to the strike, the Baton Rouge police arrested four Students United leaders and charged them with "disrupting the normal educational process." Responding later in the day, students stormed into the administration building—three hundred strong—and up to President Netterville's office.

Hearing the leaders out, President Netterville made a phone call and allegedly instructed the police to come and clear out the campus. He bolted
out of his office and left for a meeting with the state board of
education.[25]

Not long after, on November 16, 1972, the assembly of students, now
numbering three thousand, started to leave, when they saw a wave of sheriff's deputies, state troopers, and city police come onto campus. They gave
the students five minutes to disperse. It was a standoff—the students were
now not going anywhere. When the five minutes had elapsed, a state
trooper tossed a tear gas canister into the crowd. It did not explode. A
student picked it up and tossed it back over the line of state troopers and
near the sheriff's deputies. The canister exploded and sent the deputies
scurrying in a panic for their masks. Now donning masks, they turned to
the crowd of students and opened fire with more tear gas canisters. One
officer reportedly emptied a single shotgun blast that killed 20-year-old
Leonard D. Brown Jr. of Gilbert, Louisiana, and Denver A. Smith, a
20-year-old computer science major from New Roads, Louisiana.[26]

The campus immediately closed, and soon after President Netterville,
whom Students United blamed for the tragedy, resigned. In a statement
released to the press, the group said the murders were "premeditated,
plotted, and implemented." Governor Edwards tried to deflect blame
from landing on his administration and the Southern officials he allowed
to stay in power. He said over and over again, "It was the students who
initiated the confrontation" by throwing the tear gas canisters first.
Southern reopened on January 3, 1973, with a tripling of campus police
forces, loyalty oaths signed, and student leaders barred, harassed, or
disciplined.[27]

This tragedy was too much for the national student community to
endure. They still had not recovered from Jackson State. In contrast to the
previous killing of Black campus activists, sadness eclipsed fury when students around the nation heard about the shootings. The reaction was
"scattered and subdued," according to one report. Only at nearby
Grambling did students aggressively protest the killings, but memorial
services were more popular than protests. The Black Campus Movement
was history.[28]

"We, the students of Langston University, have fallen into an abyss of
apathy, where our only resolution is the condemnation of the institution."
Condemnation had not been sparking activism as in years past, irritating
Leanear Randall as he watched the movement recede into history in May

1972. The cry of apathy had been heard since 1970, but it had not been this loud. In two issues of *The Afro-Times Newsletter* in the fall of 1972, students at Mississippi State University added to the chorus. "Perhaps our biggest enemy is apathy," Edward R. Robinson wrote in September. In the November-December newsletter, Coleman Wicks alleged that Mississippi State was "rapidly earning the unheralded distinction of being one of the nation's most apathetic." Up north at Lehigh University in Pennsylvania, Nathan Harris, a Black administrator, attested in December that the "belligerently angry black student" who pressured the "University through overt actions has faded." Out West, CSU Long Beach professor and former Black campus activist J.K. Obatala asked in *The Nation*, in 1972, "What happened to the black campus revolution? Whatever happened to the gun-toting nationalist, the uncombed hair, the demonstrations, the handbills, the placards, the protests, the black leather jackets and Malcolm X sweatshirts that came to be symbols of black student militancy in the 1960s."[29]

With reports of apathy emerging from every region, the age had passed, even as Black students detested the new contradictions in higher education—substance not matching the new ideals. Derisively, on January 19, 1973, the White editors of *The Collegio* at Pittsburg State awarded Black students "first place in the age-old category of apathy. This infamous honor is presented to those with the most anger and the least action." The movement had indeed faded, but not necessarily Black student anger or action. Beginning in 1973, defensive, disconnected Black student activism, to retain the gains of the Black Campus Movement, eclipsed the offensive, connected activism that instituted a slew of new antiracist changes and rewrote the racial constitution of higher education during the previous eight years. Put differently, Black students no longer held the academy in the creative clutches of a social movement in 1973. In that sense, they were apathetic. However, they were far from apathetic in the rearguard, defending their humanity, defending their gains—a defense that continues to this day.[30]

CHAPTER 11

"A Fly in Buttermilk": Organizations and Demands

Shortly after forming the Organization of African and Afro-American Students at American University (OASATAU) in 1968, Walker "Moose" Foster clarified the group's function. "All our lives, we've been told that niggers ain't nothing." But "it does mean something to be a Negro," said the 19-year-old son of a maid and butler. "We want to appreciate our cultural differences." Since first stepping on the Washington, DC, campus, "I felt like a fly in buttermilk. I was stranded in a wasteland, in affluent Spring Valley. The only Negroes we saw up here were janitors. I mean, it could be me or my parents." In the fall of 1969, the University of Tennessee BSU circulated an orientation booklet that exclaimed, "The Black student must realize that, here at U.T., he constitutes what is analogous to the 'fly in the buttermilk.'"[1]

Black students borrowed the James Baldwin adage and habitually used it to characterize their experiences in the middle to late 1960s and early 1970s. It could be heard more at HWCUs, where, aside from Black service workers, buttermilk tended to flow everywhere. Buttermilk gushed around at Black colleges, too—the White benefactors, politicians, education bureaucrats, trustees, literature, rules, overwhelmingly White faculty bodies, and presidential Black puppets controlled by White strings. Long before the 1960s, Black students felt like flies in buttermilk, stranded in "academic wastelands." However, the contradiction had never been this pronounced. The flies were never this Black. The buttermilk never seemed

© The Author(s), under exclusive license to Springer Nature Switzerland AG 2025
I. X. Kendi, *The Black Campus Movement*, Contemporary Black History, https://doi.org/10.1007/978-3-031-37394-7_11

so White. Black campus activists, emboldened by the contradictions, fashioned SGAs and BSUs to reform the racist constitution by organizing and issuing a series of demands.[2]

ORGANIZING

Before they could transform their colleges and universities, Black campus activists first had to build organized campus bodies to wage the struggle—the chief striving during the early years of the Black Campus Movement. At HBCUs, these organized bodies were usually SGAs. By the 1967–1968 and certainly 1968–1969 academic years, most student bodies of HBCUs had elected Black campus activists as SGA presidents. Ewart Brown Jr., a native of Bermuda, gave his opening remarks as president of Howard's student body in September 1967. Sounding a chord heard from other SGA presidents at the time, he declared, "Black leadership must be developed in a Black university. This is the kind of leadership the movement needs now."[3]

North Carolina A&T students elected Vincent McCullough (president) and Nelson Johnson (vice president) in the spring of 1969. "We got elected on a pretty militant platform," said Johnson, who also helped organize and become the first national chairman of Students Organized for Black Unity (SOBU) that spring. "We took to the students as straightforward and honestly as we could, like what we felt was going on in the society and the whole question of Black Power." The whole question of Black power dominated the platform of Earl Hart, Winston-Salem State's SGA president during the 1970–1971 school year. Upon announcing his candidacy, a campus reporter styled Hart "the little man from Rocky Mount, N. C. who has been a constant thorn in the side of the administration since he has been here." Hart had continuously pricked the administration as BSU president, with a mission "to help make Winston-Salem State University a mentally Black university."[4]

Historical memory and scholarship places BSUs solely at HWCUs. However, HBCUs also had BSUs, an umbrella term for all of the groups with multiple names imbued with a Black power ideology that united and served the academic, political, social, and cultural interests of Black students during the movement and beyond. At HBCUs, BSUs were often more radical than SGAs and, thus, jockeyed with them for the direction of the struggle. Some HBCUs, including Tougaloo, had more than one BSU of differing ideological persuasion, or they had BSUs that were coalitions of many of the student groups, such as Howard's Ujamma or Students United at Southern. In the initial years of the movement, in the mid-1960s, BSUs were more likely to lead the movement, such as the Students for Academic Freedom and Black Power Committee at Howard, SOUL at North Carolina A&T, Central State's Unity for Unity, and the Informers at Grambling State. By the end of the decade, some former BSU directors had been elected to run SGAs, sometimes pushing BSUs to the margins. Paine (Afro-American Alliance), Kentucky State (Black Student Unity), Alcorn State (Black Culture Society), and Fisk (Students for a Black University) are a few of the many HBCUs that had BSUs during the movement.[5]

Nevertheless, BSUs were more ostensible at HWCUs. Black campus activists were most likely to name their BSUs *Black Student Union*—thus the reason for the use of this general appellation. The first known group to be named "Black Student Union" materialized at San Francisco State in March 1966, led by Marianna Waddy, Jerry Varnado, Benny Stewart, and Jimmy Garrett. Reportedly, San Francisco State student Tricia Navara came up with the name "Black Students Union," which spread (sometimes through San Francisco State organizers) to other institutions in California, including CSU Dominguez Hills, CSU Fresno, Mills, UC Santa Barbara, UC Davis, UC Riverside, and University of Southern California. The term moved along the Pacific Ocean into Oregon and Washington and then made its way east, appearing as Black Students Union or Black Student Union in Utah, Kansas, Kentucky, and Upstate New York. Presumably Columbia's Society for Afro-American Students, founded in 1964, popularized the name *Afro-American Society* (AAS), which many organizers along the Atlantic coast borrowed, particularly in Massachusetts and Rhode Island. Generally, Black campus activists were likely to name their BSUs after existing prominent groups in the area. *Black Student Association* was trendy in Illinois (Illinois Wesleyan, North Central College, Roosevelt, Southern Illinois University, Southern Illinois University Edwardsville, and University of Illinois) and Michigan (Michigan State, Northern Michigan University, and Eastern Michigan University). In the St. Louis area, most BSUs were named the *Association of Black Collegians*, a popular title in the Lehigh Valley of Pennsylvania as well.

Black campus activists publicly announced the founding of BSUs at press conferences and campus forums, on circulars, and in student newspapers. Ten weeks after students founded the Carleton College BSU in the fall of 1967, two college officials claimed that "a major change, some might call it a revolution, has taken place on campus." The change was a growing awareness of the "Negro's presence," as Black students sought to end the standardization of their exclusion. Organizers often knew they were part of a national social movement. The founding of the Afro-American Association at the University of Alabama emanated from a "national trend," executive Angela Jones explained in 1968.[6]

The spokesmen and spokeswomen and their founding constitutions proclaimed eight interrelated but distinct functions for BSUs at Black and White institutions. A minority of BSUs contained only one or all eight of these functions. Most expressed a few, usually based on the ideology of the organizers, the number of Black students, and the nature and location of the college.

First and most often, BSUs were guided by Black suasion, like other Black Power organizations at the time. Students founded BSUs to unite and raise the consciousness of the Black student body, which was why many started out as study groups. Monmouth College's BSU in Illinois sought to "unite the Black students on campus" and discuss and make them aware of the problems of the day. At Kentucky State in 1972, the BSU endeavored to "create Black awareness, promote Black pride, and maintain Black unity."[7]

Second, and most practically, students established BSUs at HWCUs to help them "survive the White college experience," as articulated at Franklin in 1970. Students who "could find no security in the White cotton fields of Claremont Colleges" founded the BSU, said President Franklin Peters in 1969. University of Northern Iowa students "banded together to make it easier to survive on this malevolent campus," wrote Dwight Christian in 1969.[8]

Third, solving the Black student identity crisis emerged as the inaugural objective of a few groups. This crisis took different forms. At American University, this crisis stemmed from a yearning for self-love and self-awareness. "For Negroes, the trend has been assimilative integration … the sponge theory," Foster asserted. "We're trying to ring the sponge out." In the process of exploring their Blackness and Africanity through Black Power principles, literature, and speakers, another identity crisis often surfaced: the contradiction of the contemporary ideas of Blackness—socially responsible, working class centered, politically and culturally nationalist—and the hypothesized historic notions of student identity—bourgeois, socially irresponsible, and politically and culturally assimilationist. The Black Capitalism Movement escalated the identity crisis, along with those activists who regularly told Black students that their campus activism was either irrelevant to the Black struggle or not as relevant or revolutionary as community activism. Grassroots altruism resolved this crisis for many Black students—the attempt to make their colleges vehicles of grassroots community change (with them at the steering wheel). Thus, they called for politically radical, culturally oriented, socially responsible Black Universities at HBCUs and Black Studies at HWCUs.[9]

BSUs strove to "perpetuate the interests of Blacks on campus," as the founders of a group at the University of Arkansas at Monticello stated. Imbued with the Black power principle of self-determination, Black campus activists based this fourth function on the assumption that no one on campus—not administrators, faculty, staff, or other students—no one had their interests in mind or could address them like they could. Twenty-two Black students at Franklin & Marshall unanimously voted in the spring of 1967 to form a group to "speak for our collective interests," according to their leader, Ben Bowser. Correlated with the fourth function, but taking an activist step, a fifth function of BSUs was to create an antiracist collegiate experience through the institution of "Black reforms," which the BSU at Marietta College in Ohio announced in its circular in March 1969.[10]

Sixth, Black campus activists formed BSUs to serve as an instrument of incorporation into campus life, usually at institutions where they had a small number of Black students. This organizational mission initially guided the BSUs at Utica College in New York and Morningside College in Iowa. Utilizing the civil rights code of White suasion, some BSUs formed to promote and enlighten non-Black students about African American history and culture and teach away racist ideas. This seventh purpose were more likely to guide BSUs at colleges with relatively small Black populations, such as C.W. Post Campus of Long Island University, Clarke, Thiel, and Guilford College in North Carolina, where founders struggled to get "the White student to know the Negro and his problems" in 1968. Finally, pioneers of BSUs at institutions near large Black populations functioned to relate to, support, and serve off-campus Black communities, such as Case Western Reserve's AAS in Cleveland.[11]

Each BSU tended to give prominence to different functions. Similarly, each Black campus activist gave his or her attention to the functions that mirrored his or her ideology. The radicals often devoted their energies to BSU community projects and campus activism, while many moderates spent their time educating White people and addressing their identity crises. Black campus activists of differing ideologies were generally united on the BSU duties of Black suasion, serving Black student interests, and effecting relevant campus reforms, although they sometimes differed on tactics and goals. Initially, these points of unity eclipsed areas of division. However, there were always internal ideological conflicts in BSUs that only grew as the Black Campus Movement rose in stature and matured.

Although there existed some citywide, statewide, and regionwide alliances, BSUs were fervently autonomous, focused on their own campus and local community. As Marshall junior John Shellcroft explained in March 1969, "The Black United Students organization is a local campus group with no national ties other than the bond of Black skin." There were a few national Black student organizations in the late 1960s and early 1970s, most prominently SOBU and NABS, formed in the spring and summer of 1969, respectively. SOBU, which eventually changed its name to Youth Organization for Black Unity, focused (though not totally) on off-campus matters, particularly Pan-African projects, and the NABS provided a "national and international forum ... to articulate the legitimate demands of Black students," explained its national coordinator, Gwen Patton.[12]

As BSUs at HBCUs have been historically overlooked as components of the Black Campus Movement, so too have Black SGA presidents at HWCUs. They were elected at Occidental (Don Cornwell) and St. Olaf College in Minnesota (Lee Oliver) for the 1968–1969 academic year and at Ursuline College in Ohio (Renee Jones) for the following school year. Probably the most heralded (and most improbable) SGA president at an HWCU was Harry Walker, who sported a large Afro, adored Malcolm X, and had been a BSU president at the University of South Carolina. Walker became the first Black SGA president at a college in a former Confederate state in March 1971.[13]

DEMANDS

Demands were as varied as the primary functions of BSUs and the ideologies of SGA presidents. Nonetheless, most of the BSUs and activist SGAs in the early years of the movement (1965 to 1967) issued requests, concerns, and grievances through traditional academic channels. The racist reactions to their requests, the slow pace of academic change, or outright rejections alienated many students from traditional channels by 1968 and 1969. As a preface to their list of demands in December 1969, the BSU at the University of the Pacific (California) quoted the Declaration of

Independence: "In every state of these oppressions we have petitioned for redress in the most humble terms: our repeated petitions have been answered only with repeated injury." In the demands at Duke in February 1969, Black campus activists shouted, "WE HAVE EXHAUSTED THE SO-CALLED 'PROPER' CHANNELS." Quoting Frederick Douglass, who said the "limits of tyrants are prescribed by the endurance of those they oppress," University of Houston students proclaimed in their demands, "our endurance is exhausted." In March 1969, Sally Smith of Mills told reporters, "we felt we weren't getting anywhere, so we decided to turn our requests into demands."[14]

Demands did not merely surface due to the BSU members' or SGA leaders' growing conception of the irrelevant and racist constitution of higher education. Black campus activists were inspired to issue demands by hearing about other demands, traveling speakers, conferences, and Black Cultural Weeks. They materialized after an off-campus tragedy, such as Bloody Sunday or King's assassination, or an on-campus racist action. The attack on Black students at an ROTC demonstration at New Mexico State prompted the issuance of demands in April 1969. Two crosses were burned at the University of Mount Union, in March 1970, sparking demands from Black students. Most of the demands of the Black Campus Movement were presented from the day after King's assassination through the end of the spring 1969 semester.[15]

Almost all administrators despised the term "demand," which asserted a level of Black student power they were unwilling to concede in highly hierarchical academia. Black campus activists usually wrote out their demands in essay format or as a simple numbered list. At HWCUs, they regularly addressed the demands to the president. The demands were more likely to be targeted to the trustees and governors at HBCUs, since Black campus activists were adept at speaking directly to power. Sometimes they announced their demands at a press conference, at a campus rally, in a campus forum, in the student newspaper, or during a protest.

Demands at HBCUs were very similar. It was not rare for students to submit fifty-page reports, such as at the University of Maryland Eastern Shore, or more than fifty grievances, such as at Virginia Union. First and foremost, HBCU activists demanded some derivative of what came to be known as a "Black University." Generally, they asserted that White people controlled the existing "Negro University," which merely graduated elitist, assimilationist, and conservative students. Instead, Black students envisioned that a "Black University" would connect students to African

American culture, imbue them with antiracist ideas and a social responsibility to aid the Black masses, and be a chief institutional participant in the Black Power Movement.

"The Black student is being educated in this country as if he were being programmed in White supremacy and self-hatred," began Ernest Stephens, a Tuskegee student, in a spring 1967 article. "How long will it be before Black leaders and educators take hold of Negro colleges and transform them from 'training schools for Negroes' into universities designed to fit the real needs of Black people in this nation?" Also, that February 1967, a recently formed Black Power Committee at Howard presented the "Black Power Manifesto." The manifesto called for the "overthrow of the Negro college" and its replacement by "a militant Black university which will counteract the White-washing Black students now receive in 'Negro' and White institutions." Suggesting that Howard be renamed after Nat Turner or Marcus Garvey, they wanted it to emphasize "subjects more pertinent to the present and future demands of the Black struggle in America and the world."[16]

HBCU activists demanded the firing of paternalistic, dictatorial presidents controlled by Southern segregationists. They desired presidents who would lead the transformation of their colleges into Black Universities. Students demanded the desegregation of all-White trustee boards that reigned over most of their colleges like colonial officials. As their White peers at HWCUs did, HBCU activists wanted student power. They demanded more-powerful SGAs and student involvement in decision-making bodies. Black Studies courses, programs, departments, and curricula were demanded. They wanted their dorms, dining halls, classroom buildings, athletic fields—everything on campus—to be renovated, at least to the level of facilities at HWCUs. As they had for the last forty years, they wanted better food and service in the cafeteria. They demanded improved recreational, transportation, and medical services and enhanced campus offices, such as the registrar's and financial aid offices. At many HBCUs, activists wanted extended library hours, and they also demanded more books authored by Black people. Some Black campus activists required the rehiring of fired antiracist White faculty, while at other HBCUs, including Fisk, they sought the ejection of all White people. Generally, they demanded better credentialed Black faculty, faculty power, and a clear system based on merit (as opposed to loyalty to administration or religiosity) for faculty hiring, firing, and tenure.[17]

During the formative years of the movement at HWCUs, as civil rights shifted to Black Power, Black students requested the desegregation of White Greek organizations, the desegregation of nearby campus businesses, and open campus and community housing measures. However, their most notorious demand, their most impassioned demand, their most concerted demand was for more Black students. Every other desire pivoted off of this one at HWCUs. Practically every single set of demands (and there were hundreds issued at HWCUs) listed a demand for more Black students. "The unusually small number of Black … students here frustrates our attempts to obtain a meaningful liberal arts education relevant to the society we live in today," Skidmore College activists in New York said in 1971. Some BSUs wanted their collegiate composition to represent the racial demographics of the city, state, or nation, such as at CSU Fresno and Stetson University in Florida. Others demanded quotas, including Brown activists in 1968, who demanded 11 percent, equivalent to the national Black population. Related to this demand, Black campus activists also demanded the active recruitment of Black students and that they be involved (or in control of) that process.[18]

Demonstrating their grassroots altruism, BSUs frequently demanded students from "hard core, poor areas," to use the language of Illinois Wesleyan activists in 1969. Sometimes BSUs resisted calling these students "disadvantaged," such as at University of San Francisco in 1968. They demanded remedial programs, financial aid, and scholarships, sometimes based not on academic performance, but on need, including at Goucher College in Baltimore in 1970. Collegians at institutions such as University of Virginia and Providence College wanted application fees to be waived for Black applicants. Asserting that standardized tests were racist, they demanded that the "SAT be waived for all Black applicants," as activists at Wilmington College of Ohio stated in 1971. At some institutions, BSUs demanded admissions criteria tailored to Black students, asserting, as Duke students did in 1970, that the present "criteria for entering Black students are oriented toward White middle class students." BSUs were more likely to demand the hiring of a Black admissions officer, who would not only review files from Black applicants but also effectively "sell" their colleges to Black students, as Millsaps College activists desired in 1970. They also requested student exchange programs with HBCUs (Johns Hopkins University and St. Cloud State University were examples), funds for recruiting weekends to host and convince potential applicants, and Black orientation programs for entering freshmen.[19]

After Black admissions, the next two most popular demands were for Black Cultural Centers and Black Studies in the form of courses, programs, and departments. It appears that Black Studies, specifically programs and departments, were more likely to be requested if an institution resided near a Black population center or if it had a relatively large population of Black students. In contrast, Black Cultural Centers were more likely to be requested if the colleges were removed from Black population centers or if they had a relatively low enrollment of Black Americans. So even though historians have generally labeled Black Studies as the major programmatic demand, Black Cultural Centers were demanded nearly as often, if not more often. And students fought just as fiercely for them.

Black students envisioned Black Cultural Centers as becoming the spatial nexus of Black student life that would give them a sociocultural refuge—a place to cultivate their culture, display their culture to White students—or run programs for the area Black community. Its purpose depended on the guiding ideology of the BSU. To DePauw students in 1970, a Black Cultural Center would serve as a "place to establish our cultural identity." Middlebury students needed a place in 1972 to develop their "sense of community and solidarity." University of Wisconsin-Oshkosh activists desired that it "be a place apart" in 1968.[20]

Lying at the core of demands for antiracist curricula was Black Studies. Depending on the spectrum of their ideology and how much they challenged the assimilationist curriculum, students conceptualized existing curricula as racist—as segregationist or assimilationist. In 1969, Colorado State students described their education as "tragically irrelevant and vulgarly Whitewashed," and they deplored the curriculum that taught all aspects of European civilization while dismissing people of African descent. "When the focus in these classrooms is almost exclusively Western and White … and almost never Black, dissatisfaction among those students with historical and cultural roots which are not White and European is inevitable," wrote Barbara Smith of Mount Holyoke in 1968.[21]

Black Studies would not merely have materials "relevant to their culture," as expressed by Roosevelt's BSA in 1969. Pioneers wanted it to "recognize the validity and the uniqueness of the new Black perspective," according to University of Maryland Eastern Shore activists in 1970, and to "equip us with the essentials necessary to combat the particular programs of Black people," said the University of Houston group. Courses were more likely to be demanded from 1965 to the spring of 1968.

Departments and programs were more likely to be demanded after the assassination of King.[22]

BSUs not only demanded Black Studies departments on the same level of existing departments, but periodically they demanded BSU (or Black community) control over the new department, including hiring and firing faculty at schools such as Nebraska's Creighton and Portland's Reed. Or, as at the University of Akron, Black campus activists wanted a department "independent of the university hierarchy." Students argued for control based on the argument offered by State University of New York (SUNY) Stony Brook student leader Calvin Canton. "A program for Black [people] cannot be run by people who have oppressed us," he said in February 1969. Quite a few groups of BSUs, including that at Vassar, demanded Black Studies facilities situated off campus in Black communities. At Stetson, Beloit College in Wisconsin, and Emerson College in Boston, Black campus activists wanted a Black Studies course to be required of all students to "dispel the myths about the Black man," asserted Stetson students.[23]

Some pressed against interdepartmental programs in which Black Studies faculty and courses would be cross-listed between Black Studies and other departments. Nevertheless, many radical BSUs demanding departments had to settle for these interdepartmental programs with formally or informally cross-listed professors and courses with a Black Studies director. Even more activists had to settle for (or were satisfied with) the intrusion of Black courses in existing departments.[24]

Students often demanded Black Studies courses taught by Black faculty. Many thought the "validity" of those courses "taught by Whites" was "questionable," to use the language offered at Saint Peters University in New Jersey in 1969. Some, like the San Francisco State BSU, thought it was impossible. Therefore, those BSUs that considered this impossible demanded the firing of White professors who taught some of the original Black Studies courses. At the University of North Dakota, for instance, students disrupted a Black history course in February 1969 taught by a White professor. In July 1969, Stanford's BSU demanded that its new Black Studies program be Black led and Black taught. Even at HBCUs, more Black faculty were demanded, including at Howard, where students asserted in 1970 that White faculty "stifle thoughts, stagnate imagination or curtail analysis of and by Black students."[25]

Black faculty, aside from teaching Black Studies courses, became a key demand. Students knew that professors dictated the academic direction of a university and they could serve as advisers. Students wanted their presence to "set the stereotype of Black people straight," expressed the BSU at Xavier University in Cincinnati in 1969. Just as many BSUs wanted to control Black Studies programs and departments, they also wanted "a recognized, responsive, and representative voice in the hiring and dismissal" of Black professors, as the Providence College BSU indicated in 1971. Sometimes they demanded a voice in the personnel decisions of all faculty and often requested that professors they deemed "bigoted" be terminated, as at Roosevelt. Black campus activists also listed in their demands the termination of racist HWCU presidents, while habitually demanding the firing of prejudiced nonacademic staff, such as financial aid counselors, secretaries, store clerks, and security officers. Routinely, when they demanded the firing of racist White people, they wanted them to be replaced by Black Americans. Police harassment prompted many demands for Black officers (or no officers at all).[26]

In addition to faculty changes, Black campus activists regularly demanded Black administrators. Black students, such as those at Wilmington College of Ohio, felt that they "would be able to relate to Black administrators with greater ease" and that Black administrators comprehended Black "students' needs and desires." Sometimes they simply preferred that an African American fill one of the existing administrative positions. More often, they demanded the creation of a new administrative post—vice president for minority affairs (Eastern Michigan), dean of Black student affairs (Western Connecticut State), or a Black ombudsman (Coe College in Iowa)—what today is usually called a chief diversity officer. The BSA at Rensselaer Polytechnic Institute (New York) wanted the "Black dean" to "have the final word on all Black affairs on campus and [be] responsible only to the VP," echoing their peers across the nation. More likely they wanted the Black dean responsible only to the president or the BSU.[27]

At HWCUs, Black students demanded a few Black trustees, including at the University of Massachusetts Dartmouth, while at HBCUs they wanted the boards to be controlled by Black people. Black campus activists demanded one or several Black counselors because, as an Angelo State student said in 1972, Black students have no one that will sympathize with them and know the way they feel. Some BSUs, such as at Duquesne University in Pittsburgh in 1969, reported that they spent too much time counseling each other, and therefore full-time counselors for Black students were needed so the BSU could shift its focus from "academic programs to community problems." Based on reasoning similar to that supporting their demand for Black counselors, some groups of students demanded a Black psychologist, including the Allied Blacks for Liberty and Equality in 1969 at Knox College in Illinois, "in order to help in the adjustment of Black students."[28]

To ease the adjustment, collegians demanded Black residence areas, usually Black floors, as at the University of Akron, and sometimes an all-Black, majority-Black, or African American culturally themed dormitory. "As it is your duty to secure the physical and mental well being of every student at Chatham, allow us our physical and mental well being by permitting us a separate residence for Black students" in order to avoid the "mental cruelty perpetuated against us in interracial dormitories," wrote the BSU in 1970. Black students often desired and received office space for BSUs, as at the University of Nevada, decorated with African fixtures and posters of their icons, such as Muhammad Ali and Malcolm X.[29]

Just as HBCU students wanted longer library hours, HWCU students craved something of relevance to read in their libraries. Less likely were the demands for a Black library, which occurred in 1971 at Grinnell College in Iowa. Defiance College activists in Ohio asked for 15 percent of the library budget for Black literature in 1970, while they demanded a portion of the library at Saint Peters. Black students often requested (and were given) a role in the selection of books by or about Black people. As Black campus activists desired mental food in the library, they craved soul food and Black cooks in the cafeteria at schools such as Roger Williams University in Rhode Island and Pennsylvania's Slippery Rock University. To sustain their diets and their livelihood, some BSUs, including the one at Truman State University, demanded campus jobs for Black students.[30]

Due to reports of racist professors and knowledge that members of their groups were being underprepared, BSUs demanded an overhaul of the grading system. This overhaul included the mass termination of racist professors, a pass-fail system, or even the establishment of an inquiry committee to supervise grading, to be controlled by Black students. Activists demanded the appointment of a BSU representative to the SGA, or a senate vote (or bloc) allotted to Black students, as at the University of South Alabama. BSUs demanded higher appropriations for their ambitious and expansive campus and community projects. Some groups demanded a separate budget allocation or financial autonomy, requesting that all Black student fees be deposited in their accounts. Activists at the University of

Houston and Kalamazoo College in Michigan demanded fiscal independence; as the Colorado State students explained in 1969, "the concerns of
the Black student ... will not be met by the monolithic student
association."[31]

BSUs, including at Case Western Reserve, tried to support the Black
Capitalism Movement, demanding that their colleges and universities buy
goods from Black firms. At Harvard and Princeton, they demanded divestment from companies engaged in business in apartheid South Africa.
BSUs almost always demanded amnesty for its protesters and frequently
called for the honoring of Black holidays, specifically the birthdays and
death days of Martin Luther King Jr. and Malcolm X. They demanded
that their colleges supply relevant social activities, cultural events, speakers, and Black grooming products. Like their fellow White students, Black
campus activists wanted representation on college committees, particularly those that impacted Black student life, and disciplinary committees at
schools like Northeastern Illinois State University, Cedar Crest, and East
Tennessee State University. They also desired the creation of committees
to address their demands and the dissolution of those committees if they
did not meet their expectations. In March 1968, Indiana University students demanded a new racist practices committee "composed and
approved by Black students and faculty members."[32]

Particular Black student groups made special demands. Initially, at
institutions such as the University of Texas at Austin, students demanded
more Black athletes, while at Grambling State, one of the smoothest NFL
pipelines in the 1960s, students requested the reduction of athletics. For
decades, the athletic departments at HWCUs had a miniscule number of
Black Americans, who frequently were great players. In the 1960s, as
Black students in general began enrolling in unprecedented numbers, so
too did Black athletes. But those athletes, like Black students generally,
found themselves in "brutally dehumanizing, educational and athletic
environments," wrote Harry Edwards, a former athlete turned professor.
Black athletes faced incredible pressure to succeed, supporting the weight
of the coach, the school, and the Black race on their backs. Vociferously
racist coaches assigned Black athletes inferior housing and amenities,
derided them, forced them to play injured, ordered them to trim their
Afros and beards, herded them into "Black" positions and sports, and
misled them on scholarships.

Calvin Murphy, an All-American basketball player, seriously considered
leaving the University of Niagara in March 1968. He hated being called

"boy." "The guys in the dorms—even the priests—call me this and don't realize what they are saying," said the future NBA Hall of Famer. "To me it's worse than being called nigger." White athletes called them niggers, coons, and jiggaboos six days a week, but on game day they wanted them to have team spirit. "In the social and educational areas of college life, the Black athlete is expected to function at a sub-human level. In athletics, he is expected to be super-human," Edwards revealed. Obstructed by these two opposing expectations, Black athletes dodged them repeatedly and scored athletic demands, supported by BSUs. They wanted more Black athletes, cheerleaders, counselors, and especially coaches. They demanded equal treatment to their White teammates. They advocated for the firing of racist coaches.[33]

Athletic directors and coaches were usually highly resistant to the demands, and in many cases they refused to acknowledge that racism even existed. At Michigan State in April 1968, Black athletes submitted a list for Black coaches, cheerleaders, athletic employees, and a Black academic counselor to Athletic Director Clarence "Biggie" Munn. He scanned the list, chuckled, and crossed the demands out one by one. When Munn finished, he smiled and said, "Ho, ho, I guess you want a Black ticket manager or something." The Black athletes boycotted practices—the common protest tactic (along with boycotting games) used by athletic activists—until the administration took positive steps to address their concerns.[34]

Seminary students demanded and protested for a relevant and socially responsible seminary experience with more Black Studies courses and Black professors. These students were inspired by James Cone and the Black Theology Movement. Fifty seminarians took hold of the administration building at Union Theological Seminary on May 12, 1969, in support of SNCC international affairs director James Forman's call for reparations in his 1969 "Black Manifesto." Twenty-four hours later, the students exited the building with officials having agreed to invest $500,000 in the Harlem community and raise another $1 million to be put at the disposal of the seminary's Black community. Black medical and law students formed campus and, sometimes, national organizations to improve their lot in the academy, while psychology students established the active Black Student Psychology Association. Black graduate students organized and demanded more of their own at schools such as UCLA, Johns Hopkins, and the University of Oregon. In general, though, Black campus activists tended to support the particular demands of their subset, while not losing sight of the larger Black student challenge to higher education.[35]

With booming endowments and student populations in the 1960s, urban HWCUs continued to expand, encroaching on nearby Black communities that resisted the expansion. Either community members approached BSU leaders or Black campus activists independently became aware of the discord. Most BSUs formally or informally requested or demanded the termination, slowing, or altering of this encroachment and improved community relations, facilities, and services for locals. Sometimes guided by the student-labor coalition fomented by Marxist students at the time, but more often guided by antiracist organizing, students demanded better conditions for Black nonacademic workers and campus construction workers and aided them during their strikes.

BSUs even demanded that their White colleges and universities produce a public statement acknowledging their racism and pledging to eliminate it, the origin of the now popular diversity statements. Wittenberg faced this request, along with Atlanta's Emory University, whose president announced that "racism exists" and pledged to cooperate with students, faculty, and administrators to "openly commit themselves to its eradication." In Northwestern's thirteen-page agreement in 1968, signed by seven school officials, the university confessed that "it has had in common with the White community of America the racist attitudes that have prevailed historically in this society."[36]

BSUs made sure to emphasize the urgency of their demands. They often gave administrators a week, two weeks, a month, a year—some timeline to respond to or implement their requests. Sometimes, the demands were classified as "non-negotiable," which, on top of the term demand, particularly unnerved administrators. Some BSUs refused to negotiate or to settle, feeling their academic freedom was at stake. "We will not sit here and submit. We will not sit here and conform. We will not sit here and be controlled," the BSU at the College of Saint Benedict and Saint John's University in Minnesota declared in its demands in 1970. "We know what we want and we are fighting for our survival. THEREFORE, WE WILL NOT ACCEPT A SLICE OF BREAD BECAUSE WE WANT THE LOAF."[37]

However, administrators habitually forced them to accept a slice, arguing that the loaf was impossible, too expensive, against the law, "reverse discrimination," or in opposition to academic freedom or the values of the colleges. Usually before the deadline imposed by BSUs and SGAs, presidents responded to the demands, sometimes with line-item replies after a marathon meetings with faculty and administration. On other occasions, presidents and trustees requested meetings with BSUs, in which they deliberated (sometimes peacefully, more often combatively). Most administrators and faculty members responded to demands with the creation of diversity task forces or Black student or Black Studies committees. BSUs usually contested the composition of these task forces or committees.

Customarily, administrators and BSUs exchanged letters on their demands. This occurred at Colby during a weeklong takeover of the college chapel in March 1970. Colby president Robert E.L. Strider dispatched a letter saying the college had made progress on their concerns through existing channels, demands closed rather than open doors, and the college could not engage in useful kinds of discussion during a takeover—the standard tripartite response of administrators. "Obviously, we would not now be in the CHAPEL if we were confident in the administrative mechanisms that you have instituted to bring about change," the Black students responded. They took issue with the president's classifying their demands as "complex problems." "There is nothing at all complex about the five demands," they wrote. "The complexity lies in your inability to free yourselves from the administrative paternalism and red tape which might unduly complicate a matter that is quite simple." They also argued that "the perpetuation of racism 'occasions disruption' of normal human development," which is why they felt justified in their disruptive occupation. "The matter of illegal trespass in the Chapel is pitifully irrelevant when compared to the matter of man's illegal trespass against human dignity."[38]

The issuance of demands during protests was more the exception than the rule. BSUs tended to protest as a last resort. HWCU presidents usually gave in to the demands for more Black students, administrators, counselors, faculty, library books, office space, and Black Studies courses. When they did, they regularly claimed that they acted with more haste for a plan they had already devised to promote noncoercion. HBCU presidents and trustees often agreed to extend library hours and curfews and to offer more Black Studies courses and books and better campus services and facilities. Administrators typically rejected demands for quotas, a separate admissions or grading criteria, firing of racist personnel, Black Studies departments, Black dorms, discontinuing campus expansion, requests relating to campus workers, Black holidays, divestment, BSU or SGA financial autonomy, or Black student control of anything.

Usually, BSUs and SGAs refused to let administrators' rejections end their struggle. Their language in letters and statements became more forceful, but they were frequently using a different language than administrators were. Administrators spoke about illegality, rationality, and gradualism. Black campus activists spoke on moral validity, racism, immediacy, and tangibility. Both sides usually hunkered down. Not for long, though. BSUs and SGAs regularly charged forward with protests.

CHAPTER 12

"A New Sense of My Black Self": Protests and Support

BSUs and SGAs not only set deadlines as to when they wanted demands to be addressed. They frequently issued indirect or direct threats of protests if they were not satisfied with the responses. Deadline days or days when negotiations fell apart were some of the tensest on college campuses from 1965 to 1972. Students, faculty, and administrators with urban rebellions and protests on other campuses in the forefront of their minds braced for the inevitable, for the academic apocalypse, for the end of the beginning.

If a dramatic act of campus racism had not stirred up Black students to protest or a deadline had not committed them, then the "doubletalk," lying, paternalist, or racist ideas of negotiators did the trick. Most protests, though, seemed to be relatively spontaneous affairs decided within minutes, hours, or days. But some, usually the more effective ones, such as those at Cornell and San Francisco State, were planned for weeks and months in advance.

The building takeover became the most famous type of protest associated with campus activism in the late 1960s and early 1970s. On a few occasions, Black students took over multiple buildings, as at Howard in 1969. Black campus activists seized an entire campus at LeMoyne-Owen in November 1968 and at City College in late spring 1969. Nevertheless, they were more likely to barricade themselves inside an office or floor than a building or campus.[1]

© The Author(s), under exclusive license to Springer Nature Switzerland AG 2025
I. X. Kendi, *The Black Campus Movement*, Contemporary Black History, https://doi.org/10.1007/978-3-031-37394-7_12

Black campus activists, often in the early morning, snuck into campus buildings carrying books, sleeping bags, records, and food and forced out workers with threats and sometimes minor skirmishes and small weapons. Then they barricaded all of the doors and announced to the campus community that they would not leave until their demands were met. They did not allow anyone into the buildings and took their posts at windows and doors to ensure safety for the occupiers. Often, the students plastered the inside and outside of the buildings with signs of resistance. While inside occupied buildings, Black students usually did their homework, played cards, read, listened to music and speeches, debated, debated some more, laughed, laughed some more, grew nervous and more nervous. During the Howard takeover of the administration building in March 1968, the twelve hundred students controlled the university switchboard and served a "heavy diet of Black culture ranging from … African chants to *The Autobiography of Malcolm X* and the contemporary blues of Aretha Franklin." Often "traditional" gender roles played out—with the men on guard and the women preparing food. Or gender divisions were observed, as at Hampton in April 1969, when female and male occupiers stayed on different floors. BSU and SGA members spent more of their time drawing up demands, manifestos, and press releases, occasionally stepped outside the buildings for press conferences or rallies, and deliberated with their negotiators or negotiated with administrators. Takeovers lasted a few hours, days, or weeks.[2]

It wasn't just that students change higher education by means of building takeovers, but building takeovers changed students. Before participating in the takeover in April 1968 at Columbia, one tense, unnamed sophomore from the South had been a regular in the university's counseling office, discouraged academically and estranged socially. She had made few friends and walked around campus with a straight and dejected face, and even straighter hair. A month after the building takeover, she looked almost unrecognizable to the counseling therapists. She had a large Afro. Her face was bright and alert. She looked completely at ease. She had been "completely swept up by the sense of friendship, closeness and belonging which prevailed in the occupied building," wrote a therapist. Paula Giddings, a participant in the building takeover at Howard in March 1968, "got a new sense of self, a new sense of my Black self, in terms of culture, in terms of politics, in terms of the rights to demand certain things, the right to feel good about yourself."[3]

Black students employed their early 1960s tactic of a sit-in during the movement, demanding to be served an antiracist education at many institutions, including Harvard in December 1968. Unlike during the takeovers, during sit-ins Black campus activists did not close off buildings, floors, or offices. They simply sat in place and commanded action on their demands before they moved, generally allowing normal activities to continue.[4]

When they were not taking over campus spaces or carrying out sit-ins, they were using the tactic campus activists had used throughout the Long Black Student Movement. They struck at the heart of the racist constitution. The most notable and longest student strike in American history disrupted San Francisco State for almost five months beginning on November 6, 1968. During quite a few strikes, Black campus activists did not merely stay away from classes. They held campus rallies, picketed, negotiated with administrators, kept up with their class work, and often disbanded classes. Campus walkouts were like strikes, and protesters staged walkouts at Kent State and Clemson. Most of the Black students dramatically left campus in unison, pledging to stay away until their demands were addressed.[5]

Black campus activists staged numerous campus protest rallies and marches at places such as Marshall and George Washington University. They picketed campuses and disrupted athletic events at Lehman College in New York and Northern Michigan University. Bowdoin students engaged in a silent protest for a few days in February 1970, while some BSUs silently sued universities. Students disrupted convocations, services, registration, concerts, and faculty meetings, often to recite their demands. For example, days after King's assassination, Stanford held a convocation to discuss race and racism, a common occurrence at the time. Suddenly, seventy Black students rose up in unison and walked on stage, at which point one of them snatched the mike from the shocked provost. "Put your money where your mouth is!" BSU chair Kenny Washington yelled and then gave the mike to another BSU member, who read out ten demands.[6]

Sometimes students took school officials hostage for several hours. Often, they would not allow the president, administrators, or trustees to leave their offices or meeting places until they gave in to the students' demands. Activists also burned remnants of what they considered campus racism. A dozen students at Wesleyan soaked four copies of the college's 1968 yearbook in gasoline and set it on fire. "The Olla Pod reflects the White Western racist orientation of Wesleyan which seeks to deny the existence and unique expressiveness of the Black world," the AAS wrote in a statement. As other activists had, Beloit students burned an effigy of the president and other items on successive days in spring 1969. During their December 1969 drive to rid Fisk of White people, Black campus activists burned the automobile of historian Theodore Currier, who had been at the college for so long he had taught John Hope Franklin in the 1930s. Years later, Franklin torched the students in his memoir. "At Fisk, of all places, some students were involved in some of the shoddiest activities imaginable, all done in the name of the students' rights and civil rights."[7]

However, that was not the extent of the burnings. Activists started fires at Lane College, a Tennessee HBCU, in March 1969 before burning a building to the ground. Three buildings were set ablaze at Paul Quinn College in Dallas in the summer of 1970. Bombs destroyed property at Bluefield State in November 1969 and at Hampton in May 1971. Violent, disruptive rebellions gripped many historically Black institutions, such as Prairie View A&M in February 1971. Rebelling students also gutted offices. On January 13, 1969, about fifteen students at Queens College in New York ransacked the office of Joseph P. Mulholland, director of the college's Search for Education, Elevation, and Knowledge (SEEK) program. Around 3:25 p.m., the students brushed by four employees in the outer office, who swiftly left, and charged into the main office. The Black and Puerto Rican activists picked up the director's desk, a metal conference table, and eight chairs and carried them out of the room and down a long corridor. They exited the building with furniture in hand and dumped the pieces between two parked cars on the asphalt like it was trash. Meanwhile, other students tore out phones and ripped down pictures. When the fifteen students were done, they left the room almost completely empty except for the green carpet littered with their debris.[8]

One of the most popular movies among some Black students was the 1966 film *The Battle of Algiers*, which was based on urban guerilla warfare used during the recent Algerian revolution. Some students read Ernesto "Che" Guevara's *Guerilla Warfare* or Robert Taber's *The War of the Flea* on rural guerilla warfare in Cuba. Therefore, it was not surprising that activists utilized violent and disruptive guerilla tactics during the movement. They demonstrated that normality would not return to campus until their demands were granted. In May 1968, CSU Fresno students verbally harassed the president, uprooted parking lot trees, set small fires, jumped into public fountains, and painted classroom doors black. During the Brandeis building takeover in January 1969, five Black women wearing bandanas marched into the reserve room at the library. One student activist told the students there to sit down and "nobody will get hurt." Another went to guard the door with a piece of wood. After closing the window drapes and ripping out the phones, the students scattered more than two thousand books and periodicals before a library worker forced them out. A little over a month later, about fifty Black men at Rutgers and a slightly larger number of women at Douglass Residential College entered their dining halls, stacked their trays with food, dumped the food on the floor, and left. The next day, Douglass women abruptly walked out of classes, yelled insults at instructors, ignored White students, locked bathroom doors, and stuffed toilets, while Rutgers men vandalized property, issued bomb threats, and set minor fires.[9]

It was a rare occurrence when a protest did not lead to some promise of reform. Nevertheless, campuses that experienced protests also became virtual police states. Thus, reform and repression followed protests, diminishing their likelihood of reoccurrence and forever altering the racial and policing mechanisms of the institutions. It is not known how many protests were staged during the Black Campus Movement. There is no available tally of the early years of the movement. Black campus activists disturbed more than 150 campuses during the 1967–1968 academic year, with the vast majority of the disturbances occurring after the death of King. More than 250 protests were held during the climactic year of 1968–1969, followed by more than 150 incidents the next year. Usually, the more violent and the longer the student protest, the more likely students were to achieve their more radical demands. A protest at one college inspired a protest at another university and motivated administrators to pick up the pace on meeting demands to prevent a protest. Put differently, not every institution experienced protests, but it is quite possible that administrators instituted the vast majority of changes due to protests at their schools or at others, nearby or on the other side of the nation. Presidential files across the nation are filled with reports on protests from other institutions.[10]

To stage successful protests, Black campus activists had to establish their own support system. In addition to each other, BSU members usually enjoyed the support of antiracist White students, often in the campus chapters of the Students for a Democratic Society (SDS). White campus activists, whom San Francisco State BSU members called "White mother country radicals," formed picket lines in front of seized buildings, educated White students on demands through flyers and forums, and brought BSU members food and supplies, in addition to staging their own antiracist protests. For example, in May 1968, about forty White students at Brooklyn College were expelled, arrested, and charged with criminal trespassing for a sixteen-hour takeover of the registrar's office, during which they demanded a thousand more African American and Puerto Rican students by September. At a news conference, Brooklyn League of Afro-American Collegians president Orlando Pike, sporting a dashiki, said the demonstrators highlighted "the role that White people must play in the struggle for the emancipation of Black people—to confront White racism wherever it may exist." Along with anti-war and student power activism, the support of the Black Campus Movement served as a major pillar of the White Student Movement in the 1960s.[11]

Black campus activists received vital sustenance from Black professors. Perhaps no Black professor catalyzed the movement more than sociologist Nathan Hare, who was fired for his activism at Howard in 1967 and San Francisco State in 1969, where he directed the nation's first Black Studies program. Most Black professors, specifically younger faculty and those hired as a result of student activism, tended to be sympathetic to, if not supportive of, the movement. These sympathetic and supportive faculty pressured colleagues to concede to demands, wrote explanatory press statements and open letters, and joined protests. Black and Puerto Rican students banded together for joint programs and initiatives in demands and protests in New York. Thus, there emerged Africana and Latino Studies programs and departments at institutions like the SUNY Oneonta and Baruch College and Hunter College of the City University of New York, or CUNY, system. In the Midwest and West, Black students formed activist coalitions with Latinx, Asian, and Native American students. Black and Native American students issued a stinging statement of demands at South Dakota's Augustana College in November 1969. "When the Red brethren tried to resist you called him savage and an animal. You brought the Black man from his native land to develop your ill-gotten gains. Yet we ask now for a little payment for our land and labor, and you set up committees! You, the good Christian people, did not form a committee to take the Red man's land or the Black man's labor." The most notorious actualization of these coalitions, what historian Jeffrey Ogbar terms "rainbow radicalism," occurred at San Francisco State and UC Berkeley. At these universities, Third World Liberation Fronts formed in

1968, a coalition of Black, Latinx, Asian, and Native American groups that together waged multimonth student strikes for colleges of Ethnic Studies.[12]

A sympathetic White administrator sometimes honored their demands or diffused protests. Antiracist White professors aided Black campus activists, as at Colgate, where forty White professors joined a Black student sit-in at the administration building in April 1968. "Why, that is, have we used this method to eliminate discriminatory practices from our fraternities? The answer is simple: Because no other methods have succeeded in eliminating these practices." Sometimes White alumni demonstrated support for the movement. For instance, three alumni of Ohio's Marietta College approached their president in May 1968 about recruiting more Black students and faculty and instituting Black Studies courses.[13]

But in the end, the support of nearby Black communities cannot be understated. Throughout the Brandeis takeover in January 1969, Boston area community organizations, local schools, and parents supplied the students with food. "Now if we only had as much freedom as we have food," said one of the student leaders during the occupation. Possibly as focal as community support was the aid BSUs and SGAs received from each other. Tougaloo students raised money for jailed Tuskegee activists in the spring of 1968. On December 9, 1968, the BSU at the University of Hawaii sponsored a rally in support of the San Francisco State strike. Students dispatched letters of protest from Fort Valley State, Paine, Louisiana State and Xavier University of Louisiana to the president of the University of Texas at Arlington during the campus campaign to terminate the flying of the Confederate flag and the singing of "Dixie."[14]

Support from other students and nearby Black communities, as well as from alumni, faculty, and administrators, provided some refuge for the Black Campus Movement. Because as soon as Black students started complaining about the racist constitution of higher education, opposition and repression flared up in response. That opposition and repression only compounded as the students organized BSUs and made demands and exponentially expanded as Black campus activists protested at hundreds of institutions across the United States. While Black students shook higher education with the arms of protest, Black students and their antiracist actions were shaken by the paired arms of opposition and repression.

CHAPTER 13

"American Version of Storm Troopers": Opposition and Repression, 1965–1968

The storm of student activism that forever transformed the racial ideals of higher education had to endure a storm of opposition and repression that forever transformed the activists and established the academy as a policed state. Tens of thousands of students were rebuked, derided, suspended, expelled, harassed, beaten, arrested, jailed, injured, or killed in their determined effort (or as bystanders of the struggle) to confront the racist contours of higher education. Many put their collegiate lives on the line and lost or nearly lost them. Some put their actual lives on the line and lost or nearly lost them. At the same time, though, Black campus activists fought stridently against the opposition and repression alongside their fight to revolutionize their institutions. Thus, their activism persisted on two fronts—offensive protests to implement novel measures to diversify higher education and defensive protests against the reaction their activism evoked. No depiction of the movement is complete without a discussion of this all-important rearguard and the trauma and brutality Black campus activists suffered, the form their sacrifice took, the way they gave their lives to the struggle.

Early in the movement, HBCU students faced the main brunt of the repression and opposition. One of the first Black campus protests to become national news was headlined by what would become a familiar occurrence during the movement—brutality by Mississippi state troopers, many of whom, like other troopers and police officers across the South, were suspected of being KKK members. Troopers tossed tear gas at one

© The Author(s), under exclusive license to Springer Nature Switzerland AG 2025
I. X. Kendi, *The Black Campus Movement*, Contemporary Black History, https://doi.org/10.1007/978-3-031-37394-7_13

thousand protesting students and community members at Alcorn State in April 1966 and clubbed them with nightsticks and rifle butts. "Brutality! Brutality! Brutality!" a woman shouted at one point. The shout would reverberate throughout the Black Campus Movement.[1]

It was particularly loud in 1967, when students, angered by an act of police harassment or brutality, rebelled or battled it out with the police on or near at least three HBCUs. These clashes included a four-day urban rebellion in Nashville, a skirmish at Jackson State where community activist Benjamin Brown, a 21-year-old bystander, was killed, and an hour-long clash at Central State. At Texas Southern, after a three-hour stalemate with student snipers that lasted into the early morning of May 17, the police fired more than two thousand shots from rifles and carbines into a student dormitory. After forty minutes of gunfire, which wounded at least one student, police officers stormed the dormitory. One officer was shot and killed and two others wounded during the melee. The officers then ripped apart the dorm, hospitalized several students, and found three guns. With guns pointed at their backs, almost five hundred students were compelled to lie face down on the cold, wet ground before being arrested. In the morning, resentment resonated among the student body. "What can you expect?" one student told reporters. "To them we're just apes." Another indignantly said, "I'm sorry there wasn't but one of them killed." In June, the NAACP defended and got the charges dropped for the "TSU Five"—Trazawell Franklin Jr., 20, Floyd Nichols, 25, Charles Freeman, 18, Douglas Wayne Waller, 21, and John Parker, 20. These students had been charged with first-degree murder and assault to murder, despite evidence of friendly fire killing the police officer. As it had been throughout the Long Black Student Movement, the NAACP also came to the legal aid of Black student activists who had been expelled or charged at schools such as Bluefield State.[2]

Critics rebuked the student violence in 1967. The American Civil Liberties Union condemned activists for encroaching on the academic freedom of non-participants. The *Pittsburgh Courier* editorialized in June 1967, "No amount of demonstration can take the place of good sound academic performance." Meanwhile, Black campus activists at HWCUs were not immune to the activism. NAACP executive director Roy Wilkins began his criticism in May 1967 upon hearing about the organizing of BSUs, calling it self-segregation and "puzzling, indeed."[3]

Throughout the movement, White students and faculty used similar language to censure BSUs as segregationist or isolationist and halted (or questioned) the founding of BSUs at numerous institutions, including at Morningside and Boise State University. A campus newspaper editorial in May 1967 told the newly organized Trinity Association of Negroes to beware of "establishing an atmosphere of group separateness and confrontation." After the Cornell Afro-American Society formed that spring, one professor said, "There are many people here … who felt they had been fighting for integration so long, and they just couldn't turn themselves around that fast." Often these nascent BSUs produced even more controversy when they barred White people from events, such as when Muhammad Ali spoke to only Black students at the UPENN on October 31, 1967. *The Daily Pennsylvania* called the exclusive gathering "flagrantly totalitarian behavior" and compared the Society of African and Afro-American Students (SAAS) to Nazis. "Equating Black societies in America with Nazism is a poorly constructed analogy," SAAS chairman pro tempore Billy Riley responded, "because the Nazis were oppressors, and we as Blacks are the oppressed."[4]

More often, BSUs organized two events for speakers: a publicized, open, formal speech to an interracial audience and a clandestine, closed, informal discussion with Black students. Opponents rebuked these closed meetings too, as they did any affair that prohibited White people (or was open but clearly designed for Black people). Sometimes White students and faculty forced their way into these meetings. In September 1968, two Tulane University professors and twenty students staged a "reverse sit-in" of a Black first-year orientation facilitated by the Afro-American Congress.[5]

Black nationalism and Black Power faced critiques as well, even from Black students. To refute Primus J. Mootry's piece at Chicago State University declaring "we are Afro-Americans," Chuck Riley claimed "this recently popularized term is a clever but inaccurate substitute for Negro," which "comes originally from Latin, a language used a couple thousand years ago." To Riley, "soul brother" and "Black" were also "misnomers." Black and White students at HWCUs debated Black power in newspapers in the early years of the movement. In November 1967, for instance, Madelyn Clark at Wilson College in Pennsylvania declared her support for "Black unity, identity, pride, and growth." Within a week, a "Wasp student" responded: "After having accepted the Negro as a 'thinking, creative HUMAN,' I have not been accepted by him." Many HBCU presidents and professors tried to distance themselves from Black power. Spelman president Albert E. Manley, who gave a series of anti-Black Power lectures in the fall of 1966, reasoned that "radical exponents of Black Power" were attempting "to substitute one form of racism for another."[6]

Some Black students were "puzzled" by this rejoinder from HBCU presidents and especially White students who had isolated and alienated them. On a number of campuses, when BSUs did not bar White people, Whites did not come. When BSUs barred White people, they were criticized. Often, these detractors conflated segregation, an involuntary domineering relationship, with separation, a voluntary act of solidarity. Black campus activists sometimes erringly used this language, undercutting their solidarity arguments.

Police officers and National Guard members were constantly being called to HBCUs. In late October 1967, five hundred National Guard members descended onto a protest-ridden Grambling State campus and twenty-nine students were dismissed—crushing the demonstrations and boycott. National Guard members arrived in Orangeburg, South Carolina, after South Carolina State students, embroiled in a battle to desegregate a nearby bowling alley, rebelled and battled police on February 5, 1968. By February 8, roadblocks had been set up surrounding South Carolina State, and students were urged not to leave. That night, students built a huge bonfire on campus, separating them and a massive line of hundreds of National Guard members, state troopers, and police officers. As Henry Smith, a tall sophomore standing in front of the crowd, attempted to put something into the fire, the officers began shooting for an unknown reason. Smith spun and crumbled to the ground. When the officers finally stopped shooting, three students—Smith and Samuel Hammond, both South Carolina State students, and Delano Middleton, a local high school student—were dead and at least thirty-four were wounded, mostly shot in the back.[7]

As when officers killed students at Jackson State in May 1970 and at Southern in November 1972, upon hearing of the "Orangeburg Massacre," Black Americans were furious. The presidents of six HBCUs in Atlanta wrote a letter to President Johnson, Attorney General Ramsey Clark, state governors, and law enforcement agencies urging them "to stop these invasions of college and university campuses by the American version of storm troopers." It did not stop. Two weeks after the Orangeburg Massacre, Mississippi police wounded six students at Alcorn State during a protest. Even though hundreds of students were jailed for nonviolent activism, the "storm troopers" in Mississippi and South Carolina paid no price for the killing and wounding of students in criminal or civil court.[8]

Black students also faced gunshots from students. On April 7, 1968, thirty-five members of Colgate's Association of Black Collegians occupied the Sigma Nu fraternity house for seven hours after residents shot at a Black student. Still mourning the death of Martin Luther King, they threatened to "burn the house down," until the president agreed to close the fraternity house and investigate the shooting. It was just one of numerous occasions on which Black campus activists faced harassment. A few nights after a Black student protest at Bradley University in Illinois, a White fraternity member spat on Renee Grant as he drove by her in early May 1969. Not long after, all three hundred BSA members descended on the fraternity house "ready to burn it down." The perpetrator hid for two days, until he mustered up enough courage and swallowed enough pride to apologize to Grant.[9]

In late April 1968, reports of an Ohio State bus driver's mistreatment of two Black women compelled seventy-five allegedly armed Black students to hold various officials and secretaries in the administration building hostage for eight hours. Within a year, thirty-four protesters were each indicted on eleven felonies and one misdemeanor, including five counts of unlawful detention and conspiracy to unlawfully detain. It marked one of the most serious sets of charges ever filed against a group of student protesters—what Julian Bond called "an old Southern practice—lynching." As in the Black Power Movement more generally, many male Black campus activists thought their masculinity rested on whether they defended "their women" from White racism. Harassing or harming a Black woman became one of the quickest ways to arouse Black male campus activism.[10]

Some Black leaders were particularly loud in their condemnation of the movement in the summer of 1968. Benjamin E. Mays, for one, rebuked demands for Black dorms, Black Studies, and more Black faculty at HWCUs as "working against Negro colleges" because they "would take away the best professors" and students from HBCUs. "I hope Black students will ponder this." Black students did not have much time to ponder this. They were bombarded by the strengthening recoil from educators, journalists, and politicians who were implementing measures to curb their activism. As part of the Counter-Intelligence Program (COINTELPRO), FBI director J. Edgar Hoover dispatched a message in 1970 to his staff. "Increased campus disorders involving Black students pose a definite threat to the nation's stability and security and indicate need for increase in both quality and quantity of intelligence information." BSUs were investigated by the FBI, and the FBI kept a running list of prominent activists. Organizational, personal, and ideological conflicts within BSUs were exacerbated by the FBI. It sent forged letters to endanger BSU affairs and manipulated the press. The FBI (as well as local and state police) recruited, employed, and deployed an army of spies (students and college employees) that collected data on student groups or thwarted their activities. A mole at Widener University in Pennsylvania reported to the FBI that BSU members were "not engaged in any militant type of activity on campus." Administrators also had their spies and trackers. In September 1968, "Mary" reported to her chancellor on a Black student dance attended by officers from Black student groups in St. Louis. CSU Fresno officials apparently planted plainclothes officers on campus to follow Black and Chicano activists in the spring of 1969.[11]

BSU officers received hate mail and their dorm rooms were sometimes ransacked, as occurred at Luther College in Iowa in March 1969. Phillita Carney, after becoming the University of Utah's first Black homecoming queen in October 1971, was happy "to see the shock on those sorority bitches' faces" and termed it an "opening for minorities." The story (and Carney's vulgar words) went national. "Better make that Black bastard, bitch, take back what she said or she will be crowned, but not a QUEEN of any Homecoming event, we can assure you of that," threatened a White Chicagoan in one of many nasty letters mailed to the university. A "loyal Tennessee fan" teased, "This evidently was a tree climbing contest. This is the only possible way it could win."[12]

In a letter addressed "to the NIGGERS," the "silent majority of Cal State Long Beach and the surrounding cities" stated, "if this verbal harassment of White people does not stop, the B.S.U. ... will be exterminated." Sometimes the foes of the BSUs acted on their violent threats. Three White students attacked Gene Locke at the University of Houston on the morning of March 17, 1969. In retaliation, several students rampaged through campus and were later charged with property damage. With mass opposition, charges against the so-called UH Fourteen were eventually dropped (or the accused pled out). About 250 Northern Illinois students went on a rock-throwing, window-breaking rampage through campus on March 22, 1969. This was in revenge for five White students jumping a Black male student in the presence of university police. All of DeKalb's available police officers were brought in to restore the order of racism. In a statement, the Black students declared: "The Black student body wishes to serve notice ... it will not tolerate or let go unnoticed any acts of violence committed on Black people."[13]

After fielding threatening phone calls and dodging a bullet the week before, BSU vice president Paul Whiteurs was shot in the arm at the University of South Alabama on March 9, 1971. "In my life, I have never had time to be afraid," Whiteurs said after the unsolved shooting. "My philosophy is like many people—if you have nothing worth dying for then you are already dead." Law enforcement officers also continuously harassed BSU leaders with some of the force they used to abuse Black power figures off campus. According to an undated BSU flyer, a local assistant district attorney declared, "We are going to get those Black students" at UC Santa Barbara.[14]

Similarly, the day before William Garrett of the Lawrence Police Department shot and killed Rick "Tiger" Dowdell, 19, on July 16, 1970, Garrett allegedly had told his brother he was going to "get one of you Dowdells." Dowdell, a rising University of Kansas sophomore, walked out of the Afro-House, the BSU's new Black Cultural Center. Soon after, Garrett was chasing him in his car and then down an alley, where he discharged the fatal shot. In the college town of Lawrence, the Dowdell Black power activists were respected by the activist community and despised by the law enforcement community, leading to many altercations. Rick Dowdell entered the struggle as a student activist at Lawrence High. He organized a walkout there in September 1968 around the time the University of Kansas BSU was forming. Paralleling the Black Campus Movement, a similar movement emerged in high schools across America.

Garrett claimed Dowdell shot first. Local activists dubbed it an assassination and gave Dowdell the funeral of a martyr (just as students did for the other twelve youths killed nationwide during the Black Campus Movement). The BSU vowed that the exonerated Garrett "shall reap what he has sown," and the death sparked a week-long student uprising that eventually led to the police killing of a White University of Kansas student, Harry Nicholas "Nick" Rice, and the wounding of a Black chemistry graduate student, Merton R. Olds. Unlike those at Orangeburg, Kent State, and Jackson State, the Lawrence tragedies flew under the national radar.[15]

When Black campus activists were not being harassed, injured, or killed, they were being expelled and arrested, as at the University of Wisconsin-Oshkosh, in late November 1968. For ransacking the president's office, nearly the entire Black enrollment (about ninety students) was arrested and expelled in one of the largest mass expulsions of the movement at an HWCU. The repression incited several unsuccessful student protests for their reinstatement. Instead of using their hands to damage a building, students at Bluefield State let a bomb do the damage that month, leading to several arrests.[16]

White community members and alumni often clamored for arrests. When administrators showed restraint, as did Washington University chancellor Thomas H. Eliot, who ended a ten-day sit-in in December 1968 with a peaceful agreement, they usually received a stack of fuming letters. "Put your foot down," ordered one letter writer. C.L. Husbands of Littleton, Colorado, declared the university was "no longer … worthy of the name Washington" due to its "ignoble surrender to the forces of riot and anarchy." An alumnus in St. Louis condemned Eliot's "outrageous concessions to inarticulate and illiterate Negroes."[17]

These writers probably desired someone like San Francisco State president S.I. Hayakawa, a Japanese American semanticist. He took over for Robert Smith in late 1968 as the embattled college's third president that year with orders to crush the several-week-long student strike. Hayakawa instituted new rules for the college, including a ban on amplification equipment and noon rallies. Strikers ignored the rules on December 2, 1968. When Hayakawa heard the usual early morning strike refrains amplified from a sound truck, he stormed out of his office with mimeographed copies of his "emergency regulations," followed by police, photographers, and reporters. He leaped onto the top of a truck, tried unsuccessfully to snatch the microphone out of the White students' hands, then looked around angrily until he saw the wires of the amplifier. He grabbed at them until the sound stopped. Some students tried to remove Hayakawa. "Don't touch me, I'm the President of this college!" A crowd hurriedly gathered to watch their new president before the police arrived and hustled him back to his office. The national media caught wind of and reported the entire scene. With that single spontaneous act, Hayakawa became the symbol of presidential defense of the racist status quo. He projected himself as a pillar that could not be pushed around or swayed by the movement. BSU leader Jerry Varnado would later say, "He would never have dared to do that to us. We would have trampled all over him."[18]

The next day—December 3, 1968—turned out to be even worse at San Francisco State. On Bloody Tuesday, as it has been designated, the police had a new directive—prevent any large gathering on campus. In the morning, officers arrested and clubbed fifty picketers and chased one of them into the cafeteria, where they brutalized more students. A White male student was hauled out with blood streaming down his face. When an enraged crowd mobilized at the administration building upon hearing about the cafeteria brutality, the police scattered and clubbed them, too. After the regular noon rally, students marched on the behavioral science building. Hundreds of police officers stopped their advance with batons, sparking a battle at the center of campus. Students used pieces of campus furniture as defensive weapons. Over the campus loudspeaker, Hayakawa ordered students to disperse. "If some of you want to make trouble, stay right there. The police will see that you get it." Hayakawa was not lying. Four officers jumped Don McAllister, a Black student, creating a gash that bled profusely and almost killed him. Collegians beat so brutally by police clubs that they could not get up were thrown into paddy wagons. Two ambulances made regular runs to the hospital. At an afternoon press conference, after the ferocious melee, Hayakawa praised the police for their "restraint and professionalism" and declared, "This has been the most exciting day of my life since my tenth birthday, when I rode on a roller coaster for the first time!" The press stood stunned.[19] The opposition and repression only got worse in 1969 and during the final years of the movement.

CHAPTER 14

"Black Jim Crow Studies": Opposition and Repression, 1969–1972

During a twenty-four-hour takeover of the University of Minnesota administration building in January 1969, activists turned a fire hose on counter-demonstrators who had brandished White supremacist signs and shouted epithets such as "go home and take a bath." White students ridiculed protesters or tried to end protests at the UC Santa Barbara in October 1968 and at the University of Wisconsin-Madison in February 1969. Some of those counterdemonstrators at the University of Wisconsin-Madison were members of the right-wing Young Americans for Freedom (YAF) and wore "H" armbands to identify with San Francisco State President S.I. Hayakawa, an alumnus. YAF members and conservative students in other groups, such as the Young Republicans and the John Birch Society, tried to slow the movement at several other institutions, including CSU Stanislaus and Marquette. At Delta State, White students cheered and sang "Dixie" on March 10, 1969, when the police arrived to arrest rebelling campus activists.[1]

Hayakawa probably cheered on January 23, 1969. During a campus rally, police arrested more than four hundred San Francisco State strikers, including Nathan Hare and almost the entire leadership of the BSU and its allied groups. Police used every paddy wagon in the city for the biggest single arrest in San Francisco history. Meanwhile, threats from the movement's detractors rose in volume in early 1969. The House Special Education Subcommittee held hearings on student unrest in February. Roy Wilkins threatened to sue institutions that established separate dorms

© The Author(s), under exclusive license to Springer Nature Switzerland AG 2025
I. X. Kendi, *The Black Campus Movement*, Contemporary Black History, https://doi.org/10.1007/978-3-031-37394-7_14

or "autonomous racial schools within colleges and universities"—ironic, since local NAACP chapters were defending Black campus activists. For CORE's Roy Innis, Wilkins's latest reproach became "the last straw. If Wilkins can use funds supposedly earmarked for Black people to fight against those same people, then CORE will commit its resources to defend and safeguard the students in their demands."[2]

Nathan Hare continued Innis's assault on Wilkins in *Newsweek* in February 1969. In the "Black Perspective," Hare wrote that he was appalled by "the sneaky way in which critics like Roy Wilkins accuse us of 'separatism.'" He added, somewhat accurately, "Our cries for more Black professors and Black students have padded White colleges with more Blacks in two years than decades of whimpering for 'integration' ever did." Wilkins sympathized "with the frustration and anger of today's Black students" in *Newsweek*. But "in demanding Black Jim Crow studies … and exclusively Black dormitories or wings of dormitories, they are opening the door to a dungeon."[3]

Shortly after Black students at Duke opened the door and walked out of their barricaded building on February 13, 1969, hundreds of mostly White supporters and spectators started to disperse. To accelerate them, police drove cars through them, whipping the students into a frenzy. The students banged on the cars and tried to set them aflame. Officers launched a barrage of tear gas, which ignited a social fire on campus, with police clubs fanning the flames. Students defended themselves. One Black student even reportedly lashed out at the police with a chain. When the police finally retreated into the administration building (and ultimately left the campus), the students numbered three thousand. Forty-five people, including two officers, required medical treatment. Mostly White students were also brutalized a week later at UC Berkeley during the notorious strike for Ethnic Studies.[4]

By late February and early March 1969, the opposition rhetoric had reached a fever pitch. Criticisms were voiced. Instituting the demands would be "like levitating the University Tower 30 feet off the ground," a dean at University of Texas at Austin told students. After the BSA issued its demands, Eastern Michigan professors mockingly circulated eleven similar demands "for the Welsh Minority on this campus." In 1968, White students wrote similar lists at William Penn in Iowa and the University of Wisconsin-Oshkosh. President Nixon endorsed taking a tough stand against activists, as did many professors and seemingly the majority of Americans. NBC News' Chet Huntley called the ferment for Black Studies departments another "college fad" that he hoped did not get out of hand. Bayard Rustin, the executive director of the A. Phillip Randolph Institute, condemned the "separatist demands" of the struggle. The National Governors' Conference passed a resolution pledging to keep colleges open and safe. In the name of academic freedom or, more appropriately, academic power, faculty unrelentingly slammed student protesters "who would subordinate intellectual freedom to political ends," as Cornell professors wrote in March 1969.[5]

On March 5, 1969, the US Department of Health, Education, and Welfare (HEW) warned all colleges and universities receiving federal assistance not to institute separate Black Studies programs, "separate housing," or "separate social activity" spaces that excluded White students. In particular, in late February, HEW told thirteen private institutions, including Antioch, that they could be violating the Civil Rights Act of 1964. HEW gave Antioch President James P. Dixon two weeks to explain how its Afro-American Studies Institute for Black students was not against the law. A literal interpretation of the Civil Rights Act on this "deliberate and crucial question" might deny Black students rights that White students long have had at Antioch, President Dixon wrote back to HEW. In most cases, activists did not demand total White exclusion in their programs, but they did want Black people controlling their programs.

This interaction between HEW and Antioch was leaked to the press. "In defending the 'Crow-Jim' policy, Dr. Dixon gave HEW the greatest line of double talk I have ever read," stated a *The Chicago Defender* columnist. Psychologist Kenneth B. Clark resigned from his trusteeship at Antioch. "It is Whites who need a Black studies program most of all," Clark said, echoing a view of White suasionists, who showed mild support for Black Studies. Presidents were trying to satisfy the conflicting wishes of antiracist and assimilationist members of their college communities. They castigated Black students for forcing them into this untenable position, saying their protests prompted the reaction that curtailed their efforts at reform. Paradoxically, some presidents did not enact reforms until protests were held.[6]

On April 9, 1969, seven Southern students on the New Orleans campus walked to a flagpole with their Pan-African flag as a sizeable police force looked on. They opened up their flag, explained its meaning, read their demands, pulled down the American flag, and raised the Pan-African flag. When it was lifted, the police had to fight through a crowd of two hundred observers and supporters to make twenty arrests. Black students, in late spring 1969, were also arrested at University of Memphis (109), Voorhees (25), Howard (20), Brooklyn's Pratt Institute (11), and Alabama State (365), where they were hauled away in three trucks for demonstrating at the state capitol for the termination of their president.[7]

Minutes before the Cornell University judicial board decided to reprimand three of the six Black students involved in an earlier protest, the first of eleven fire alarms in nine dormitories and two halls awakened the campus. In between alarms, at around 2:00 a.m. on April 18, 1969, a frantic Black student called the police to report a six-foot-high cross burning on her dorm's front porch and the rock someone had tossed through her front window. Black students were livid about the attacks on Wari, a Black women's cooperative. For the rest of the day, rumors swirled about what they were planning. Everyone knew that the bubble that had been expanding with each new cohort of Black students over the previous few years was about to burst. They just did not know when or where.[8]

It happened early the next morning. Members of the Afro-American Society (AAS) seized Willard Straight Hall, the student hub of Cornell. By 7:00 a.m., the AAS controlled the building, and White students in the Cornell Students for a Democratic Society (SDS) chapter were picketing the hall. They chanted "the revolution has come … time to pick up the gun," echoing the popular mantra of the Black Panther Party. Settling in, AAS members called their parents, studied for upcoming exams, slept after a night of planning and partying, and contacted friends and urged them to join the occupation. Calls were coming into the hall, too, primarily from Cornell's vice provost, Keith Kennedy, who at around 9 a.m. made his way over to the hall along with Eugene Dymek, head of campus security, and Cornell legal counsel Neal Stamp. They navigated through the SDS picket line. With a bullhorn, Dymek commanded the students to leave. During the exchange, Black students heard a commotion coming from the rear of the hall. Everyone raced to the scene.[9]

About ten White Delta Upsilon International Fraternity (DU) members had snuck in through unguarded rear windows to "liberate" the hall. As they reached the main lobby area and announced their intention to open the hall's front doors, AAS members sprinted out of rooms and corridors and fought them. The DU members retreated through the windows. "We're coming back! We're going to burn it down next time!" screamed a DU brother. "If you do, then we will fill y'all with lead," shouted a seething Black student. During the next few hours, while a stream of telephone reports about copycat invaders unnerved them, AAS members smuggled guns into the hall for protection. What was planned as a festive, peaceful, and short-lived takeover of a building became a protracted, tense, and hostile confrontation. White fraternity members pushed Cornell student opinion to back the AAS occupiers, who in the early afternoon issued four demands: nullify the three reprimands, reopen the question of housing, and conduct thorough investigations of the cross burning and DU attack.[10]

The next morning, April 20, 1969, the national media arrived and calls by reporters kept a constant tune in the information office. Everybody wanted to verify leaked reports of the guns. The minds of Cornell officials were elsewhere, though. It was Sunday, and all they could think about was forcing those students out before classes resumed on Monday. AAS and Cornell officials reached an agreement that afternoon: amnesty, a faculty motion for nullification of the reprimands, twenty-four-hour protection of the occupiers and the AAS's office, legal action against the White fraternity brothers, a list of the invaders, and university assistance in securing legal help for AAS. During the final negotiations, students informed the

Photo 14.1 Heavily armed African American students leave Straight Hall at Cornell on April 20, 1969 (AP Photo/Steve Starr)

administrators that they wanted to sign the agreement at their headquarters after a procession across campus. The administrators tried to disarm the Black students. In the era of ostentatious self-defense, it proved impossible.[11]

Eighty students lined up in military formation with women in the center, so they could be "guarded." "Breeches open, no ammo!" AAS president Edward Whitfield shouted. When word quickly spread around campus that they were coming out, reporters and photographers sprinted to the entrance. Within minutes, the two hundred people outside became two thousand. The heavy, wooden doors flew open. SDS members safeguarding the entrance scattered to the sides. One by one, at 4:10 p.m. on April 20, 1969, Black students, brandishing their rifles, shotguns, knives, clubs, spears, and expressions of seriousness, victory, fear, and wonder, trotted out of the dark Gothic structure into a sea of bright cameras that latched onto their seventeen rifles and shotguns like leeches. "Oh, my God, look at those goddamned guns!" shouted Steve Starr, an Associated Press photographer, before snapping "The Picture," a Pulitzer Prize winner in 1970.

When the procession crossed the large porch of the building, SDS members raised clenched fists and cheered, while hundreds of onlookers watched, stunned into silence. They marched across the rolling Arts Quadrangle, over a gorge, and across a bridge to 320 Wait Avenue—the home of Black students. People in cars and on foot abruptly stopped as the marchers approached, looking on in amazement, confusion, and anger. When they reached the house, most of the students congregated on the porch. Riflemen took up strategic positions on the steep lawn and steps, staring at onlookers and reporters.[12]

After hammering out some final details, Whitfield read the signed agreement to the press. When he finished, it was Eric Evans's turn. He pulled out a prepared statement, fixed his glasses, and faced the reporters. With bandoliers crossing his chest and waist, his shotgun cradled in his left hand, and dozens of armed Black students scattered on the lawn surrounding him, he proclaimed, "We only leave now with the understanding that the University will move fairly to carry out its part of the agreement that was reached. Failure on the part of the University to do so may force us to again confront the University in some manner."[13]

The next evening, still reeling from the spectacle of guns, the Cornell faculty refused to sanction the "coerced" agreement. Many students rallied around the AAS, who lashed out with incendiary threats toward the professors. Several campus groups were armed or arming. There was talk about taking another building. With severe pressure coming from students and the specter of violent clashes between police and students, the faculty reversed its earlier decision two days later, while also giving students more power and establishing an autonomous Black Studies department.[14]

The Monday morning after students exited the building, "The Picture" appeared on front pages around the nation. Although guns had been used by previous groups of Black campus activists, it had never been displayed so publicly. State and federal politicians censured the AAS. Several Cornell professors resigned in protest, including Thomas Sowell, one of the college's few Black faculty, saying he could not be a part of a college that was so "interested in its image—anything to keep the black students happy." *The Chicago Defender* characterized it as the most "frightful and damnable" demonstration of the year. *The New York Times* amazingly compared the AAS to the "jackbooted students" of Hitler's Germany.[15]

Black students at Cornell had to withstand opposition and repression seemingly coming from everywhere. The Black and White press, Black professors and leaders, White administrators, students, faculty, politicians, campus judiciary, and security personnel all clamped down at some point on Black campus activism at Cornell in the spring of 1969. Opposition and repression generated the protest in April 1969, and opposition and repression doggedly stalked the protest.

Black campus activists were fighting White students at other colleges, including at City College when it reopened on May 6, 1969, after a two-week takeover by Black and Puerto Rican students. Students also brawled at Queens College in early May. As Black and Puerto Rican students ran from building to building smashing windows, jeering White students chased them, shouting "animals," "criminals," and "get back to the jungle." While the NYPD mobilized five hundred officers in six buses, seven paddy wagons, and a dozen patrol cars, more than a hundred angry White people converged on twenty Black students. Outnumbered, the Black students stood their ground. Punches and rocks were thrown until security guards put up a chain-link fence between the groups.[16]

In late spring 1969, Bayard Rustin, once again deriding the movement, implored college officials to "stop capitulating to the stupid demands of Negro students" and "see that they get the remedial training that they need." At a two-day law institute sponsored by the NAACP in May 1969, Columbia student Leon Denmark was not at all surprised at Rustin's criticism. "Given his hookups and where he gets his money, he can't do anything else but come out against Black student demands." Charles Duncan from Cheyney could not understand why Rustin had been calling them stupid. "We're the most educated Black generation" this nation has had, he said. Activists in particular were usually the most accomplished students, as the US commissioner of education James E. Allen Jr. announced in late May.[17]

Down South, after police drove out building occupiers (eight of whom were expelled) at the University of Louisville in early May, Kentucky Governor Louis B. Nunn told reporters, "I'm damned sick and tired of this kind of thing." The tactic of taking over a building had steadily lost its effectiveness, as more presidents used court orders and the police to force out students they refashioned as "militants." Apparently, the words of President Nixon in late April—"it is time for the faculties, board of trustees and school administrators to have the backbone to stand up against this kind of situation"—his strongest public comments on Black campus activism to date, had been fully digested.[18]

The backbone produced what some administrators feared—a tragedy. The campus that accelerated the Long Black Student Movement early in the decade by imitating nonviolent protests concluded the decade with violence. Under the cover of night, in late May 1969, police officers and members of the National Guard descended on a protest-rocked North Carolina A&T campus only to be met by sniper fire from a dormitory. The officers fired back. "It's just like guerillas in Vietnam," said Greensboro mayor Jack Elam. The battle scene grew more intense when activists found 20-year-old honor student Willie Grimes dead in a clump of bushes with a gunshot wound in the back of his head. Students believed the police had executed him.[19]

The next day, May 24, students exacted their revenge. Seven police officers were shot by snipers from a dorm room, the worst critically injured in the back and lung by a 0.45-caliber slug. A student was also shot that day in the groin. On the third day of the shootout, Police Major E.R. Wynn resolved to end it. He declared a state of emergency and told the students they had five minutes to "get out of here." The students answered with a spatter of gunfire, wounding a sergeant. Guard members returned fire, while a plane and helicopter flew low over the dorm and executed one of the government's new counterinsurgency techniques. It had been tried for the first time three days earlier on White campus activists at UC Berkeley. The plane and helicopter unleashed swirling clouds of tear gas into the dorms. Coughing and choking, the students spilled out like bugs gassed out of cracks. The police swept the building and found nine rifles and arrested two hundred students. Soon after, the students were all released when the police could not compel any of them to disclose the shooters, ending one of the most violent confrontations ever to occur at a college in the nation's history.[20]

After all of the violence, many of the remarks from leaders that summer were unfavorable. Supreme Court Justice Thurgood Marshall said, "Many of us are not going to let [the nation] go down the drain and stand for anarchy, which is anarchy, which is anarchy." Andrew F. Brimmer, the sole Black member of the Federal Reserve Board, suggested focusing on traditional courses, rather than advocating for Black Studies, if students wanted a future career. Harvard government professor Martin Kilson said at the annual NAACP convention that summer of 1969 that he was "opposed to proposals to make Afro-American studies into a platform for a particular ideological group." In early September, Kilson described Black Studies as "a frightful experience of strangeness and alienation," sordidly and indirectly positing that the overwhelmingly White curriculum did not (or rather should not) cause alienation. Another Ivy League Black professor, Arthur Lewis, called Black Studies a "folly of the highest order," because "employers will not hire the students who emerge from this process, and their usefulness even in Black neighborhoods will be minimal."[21]

White opponents used these ideas to legitimate their opposition on their campuses and to remove the cloak of racism from their critiques. Citing Lewis, Rustin, and Brimmer, Robert H. Mills, a White accounting professor, asserted in September 1969 that "under no condition should Lehigh establish" a Black Studies major, suggesting it will not prepare African Americans to live in an integrated society. Responding to a Black student request for more Black history courses, University of Missouri–St. Louis chancellor Glen R. Driscoll explained his personal opposition to a "proliferation of Afro-American courses … I am impressed that American development is the result of an intertwining and interacting of many streams, and I would prefer that each course reflect this fact." As the Black Studies idea rose up from the desegregation of existing courses, to new courses, to interdepartmental programs, to autonomous departments, to colleges, to a unique discipline, racist opposition reached new heights. Black students on many occasions were forced to settle for new courses in interdepartmental programs—a significant transformation of many curricula, which before the movement had zero Black Studies courses.[22]

Black Cultural Centers, the other major demand of BSUs, were opposed as well, though with less intensity than Black Studies. They were described as a form of segregation. More than two hundred students at Morningside signed an oppositional petition in early 1970. In November 1968, an anonymous St. Cloud State student asserted that the center indicated "reverse discrimination." "As they slink into their Black sanctuary … they alienate all but a few well-chosen Whites," another anonymous student proclaimed at St. Olaf. "The door is open, from 10 a.m. to 10 p.m., to us and our Blackness," the Cultural Union for Black Expression responded. The vast majority of BSUs kept their Black Cultural Centers open to all members of the campus community, placing the onus on White students to keep them interracial. Usually, they did not do so.[23]

While Black leaders and academics censured the movement in the summer of 1969, local, state, and federal legislators continued writing and passing laws to slow the campus activism of all races. The laws regulated student codes of conduct, revoked financial aid funds or scholarships for protesters, outlawed specific tactics (such as building takeovers), and empowered governors and presidents to declare a state of emergency if students threatened campus property (Oregon) and to proclaim "closed periods," barring people from setting foot on university property (Wisconsin).

Campus officers seemed to be preparing for war that summer of 1969. At the annual Convention of College and University Security Directors, some 180 campus law enforcement officials sought the latest riot-control equipment. They advocated using a heavy hand to squash protests. That is "the only way to handle disruptions," said Wayne O. Littrell, the association's president. "This view is shared by other security directors, but unfortunately not by many administrators," who realized, like many police departments that summer, that police brutality invigorated student activism.[24]

Administrators greeted the incoming class in the fall of 1969 with stern warnings against disruption, as they would for the next few years. Many colleges adopted or revised their disciplinary codes and circulated them widely for the first time. Colleges increased their police forces, increases that continued in the early 1970s. For example, Temple formed its own 125-person security force after previously relying on an outside detective agency, and Ohio State doubled and Southern Illinois almost quadrupled its roster of officers. Universities let it be known that they would seek injunctions against protests. Ohio University president Claude R. Sowle informed students in the early fall of 1969 that "unlawful force is not an acceptable substitute for reason. It must be met with lawful force—promptly and without hesitation." Administrators received training during the summer of 1970 on how to deal with protests. The US Army ran one of the programs.[25]

Many Black campus activists could not return to their institutions in the fall of 1969. Some protesters left because their financial aid had been cut off as punishment for their activism. The courts and prisons further hobbled the movement that summer and fall. Hundreds of Black students faced criminal charges and were jailed, including students at the University of Minnesota and San Francisco State. For their role in seizing the administration building in November 1968, ten women and fourteen men at CSU Northridge went on trial in September 1969. They faced seventy-five felony counts of "willfully, unlawfully, feloniously and knowingly" conspiring to commit kidnapping, robbery, false imprisonment, and burglary. In total, they were charged with 1,730 felonies—a record for the movement. The NAACP retained the services of a Los Angeles law firm to defend the students. The case received national exposure, since the government attempted, for the first time, to convict protesters of conspiracy, which, according to the students' lawyers, "has significant ramifications for the entire nation. If the district attorney is successful in arguing that a conspiracy existed, the Black protest movement is in serious difficulty."[26]

In January 1970, twenty students were convicted of conspiracy, kidnapping, and false imprisonment. In announcing his verdict, Judge Mark Brandler said, "We dare not and will not sanction or tolerate the use of force, violence, or other illegal acts to effect desired changes." In effect, negotiating had *not* brought the desired changes and now more effectual protesting became virtually illegal. Archie Chatman (the BSU leader) and Robert A. Lewis, both 22 years old, and 21-year-old Eddie Lee Dancer were sentenced to one to twenty-five years in state prison—the stiffest prison sentences for nonviolent campus activism in American history. Eight other students were held in the county jail for periods ranging from three months to a year, seven students were fined, one was placed on probation, and the final student had her charges dismissed. One of the students' lawyers described the sentences as a "judicial lynching." *The Chicago Defender* called it "an OUTRAGE."[27]

The major work of athletic activism that fall and spring of the 1969–1970 academic year occurred in the Western Athletic Conference (WAC). Black football players at the University of Wyoming considered the Mormon Church, and the Mormon-affiliated Brigham Young University, to be racist. For suggesting they would boycott an upcoming game against BYU, University of Wyoming football coach Lloyd Eaton revoked the scholarships of fourteen Black players. He kicked them off the team in October 1969, all the while saying they now had to go on "Negro relief" or back "on the streets hustling." Six of the athletes were starters on the University of Wyoming's undefeated and twelfth-ranked team. At a press conference a week after dismissing the so-called Black 14, university president Bill Carlson told reporters that football was more important than civil rights. With NAACP assistance, the Black 14 filed an unsuccessful civil suit against Coach Eaton and the University of Wyoming. Ten graduated from other colleges, and four played professional football.[28]

In the midst of the Black 14 affair, Black students at Harvard, demanding better pay for Black construction workers, shut down a construction site in December 1969, leading to campus disciplinary charges. Thirty-six Harvard students did not report to the hearings and conducted their own "fact finding hearing" in January 1970. Several university officials were invited to defend themselves. None attended. LeRoy Boston of the New England Consulate of the Republic of New Africa served as judge and found Harvard negligent and racist.[29]

In February 1970, police arrested 894 Mississippi Valley State activists, the largest mass arrest in higher education history, 89 at Ole Miss, and 351 students at Bishop College in Dallas. Mississippi Valley State president White did not file criminal charges, but he did expel the students—close to a third of the student body—and required them to sign a statement pledging to not take part in protests in order to reenroll, a tactic also used at Tuskegee in April 1968 and throughout the Long Black Student Movement. By late February 1970, only a few dozen students had signed the pledge. "Anyone who signs this should be enslaved," one Mississippi Valley State student leader stated.[30]

Sometimes the suppression came from parents, prompted by media coverage of protests or letters from administrators. On February 23, 1970, a dean of students at Pennsylvania's Thiel College sent a letter to the parents of Black campus activists. "We are certain that you wish your child's education to continue uninterrupted. Your advice and counsel to your child will be greatly appreciated." In this case, the parents stood behind their grown children, and many parents were reportedly aggravated by the condescending letter. In other cases, parents were incensed when they learned that their grown children were throwing away (or, from the students' perspective, improving) their education. On January 14, 1969, a mother heard that her child had occupied a building at Brandeis University outside of Boston. She raced to the campus, walked up to the hall, and pounded on the doors with her fists and umbrella. "Christopher Carombo, come out! Christopher Carombo, come out! I don't believe in Black Power!" she screamed. A few moments later, a student hurried down the fire escape and ran into his mother's arms, and car, which quickly sped away.[31]

During the 1970–1971 academic year, suspensions or expulsions of protesters led to campus activism and often police retaliation at Norfolk State, Syracuse, University of Florida, and Hampton, where administrators suspended five activists, including SGA vice president Roxanne E. Sinclair. The "Hampton Five" freedom campaign staged a 90 percent effective class boycott, and by early May the historic institution became a war zone. President Roy Hudson cancelled commencement and shut down the campus because he "didn't want to wait until someone was killed."[32]

Hudson had ample reason to think someone would be killed, as Black youths were slain at Tuskegee, South Carolina State, North Carolina A&T, Jackson State, University of Kansas, Pepperdine, and Southern. At least thirteen youths (nine collegiate, three high schoolers, and one community activist) were killed by police during the Black Campus Movement. And then there were the dozens of students injured by police bullets, the thousands arrested and jailed, the tens of thousands brutalized, suspended, expelled, and tracked by the intelligence community, and the millions who opposed the movement and endorsed these atrocities. With all the opposition from segregationists and assimilationists, it is remarkable that Black students were able to win so much and to change the racial constitution of higher education. Their persistence gave life to the words of San Francisco State BSU chairman Benny Stewart, which he often repeated to his members during their 134-day strike: "The only way a people can be defeated is when they lose their determination to fight."[33]

CHAPTER 15

"Black Students Refuse to Pass the Buck": The Racial Reconstitution of Higher Education

Two days after armed Black Cornell students marched out of their occupied building, professors at Harvard walked into a faculty meeting prompted by the Black Campus Movement. In January 1969, a Harvard committee recommended the establishment of an Afro-American Studies major in an interdepartmental center. *The New York Times* praised the "important step in depoliticizing an issue that has become enmeshed in unnecessary controversy at many colleges." Harvard's Black students were not nearly as pleased, especially in early April when they came across an outline of the new program. They were dismayed that Afro-American Studies majors had to combine their studies into one of the existing, and to the students' thinking, "racist" disciplines. The setup presupposed that "Afro-American Studies is less than a legitimate and valid intellectual endeavor," said sophomore Fran Farmer. In turn, members of the African and Afro-American Association (AAAS) demanded an autonomous department to give the academy's latest intellectual endeavor that legitimacy and validity.[1]

As Harvard professors walked into the meeting room to decide the fate of Black Studies on April 22, 1969, most did not like the ultimatum issued by AAAS president "Skip" Griffin in one of the meeting's first talks. "Not to make a decision in favor of the proposal that we have put here before you is to commit a serious mistake … creating a tragic situation which this university may never be able to recover from." As the professors hissed, rumors were already circulating about the impending doom coming to the

© The Author(s), under exclusive license to Springer Nature Switzerland AG 2025
I. X. Kendi, *The Black Campus Movement*, Contemporary Black History, https://doi.org/10.1007/978-3-031-37394-7_15

campus. Officials stood guard at the library and the museum. According to one Harvard professor, "the shadow of Cornell was spreading to Cambridge, Massachusetts."[2]

A heated debate followed Griffin's threat. Two hours later, the moment of truth arrived. "All in favor, please rise," Harvard president Nathan Pusey requested. "All opposed." It was too close to judge. A head count ensued, as more than seventy-five nervous Black students huddled together around their radios outside the meeting room. "The motion is carried by a vote of two fifty-one for, one fifty-eight against …" Before the president could finish, a cheer drowned him out. "I consider this a great victory for Black students and for American education," senior Clyde Lindsay told reporters. Indeed, it was one of the greatest victories of the Black Campus Movement.[3]

Harvard's Black students partied through the night, letting out collective sighs of joy, while the faculty let out collective sighs of relief. Some of the professors voted in favor of Black Studies due to their sympathy for the budding discipline. With the Cornell guns and AAAS threats on their mind, others were scared into voting. Whatever the reason—the debate on the legitimacy of Black Studies, the signature intrusion of the movement—received a boost with that Harvard vote. Furthermore, the faculty placed six students on the thirteen-member committee to develop the department, the first time in the university's history that students had ever been given a direct role in the selection of faculty.[4]

Two weeks after the historic decision at arguably the most illustrious HWCU, students forced a historic decision at arguably the most illustrious HBCU. On May 8, 1969, what Harvard professors had feared became a reality at Howard during the student fight to transform their "Negro university" into a "Black university." Six buildings were occupied by Black campus activists, compelling its president, James Nabrit, to close the university. The students barricaded themselves inside buildings and they also barricaded the main gate with boards, chairs, and desks to repel a police invasion. Students who were not inside buildings broke into the campus restaurant and smashed doors, windows, and vending machines. A fire gutted the ROTC building. The university had a temporary restraining order against building takeovers. The Howard students did not care, defying the order and Nabrit's threats to "call on outside forces."[5]

The warning was actualized on May 9. More than a hundred federal marshals sporting riot gear charged onto the campus and smashed, sawed, and cut their way into buildings to drive out the remaining students. In their first target, Frederick Douglass Memorial Hall, seventeen students were holed up in a second-floor office with a sign on the door that read "This is a Black struggle." Two husky marshals had to kick the locked door in unison to break it down. Seventeen students were led out to police cars shouting, "Black Power!" The marshals moved onto Locke Hall and entered through the frame of a plate-glass door, which they smashed in. It was empty, save a simple note: "Welcome pigs ... Unity is the Way."[6]

In all, during the sweep of the six buildings, twenty-one students were arrested and charged with "criminal contempt of court." Two of those students ended up serving two weeks in jail. But that did not stop their activism. At the end of the month, twenty Howard students pushed past two police officers into a trustees meeting and suggested they appoint Kwame Nkrumah, the deposed president of Ghana, as Howard's next president. *The Chicago Defender* endorsed the students' suggestion: "He would bring dignity and leadership of the highest order to embattled Howard." The trustees passed on Nkrumah. But they did replace Nabrit with James E. Cheek, who endorsed aspects of the Black University concept. In the summer, Cheek outlined a program for the future of Howard that included "creative and imaginative ways to deal with the problems of the cities, the economically disadvantaged, health care, Black Americans and Black people throughout the world." He presented his "new humanism" at the opening convocation in the fall of 1969, as Harvard opened its Black Studies department with Ewart Guinier as chair.[7]

The weekend after the Howard protests, *The New York Times* reported that "colleges and universities across the country are hurriedly instituting changes and reforms, as administrators attempt to deal with student restiveness and to avoid the kind of demonstrations that have shaken Ivy League and other major universities," the story opened. With a team of correspondents issuing reports from forty-two campuses, the newspaper found that one of the most significant changes and reforms was the establishment of "Black studies programs and increased effort to recruit Negroes and other minority groups." American Council on Education vice president Kenneth Roose informed the *Times* that "even in areas where faculty resistance was strong, the walls are crumbling." This assessment was not new. Educational pundits and officials had seen the walls crumbling in 1968. Black campus (and other) activists had stoked a crisis of "educational authority." F. Champion Ward, the Ford Foundation's vice president for research and education, declared in 1968 that the crisis "has strained the institutional fabric of American universities and colleges. Strengthening that fabric is now the first order of business if higher education is to make its aims clear and quicken its responses under stress." Moreover, in July 1969, after surveying educators from forty leading colleges and universities, the *Wall Street Journal* reported that "Black students are an identifiable, relatively cohesive group ... [that] have become the cutting edge for much of the academic and social experimentation sweeping the schools these days." Researchers, who studied innovations in 1969 at almost a thousand liberal arts colleges, found evidence "from every quarter ... suggesting that the 1970s will see vastly different colleges and universities than those of the 1960s."[8]

These vastly different colleges and universities did not come about as a result of the 1954 *Brown* decision or the Civil Rights Act of 1964. It was the Black Campus Movement that forced the rewriting of the racial constitution at the country's institutions of higher education and an implementation of antiracist changes that is without parallel in higher education history. Academics started conceiving of grassroots altruism as foundational to higher education's function, as opposed to ladder altruism. Diversity and the standardization of professed inclusion eclipsed the long-held standardization of exclusion. Some scholars started to move away from an assimilationist curriculum, conceding that Black ideas, assumptions, perspectives, methodologies, methods, and scholarship were academically legitimate and should be taught. Moral freedoms for HBCU students had in many cases replaced the moralized contraption.

MORAL FREEDOM

At HBCUs in the mid-1960s, there were still remnants of the moralized contraption that students furiously challenged throughout the Long Black Student Movement. The contraption of rules and regulations was based on the racist, sexist, and ageist notion that these Black students were incapable of acting responsibly with academic, social, and political freedom. HBCU activists began to conceptualize in unprecedented fashion the totality of the contraption and its ideological basis in the mid-1960s. The ideas undergirding the rules became just as germane to their activism. In his "State of the Campus" address on February 24, 1966, SGA president Charles E. Daye of North Carolina Central declared, "We are engaged in great revolution on this campus." He referenced the previous year's strike against the rules. "We seek to overthrow the system of ideas that refuse to permit us to grow into adulthood. If our college administration spent greater time administrating and less time trying to baby-sit for grown men and women, Negro colleges would not be so far behind." A booming applause from student congress members interrupted this speech, one that SGA presidents and BSU presidents at HBCUs across the South replicated throughout the early years of the movement. As historian Joy Ann Williamson revealed, "Their arguments mirrored the burgeoning Black freedom struggle's demands for participatory democracy."[9]

By the end of the movement, the moralized contraption was largely history at many HBCUs, aside from cross-gender room visitation. Women, at least on paper, began to be regulated somewhat equally. Chapel, class, and ROTC mandates had been abolished on most campuses. The efforts of faculty and administrators to raise the academic acumen of students surged ahead of moral advancement. Black campus activists had driven from office many of the dictatorial, paternalistic, conservative presidents, who openly treated students like children.

STANDARDIZATION OF INCLUSION

"The freedom to learn depends upon appropriate opportunities and conditions in the classroom, on the campus, and in the larger community, which we have been denied," said one of the organizers of a building takeover by two hundred students (a third of the body) at Bowie State days before Martin Luther King's death in 1968. Like the speech from the North Carolina Central SGA president, the avowal from the Bowie State organizer echoed from the lips of most Black campus activists at HBCUs during the movement. In February 1969, Calvin Matthews, SGA president at North Carolina A&T, mourned his school's "archaic and dilapidated system," while students the following year at the University of Maryland Eastern Shore called their HBCU a "poor attempt at an institution" in their roughly fifty pages of "demands and recommendations."[10]

In addition to conceiving of their lack of freedom in connection with the moralized contraption, Black college students recognized how poor campus facilities and services at HBCUs standardized their exclusion from adequate learning environments and, thus, their "freedom to learn." Collegians grieved over inadequate housing, understaffed campus offices, short operating hours for campus facilities, including the library and student center, and meager medical, transportation, laundry, and telephone services. HBCU students faulted their faculty, administrators, governors, education bureaucrats, trustees, and benefactors. Public HBCU activists regularly compared their campus facilities and services to those at nearby public HWCUs, demonstrating the racial inequity. In 1966, Alcorn State had one professor for every twenty-two students, compared to the University of Mississippi's ratio of thirteen to one. Alcorn State had fourteen library books for each student, while there were sixty books for every University of Mississippi student. "This state of affairs," wrote a member of the Southern Student Organizing Committee in a pamphlet on Alcorn, "is only the final step in a totally inferior and almost totally segregated education system for Mississippi Negroes." The writer classified Alcorn State as a "plantation college," the same label sophomore Guinnevere Hodges pinned on University of Oklahoma in 1967.[11]

Campus activists charged that American racism produced the inequities between HBCUs and HWCUs—of state appropriations, private credit lines, and wealth of alumni, the deliberate appointment of incompetent administrators at HBCUs, and HBCU administrators and faculty personally benefitting from their accommodation to a racist order that mandated a bottom-tier position for HBCUs. During the era of Black pride and self-love and its concomitant psychological attack on Black inferiority complexes, HBCU activists distanced themselves from the racist idea that the inferiority of Black people produced the inferiority of HBCUs. Black campus activists rejected the racist justifications for the inferior quality of HBCUs: financial mismanagement, administrative incompetence, alumni giving, and student comportment. If HBCUs were failing, trustees, politicians, and presidents wanted them to fail, since failure and inferiority reckoned their proper places in the academy and in society, students argued. The "guardians," as one student called them, endeavored to keep the standardization of HBCU exclusion from an equal academic playing field, from achievements, and from progress.

Yet the guardians failed to keep Black students from effecting change. Echoing the demands of Black students, although for not quite the same reasons, the Southern Regional Education Board in the early summer of 1969 circulated a report to trustees, foundations, and government agencies proposing that HBCUs needed special operating funds in addition to their regular allotments. As Black campus activists asserted, Black colleges were deficient in faculty salaries, administrative services, curriculum change, and a range of remedial and compensatory education programs.

"It is essential that a systematic procedure be adopted for removing these deficiencies over a period of years," the report stated.[12]

By the early 1970s, HBCU officials were making demands on the federal government for more funds. Representatives from forty-six institutions came to Washington, DC, in May 1971 to criticize the Nixon administration during a salute to Black colleges sponsored by the Capital Press Club. Even though not even two decades had passed, it seemed like ages ago that HBCU officials were putting on campus shows of humility for public and private benefactors. Their begging had turned into decrees. Lincoln (PA) president Herman Branson called it "immoral" and "dirty" that Black colleges had received a mere 3 percent of the $4 billion in overall funds for higher education that year. This is what Black students had demanded for several years—assertive and aggressive administrators unwilling to allow state and federal racism to hold back their HBCUs.[13]

Black students also demanded the elimination of their exclusion from campus decision-making bodies, such as university committees, and the desegregation and Black domination of HBCU trustee boards. Many HBCUs gave students an unprecedented amount of power in newly written student constitutions, and the trustee boards were made over, often with student trustees. Clark Atlanta named student trustees and placed students on policymaking committees "with the clear understanding that these were not short-term responses to the national campus crisis, but ideas whose time had come," wrote President Vivian W. Henderson in 1974. The administration and student body at Alabama A&M agreed in 1969 to establish a faculty-student evaluation committee in order to assess teaching performance. At North Carolina A&T, in the fall of 1969, trustees unanimously voted John S. Stewart, president of the Mutual Savings and Loan Association, chairman of the board. He became the first Black chairman since the Greensboro institution had opened in 1891. North Carolina A&T trustees also approved the creation of a student legislature, a student judicial system to handle disciplinary cases, and a new student code of conduct. They even allowed 21-year-old students to have alcohol in their rooms—a stunning development, since a decade earlier alcohol consumption would likely have led to immediate expulsion.[14]

On December 1, 1969, Case Western Reserve president Robert W. Morse responded to a few concerns voiced by AAS president Raymond

A. Henry, including one regarding racism at the university. "There has been injustice to minorities and denial of equal opportunities in many institutions of American life, including universities. With your cooperation, we have been trying to make advances at this University to create a more responsive atmosphere for all, and to redress those inequities which particularly affect Black students on this campus." Morse proceeded to list the "record of some of the developments in this University during the past year." The Black student population had nearly quadrupled, from twenty in the fall of 1967 to seventy-two in the fall of 1969. There were six and seven more Black professors and Black administrators, respectively, than the previous December. A "large number of new books" on African Americans had been added to the library.[15]

The change at Case Western Reserve reflected higher education in general at HWCUs. Black students poured into the academy at a growth rate of 50,000 per year between 1965 and 1973—what two scholars called the "golden age of Black educational opportunity." Tuition increases, financial aid cuts, and the end of the movement in 1973 reversed the rate, as the percentage of Black freshmen dropped from its peak in the fall of 1972 at 8.7 percent to 7.8 percent in the fall of 1973. However, it increased again in the fall of 1974, marking the first time the number of Black Americans in the academy breached the 800,000 mark, at 814,000. That fall, Black Americans made up about 9 percent of the total student body (compared to 5 percent in 1964) and 12 percent of the freshman class, comparable to 11 percent of Black people in the country's population. Black student enrollment would reach 10.3 percent by 1976. But the number of incoming Black students started to come down from the mountaintop they had reached in the mid-1970s, such that they accounted for a mere 4.9 percent of the fall class of 1978.[16]

During the apex academic year of 1968–1969, more than three hundred schools established admissions programs tailored to African Americans. By 1970, after the three most protest-ridden years of the movement, almost a thousand colleges had adopted more open admissions policies to admit Black people, had a tutoring program for Black students, were providing diversity training for workers, and were actively recruiting Black professors and staff. Almost three hundred colleges offered financial aid to African American students and had developed diversity policy statements. In addition, during the 1970–1971 academic year, almost two hundred institutions hired Black professors, and over a hundred established admissions programs for Black students. Almost every college with a substantial Black student population hired Black counselors, admissions staff, and administrators—often Black deans or diversity officers. Black Cultural Centers were opened at hundreds of institutions. Usually, public colleges and universities, Western and Northeastern institutions, higher ranking schools, and large urban institutions were the most responsive to the demands of Black campus activists. Meanwhile, the private church colleges, the Southern colleges, and the lower ranking schools were the least responsive.[17]

The Black Campus Movement compelled HWCUs to move away from the standardization of exclusion. In its place rose diversity statement after diversity statement and professed commitment after professed commitment—demonstrating new ideals, a new constitution. The gains from the movement have been immense. However, individual gains do not necessarily mean institutional progress, just as writing a new racial constitution does not mean that constitution has been actualized.

ANTIRACIST CURRICULA

As campus activists conceptualized the standardization of exclusion, they also uncovered the assimilationist ideas that had concealed racist or Eurocentric thought as the norm in American higher education since its inception. American higher education had dominant political persuasion, cultural expression, and class positions, many students contended. Black campus activists usually termed institutions White or Negro universities—with curricula, programs, and personnel that indoctrinated and socialized assimilation into political docility, a bourgeois class perspective, and White American culture. They were no longer willing to stay in the academy "dislocated" on "borrowed European terms." They wanted to think on their "own terms," to use scholar Ama Mazama's words. They wanted something of relevance to their sociocultural experience.[18]

"We feel that the University of Houston is a White Anglo-Saxon Protestant institution," read a statement by Afro-Americans for Black Liberation on February 7, 1969. In 1970, New Mexico State Black Students Organization President Hardy Murphy said the curriculum prepared them for life as middle-class White men. Meanwhile that year, a student in the Howard Students Organized for Black Unity chapter said that from the institution's "inception," it had had "a calculated program of assimilation and degradation for Black people." Hampton had been "geared to fitting us for a 'nice, comfortable, middle-class' existence with a nice-paying job in some huge impersonal corporation—that is unobtrusive assimilation into White bourgeois society (Booker T. rides again)—rather than teaching us to think … and to preserve our cultural integrity in a hostile society," said sophomore activist Sharon Masingale. "All the University of Georgia offers its Black students is indoctrination into White society," read a BSU news release in 1969. It continued, "Neo-slavemasters have declared that it is illegal, unnecessary and educationally unsound for Black people to obtain a meaningful education." According to Fisk's Students for a Black University, the storied HBCU "had been known to cater to 'Negro' scholars who have aspired to assimilate." At the height of the movement, in 1969, Paul E. Wisdom and Kenneth A. Shaw captured the Black student presumption in the *Educational Record*. "What the universities have failed to realize in almost every case is that the American educational experience is a White experience, an experience based on White history, White tradition, White culture, White customs, and White thinking, an education designed primarily to produce a culturally sophisticated, middle class, White American." In the "Black Challenge to Higher Education," the two collegiate deans added that "the key word to Black students today is the same one most often used by White critics of our universities: relevance."[19]

Antiracist education was rare at White colleges and universities, while Black Studies courses were rarer, and Black Studies programs and departments were nonexistent in 1965. Until Black students called this into question, the paucity of courses and literature dealing with African Americans was normalized for higher education. Normalized as opposed to normal, since these curricula were deliberately created and recreated over the years, ignoring Black scholarship from W.E.B. Du Bois, Anna Julia Cooper, Zora Neale Hurston, J.A. Rogers, and Alain Locke—to name a few. It was no coincidence or oversight. To White and quite a few Black academics, scholars had not been reading and discussing "White American" or "European" literature over the years. A basic assumption was that these "objective" professors were reading and discussing "literature."

The same assimilationist conceptions rationalized the exclusion of Black scholarship at HBCUs. A graduate dean at North Carolina A&T knew of few courses "oriented to the Negro" at HBCUs in 1968. Most HBCUs merely had one "Negro history" and "Negro literature" course at the most. Activists constantly brought to light this glaring contradiction of few Black courses at institutions with practically all Black students, including Earl Hart at Winston-Salem State in 1969. In the physical education department, they only taught the "fox-trot and all those other European dances," he said. "In the music department we are still fooling around with Bach and the rest of those pigs when we have soul musicians." Ultimately, "Black students emerge after four years of college completely Europeanized." Black campus activists also endeavored to make European thinkers relevant by ascertaining their utility to the antiracist struggle. "Like a Black Midas' wand, this movement imbues everything it touches with an ebony hue," explained Robert Goodman, a Morehouse instructor in 1968. "A discussion of Descartes in Western civ is likely to wind up in heated debate over how Descartes would have analyzed Black Power or whether White philosophers are relevant to Black people anyway."[20]

The Black Studies idea conceived and injected into the academy by Black students challenged head-on the assimilationist curricula at both HBCUs and HWCUs. In one of the first issues of *The Black Scholar* in 1970, its editors wrote that Black campus activists had blasted the "archaic illusions of scholarly objectivity, of the sanctity of the ivory tower, of the almost churchlike serenity of the college." Black students "demonstrated that American colleges were as racist and oppressive as any other of this country's institutions." Black students also challenged the notion of knowledge for knowledge's sake. Black campus activists drew a line in the academic sand and claimed that all knowledge either reinforces or challenges the status quo. And therefore, knowledge for knowledge's sake has been utilized to justify scholarship that maintains an assimilationist curricula and White supremacy in the community.[21]

Racist mainstream scholarship, which had long been refuted by Black scholars, were refuted with a new vigor by Black students—ideas such as the historical and cultural backwardness of Africa, African American incompetence during Reconstruction, the humaneness of slavery, and the docility of enslaved Africans. In addition, Black campus activists' notion of a "Black perspective" challenged the idea of a universal scholarly perspective that masked a Eurocentric perspective. They de-universalized the European ideas that had been spread over much of the globe. Like Third World revolutionaries stopping imperialists dead in their tracks in the 1960s, so too did students challenge imperial ideas. "Through perspectival elimination you have necessarily de-emphasized some aspects of reality," wrote Genna Rae McNeil to the Kalamazoo faculty and administration in Michigan on May 19, 1969. "You do not focus on total reality. No human being or social group does. Black people are not demanding the impossible. Black people are affirming the need to look at reality again.

For in looking more closely with us you, too, may build a construct of more details from which you, too, may see new patterns of possibilities."[22]

Black students provided the vision for Black Studies. Their activism led to its institutionalization. By 1970, after the three most active years of the movement, nearly a thousand colleges had organized Black Studies courses and more than two hundred had interdepartmental programs or autonomous departments. Although interest waned and attacks increased from segregationists and assimilationists, by mid-decade the discipline of Black Studies was very much alive. In 1972, *The New York Times* reported that "although divided on what Black studies are, what they should be and whom they should reach, a number of Black educators, social scientists and intellectuals agree that the discipline has forever changed some aspects of American higher education." The *Times* added that "the adherents of Black studies have questioned and broken a number of long-accepted academic rules." The United Press International, the American Association of State Colleges, and Nick Aaron Ford's groundbreaking study on the discipline all demonstrated the success of Black Studies. Even *the Chronicle of Higher Education*'s report on "The State of Black Studies" in late 1975 reported that the demise of the discipline proved to be exaggerated. The programs and departments "are not where they thought they would be by this time, but they're slowly becoming more established," wrote Elias Blake.[23]

The Black Studies idea and the movement generally—along with student activism from other races and the innovation of antiracist faculty—profoundly affected the existing disciplines. Five dissident factions—Psychologists for a Democratic Society, Psychologists for Social Action, Women's Consortium of Psychologists for Social Action, the Association of Black Psychologists, and the Association of Black Psychology Students—actively sought to reform or revolutionize their discipline and its affairs at the American Psychological Association's annual convention in 1969. The newly organized Association of Black Psychologists and a group of twenty-five Black psychology students raised concerns about the discipline's relationship to the Black community and wanted the association to actively recruit Black students and faculty into the area of inquiry. Delegates established a committee to study the issue and provide funds for students to travel to campuses to discuss problems.

The American Sociology Association convened the "most politicized meeting" in the organization's sixty-four-year history in 1969. A Black caucus condemned it as racist, saying the "association has profited parasitically by victimizing the Black community, by using the Black community as a research laboratory for White experimentation, by using Black people as human guinea pigs for publishing books, surveys, and the earning of Ph.D.'s for Whites, and for gathering data on Black people for the purpose of oppression, exploitation, and control." To revamp the association, the Black caucus demanded, among other things, that it appoint Black members to its decision-making bodies.

Activist members of the American Political Science Association formed a caucus and won several victories at their annual conference in 1969. Black Americans received more influence in the association's affairs, while David Easton of the University of Chicago devoted his presidential address to the "revolution in political science" based on the "credo of relevance." He proclaimed that the revolution does not seem to be a passing phenomenon, "but rather ... a specific and important episode in the history of our discipline, if not in all the social sciences." A progressive caucus formed at the annual convention of the Association of American Geographers to make their discipline more relevant. "We're changing from just looking at the way man uses the land to trying to figure out why he uses it the way he does," said one geographer. Similar shifts and caucuses were formed in several other social sciences, with their activity coming to a head at the 1969 conventions.[24]

Their college administrations, their presidents—were they relevant to Black people? Aside from the curriculum, it was another question HBCU campus activists debated in the mid-1960s. They had reached a general consensus by the end of the decade. Many of their Black presidents were assimilationists at HBCUs. Deeply immersed in colonial literature and news, students compared their presidents to the White-controlled "puppet presidents" who had "sold out" their people in the Third World in the mid-twentieth century. Activists had long demonstrated against these "puppets," since these assimilationist executives increasingly took the helms of HBCUs in 1920s. Yet by the 1960s, it was no longer enough for these presidents to be Black, especially when some of these HBCU presidents clamped down on civil rights protests as if they were White segregationists. To Charles Daye, SGA president at North Carolina Central, HBCUs in 1966 were propagated by a coalition of White Southerners and African American elites who gained "personal aggrandizement and social prestige." The deplorable conditions persisted at Prairie View A&M

because a group of Black administrators was "willing to do the bidding of their White mentors" for "authority and affluence."[25]

By the early 1970s, many of the assimilationist and accommodating HBCU presidents had resigned or been let go. One example was the forced resignation in 1969 of J.D. Boyd. He had served as president of a protest-ridden Alcorn State for a dozen years. Students staged major protests calling for his termination in 1964, 1966, 1968, and 1969. Walter Washington took over for Boyd and proclaimed that he would create "The New Alcorn." In July 1969, Washington's administration met with student leaders on the list of forty grievances they had drawn up for Boyd in the spring. He agreed to improve the dining hall, extend library hours, and grant dancing privileges. He hired two physicians, beautified the campus, requested more capital for the restoration of facilities, and, most importantly from the students' perspective, yielded "the responsibility of young adulthood to the students of Alcorn." He was not like Boyd, who "maintained a conservative viewpoint to retain his empire," explained Alcorn student Ervin Barnes Jr. in October 1969. "Suddenly, out of despair there came hope, out of confusion there came logical reasoning, and out of unfairness there came justice. This was all a realization as a result of new president Dr. Walter Washington."[26]

GRASSROOTS ALTRUISM

In its totality, the Black Campus Movement critiqued the purpose of higher education. Black campus activists on almost every campus indicted higher education for perpetuating the status quo of racism. The university bears a "large responsibility" in "influencing the creation of an equitable society for all," proclaimed the BSU at Indiana University Northwest in 1969. The Association of Black Collegians at the University of Missouri–St. Louis described colleges and universities as "wholesale producers of a designated mentality conducive to the perpetuation and continuation of America's present national life—a national life which we have witnessed to be in total and complete contradiction to the wholesome development and survival of our people." Students, including those at Mississippi State and Michigan State, continuously argued that their colleges programmed or indoctrinated them into a Eurocentric, capitalistic, patriarchal, or assimilationist ideology. Robin Gregory, Howard's first homecoming queen with an Afro, who spoke out against sexism during her 1966 campaign, particularly despised Howard's special assemblies for women. "We had this lecture on etiquette, and how we were supposed to dress, and how we were supposed to behave. And we were supposed to be ladies [laughs]." Barbara Garrison of the Alliance of Black Students at the University of Wisconsin-Milwaukee declared on February 13, 1969, that "Black students refuse to pass the buck and become the colonial buffer-zone niggers emasculate reincarnation."[27]

Their colleges were like ladders, removing them from the struggles of their people, many Black campus activists claimed. At a mass meeting concerning their twelve "non-negotiable demands" at Stetson in May 1970, an elder professor advised Black students to focus their energies on their careers. A leader "rejected the idea vociferously," according to a university biography, and instead announced that their chief purpose at the school should be to prepare to "work for justice" in Black communities. The pervasive notion of ladder altruism, as projected by Stetson's elder professor, resulted in Black collegians leaving their communities, spatially and psychologically. "His community has thereby been left without the element most essential to its regeneration and construction—its aware young people," asserted University of Missouri–St. Louis's Association of Black Collegians in its Black Studies proposal. "Henceforth, our education must speak to the needs of our community and our people. We can no longer prostitute our minds to the vain and irrelevant." Serving as professional role models on the ladder of success did not speak to the community's needs as much as it satiated the conscience of the professional Black people who believed the community's livelihood rose as they trekked up the ladder, Black campus activists argued.[28]

Graduates in the 1950s and early 1960s were not interested in relating to the poor Black community and instead strove to be "as 'middle class' as possible," according to Black United Students at the University of Akron in 1970. Elaborating on the point, Roosevelt's Black students attested, in their 1969 "Minority Report," that Black students were disallowed from studying matters of housing, relief, social welfare, education, and other matters germane to their people. Expressing an ideology of grassroots altruism, Black students asserted (and were supported by many Black power speakers across the ideological spectrum) that they must become the "dominant force in improving the conditions of the poor Black community," as the University of Akron's Black United Students exclaimed. Shortly after the Orangeburg Massacre in February 1968, the University of Chicago Black Student Alliance, "as the future leaders of the American Black community," felt "compelled to go on record that our primary commitment is to our people" in a letter to President Johnson. "Blacks no longer want college degrees to escape from the Black community," said Ken Blackwell, president of the Afro-American Student Organization at Cincinnati's Xavier University in March 1970. "We want degrees to aid it." The weight of this aid rested on the "shoulders of young Black Americans in our colleges and universities," since Eldridge Cleaver was in exile, Huey P. Newton was in jail, and both Martin Luther King Jr. and Malcolm X were dead, read a 1969 pamphlet created by the National Association of Black Students.[29]

Black campus activists were fairly united on their push for an antiracist education for liberation. To be relevant, the antiracist pedagogy must allow them to intensely study and figure out methods to improve the complex condition of people of African descent, ultimately training them to be antiracist servant-leaders of the masses of Black people. That was the rationale Black students usually laid out for Black Universities and Black Studies. The Claremont Colleges BSUs proclaimed in their demands in May 1968 that an "adequate education will provide them with the tools to combat racism, discrimination, and inequality." "Our first goal should be to obtain an education relevant to the needs of the mass of Black people in this country," asserted Tougaloo's Irma Watkins in February 1969.[30]

Before this movement took hold, ladder altruism thrived as a constituent element of the racist constitution of higher education. Colleges were like ladders, disassociating from the communities and professing to serve as enlightened models for the development of society. Black college graduates utilized these ladders to individually make their ascent in society, while also claiming that they were helping the entire race by smashing ceilings and serving as positive role models. Black campus activists theorized that if colleges and universities were like ladders, or tools of removal, then students would use them accordingly. However, if higher education tossed the ladder aside and directed itself openly to grassroots community advancement, then students would follow. This was the most unyielding aim of the Black Campus Movement—revolutionizing the function of higher education from ladder altruism, which largely maintained the status quo while helping out a select few Black people, to grassroots altruism, which students speculated would transform the academy into an organ of the antiracist revolution.

Black campus activists were unable to revolutionize higher education. But they did help rewrite the racial constitution of higher education, replacing ladder altruism with grassroots altruism. Many HWCU officials and academics, particularly at public, Christian, and prestigious institutions, said higher education had to come down from the tower (or ladder) and assumed a social responsibility in the late 1960s and early 1970s. "No longer is it possible to separate the world of scholarly pursuit from the world of reality," wrote Marquette president John P. Raynor in 1967. "The two have firmly intertwined, and we (Marquette University) would have it no other way." Marquette's Students United for Racial Equality praised Raynor's words but then challenged him to turn his words into action in a November 1967 letter. When he failed to do so, Black campus activists pressured him with weeks of protests in May 1968. After the campus crisis was finally resolved, a widely circulated Associated Press story reported that many were saying the Catholic institution would never be the same. "Some say it was a permanent sense of 'Christian commitment' that will make unmistakably clear that Marquette as an urban institution has an inescapable need to help find solutions to Milwaukee's social problems."[31]

In a spring 1969 speech at the forty-ninth annual meeting of the American Association of Junior Colleges, William M. Birenbaum, president of Staten Island Community College, said, "Those who cry out most loudly now against politicization of the university are really making a last-ditch defense of the present political rigging of academic privilege and vested interest." SUNY chancellor Samuel B. Gould gave three lectures on "The Academic Condition" in the early fall of 1969. "We can no longer consider the university as an enterprise largely removed from the main concerns of society, but now must see it as one part of a complex web of social institutions, each of which is rapidly and perceptively changing in character and direction, while [at] the same time interacting with all the other forces," Gould argued at Colgate. The "conscience of the academic community has been aroused, and in small towns and big cities our institutions are searching for ways to be 'part of the action,'" elucidated Cleveland State University president Harold L. Enarson in a prepared paper for the American Council on Education's 1969 annual meeting. HEW secretary Robert Finch, in a paper for the same meeting, suggested new expectations and responsibilities for higher education. As "great equalizers of opportunity," they should "exercise a sort of providential influence over people's lives" and tackle "the most intractable problems of our society."[32]

During the movement, Black campus activists at HWCUs and HBCUs did not merely project a new grassroots vision for the academy. They led the way through their scholarship, initiatives, and programs. Using BSUs,

SGAs, Black Studies offices, and Black Cultural Centers as bases, Black students entered Black communities and lectured on Black Studies, launched food drives, organized tutoring programs, sickle cell anemia campaigns, and student recruitment programs, initiated Kwanzaa celebrations, helped establish day care centers, lent their money and time to a series of urban and rural Black political campaigns, and campaigned to free political prisoners. They engaged in many forms of reformist and revolutionary community activism, joining most of the local and national Black Power organizations, including SNCC, CORE, RAM, the National Black Feminist Organization, Congress of African People, US Organization, and the Black Panther Party.

Many HBCUs were barely surviving on their dwindling lifelines due to the fact that Black students were increasingly choosing White colleges and government and corporate funds followed them in the late 1960s. HBCUs were searching in those treacherous, ever-changing waters for a new identity. HBCU officials heard the loud calls for their elimination. They heard their alumni and students match that volume with demands for their continuance. The new crop of HBCU administrators installed by the Black Campus Movement were searching for a new identity for their colleges. They had to look no further than to what their students had been requesting, demanding, and protesting for since the spring of 1965.

In 1969, some HBCU administrators, once some of the fiercest opponents of the Black University concept, started crafting a mission for HBCUs out of its main tenet—grassroots altruism. As Lucius Pitts, president of Miles College, explained in October 1969, "We're taking students whom no one else will take, and we're designing programs for the whole spread of students."[33]

Morehouse launched a project in 1969 in an Atlanta storefront. Termed Project CURE, it endeavored to organize credit unions and buy clubs and to form cooperative stores. Most HBCUs enacted grassroots altruism by supporting the most conservative movement within the Black Power Movement, the Black Capitalism Movement. Yet they were in the Black Power orbit, a dramatic shift from just a decade prior. There were other grassroots experiments at HBCUs, which, according to the *Boston Globe*, "are symptomatic of a larger shift in emphasis at Black schools to train students for a wide range of functions that will aid in the uplifting of Black communities. It is not scientists that are needed, but social workers, community organizers, teachers." Clark Atlanta strengthened its focus on urban and rural problems in its curriculum "when student pressure built," according to President Vivian W. Henderson. And, with the help of the Voter Education Project, Clark Atlanta, Talladega, Miles, and Southern established instructional and technical assistance centers for Black elected officials in the early 1970s. "Students and professors became more systemically involved in the voting, political, and policy processes and in providing technical assistance to public officials," Henderson added in 1974. North Carolina A&T president Lewis C. Dowdy also articulated elements of the Black University concept. "We want you," speaking to the students in 1969, "to assist us in making our programs relevant. I think some of our programs are obsolete and should be replaced with courses that are relevant to us. Change is inevitable and we must face it with perseverance and responsibility."[34]

EPILOGUE: BACKLASH AND FORWARD LASHES

Malcolm X once reasoned, "You don't stick a knife in a man's back nine inches and then pull it out six inches and say you're making progress." The Black Campus Movement pulled out the knife several inches. The new ideals, the new antiracist constitution, gave higher education the tools to fully extract the knife and heal the wounds. Several decades have passed since the demise of the Black Campus Movement. Has the knife been fully removed? Have the wounds healed? Has higher education eradicated racism? Are we making progress?[1]

Most would agree that the new ideals put forth by the Black Campus Movement, exemplified now in one catch word—diversity—echoes from higher education. Almost every college and university in America has a public statement or mission on its website or in its literature declaring a commitment to diversity, equity, and inclusion, a public commitment unheard of sixty years ago. There are "signs" the knife has been removed. Nevertheless, the debate lies in whether the statements are merely statements, ideals remain ideal, or whether they have been (or are trying to be) implemented, whether college and university administrators and faculty are truly devoted to diversity, or whether their public commitments simply pay lip service to the order of the day.

There are without question new racial ideals, but some of those new ideals have been used to justify racism against Black people since 1973. Ideals are rhetoric. The rhetorical tools that students forced onto the academy to pull out the knife have been used to keep it in higher

© The Author(s), under exclusive license to Springer Nature
Switzerland AG 2025
I. X. Kendi, *The Black Campus Movement*, Contemporary Black
History, https://doi.org/10.1007/978-3-031-37394-7

education. The Black Campus Movement created new contradictions in the racial constitution of higher education—the use of new ideals, supposedly to eliminate the old, to maintain the old.

We live in an era in which pleas of (reverse) racism are used to substantiate racism, as in the justification for the US Supreme Court effectively banning affirmative action in June 2023. Integration segregates. The rhetoric of color blindness veils racism. The Civil Rights Act and the Fourteenth Amendment are being used to extinguish Black rights on campuses. Standardized testing standardizes the class and race of students.[2] Black college athletes generate billions for historically White universities, while the HBCUs that some of these athletes socialize at flounder financially. The racist claims that an institution must lower its standards to draw Black students and faculty remain popular mythology. The titled champions of diversity sometimes limit diversity. Some Black members of boards of trustees at HBCUs have become as assimilationist and accommodationist as the White trustees they replaced. White cries of racism maintain White privilege. Some Americans classify HBCUs as inferior based on false claims and demean HBCUs for complications that regularly occur at similarly funded HWCUs. Assimilationist ideas still fuel remnants of the moralized contraption. The professed standardization of inclusion excludes. Assimilationist curricula mask racist ideas. Grassroots altruism veils ladder altruism.

These contradictions—this *egalitarian exclusion*—appeared during the movement. Most of the campus activism of Black students since the Black Campus Movement has been devoted to defending the gains of the movement and fighting the new contradictions that surfaced during the movement. While White students were members of exclusive groups, barring or limiting African Americans, White students criticized the racial makeup of the BSUs in the late 1960s, calling them racist, separatist, and forms of reverse racism. White students at Dickinson called the Afro-American Organization (AAO) racist and segregationist when it formed in 1967. Mike Floyd, AAO prime minister, replied, "When we organize ourselves, when we direct our actions towards racism, it is a defense mechanism."[3]

When White organizations desegregated and welcomed a handful of African Americans, Black organizations had no reason to exist and certainly no reason to form, the argument went (and continues to go). Black organizing restrictions also operated at HBCUs in the late 1960s and early 1970s. As soon as HBCUs started transforming into institutions geared toward the development (as opposed to the submission) of African

America, racist Americans questioned their need to exist, since HWCUs had desegregated. These questions (and outright calls for their destruction) still occur even while the majority of American colleges and universities remain predominantly White. Existential critiques of predominantly Black institutions, specifically those that are struggling financially, have been constant.

During the movement, one of the major rearguard actions of HBCU activists was their defense of HBCUs. Threats of mergers and closures were steady in the early 1970s (and continue today). Believing that North Carolina Governor Bob Scott's proposal to merge all state institutions under one centralized board could lead to the phasing out of the five public HBCUs, more than five thousand Black students met at Shaw on October 25, 1971. They marched to the state capitol, where they gave passionate pleas to "Save Black Schools." Students Organized for Black Unity spearheaded this defense, preparing a report earlier in the year on the "crisis" with the heading "Save Black Schools." The creation of a centralized board in Arkansas that year also sparked a capitol invasion, specifically by students from Arkansas A&M. SGA president Woodson Walker argued that other state institutions were just as White as his college was Black, but they were not in the hot seat. Depriving students of voices "in the future of AA&M is an unethical and insidious act that demonstrates aggression against the welfare of Black people in this state," Walker wrote in a letter to Arkansas Governor Dale Bumpers. Students in the "Save Black Schools" struggle contended that the inclusion of HBCUs in centralized state systems controlled mainly by White people may have led to more forms of equality between White and Black public institutions but at the same time stripped any Black power that did exist over HBCUs. This egalitarian exclusion of HBCUs within state systems endures to this day.[4]

At HWCUs, egalitarian exclusion is the prohibition or limiting of people of color, their authority, or antiracist initiatives using derivatives of "equality" or "reverse racism" or "race neutral" as justifications. Egalitarian exclusion first rose to prominence in the spring of 1969 when the federal government threatened to pull funding from institutions that agreed to some demands of Black students. In order not to violate the "compliance requirements of Title VI of the Civil Rights Act of 1964," HEW ordered that housing, social activity spaces, and Black Studies units "must be available to all students without regard to race" and that assignments must be made "in a nondiscriminatory manner." Presidents used this reasoning to reject demands, even when student activists planned to allow non-Black students into the units they were demanding. For instance, UNC Chapel Hill Chancellor J. Carlyle Sitterson responded to the Black Student Movement's demands in late January 1969, saying, "the University cannot, in policy or in practice, provide unique treatment for any single race, color, or creed; to do so would be a step backward." In reaction, the seemingly multiracial student and faculty New University Conference at Chapel Hill argued that "discrimination is a meaningless term unless one considers the intention and results of discriminatory practices. Discrimination that results in the subordination of one group to another is a far different thing from discrimination that leads to the equality of all people." Meanwhile, Black Student Movement chairman Preston Dobbins announced that he hoped "Sitterson is not foolish enough to think that this is the end of the line." It was not. On February 21, 1969, about thirty-five Black students marched across campus chanting, "We're going to burn this place down."[5]

Inequities and injustices have been apparent and a problem in higher education and beyond. But some Black student demands to reduce or eliminate the inequity or injustice have been classified as "racist." The intent of those who opposed Black student demands—in the name of "equality"—was not to produce equity and justice but to preserve inequality.

The use of egalitarian exclusion came to a head in 1978, after five years of defensive Black student activism to resist cuts to their programs at schools such as Macalester College in Minnesota, the University of Michigan, Harvard, UC Santa Barbara, and the University of Alabama. Allan Bakke believed that a special admissions program that set aside sixteen seats for students of color at the UC Davis medical school violated his civil rights when he was denied admission. He appealed to the courts. In 1978, the US Supreme Court mandated the thirty-seven-year-old White male's admission to UC Davis, ruling in *University of California Regents v. Bakke* that affirmative action can be used as one of many factors to achieve diversity. The court ruled the medical school was being racist toward White people because it disqualified them from sixteen seats due only to their race. The court deemed this "quota" unconstitutional under the Equal Protection Clause of the Fourteenth Amendment. The court ignored—and still ignores—the other admissions metrics that gave (and give) preferential treatment to White students. The court severely weakened the legality of affirmative action to heal past and present manifestations of racism.[6]

Many Black students, particularly those studying law, did not need to have the long-term effects of the *Bakke* decision explained. They were livid, rising up around the nation. They often perceived the ruling as an "attack on" their "civil rights," as a poster shouted from a demonstration organized by the BSU at Roosevelt in 1978. Even before the ruling, on April 15, 1978, upwards of 30,000 mostly Black students from along the Eastern Seaboard marched down Pennsylvania Avenue in Washington, DC, chanting, "We won't go back. Send Bakke back!" The DC coordinator of the demonstration was Jimmy Garrett, who organized the first BSU at San Francisco State in 1966 and at the time taught political science at Howard. He gave a thrilling speech. "We said no to racism. We said no to sexism. We said no to Carter. We said no to those eight old White men on the Supreme Court." Carrier Fairley, a student at Rutgers University-Newark, asked the press, "How can there be reverse discrimination when minorities aren't free now? That (Bakke) thing is crazy."[7]

According to Mary Frances Berry, who served as the assistant secretary of education from 1977 to 1980 in the Carter administration, the climate had shifted by the late 1970s. The "reaction" came from "everywhere, the backlash against the progress that had been made" with "rationales for why nothing more needed to be done." These rationales for nothing or for equality or to reverse "reverse racism" amplified in the 1980s and eventually became standardized by the end of the century. The professed standardization of inclusion now too often excludes antiracist policymakers from instituting antiracist programs, the primary way to eliminate past (not to mention present) inequities.[8]

Black student activists have continued to defend the gains of the movement from this progression of racism. At the same time, as the movement recedes ever more into the past, the avowals of Black student apathy have grown louder. And yet, generating a new social movement usually necessitates a consciousness of the prevailing conditions. Twenty-first-century higher educational racism seems to be largely unknown to many students, largely unknown to many members of campus communities. In addition, compared to students in the Long Black Student Movement, Black students seem to be more elitist, more fearful (coming after 1960s repression and growing up in a carceral state), and more imbued with a sense of freedom, since they do not see "Whites only" signs. Many seem to have bought into the notion that there is something progressive, selfless, and antiracist about ladder altruism, the idea their personal success as distant role models generates Black community success. As the movement has faded further into history, so too has the widespread student ideal of grass-roots altruism, the drive to use the campus to build antiracist community programs and servant-leaders.

The pre-Black Campus Movement moralized contraption seems to have been refashioned into the operation of the "familial environment," a principal element of the twenty-first century HBCU brand. Is this "familial environment" due to a genuine concern among administrators and professors who want to provide a home away from home? Or is it (also) a result of a racist paternalism from the pre-Black Campus Movement idea that Black students need extra help, care, and supervision? Moreover, quite a few HBCUs still do not have co-ed dormitories or cross-gender room visitation for first-year students, and some schools still try to regulate more than the academic lives of their students. Years ago, Hampton turned students away from various functions for inappropriate dress and prohibits "at all times ... except in the privacy of the student's living quarters ... do-rags, stocking caps, skull caps and bandanas." This, and other elements of the dress code, "is based on the theory that learning to use socially acceptable manners" is a critical factor "in the total educational process."[9]

As some HBCUs still attempt to moralize and civilize their students into "socially acceptable manners," diversity workers have become staples at HWCUs. And yet, these diversity workers occupy staff or administrative posts, sometimes close to (and only reporting to) presidents. Thus, sometimes it is in their self-interest to diffuse the very campus activism that once brought measurable diversity to their institution. Black students and higher education have nevertheless given diverse workers the keys to the movement during the last fifty years. Some diversity officers have boldly challenged their institutions over the years, usually confident that antiracist students will protest if they are dismissed. Most try to toe a treacherous line, keeping antiracist students *and* racist administrators pleased with their work. However, some do not have (and do not desire) student support and find backing from the very campus officials who do not support curricula, programs, and the campus community reflecting the physical, cultural, and ideological diversity of the regions, states, or national spaces from which colleges draw students. They can quickly picture the exodus of White alumni funding, students, and capital. Therefore, some diversity officers are administrators performing administrative duties, representing the interests of the college or university, and defending it against charges of racism, while occasionally ruffling feathers with serious questions and programs.[10]

At the same time, blame cannot be placed solely on diversity workers any more than it can be placed on politicians for catering to benefactors to fund their reelection bids. Ridicule needs to be directed at the structure that caused their paradoxical position. Many diversity workers are doing the best they can in their positional anomaly, one that Black students did not envision when they demanded the hiring these administrators and staff, some of whom were former Black campus activists. It is the responsibility of the students (and faculty and administrators) to create a political atmosphere that empowers diversity officers with the freedom to build a truly antiracist college. This is what occurred when diversity officers were first hired at HWCUs during the Black Campus Movement.

Progress is vibrant at HBCUs in the twentieth-first century. While some remain havens for Black subordination, and many are toiling to stay afloat, quite a few are progressive sites of innovative, socially responsible, concerned learning, magnificent Black cultural production, and relevant, didactic, and antiracist scholarship with talented faculty, administrators, and students who constantly and consciously turn down HWCUs for HBCUs. Amid the criticism, many students have a fertile love for HBCUs, growing from enriching social, cultural, academic, and political experiences. In addition, at HBCUs and HWCUs, some meaningful diversity has emerged in terms of nationwide undergraduate Black enrollment. After doubling during the movement, between 1976 and 2021, Black undergraduate enrollment rose from 943,000 to 1.9 million, and the share of the overall enrollment increased from 10 to 12.3 percent (13 percent for graduate schools in 2021). Still, too many African Americans are being herded into lesser resourced colleges and universities, and for-profit institutions. The share of Black foreign-born bachelor's degree holders is growing faster than the share of Black US-born bachelor's degree holders. Black students, especially Black women, are underrepresented among bachelor's degree recipients in STEM (science, technology, engineering, and mathematics) fields. Additionally, Black STEM majors are more likely than White STEM majors to switch concentrations and to drop out of college altogether. Only a slightly higher percentage (38 percent) of Black eighteen- to twenty-four-year-olds lived in college dorms compared with the total percentage of Black Americans who lived in prison cells (32 percent) in 2021. It is a "mass incarceration" that Michelle Alexander labels "The New Jim Crow."[11]

Black Americans remain woefully underrepresented in the fairly permanent positions—administration and executive leadership (less than 8 percent in 2020) and full-time faculty (7 percent in 2020)—that comprise and guide the car of higher education that temporarily taxis students. The faculty figure, not even three percentage points higher than its mark of 4.4 percent in 1975, is alarming, since faculty diversity leads directly to diverse academic leadership, curricular diversity, and an assortment of ideas and scholarship—all vital to transforming assimilationist curricula into antiracist curricula. The current pace of faculty diversity must be increased 3.5 times for the American professoriate to be consistent with the national racial demographics by 2050. These poor numbers are partly due to the low number of doctorates, as Black Americans and African Americans earned 7.7 percent of all doctorates in 2021. However, the faculty underrepresentation is also the result of White networks that clandestinely exclude Black Americans; and Black positions, specifically in the humanities and social sciences. Many departments at HWCUs have an unofficial quota (or number of positions) for Black faculty (as they do for other underrepresented groups). These are usually the positions that research and teach about the Black experience and are cross-listed with Black Studies programs, a minute percentage of the faculty. It is difficult for Black Americans to receive other positions, such as general Americanist positions, specifically when African American history is not considered American history, specifically when faculties have no pressure to diversify. Thus, these Black positions, forced on the academy by the movement, have created an egalitarian exclusion of Black professors.[12]

Using Black Studies faculty to ostensibly diversify is not a new pattern or policy. In May 1968, the Yale Black Student Alliance organized the nation's first Black Studies symposium, welcoming several scholars to provide a well-defined charge for the academy's newest discipline. The Ford Foundation's McGeorge Bundy, an alumnus of Yale, advised that "the strength of Black Studies was ... in its ability ... to desegregate the faculty and curriculum of traditionally 'White' disciplines." Using this "integrationist rationale," Bundy and the Ford Foundation granted $10 million to support two dozen interdepartmental programs over the next two years. As *The Black Scholar* editor Robert Allen noted, "With hundreds of such programs competing for limited funds, effective control of the future of Black Studies was thereby shifted away from Black scholars and students, and instead ... to the funding agencies—college administrations, government and foundations."[13]

Interdepartmental programs arose with cross-listed professors in conflicting positions, like the diversity officers. Their "traditional" departments and Black Studies programs have often competed for majors, prominence, and resources, while also having some opposing ideas. Black campus activists were aware of this paradox, which compelled them to habitually demand autonomous Black Studies departments. "Cross listing may be better described as academic double cross," said activist Robert McCray at the University of Illinois at Chicago in March 1973. Many Black professors and interdepartmental programs have remarkably toed the line to make lasting contributions to the academy.[14]

At the same time, though, with their doctorates, supervision, tenure, and often institutional legitimacy in the existing disciplines, it is not hard to figure out where some of these cross-listed scholars' academic loyalty lies. More important, students during the movement framed the discipline of Black Studies as different than studying Black people using the assumptions, perspectives, methods, and methodologies that scholars in the existing disciplines had long used to validate Black exclusion and inferiority. Many scholars have managed to carve out a space in the "traditional" disciplines and have used traditional methods to produce scholarship that has exposed assimilationist ideas as racist. This contested Africana Studies sociologist Fabio Rojas terms a "counter center," or a "formalized space for oppositional consciousness." This "counter center" has inspired the carving out of other counter centers that are removing the mask and denormalizing Whiteness (Chicana/o Studies, Latina/o Studies, Native American Studies, Asian Studies, and Whiteness Studies), patriarchy (Women's Studies, Men's Studies, and Gender Studies), and heterosexuality and cisgenderism (Queer Studies). In addition, Black Studies has increasingly engaged in the all-important disciplinary process of reproducing itself through at least nineteen doctoral programs founded in the last thirty-five years, first in 1988 at Temple University by Molefi Kete Asante and most recently at Emory (2023), the University of Pittsburgh (2023), and the University of North Carolina at Chapel Hill (2025).[15]

In the twenty-first century, popular definitions of racism and, more importantly, what proves racism have not caught up with the presentation of racism. In other words, Americans are using racism's spectacles from the 1950s to see racism in the twenty-first century. Americans are looking for racist public statements, and laws and policies with racial language, like those that harnessed the educational mainstream before civil rights and Black Power, to prove racism at a time when racist laws and policies rarely use racial language. White overrepresentation within a campus body of administrators, faculty, students, and staff does prove intent, incompetence, or acceptance. Intention and acceptance are virtually the same when it comes to racism. There is no major difference between a college that intends to keep its faculty below 5 percent Black and a college that accepts a proportion of Black faculty that is perpetually below 5 percent. By acceptance, the college or university chooses not to divert resources to dramatically change that figure, to become truly diverse, to live up to the diversity statement it keeps broadcasting. Astute administrators speak regularly about diversity, say they want to be diverse, say they are trying, but send little money and power in that direction, demonstrating their acceptance.

One of the first to discuss these empty avowals, this egalitarian exclusion, was San Francisco State's Nathan Hare in his groundbreaking Black Studies proposal of April 29, 1968. "It will be an irony of recorded history that 'integration' was used in the second half of this century to hold the Black race down just as segregation was so instigated in the first half." With the second half of that century now recorded history, Hare's irony has become reality. While the ideals put forth by Black students have been somewhat implemented, the ideals of a racist movement have kept the "Black race down" in the name of "equality" and "integration." The contradictions will not be confronted by an imitation of the movement (1965–1972)—the collective Black student thrust of antiracist SGAs, BSUs, BSAs, AASs, of demands, of deadlines, of Black Power shrieks, of strikes, of building takeovers by five or five hundred, of ten-person student meetings, of ten-thousand-student marches, of arrests, of expulsions, of students feeling emboldened by the sights and sounds and words and pulse of their living and deceased heroes. These Black students stood high on the shoulders of the Long Black Student Movement and for eight long years forced higher education to look upward to raised fists, Afros, Pan-African flags, and educational change. Likewise, student activists today and tomorrow must build on the Black Campus Movement.[16]

Acknowledgments

The first edition of this book was five years in the making. During that time numerous people and institutions contributed to its development; they are so numerous that it would be impossible to acknowledge everyone. But I would like to offer a general thanks to all those who aided me in producing this manuscript. I would like to give special thanks to the major funding sources (and the archivists and officials I worked with there): UCLA (Charlotte Brown), Washington University (Sonya Rooney), Michigan Tech University (Julie Blair), Kentucky History Society (Darrell Meadows), Lyndon Baines Johnson Library and Museum (Allen Fisher), Wake Forest University (Megan Mulder), Historical Society of Southern California, SUNY College at Oneonta, and Temple University. Research fellowships were crucial as well, so thank you Deborah Gray White and Donna Murch for allowing me to contribute to the Rutgers Center for Historical Analysis, Vera Davis at the Black Metropolis Research Consortium, and Carolyn Brown for treating me so kindly during my J. Franklin Jameson Fellowship in American History at the Library of Congress, supported by the American Historical Association. Your support and guidance during this process were immeasurable. I must also sincerely thank the hundreds of archivists and librarians who I corresponded with. Your kindness, generosity, and knowledge have eased this trying task of writing a national story. I was told before I started my

© The Author(s), under exclusive license to Springer Nature Switzerland AG 2025
I. X. Kendi, *The Black Campus Movement*, Contemporary Black History, https://doi.org/10.1007/978-3-031-37394-7

research that college archivists are usually a pleasure to work with. I now see why they have that much-deserved reputation.

To my parents and parents-in-law, all of whom were involved in the Black Campus Movement—and my brothers, I am forever grateful for your love, support, compassion, and positive energy. My aunts and uncles: thank you for your constant love and encouragement. My loving and funny cousins, who are full of life and too numerous to name (so I will not, in fear of leaving someone out), thank you for being my role models and for always challenging me and keeping me grounded. To all of my family members and countless friends, thank you for always being there for me and regularly giving me a reason to believe in myself and the goodness of our world. I would like to acknowledge Sadiqa for patiently listening as the ideas for this book came to life. Thank you for our partnership, companionship, understanding, and love throughout this process. I would like to thank Weckea Lilly, H. Zahra Caldwell, Jasmin Young, and Robert Chase for reading portions of the manuscript.

My colleagues at Boston University and former colleagues at SUNY College at Oneonta, University at Albany, University of Florida, and American University—thank you for opening your minds and hearts to my academic and personal companionship. Most especially, I want to thank Heather Sanford and Hunter Moyler for assisting me in revising this book. I would like to express my gratitude to my admirable dissertation adviser, Ama Mazama, for supporting me as it transformed my dissertation into this book. I have been grateful for being able to learn from you—and the venerable Molefi Kete Asante—and receiving critical wisdom and inspiring knowledge from each of you. At Temple University, I would also like to thank Muhammah Ahmad (Maxwell Stanford Jr.), Sonja Peterson-Lewis, Anthony Monteiro, and Kathy Walker for assisting my intellectual development. I must express my thanks to Yohuru Williams for encouraging me and providing essential assistance during this scholarly endeavor. To Peniel Joseph and the late Manning Marable, thank you for allowing me to claim a small part of this tremendous scholarly series and for forging a path for this research.

I would like to thank the former members of the San Francisco State Black Student(s) Union (BSU), who I have had the pleasure of meeting and informally conversing with, including Bernard Stringer, Vern Smith, Benny Stewart, Jimmy Garrett, and Jerry Varnado. To the dozens of other participants with whom I have discussed the Black Campus Movement during my travels and research—thank you for making this book a reality. To the countless more living and passed Black campus activists who thought outside the box and fought inside higher educational boxes that had confined Black students for decades—thank you for carving out a space for me to now be able to tell your story.

Ibram X. Kendi

Abbreviations Used in the Notes

The following abbreviations are used in the notes.

College and University Archives and Special Collections

AAMU Archives	Alabama A&M University Archives, Normal, Alabama
ACSD Archives	Augustana College Archives, Sioux Falls, South Dakota
ADU Archives	Adelphi University Archives, Garden City, New York
ALSU Archives	Alabama State University Archives, Montgomery, Alabama
ASU Archives	Alcorn State University Archives, Alcorn State, Mississippi
AU Archives	American University Archives, Washington, DC
BERC Archives	Berea College Archives, Berea, Kentucky
BOW Archives	Bowdoin College Archives, Brunswick, Maine
BRWU Archives	Brown University Archives, Providence, Rhode Island
BSU Archives	Boise State University Archives, Boise, Idaho
BUTU Archives	Butler University Archives, Indianapolis, Indiana
CARC Archives	The Staubitz Archives, Carthage College, Kenosha, Wisconsin
CATU Archives	American Catholic History Research Center and University Archives, The Catholic University of America, Washington, DC
CHU Archives	Chatham University Archives, Pittsburgh, Pennsylvania
CLAC Archives	The Claremont Colleges Archives, Claremont, California
CLAU Archives	Clarke University Archives, Dubuque, Iowa

(continued)

© The Author(s), under exclusive license to Springer Nature Switzerland AG 2025
I. X. Kendi, *The Black Campus Movement*, Contemporary Black History, https://doi.org/10.1007/978-3-031-37394-7

(continued)

CLEU Archives	Clemson University Archives, Clemson, South Carolina
COC Archives	Colby College Archives, Waterville, Maine
COLU Archives	Colgate University Special Collections and Archives, Hamilton, New York
CSTU Archives	Chicago State University Archives and Special Collections, Chicago, Illinois
CSU Archives	Colorado State University Archives and Special Collections, Fort Collins, Colorado
CSUFRES Archives	California State University, Fresno University Archives, Fresno, California
CSUP Archives	Colorado State University Pueblo Archives, Pueblo, Colorado
CSUSTAN Archives	California State University, Stanislaus Archives, Turlock, California
CU Archives	Creighton University Archives, Omaha, Nebraska
CWPLIU Archives	Archives of C. W. Post Campus of Long Island University, Brookville, New York
CWRU Archives	Case Western Reserve University Archives, Cleveland, Ohio
DARC Archives	Dartmouth College Archives, Hanover, New Hampshire
DEC Archives	Defiance College Archives, Defiance, Ohio
DEPW Archives	DePauw University Archives, Greencastle, Indiana
DICC Archives	Dickinson College Archives, Carlisle, Pennsylvania
DKU Archives	Duke University Archives, Durham, North Carolina
DKU SC	Rare Book, Manuscript, and Special Collections Library, Duke University, Durham, North Carolina
DQU Archives	Duquesne University Archives and Special Collections, Pittsburgh, Pennsylvania
DSU Archives	Delta State University Archives, Cleveland, Mississippi
ECSU Archives	Elizabeth City State University Archive, Elizabeth City, North Carolina
EMU Archives	Eastern Michigan University Archives, Ypsilanti, Michigan
ETSU Archives	East Tennessee State University Archives, Johnson City, Tennessee
F&MC Archives	Franklin & Marshall College Archives and Special Collections, Lancaster, Pennsylvania
FARU Archives	Fairfield University Archives, Fairfield, Connecticut
FASU Archives	Charles W. Chesnutt Library Archives and Special Collections, Fayetteville State University, Fayetteville, North Carolina
FC Archives	Franklin College Archives, Franklin, Indiana
FU SC	Fisk University Special Collections and Archives, Nashville, Tennessee
GAU Archives	Gannon University Archives, Erie, Pennsylvania
GC Archives	Guilford College Archives, Greensboro, North Carolina
GOC Archives	Goucher College Archives, Baltimore, Maryland
GWU SC	George Washington University Special Collections Research Center, Washington, DC
HARU Archives	Harvard University Archives, Cambridge, Massachusetts
HEC Archives	Hendrix College Archives, Conway, Arkansas

(*continued*)

(continued)

HEIU Archives	Heidelberg University Archives, Tiffin, Ohio
IIT Archives	Illinois Institute of Technology Archives, Chicago Illinois
ISU Archives	Iowa State University Archives, Ames, Iowa
IUN Archives	Calumet Regional Archives, Indiana University Northwest, Gary, Indiana
IWESU Archives	Tate Archives and Special Collections, Illinois Wesleyan University, Bloomington, Illinois
JHU Archives	The Ferdinand Hamburger University Archives, The John Hopkins University, Baltimore, Maryland
KAC Archives	Kalamazoo College Archives, Kalamazoo, Michigan
KC Archives	Special Collections and Archives, Knox College, Galesburg, Illinois
KSU Archives	Kentucky State University, Frankfort, Kentucky
KUP Archives	Kutztown University of Pennsylvania Archives and Special Collections, Kutztown, Pennsylvania
LAFC Archives	Lafayette College Special Collections and Archives, Easton, Pennsylvania
LAWU Archives	Lawrence University Archives, Appleton, Wisconsin
LEHIU SC	Lehigh University Special Collections, Bethlehem, Pennsylvania
LGU Archives	Langston University Archives, Langston, Oklahoma
LUTC Archives	Luther College Archives, Decorah, Iowa
MAC Archives	Marietta College Archives, Marietta, Ohio
MARSU Archives	Marshall University Archives, Huntington, West Virginia
MARU Archives	Marquette University Archives, Milwaukee, Wisconsin
MHC Archives	Mount Holyoke College Archives and Special Collections, South Hadley, Massachusetts
MIDC Archives	Middlebury College Archives, Middlebury, Vermont
MILLC Archives	Millsaps College Archives, Jackson, Mississippi
MITU Archives	Michigan Technological University Archives, Houghton, Michigan
MMC Archives	Marymount Manhattan College Archives, New York, New York
MONC Archives	Monmouth College Archive, Monmouth, Illinois
MORC Archives	Morningside College Archives, Sioux City, Iowa
MSSU Archives	Mississippi State University Archives, Mississippi State, Mississippi
MSU Archives	Michigan State University Archives and Historical Collections, East Lansing, Michigan
NATU Archives	North Carolina A&T State University Archives, Greensboro, North Carolina
NCCU Archives	North Carolina Central University Archives and Records, Durham, North Carolina
NCSU Archives	North Carolina State University Archives, Raleigh, North Carolina
NEIU Archives	Northeastern Illinois University Archives, Chicago, Illinois

(*continued*)

(continued)

NIAU Archives	University of Northern Iowa Special Collections and University Archives, Cedar Falls, Iowa
NMSU Archives	Hobson-Huntsinger University Archives, New Mexico State University, Las Cruces, New Mexico
NMU Archives	Northern Michigan University Archives, Marquette, Michigan
NOWU Archives	Northwestern University Archives, Evanston, Illinois
OC Archives	Occidental College Archives, Los Angeles, California
OSU Archives	Oregon State University Archives, Corvallis, Oregon
OTTU Archives	Ottawa University Archives and Collections, Ottawa, Kansas
PC Archives	Special and Archival Collections, Providence College, Providence, Rhode Island
PSU Archives	Pittsburg State University Archives, Pittsburg, Kansas
ROSC Archives	Rosemont College Archives, Bryn Mawr, Pennsylvania
ROSU Archives	Roosevelt University Archives, Chicago, Illinois
RPI Archives	Rensselaer Polytechnic Institute Archives and Special Collections, Troy, New York
RWU Archives	Roger Williams University Archives, Bristol, Rhode Island
SAPC Archives	St. Andrews Presbyterian College Archives, Laurinburg, North Carolina
SIUC SC	Southern Illinois University Carbondale Special Collections Research Center, Carbondale, Illinois
SJU Archives	Saint John's University Archives, Collegeville, Minnesota
SKIC Archives	Skidmore College Archives, Saratoga Springs, New York
SORU Archives	Southern Oregon University Archives, Ashland, Oregon
SPC Archives	Saint Peter's College Archives, Jersey City, New Jersey
SRU Archives	Slippery Rock University Archives, Slippery Rock, Pennsylvania
STAU Archives	The Special Collections and University Archives Department, St. Ambrose University, Davenport, Iowa
STCST Archives	St. Cloud State University Archives, St. Cloud, Minnesota
STCU Archives	St. Catherine University Archives, St. Paul, Minnesota
STOC Archives	St. Olaf College Shaw-Olson Center for College History, Northfield, Minnesota
SUNYB Archives	College Archives, The College at Brockport, State University of New York Archives, Brockport, New York
TCU Archives	Texas Christian University Archives and Historical Collection, Fort Worth, Texas
THIC Archives	Thiel College Archives, Greenville, Pennsylvania
TOGC Archives	Tougaloo College Archives, Tougaloo, Mississippi
TRAN Archives	Transylvania University Archives, Lexington, Kentucky
TRIC Archives	Trinity College Archives, Trinity, Connecticut
TRIU Archives	Trinity University Special Collections and Archives, San Antonio, Texas
TRSU Archives	Truman State University Archives, Kirksville, Missouri
TSTC Archives	H. Council Trenholm State Technical College Archives, Montgomery, Alabama

(*continued*)

(continued)

TUU Archives	Tulane University Archives, New Orleans, Louisiana
UA Archives	University of Alabama Archives, Tuscaloosa, Alabama
UAF Archives	University of Arkansas at Fayetteville Archives, Fayetteville, Arkansas
UAK Archives	Archival Services of University Libraries, The University of Akron, Akron, Ohio
UC Archives	Ursuline College Archives, Pepper Pike, Ohio
UCLA Archives	University of California, Los Angeles Archives, Los Angeles, California
UCSAN Archives	University of Santa Barbara Archives, Santa Barbara, California
UDAY Archives	University of Dayton Archives, Dayton, Ohio
UGA Archives	University of Georgia Archives, Athens, Georgia
UHOU Archives	University of Houston Archives, Houston, Texas
UIA Archives	The University of Iowa Archives, Iowa City, Iowa
UIC Archives	University of Illinois at Chicago Archives, Chicago, Illinois
UKS Archives	University of Kansas Archives, Lawrence, Kansas
UMAD Archives	University of Massachusetts Dartmouth Archives and Special Collections, North Dartmouth, Massachusetts
UMES Archives	University of Maryland Eastern Shore Archives, Princess Anne, Maryland
UMSTL Archives	University of Missouri–St. Louis University Archives, St. Louis, Missouri
UMT Archives	The University of Montana Archives and Special Collections, Missoula, Montana
UMU Archives	Robert Herman Carr Historical Room, University of Mount Union, Alliance, Ohio
UMW Archives	University of Mary Washington Archives, Fredericksburg, Virginia
UNAL SC	University of North Alabama Special Collections, Florence, Alabama
UNC Archives	The University of North Carolina at Chapel Hill Archives, Manuscripts Department, Chapel Hill, North Carolina
UNCC Archives	The University of North Carolina at Charlotte Archives, Charlotte, North Carolina
UND Archives	The University of North Dakota Archives, Grand Forks, North Dakota
UO Archives	University of Oregon Archives, Eugene, Oregon
UP Archives	University of the Pacific Archives, Stockton, California
USA Archives	University of South Alabama Archives, Mobile, Alabama
USF Archives	University of San Francisco Archives, San Francisco, California
UTA Archives	University of Texas at Arlington Archives, Arlington, Texas
UTC Archives	Utica College Archives, Utica, New York
UTNK Archives	University of Tennessee Archives, Knoxville, Tennessee
UTXA Archives	University of Texas at Austin Archives, Briscoe Center for American History, Austin, Texas
UUTAH Archives	University of Utah University Archives, Salt Lake City, Utah
UVA SP	Albert and Shirley Small Special Collections Library, University of Virginia, Charlottesville, Virginia

(*continued*)

(continued)

UWM Archives	University of Wisconsin at Milwaukee Archives Department, Milwaukee, Wisconsin
UWOSH Archives	University of Wisconsin at Oshkosh Archives, Oshkosh, Wisconsin
VC Archives	The Catherine Pelton Durrell '25 Archives and Special Collections Library, Vassar College, Poughkeepsie, New York
VTU Archives	Virginia Polytechnic Institute and State University Archives, Blacksburg, Virginia
VU Archives	Vanderbilt University Archives, Nashville, Tennessee
WARC Archives	Wartburg College Archives, Waverly, Iowa
WC Archives	Wellesley College Archives, Wellesley, Massachusetts
WCSU Archives	Western Connecticut State University Archives, Danbury, Connecticut
WEBU Archives	Webster University Archives, St. Louis, Missouri
WFU Archives	Wake Forest University, Winston-Salem, North Carolina
WIC Archives	Wilmington College Archives, Wilmington, Ohio
WILC Archives	Wilson College C. Elizabeth Boyd '33 Archives, Chambersburg, Pennsylvania
WPU Archives	Wilcox Library Archives, William Penn University, Oskaloosa, Iowa
WSSU Archives	Winston-Salem State University Archives, Winston-Salem, North Carolina
WU Archives	Washington University Archives, St. Louis, Missouri
XUO Archives	Xavier University Archives, Cincinnati, Ohio

RESEARCH VENUES

CEMA	California Ethnic and Multicultural Archives, Department of Special Collections, University of California at Santa Barbara, Santa Barbara, California
CESKAA	The Center of Excellence for the Study of African Americans, Blazer Library, Kentucky State University, Frankfort, Kentucky
KHS	Special Collections and Archives, Kentucky Historical Society, Frankfort, Kentucky
LBJL	Lyndon Baines Johnson Library and Museum, Austin, Texas
PALL	Paley Library, Temple University, Philadelphia, Pennsylvania
SCHBG	Schomburg Center for Research in Black Culture, New York Public Library, New York, New York
SHC	Southern Historical Collection, The Wilson Library, The University of North Carolina at Chapel Hill, Chapel Hill, North Carolina
WTXC	The Dr. Ralph R. Chase West Texas Collection, Porter Henderson Library, Angelo State University, San Angelo, Texas

CAMPUS PERIODICALS (WITH ABBREVIATIONS
OF INSTITUTIONAL ARCHIVES)

AH	*Alcorn Herald*, ASU Archives
AJR	*The A&J Register*, NATU Archives
ARR	*The Arrow*, CSUP Archives
AT	*Arkansas Traveler*, UAF Archives
ATN	*Afro-Times Newsletter*, MSSU Archives
BDH	*Brown Daily Herald*, BRWU Archives
BQ	*The Bristol Quill*, RWU Archives
BUTM	*Butler Magazine*, BUTU Archives
BW	*The Brown & White*, LEHIU SC
CC	*College Chips*, LUTC Archives
CE	*Campus Echo*, NCCU Archives
CHO	*Choragos*, MHC Archives
CP	*The College Profile*, HEC Archives
COE	*The Colby Echo*, COC Archives
COR	*College Reporter*, F&MC Archives
CR	*Collegian Reporter*, MORC Archives
CRW	*Crimson-White*, UA Archives
CUR	*Currents*, MMC Archives
CW	*Catherine Wheel*, STCU Archives
DB	*Daily Bruin*, UCLA Archives
DC	*Duke Chronicle*, DKU Archives
DCK	*Dickinsonian*, DICC Archives
DCN	*Defiance Crescent-News*, DEC Archives
DI	*The Daily Iowan*, UIA Archives
DN	*Daily Nexus*, UCSAN Archives
FLU	*Flush*, MITU Archives
GK	*Gannon Knight*, GAU Archives
GUI	*The Guilfordian*, GC Archives
HARD	*Harambee*, DKU Archives
HC	*The Harvard Crimson*, HARU Archives
HEIA	*Heidelberg Alumni*, HEIU Archives
HT	*Hornet Tribune*, ALSU Archives
KEY	*The Keystone*, KUP Archives
KT	*The Kentucky Thorobred*, KSU Archives
LA	*Lawrence Alumnus*, LAWU Archives
LAFA	*Lafayette Alumnus*, LAFC Archives
LUG	*The Langston University Gazette*, LGU Archives
MM	*The Manitou Messenger*, STOC Archives
MNL	*Middlebury News Letter*, MIDC Archives
MTL	*Michigan Tech Lode*, MITU Archives
NI	*Normal Index*, AAMU Archives
NIA	*Northern Iowan*, NIAU Archives

(*continued*)

(continued)

NS	*The Northwest Student*, IUN Archives
OGB	*Old Gold and Black*, WFU Archives
OTTC	*The Ottawa Campus*, OTTU Archives
PP	*Post Pioneer*, CWPLIU Archives
PSAC	*The Paper SAC*, STAU Archives
RA	*Ra* (Claremont Colleges Black Studies newspaper), CLAC Archives
RB	*The Red and Black*, UGA Archives
RP	*The Ram Page*, WTXC
RU	*Round Up*, NMSU Archives
SFF	*The Skiff*, TCU Archives
STA	*The Stag*, FARU Archives
STY	*The Stylus*, SUNYB Archives
TA	*The Arbiter*, BSU Archives
TAN	*Tangerine*, UTC Archives
TAR	*The Arrow*, CARC Archives
TB	*The Billboard*, WILC Archives
TBC	*The Black Collegian*, WU Archives
TC	*The Chronicle*, TOGC Archives
TCC	*The College Chronicle*, STCST Archives
TCE	*The Creightonian*, CU Archives
TCO	*The Cowl*, PC Archives
TCOL	*The Collegio*, PSU Archives
TCOR	*The Courier*, CLAU Archives
TDAR	*The Dartmouth*, DARC Archives
TDC	*The Daily Cougar*, UHOU Archives
TDEL	*The Delphian*, ADU Archives
TDP	*The DePauw*, DEPW Archives
TDS	*The Dakota Student*, UND Archives
TDT	*The Daily Texan*, UTXA Archives
TE	*The Eagle*, AU Archives
TECH	*The Technician*, NCSU Archives
TELB	*Tel-Buch* (yearbook), UAK Archives
TEM	*Tempo*, CSTU Archives
TF	*The Franklin*, FC Archives
TFA	*The Flor-Ala*, UNAL SC
TFOG	*The Foghorn*, USF Archives
THAT	*The Hatchet*, GWU SC
TIN	*The Index*, TRSU Archives
TL	*The Lance*, SAPC Archives
TLAF	*The Lafayette*, LAFC Archives
TMAR	*The Marcolian*, MAC Archives
TMIR	*The Mirror*, ACSD Archives
TMN	*The Miscellany News*, VC Archives
TN	*Technology News*, IIT Archives
TNA	*The News Argus*, WSSU Archives
TO	*The Occidental*, OC Archives

(*continued*)

(continued)

TOW	*Tower*, CATU Archives
TPAR	*The Parthenon*, MARSU Archives
TPC	*The Penn Chronicle*, WPU Archives
TQ	*The Quill*, UC Archives
TRA	*The Rambler*, TRAN Archives
TRAM	*The Rambler*, ROSC Archives
TREF	*The Reflector*, MSSU Archives
TRI	*Trinitonian*, TRIU Archives
TS	*The Signal*, UTXA Archives
TSL	*The Student Life* (Pomona College student newspaper), CLAC Archives
TT	*Trinity Tripod*, TRIC Archives
TTH	*The Thielensian*, THIC Archives
TTIG	*The Tiger*, CLEU Archives
TTO	*The Torch*, ROSU Archives
TV	*The Voice*, FASU Archives
VA	*Vanguard*, USA Archives
WAT	*Watani*, UMT Archives
WEB	*The Web*, WEBU Archives
WEL	*Wellesley* (magazine), WC Archives
WIT	*Witness*, WIC Archives
WT	*The Wartburg Trumpet*, WARC Archives
XUN	*Xavier University News*, XUO Archives

COMMUNITY PERIODICALS

AA	*Afro-American*, Baltimore, Maryland, ProQuest Historical Newspapers (hereafter PHN)
AR	*The Alliance Review*, Alliance, Ohio
ADW	*Atlanta Daily World*, Atlanta, Georgia, PHN
BG	*Boston Globe*, Boston, Massachusetts, PHN
BSB	*Bay State Banner*, Boston, Massachusetts, ProQuest Ethnic NewsWatch: A History (hereafter ENWH)
CD	*The Chicago Defender*, Chicago, Illinois, PHN
CH	*Clarion Herald*, New Orleans, Louisiana
CHE	*The Chronicle of Higher Education*, Washington, DC
CJ	*The Courier-Journal*, Louisville, Kentucky
CRP	*The Cedar Rapids Gazette*, Cedar Rapids, Iowa
CT	*Chicago Tribune*, Chicago, Illinois, PHN
EB	*Ebony*, Chicago, Illinois
FPM	*Fish Piss Magazine*, Montreal, Quebec
JG	*The Journal & Guide*, Norfolk, Virginia
LK	*Look*, Des Moines, Iowa
NBH	*The New Britain Herald*, New Britain, Connecticut
NE	*Newsweek*, New York, New York

(*continued*)

(continued)

NYAN	*New York Amsterdam News*, New York, New York, PHN
NYE	*New York Evangelist*, New York, New York, Pro-Quest American Periodical Series Online (hereafter PAPS)
NYOC	*New York Observer and Chronicle*, New York, New York, PAPS
NYT	*New York Times*, New York, New York, PHN
NYTM	*New York Times Magazine*, New York, New York, PHN
OP	*The Oakland Post*, Oakland, California, ENWH
PC	*Pittsburgh Courier*, Pittsburgh, Pennsylvania, PHN
PT	*Philadelphia Tribune*, Philadelphia, Pennsylvania, PHN
SFC	*San Francisco Chronicle*, San Francisco, California
SNS	*Springfield News-Sun*, Springfield, Ohio
SO	*The Sacramento Observer*, Sacramento, California, ENWH
SOBUN	*SOBU Newsletter*, Greensboro, North Carolina, SOBU Publications, Box 2, folder: newsletters, ECSU Archives
SR	*Sun Reporter*, San Francisco, California, ENWH
ST	*The Seattle Times*, Seattle, Washington
TB	*The Blade*, Toledo, Ohio
TBS	*The Baltimore Sun*, Baltimore, Maryland, PHN
TC	*The Crisis*, New York, New York
TH	*The Herald*, Rock Hill, South Carolina
TL	*The Liberator*, Boston, Massachusetts, PAPS
TMG	*The Guardian*, London, England, PHN
TN	*The Nation*, New York, New York
TNR	*The New Republic*, Washington, DC
TP	*The Philanthropist*, Cincinnati, Ohio, PAPS
TSD	*Tri-State Defender*, Memphis, Tennessee, ENWH
TWP	*The Washington Post*, Washington, DC, PHN
WSJ	*The Wall Street Journal*, New York, New York, PHN
WT	*Watertown Times*, Watertown, Wisconsin

NOTES

INTRODUCTION

1. "Troops Sent to U. of Wisconsin," *NYT*, February 13, 1969; Calvin B. T. Lee, *The Campus Scene, 1900–1970: Changing Styles in Undergraduate Life* (New York: McKay, 1970), pp. 147–148; Judith Lyons and Morgan Lyons, "Black Student Power," in *Academic Supermarkets: A Critical Case Study of a Multiversity* (San Francisco: Jossey-Bass, 1971), pp. 303–321; "Troops Use Tear Gas at U. of Wisconsin," *NYT*, February 14, 1969.
2. Rodney Stark, "Protest + Police = Riot," in *Black Power and Student Rebellion*, eds. James McEvoy and Abraham Miller (Belmont, CA: Wadsworth, 1969), p. 170; "BSA Asks Black Studies," *TTO*, February 17, 1969, ROSU Archives; Joy Ann Williamson, *Black Power on Campus: The University of Illinois, 1965–75* (Urbana, IL: University of Illinois Press, 2003), pp. 94–97.
3. Allan Kornberg and Joel Smith, "'It Ain't Over Yet': Activism in a Southern University," in *Black Power and Student Rebellion*, pp. 107–109.
4. Conrad M. Dyer, "Protest and the Politics of Open Admissions: The Impact of the Black and Puerto Rican Students' Community (of City College)" (PhD. diss., City University of New York, 1990), pp. 105–110; "Vandals Attack C.C.N.Y. Buildings," *NYT*, February 18, 1969.

© The Author(s), under exclusive license to Springer Nature Switzerland AG 2025
I. X. Kendi, *The Black Campus Movement*, Contemporary Black History, https://doi.org/10.1007/978-3-031-37394-7

5. Joy Ann Williamson, *Radicalizing the Ebony Tower: Black Colleges and the Black Freedom Struggle in Mississippi* (New York: Teachers College Press, 2008), pp. 140–141; Daniel Harris and Joseph Honcharik, *Staff Study of Campus Riots and Disorders, October 1967–May 1969* (Washington, DC: U.S. Government Printing Office, 1969), p. 25.

6. I did not find any record of Black campus activism at any of the institutions in Alaska.

7. Darlene Clark Hine, William Hine, and Stanley Harrold note that "some observers describe the period of activism between 1968 and 1975 as the 'second phase' of the black students' movement." See Darlene Clark Hine, William C. Hine, and Stanley Harrold, *The African-American Odyssey, Combined Volume* (Upper Saddle River, NJ: Prentice Hall, 2008), p. 625.

8. Ibram H. Rogers, "The Black Campus Movement: The Case for a New Historiography," *The Sixties: A Journal of History, Politics and Culture* 4 (December 2011), pp. 169–184; Larry Neal, "The Black Arts Movement," *The Drama Review: TDR*, 12 (Summer 1968), pp. 29–39; James H. Cone, *Risks of Faith: The Emergence of a Black Theology of Liberation, 1968–1998* (Boston, 1999); Kimberly Springer, *Living for the Revolution: Black Feminist Organizations, 1968–1980* (Durham, NC: Duke University Press, 2005), p. 8. In addition, quite a few scholars have already described this struggle as a movement. See William W. Sales Jr., *From Civil Rights to Black Liberation: Malcolm X and the Organization of Afro-American Unity* (Boston: South End Press, 1994), p. 169; Manning Marable, *How Capitalism Underdeveloped Black America: Problems in Race, Political Economy, and Society* (Boston: South End Press, 1983), p. 218; William L. Van Deburg, *New Day in Babylon: The Black Power Movement and American Culture, 1965–1975* (Chicago: University of Chicago Press, 1992), p. 71. For the *NYT* citation, see "The Campus Revolutions: One Is Black, One White," *NYT*, May 12, 1969. For the scholars who distinguished between the two racial movements, see Andrew Barlow, "The Student Movement of the 1960s and the Politics of Race," *Journal of Ethnic Studies* 19 (Fall 1991), p. 1; John Erlich and Susan Erlich, "Introduction," in *Student Power, Participation and Revolution*, eds. John Erlich and Susan Erlich (New York: Association Press, 1971), p. 12.

9. There were interrelated, age-old gender, class, and sexual aspects of the constitution of higher education, which the New Left movements

probably changed as well; these changes will not be intimately cov-
ered in this study. For example, capitalist and patriarchal ideas have
also been presented and masked as normal.

10. There was a lot of black campus activism during the BCM at urban
community colleges, activism that is not explored in this work. For
Black Power marginalization, see Ibram Kendi, "The Marginalization
of the Black Campus Movement," *Journal of Social History* 42 (Fall
2008), pp. 175–182. For examples of marginalization in studies on
"student" activism, see David C. Nichols, *Perspectives on Campus
Tensions: Papers Prepared for the Special Committee on Campus
Tensions* (Washington, DC: American Council of Education, 1970);
Gerald J. De Groot, *Student Protest: The Sixties and After* (Reading,
MA: Addison Wesley Publishing, 1998); Philip G. Altbach, Robert
S. Laufer, and Sheila McVey, ed., *Academic Supermarkets*; Lee, *The
Campus Scene*; Elvin Abeles, *The Student and the University: A
Background Book on the Campus Revolt* (New York: Parents' Magazine
Press, 1969); Roger Rapoport and Laurence J. Kirshbaum, *Is the
Library Burning?* (New York: Random House, 1969). For these cam-
pus studies, see Williamson, *Black Power on Campus*; Wayne Glasker,
*Black Students in the Ivory Tower: African American Student Activism
at the University of Pennsylvania, 1967–1990* (Amherst, MA:
University of Massachusetts, 2002); Stefan M. Bradley, *Harlem vs.
Columbia University: Black Student Power in the Late 1960s* (Urbana,
IL: University of Illinois Press, 2009); Richard P. McCormick, *The
Black Student Protest Movement at Rutgers* (New Brunswick, NJ:
Rutgers University Press, 1990); Donald Alexander Downs, *Cornell
'69: Liberalism and the Crisis of the American University* (Ithaca, NY:
Cornell University Press, 1999); William H. Exum, *Paradoxes of
Protest: Black Student Activism in a White University* (Philadelphia:
Temple University Press, 1985; Dikran Karagueuzian, *Blow It Up!:
The Black Student Revolt at San Francisco State and the Emergence of
Dr. Hayakawa* (Boston: Gambit, 1971); Jack Bass and Jack Nelson,
The Orangeburg Massacre (Macon, GA: Mercer, 1984); Tim Spofford,
Lynch Street: The May 1970 Slayings at Jackson State College (Kent,
OH: Kent State University Press, 1988). There are merely two books
that include national examinations of black student activism in this
period at HWCUs—a monograph and an anthology, both published
during the movement. See Harry Edwards, *Black Students* (New

York: Free Press, 1970); James McEvoy and Abraham Miller, eds., *Black Power and Student Rebellion*.

11. For a recent text on activism in the late 1960s at HBCUs, see Jeffrey Alan Turner, *Sitting In and Speaking Out: Student Movements in the American South, 1960–1970* (Athens, GA: University of Georgia Press, 2010). For a few of the many recent studies on Black Power women, see Bettye Collier-Thomas and V. P. Franklin, eds., *Sisters in the Struggle: African American Women in the Civil Rights—Black Power Movement* (New York: New York University Press, 2001); Dayo F. Gore, Jeanne Theoharis, and Komozi Woodard, eds., *Want to Start a Revolution?: Radical Women in the Black Freedom Struggle* (New York: New York University Press, 2009); Rhonda Y. Williams, "Black Women and Black Power," *OAH Magazine of History*, 22 (July 2008), pp. 22–26; Rhonda Y. Williams, "'We're Tired of Being Treated Like Dogs': Poor Women and Power Politics in Black Baltimore," *The Black Scholar*, 31 (Fall 2001), pp. 31–34.

12. For scholars who claimed that the movement began in 1967 or 1968, see Robert Allen, *Black Awakening in Capitalist America: An Analytical History* (Garden City, NY: Doubleday, 1969), pp. 101–102, 216–221; Fabio Rojas, "Social Movement Tactics, Organization Change and the Spread of African-American Studies," *Social Forces* 84 (2006), pp. 2147–2166; John H. Bunzel, "Black Studies at San Francisco State," *The Public Interest* 13 (Fall 1968), pp. 22–38; Lawrence Crouchett, "Early Black Studies Movements," *Journal of Black Studies* 2 (December 1971), pp. 189–200; William H. Exum, *Paradoxes of Protest: Black Student Activism in a White University* (Philadelphia: Temple University Press, 1985), p. 7; Edwards, *Black Students*, pp. 3, 62; Earl Anthony, *The Time of the Furnaces: A Case Study of Black Student Revolt* (New York: Dial Press, 1971), p. 11. For claims that the Orangeburg Massacre and King's death triggered the movement, see (respectively) Hine, Hine, and Harrold, *The African-American Odyssey*, p. 625; Martin Kilson, "The Black Student Militant," *Encounter* 37 (1971), pp. 80–85.

1. An "Island Within": Black Students and Black Higher Education Prior to 1965

1. George James, *Stolen Legacy: Greek Philosophy Is Stolen Egyptian Philosophy* (Trenton, NJ: Africa World Press, 1993); John G. Jackson, *Introduction to African Civilizations* (Secaucus, NJ: Citadel Press, 1997), 21, 215.

2. John Fleming, "Blacks in Higher Education to 1954: A Historical Overview," in *Black Students in Higher Education: Conditions and Experiences in the 1970s*, ed. Gail E. Thomas (Westport, CT: Greenwood Press, 1981), p. 11; Henry N. Drewry and Humphrey Doermann, *Stand and Prosper: Private Black Colleges and Their Students* (Princeton, NJ: Princeton University Press, 2001), p. 32.

3. Joanne Pope Melish, *Disowning Slavery: Gradual Emancipation and "Race" in New England, 1780–1860* (Ithaca, NY: Cornell University Press, 1998), pp. 39–41. Drewry and Doermann, *Stand and Prosper*, p. 32; Peter J. Knapp, *Trinity College in the Twentieth Century: A History* (Hartford, CT: Trustees of Trinity College, 2000), p. 337.

4. Frank Bowles and Frank A. DeCosta, *Between Two Worlds: A Profile of Negro Higher Education* (New York: McGraw-Hill, 1971), p. 13; Carter G. Woodson, *Education of the Negro Prior to 1861: A History of the Education of the Colored People of the United States from the Beginning of Slavery to the Civil War* (Washington, DC: Associated Publishers, 1919), p. 257.

5. Woodson, *Education of the Negro*, pp. 256–260, 290 (first quote); Herbert Aptheker, *Nat Turner's Slave Rebellion* (Mineola, NY: Dover Publications, 2006), pp. 23–24.

6. Emeline Burlingame-Cheney, *The Story of the Life and Work of Oren B. Cheney: Founder and First President of Bates College* (Boston: Morningstar, 1907), p. 32–33 (last quote); Bowles and DeCosta, *Between Two Worlds*, p. 23.

7. Woodson, *Education of the Negro*, pp. 265, 268–269.

8. Ibid., pp. 266–273. See also "Avery College Historical Marker," ExlporePAhistory.com, accessed July 31, 2011, http://explorepahistory.com/hmarker.php?markerId=1-A-37E.

9. Drewry and Doermann, *Stand and Prosper*, p. 33.

10. "Educating Colored Students," *NYOC*, November 15, 1845.

11. Robert Johnson Jr., "The African-American Legacy at Bowdoin" (unpublished manuscript, February 26, 1997), African American Society Records, Box 1, Folder 12, BOWU Archives; William H. Watkins, *The White Architects of Black Education: Ideology and Power in America, 1865–1954* (New York: Teachers College Press, 2001), pp. 18–29; Anthony R. Mayo, "Charles Lewis Reason," *Negro History Bulletin* 5 (June 1942), pp. 212–215; Stephanie Y. Evans, *Black Women in the Ivory Tower, 1850–1954: An Intellectual History* (Gainesville, FL: University Press of Florida, 2007), pp. 22–23.

12. Dorothy Sterling, *The Making of an Afro-American: Martin Robison Delany* (Garden City, NY: Doubleday, 1971), pp. 122–135

13. Ibid.

14. Robert Samuel Fletcher, *A History of Oberlin College*, Vol. 2 (Oberlin, OH: Oberlin College, 1943), pp. 534–535; Ellen N. Lawson, "Sarah Woodson Early: Nineteenth Century Black Nationalist 'Sister,'" *Umoja: A Scholarly Journal of Black Studies* 5 (Summer 1981), pp. 15–26; Christopher J. Lucas, *American Higher Education: A History, Second Edition* (New York: Palgrave Macmillan, 2006), p. 122.

15. James D. Anderson, *The Education of Blacks in the South, 1860–1935* (Chapel Hill, NC: University of North Carolina Press, 1988), p. 5 (AMA quote); W. E. B. Du Bois, *Black Reconstruction in America: An Essay Towards a History of the Part Which Black Folk Played in the Attempt to Reconstruct Democracy in America, 1860–1880* (New York: Atheneum, 1971), p. 123.

16. Lucas, *American Higher Education*, pp. 168–169.

17. Ibid., pp. 165.

18. Anderson, *The Education of Blacks in the South*, p. 34, 39.

19. Lucas, *American Higher Education*, pp.168–169.

20. Drewry and Doermann, *Stand and Prosper*, pp. 58–59.

21. Anderson, *The Education of Blacks in the South*, p. 29–30 (quote).

22. "Maryville College," *NYE*, July 6, 1876; Elisabeth S. Peck, *Berea's First Century: 1855–1955* (Lexington, KY: University of Kentucky Press, 1955), pp. 40–43; Maurice W. Britts, *Blacks on White College Campuses* (Minneapolis, MN: Challenge, 1975), p. 3. When the University of Arkansas was established in 1871, it was theoretically open to all races. But even though the state superintendent of public instruction was black at the time, the attendance of blacks was discouraged until it was written into law two years later. See Robert A. Leflar, *The First 100 Years: Centennial History of the University of*

Arkansas (Fayetteville, AK: University of Arkansas Foundation, 1972), pp. 273–274.

23. Booker T. Washington, *Up From Slavery: An Autobiography* (Garden City, NY: Doubleday, 1963), pp. 30–44; Mark S. Giles, "Special Focus: Dr. Anna Julia Cooper, 1858–1964: Teacher, Scholar, and Timeless Womanist," *The Journal of Negro Education* 75 (Fall 2006), pp. 623–625; Jeanne L. Noble, *The Negro Woman's College Education* (New York: Columbia University, Teachers College, 1956), pp. 22–24; Bowles and DeCosta, *Between Two Worlds*, p. 33.

24. W. E. B. Du Bois, *Dusk of Dawn: An Essay Toward An Autobiography of a Race Concept* (New York: Harcourt, Brace and Company, 1940), pp. 22–24, 32–33, 34–37.

25. Ibid.

26. "Closed Against Negro Students," *CT*, September 15, 1890 (Maryland quote); Ralph Waldo Lloyd, *Maryville College: A History of 150 Years, 1819–1969* (Maryville, TN: Maryville College Press, 1969), p. 200; Peck, *Berea's First Century*, pp. 51–53; Jacqueline Anne Goggin, *Carter G. Woodson: A Life in Black History* (Baton Rouge, LA: Louisiana State University Press, 1993), p. 13; "Notes," *TN*, May 10, 1888; Andrew Baskin, "Berea College and Interracial Education: The First 150 Years, Stages Three and Four," Berea College, April 20, 2020, https://libraryguides.berea.edu/interracial_education_essay.

27. Joy Ann Williamson, *Radicalizing the Ebony Tower: Black Colleges and the Black Freedom Struggle in Mississippi* (New York: Teachers College Press, 2008), pp. 24–26 (Alcorn quote); "Negroes in a Normal School," *NYT*, September 16, 1894 (Council quote); Raymond Wolters, *The New Negro on Campus: Black College Rebellions of the 1920s* (Princeton, NJ: Princeton University Press, 1975), pp. 192–193.

28. W. E. B. Du Bois, "The Talented Tenth," in *Du Bois Writings*, ed. Nathan Huggins (New York: The Library of America, 1986), p. 842; Washington, *Up From Slavery*, p. 161. Also, for his activities concerning civil rights causes, see David H. Jackson, *Booker T. Washington and the Struggle Against White Supremacy: The Southern Educational Tours, 1908–1912* (New York: Palgrave Macmillan, 2008) and *A Chief Lieutenant of the Tuskegee Machine: Charles Banks of Mississippi* (Gainesville, FL: University Press of Florida, 2002).

29. Watkins, *The White Architects of Black Education*, pp. 18–20, 23.

30. Ibid.

2. "WE WERE INVISIBLE": BLACK STUDENTS IN THE TWENTIETH CENTURY

1. Barbara Ransby, *Ella Baker and the Black Freedom Movement: A Radical Democratic Vision* (Chapel Hill, NC: University of North Carolina Press, 2003), pp. 60–61; "Why A Student 'Strike,'" *AA*, February 28, 1925; "Carnegie at Tuskegee," *TWP*, April 6, 1906; "Tuskegee Celebrates its Twenty-Fifth Year," *NYT*, April 5, 1906.
2. Allen B. Ballard, *The Education of Black Folk: The Afro-American Struggle for Knowledge in White America* (New York: Harper & Row, 1973), pp. 23–24.
3. Christopher J. Lucas, *American Higher Education: A History, Second Edition* (New York: Palgrave Macmillan, 2006), p. 181; "Won't Study with Negroes," *NYT*, November 21, 1908; "Medical Students Stir Up Race Issue," *NYT*, January 15, 1911; "University of Michigan," *NYT*, December 15, 1912; "African Americans," in Encyclopedia Brunoniana, ed. Martha Mitchell (Providence, RI: Brown University Library, 1993), http://www.brown.edu/Administration/News_Bureau/Databases/Encyclopedia/search.php?serial=A0080, accessed November 3, 2011; "Textures: Perspectives on African-American History at Butler," *BM*, Fall 2001, BUTU Archives; John R. Anderson, "Impacts of Iowa State University: Its National and International Presence and Its Enduring Legacies," in *A Sesquicentennial History of Iowa State University: Tradition and Transformation*, eds. Dorothy Schwieder and Gretchen Van Houten (Ames, IA: Iowa State University, 2007), p. 310.
4. Pamela Riney-Kehrberg, "Foundations of the People's College: The Early Years of Iowa State," in *A Sesquicentennial History of Iowa State University*, pp. 17–18; Raymond Wolters, *The New Negro on Campus: Black College Rebellions of the 1920s* (Princeton, NJ: Princeton University Press, 1975), pp. 322–323.
5. "Student Snowballed and Stoned, Knifes an Assailant," *PT*, February 21, 1914; "Disarmed Negro students," *TBS*, December 14, 1906.
6. Martin Bauml Duberman, *Paul Robeson* (New York: Ballantine, 1989), pp. 19–23.
7. Lawrence C. Ross Jr., *The Divine Nine: The History of African American Fraternities and Sororities* (New York: Kensington, 2000), pp. 5–7.

8. W. E. B. Du Bois, *The College-Bred Negro American* (Atlanta: Atlanta University Press, 1910).

9. Paula Giddings, *In Search of Sisterhood: Delta Sigma Theta and the Challenge of the Black Sorority Movement* (New York: William Morrow and Company, 1988), pp. 29–30, 43–44.

10. Ross, *The Divine Nine*, pp. 46–48, 102–103, 133–134, 266, 298; Giddings, *In Search of Sisterhood*, pp. 46–53; "Textures," BUTU Archives.

11. Giddings, *In Search of Sisterhood*, pp. 18–19, 21.

12. Fleming, "Blacks in Higher Education to 1954," p. 13; Wolters, *The New Negro on Campus*, p. 257; Joy Ann Williamson, *Radicalizing the Ebony Tower: Black Colleges and the Black Freedom Struggle in Mississippi* (New York: Teachers College Press, 2008), p. 17; Henry N. Drewry and Humphrey Doermann, *Stand and Prosper: Private Black Colleges and Their Students* (Princeton, NJ: Princeton University Press, 2001), pp. 59–60.

13. Langston Hughes, *The Big Sea* (New York: Hill and Wang, 1963), pp. 306–310; Langston Hughes, "Cowards from the Colleges," *TC*, August 1934, pp. 226–228.

14. Frederick Rudolph, *The American College and University: A History* (New York: Vintage Books, 1962), pp. 329–354; George Ruble Woolfolk, *Prairie View: A Study in Public Conscience, 1878–1946* (New York: Pageant Press, 1962), pp. 187, 197; Yolanda L. Watson and Sheila T. Gregory, *Daring to Educate: The Legacy of the Early Spelman College Presidents* (Sterling, VA: Stylus, 2005), p. 92; Williamson, *Radicalizing the Ebony Tower*, p. 27; Drewry and Doermann, *Stand and Prosper*, p. 128.

15. Jeanne L. Noble, *The Negro Woman's College Education* (New York: Columbia University, Teachers College, 1956), pp. 28–30.

16. The information on the NACW is from Linda M. Perkins, "The National Association of College Women: Vanguard of Black Women's Leadership and Education, 1923–1954," *Journal of Education* 172 (September 1990), pp. 65–75.

17. Drewry and Doermann, *Stand and Prosper*, p. 75; Charles S. Johnson, *The Negro College Graduate* (Chapel Hill, NC: University of North Carolina Press, 1938), pp. 10, 13, 20; B. Baldwin Dansby, *A Brief History of Jackson College: A Typical Story of the Survival of Education Among Negroes in the South* (Jackson, MS: Jackson College, 1953), pp. 83–84 (quote).

18. Joe M. Richardson and Maxine D. Jones, *Education for Liberation: The American Missionary Association and African Americans, 1890 to the Civil Rights Movement* (Tuscaloosa, AL: University of Alabama Press, 2009), p. 136; Paul Cooke, "Desegregated of Higher Education the District of Columbia," *The Journal of Negro Education* 27 (Summer 1958), p. 344; Glasker, *Black Students in the Ivory Tower*, pp. 20–21; "Columbia Negro Student Gets Two 'Death' Letters," *TBS*, April 6, 1924; "Threats Reach Negro Student," *BG*, April 5, 1924; "Columbia Whites in Arms Against Colored Student," *PT*, April 5, 1924; Charles Hamilton, *Adam Clayton Powell, Jr., The Political Biography of an American Dilemma* (New York: Maxwell Macmillan International, 1991), pp. 47–51.

19. George M. Waller, *Butler University: A Sesquicentennial History* (Bloomington, IN: Indiana University Press, 2006), pp. 192–194; "Textures," BUTU Archives (quote).

20. "Negro Graduates Protest," *NYT*, January 13, 1923 (bulletin quote); Lani Guinier, *Lift Every Voice: Turning a Civil Rights Setback into a Strong New Vision of Social Justice* (New York: Simon & Schuster, 1998), pp. 58–61.

21. "Plan to Stop Segregation at Univ. of Michigan," *PC*, February 21, 1931; "Supreme Court Forces Ohio U. to Accept Negro Students," *PT*, February 9, 1933; "'Big Ten' Universities Are Full of Prejudice," *PC*, October 13, 1934; "Color Bar Is Up at Williams College Now," *AA*, October 5, 1935; "California," *CD*, September 26, 1936; "California News," *CD*, March 24, 1934; "California Students Lodge Protest," *PT*, March 14, 1935; "Bar Discrimination on U. of Cal. Campus," *PC*, March 16, 1935; "California State News," *CD*, December 5, 1936; "Metropolitan Oakland Newsettes," *CD*, September 14, 1940. "San Francisco, Cal.," *PC*, October 16, 1937; "San Francisco, Cal.," *PC*, October 16, 1937; John H. Johnson, "What the People Say," *CD*, October 30, 1937; "Attend Negro History Week Tea," *CD*, February 24, 1940; "Cast Will Be Entertained on U. of Chicago Campus," *CT*, January 29, 1945; "Howard U. Professor Thrills Big Audience at Univ. of Chicago," *CD*, February 6, 1937.

22. Florence Ridlon, *Black Physician's Struggle for Civil Rights: Edward C. Mazique, M.D.* (Albuquerque, NM: University of New Mexico Press, 2005), pp. 67–68; "Atlanta Aroused By a Murder Case," *NYT*, August 3, 1930; "Guilty of Killing Negro Student," *BG*, July 29,

1930; Leroy Davis, *A Clashing of the Soul: John Hope and the Dilemma of African American Leadership and Black Higher Education in the Early Twentieth Century* (Athens, GA: University of Georgia Press, 1998), p. 313.

23. Drewry and Doermann, *Stand and Prosper*, p. 58.

24. Ibid., pp. 74–77; Fleming, "Blacks in Higher Education to 1954," p. 14; Albert N. Whiting, *Guardians of the Flame: Historical Black Colleges Yesterday, Today, and Tomorrow* (Washington, DC: American Association of State Colleges and Universities, 1991), p. 19.

25. Drewry and Doermann, *Stand and Prosper*, p. 78; "End of Exploitation Asked By First Lady," *NYT*, October 8, 1943; Frederick D. Patterson, "Would It Not Be Wise For Some Negro Schools to Make Joint Appeal to Public For Funds?" *PC*, January 30, 1943; Richard L. Plaut, "Prospects for the Entrance and Scholastic Advancement of Negroes in Higher Educational Institutions," *Journal of Negro Education* 36 (Summer 1967), p. 230 (NSSFNS quote).

26. Joy Ann Williamson, *Black Power on Campus: The University of Illinois, 1965–75* (Urbana, IL: University of Illinois Press, 2003), p. 10; "More Negro Students," *NYT*, April 18, 1945.

27. Whiting, *Guardians of the Flame*, p. 16.

28. Paul Drederic Lawrence, *College Primer for Negro Students* (Palo Alto, CA: PepsiCola Scholarship Board, 1948); W. E. B. Du Bois, "The Talented Tenth: Memorial Address," *Boule Journal* 15 (October 1948), pp. 3–13.

29. Du Bois, "The Talented Tenth," p. 3–13; Martha Biondi, *To Stand and Fight: The Struggle for Civil Rights in Postwar New York City* (Cambridge, MA: Harvard University Press, 2003), pp. 98–99; Edward N. Saveth, "Fair Educational Practices Legislation," *Annals of the American Academy of Political and Social Science* 275 (May 1951), p. 41; "College Color Line Cracking in South," *NYT*, October 23, 1950; "Approximately 200 Colored Students in Dixie Colleges," *PT*, November 11, 1950; "In Two Decades: What Progress in Faculty Desegregation?" *CHE*, May 20, 1968; Tommy L. Bynum, "'Our Fight Is For Right': The NAACP Youth Councils and College Chapters' Crusade for Civil Rights, 1936–1965" (Ph.D. diss., Georgia State University, 2007), pp. 99–100.

30. Robert C. McMath Jr., Ronald H. Bayor, James E. Brittain, Lawrence Foster, August W. Giebelhaus, and Germaine M. Reed, *Engineering the New South: Georgia Tech, 1895–1995* (Athens, GA: University of

Georgia Press, 1985), p. 281; Lucas, *American Higher Education*, p. 261.

31. Thomas D. Hamm, *Earlham College: A History, 1847–1997* (Bloomington, IN: Indiana University Press, 1997), p. 203; "Northwestern U. Dean Upholds Segregation of Negro Students," *CD*, March 8, 1947; "Racism and the University of Illinois," *CD*, September 22, 1945; "Klan Cross Is Burned on Harvard U. Campus," *AA*, March 1, 1952; "Rocks Thrown in Windows of LSU Negro Students," *ADW*, March 19, 1953; Donald Landon, *Daring to Excel: 1905–2005: The First 100 Years of Southwest Missouri State* (Marceline, MO: Walsworth, 2004), p. 236.

32. Richard Robbins, *Sidelines Activist: Charles S. Johnson and the Struggle for Civil Rights* (Jackson, MS: University Press of Mississippi, 1996), pp. 150–154.

33. Frank Bowles and Frank A. DeCosta, *Between Two Worlds: A Profile of Negro Higher Education* (New York: McGraw-Hill, 1971), p. 53; Arnold H. Taylor, *Travail and Triumph: Black Life and Culture in the South Since the Civil War* (Westport, CT: Greenwood, 1976), pp. 130–135; "The End of Uncle Tom Teachers," no date, circa early 1960s, General Files, ASU Archives.

34. McMath et al., *Engineering the New South*, p. 312; "Five Colleges, Universities This Summer Have for the First Time Admitted Negro Students," *CD*, July 14, 1962; "Chicago Appoints Negro Professor," *NYT*, April 14, 1963.

35. Charles Rogers to Harold Levy, April 26, 1965, Papers of Lyndon B. Johnson: Presidential Papers, White House Central Files, 1963–1969 (hereafter WHCF): Human Rights, box 50, folder: HU 2-5 Education—Schooling 11/22/63—9/6/65, LBJL.

36. Alford A. Young, *Revolt of the Privileged: The Coming Together of the Black Community at Wesleyan University, 1965–1976* (Middletown, CT: Wesleyan University, 1988), pp. 5–6; Richard McCormick, *The Black Student Protest Movement at Rutgers* (New Brunswick, NJ: Rutgers University Press, 1990) pp. 14; "More Negroes Accepted by Exclusive Colleges," *CD*, May 5, 1965; "Colleges Beckon Negro Students," *NYT*, May 15, 1966; "Strongest Minority Representations in Oxy History Due to Little-Publicized Committee," *TO*, September 24, 1965, OC Archives; "UCLA Drive Seeks More Negro Grads," *DB*, August 27, 1963, UCLA Archives.

37. For a few examples of exchange programs, see "Xavier Begins Exchange Program," *CH*, November 4, 1965; "Submersion in Negro Culture Reveals Need for More Exchange Programs," *CW*, May 9, 1969, STCU Archives; "Fisk Exchange," *TDEL*, January 15, 1969, ADU Archives; "White on Black," *TSL*, November 4, 1969, CLAR Archives; "Southern Colleges Seek Top Negroes," *NYT*, January 29, 1967; "Thurgood Marshall Scholarship Opens," *PC*, March 28, 1964; "Firms, Roosevelt U. Launch Unique Scholarship Program," *CD*, August 11, 1964; "Chicago Youth Gets 4-Year College Grant," *CD*, July 14, 1965; "V.P.I. to Recruit Negroes," *NYT*, November 28, 1965; "Negroes Get Free College Admissions," *NYAN*, October 30, 1965; "250 Top Students Awarded 4-Year College Scholarships," *CD*, February 8, 1966; "NAACP Education Committee Awards College Scholarships to 38 Students," *BSB*, June 22, 1967; Antoinette Frederick, *Northeastern University: An Emerging Giant, 1959–1975* (Boston: Northeastern University, 1982), pp. 344–345; John Egerton, *State Universities and Black Americans: An Inquiry into Desegregation and Equity for Negroes in 100 Public Universities* (Atlanta: Southern Education Reporting Service, 1969), pp. 4, 6.

3. "FIGHTING BACK!": THE MAKING OF THE NEW NEGRO

1. Jacquelyn Dowd Hall, "The Long Civil Rights Movement and the Political Uses of the Past," *Journal of American History* 91 (March 2005), p. 1235.
2. Peniel E. Joseph, "Introduction: Community Organizing, Grassroots Politics, and Neighborhood Rebels: Local Struggles for Black Power in America," in *Neighborhood Rebels: Black Power at the Local Level*, ed. Peniel E. Joseph (New York: Palgrave Macmillan, 2010), pp. 10–11.
3. John Newton Templeton, *The Claims of Liberia* (Athens, OH: Maurice Press, 1980) https://web.archive.org/web/20100713184900/http://www.seorf.ohiou.edu/xx057/john_newton_templeton.htm.
4. Ibid.
5. "Speech of Thomas Paul," *TL*, February 29, 1841.
6. Lucy Stanton, "A Plea for the Oppressed," in *Lift Every Voice: African American Oratory, 1787–1900*, eds. Philip S. Foner and Robert James Branham (Tuscaloosa, AL: University of Alabama Press, 1998), pp. 220–223.

7. Vincent Harding, *There Is a River: The Black Struggle for Freedom in America* (New York: Harcourt Brace & Company, 1981), pp. 210–213; Stephanie Y. Evans, *Black Women in the Ivory Tower: 1850–1954* (Gainesville, FL: University Press of Florida, 2007), p. 23.

8. Joy Ann Williamson, *Radicalizing the Ebony Tower: Black Colleges and the Black Freedom Struggle in Mississippi* (New York: Teachers College Press, 2008), pp. 24–25.

9. "No War of Races," *NYT*, March 3, 1887; "War in a University," *NYT*, March 2, 1887; Leroy Davis, *A Clashing of the Soul: John Hope and the Dilemma of African American Leadership and Black Higher Education in the Early Twentieth Century* (Athens, GA: University of Georgia Press, 1998), pp. 70–71.

10. James D. Anderson, *The Education of Blacks in the South, 1860–1935* (Chapel Hill, NC: University of North Carolina Press, 1988), 60–62.

11. Rackman Holt, *Mary McLeod Bethune: A Biography* (New York: Doubleday, 1964), pp. 33–37.

12. Grif Stockley, *Ruled By Race: Black/White Relations in Arkansas from Slavery to the Present* (Fayetteville, AR: University of Arkansas Press, 2009), pp. 135–136.

13. "Negro Students in Riot," *CT*, December 9, 1905; "Howard's President Resigns," *TBS*, December 28, 1905; "Howard's New President," *TWP*, May 8, 1906; "Trustees Remain Firm," *TWP*, January 27, 1906; "Negro Students Strike," *TBS*, January 25, 1906.

14. "Atlanta Massacre," *TMG*, September 26, 1906; Darlene Clark Hine, William C. Hine, and Stanley Harrold, *The African American Odyssey, Combined Volume* (Upper Saddle River, NJ: Prentice Hall, 2008), pp. 431–432; Rebecca Burns, *Rage in the Gateway City: The Story of the 1906 Atlanta Race Riot* (Athens, GA: University of Georgia Press, 2009), pp. 136, 161–162.

15. "Negro Students Rebel," *TBS*, October 22, 1911; "Expels Negro Students," *NYT*, October 23, 1911; "Color Line at Cornell," *TWP*, March 8, 1911 (tired and Clark quote); "Color Line at Cornell," *NYT*, March 13, 1911 (Martin quote); "Race Issue at Cornell," *NYT*, March 28, 1911; "Colored Co-Eds Explain," *NYT*, April 3, 1911 (Ray and Vassar statement); "No Race Line at Cornell," *TWP*, April 11, 1911.

16. Paul Giddings, *In Search of Sisterhood: Delta Sigma Theta and the Challenge of the Black Sorority Movement* (New York: William Morrow and Company, 1988), pp. 27–28, 43, 55–60.

17. "Negro Students Revolt," *BG*, January 4, 1914; "Students Go on Strike at Shaw University," *AA*, January 10, 1914; "Striking Students Return," *AA*, January 24, 1914; "700 Students at Howard Go on a Strike," *AA*, April 8, 1916; Raymond Wolters, *The New Negro on Campus: Black College Rebellions of the 1920s* (Princeton, NJ: Princeton University Press, 1975), p. 276.
18. James R. Grossman, "A Chance to Make Good: 1900–1929," in *To Make Our World Anew, Volume Two: A History of African Americans Since 1880*, eds. Robin D. G. Kelley and Earl Lewis (New York: Oxford University Press, 2000), pp. 118–120.
19. Herbert Aptheker, "The Negro College Student in the 1920s—Years of Preparation and Protest: An Introduction," *Science and Society* 33 (Spring 1969), p. 151.
20. *Pearson's Magazine* (September 1918), p. 276, quoted in Wayne Cooper, "Claude McKay and the New Negro of the 1920's," *Phylon* 25 (1964), p. 299.
21. Valerie Boyd, "Zora Neale Hurston: The Howard University Years," *Journal of Blacks in Higher Education* 39 (Spring 2003), p. 107.
22. Carter G. Woodson, *A Negro in Our History* (Washington, DC: Associate Publishers, 1922); Benjamin Brawley, *A Social History of the American Negro* (New York: The Macmillan Company, 1921), p. 386; Alain LeRoy Locke, ed., *The New Negro* (New York: Albert and Charles Boni, 1925); Alain Locke, "The New Negro," in *The New Negro*, p. 3 (Old Negro quote); Aptheker, "The Negro College Student," p. 156 (McKay quote).

4. "God Speed the Breed": New Negro in the Long Black Student Movement

1. The following section, particularly the major protests at Wilberforce, Fisk, FAMU, Howard, Lincoln (MO), and Hampton, aside from the discussion on the American Federation of Negro Students, is from Wolters, *The New Negro on Campus*, boosted by citations. Christopher J. Lucas, *American Higher Education: A History, Second Edition* (New York: Palgrave Macmillan, 2006), p. 210 (flappers quote); "Students Strike at Biddle University," *CD*, March 12, 1921.
2. Herbert Aptheker, "The Negro College Student in the 1920s—Years of Preparation and Protest: An Introduction," *Science and Society* 33

(Spring 1969); Mary Church Terrell, *The New Student* 2 (February 24, 1923), p. 1.

3. W. E. B. Du Bois, "Harvard," *Crisis* 25 (March 1923), p. 199; "Negro Graduates Protest," *NYT*, January 13, 1923; "Harvard Overseers Ban Discrimination in Race or Religion," *NYT*, April 10, 1923.

4. "Storer College Boys Quit, Say Ku Klux Threatened," *AA*, November 17, 1922.

5. Barbara Ransby, *Ella Baker and the Black Freedom Movement: A Radical Democratic Vision* (Chapel Hill, NC: University of North Carolina Press, 2003), pp. 59–60; Lisa Frederiksen Bohannon, *Freedom Cannot Rest: Ella Baker and the Civil Rights Movement* (Greensboro, NC: Morgan Reynolds Publishing, 2005), pp. 29–33.

6. "Students Hold National Meet in Washington," *CD*, April 21, 1923; J. Alpheus Bulter, "The Negro Youth Awakening," *The New Student* 2 (April 21, 1923), p. 4.

7. "Initiate Mammoth Business Scheme," *PT*, December 1, 1923; "Youth Movement Begun By Lincoln Student Spreading Over the Entire Country," *PT*, March 15, 1924; "'Ten Greatest Negroes American Has Produced,'" *PT*, March 29, 1924; "Annual Youth Movement Ends in Dixie City," *CD*, April 19, 1924, 9.

8. "Federation Urges Youth to Cease Selling Labor," *CD*, June 7, 1924; "Youth Movement Debates Votes on 'Ten Greatest Negroes,'" *PC*, March 15, 1924; "Abbott is Names Among Big 10," *CD*, May 3, 1924; "President of Youth Movement Strikes Back at Tirade of Local Columnist," *PC*, December 27, 1924; "The Prominent Men to Address Youth Movement Conference," *PC*, August 8, 1925.

9. Raymond Wolters, *The New Negro on Campus: Black College Rebellions of the 1920s* (Princeton, NJ: Princeton University Press, 1975), pp. 193–199.

10. Ibid., pp. 200–202.

11. Ibid., pp. 30–34, 37–39.

12. W. E. B. Du Bois, "Diuturni Silenti," in *The Education of Black People, Ten Critiques, 1906–1960*, ed. Herbert Aptheker (Amherst, MA: University of Massachusetts Press, 1973), pp. 41–60.

13. W. E. B. Du Bois, "The Dilemma of the Negro," *The American Mercury* 3 (October 1924), pp. 183–184.

14. Wolters, *The New Negro on Campus*, pp. 39, 45–50.

15. Ibid., pp. 51–56, 60–67.

16. "Why A Student 'Strike,'" *AA*, February 28, 1925.
17. Wolters, *The New Negro on Campus*, pp. 112–118.
18. "New Strike Threatened at Howard," *CD*, August 1, 1925.
19. "Another Student Strike," *CD*, May 23, 1925; "School Disturbances," *PC*, May 23, 1925; "Dean Flees School as Students Stage Revolt," *CD*, November 7, 1925; "Students at Knoxville in Faculty Row," *CD*, December 12, 1925.
20. Oakley C. Johnson, "The Negro-Caucasian Club," *Negro History Bulletin* 33 (February 1970), pp. 35–41; Aptheker, "The Negro College Student," pp. 162–163, 165.
21. Ibid.
22. Ibid.
23. "Another Student Strike," *CD*, May 23, 1925; George Ruble Woolfolk, *Prairie View: A Study in Public Conscience* (New York: Pageant Press, 1962), pp. 207–208, 246.
24. "Another Student Strike," *CD*, May 23, 1925; Woolfolk, *Prairie View: A Study in Public Conscience*, pp. 207–208, 246; "College Students Strike," *PC*, November 6, 1926; Bohannon, *Freedom Cannot Rest*, p. 33; "St. Augustine Students Out On A Strike," *AA*, November 26, 1927; "St. Augustine Strike Ends," *AA*, December 3, 1927.
25. "Howard U. Football Squad on Strike," *CD*, October 8, 1927; "Howard Strike Unsettled," *PC*, October 15, 1927.
26. Wolters, *The New Negro on Campus*, pp. 203–221.
27. Ibid., pp. 254–259.
28. Ibid., pp. 257, 262–263.
29. Ibid., pp. 263–275.
30. "Student Strikes," *PC*, October 29, 1927.
31. "Negroes Complain of Bias at N.Y.U.," *NYT*, December 31, 1927.
32. Wolters, *The New Negro on Campus*, pp. 319–320.
33. "Western University Student Strike Ends," *AA*, January 28, 1928; "Kittrell College Girls Accused Prexy," *AA*, February 25, 1928; Zella J. Black Patterson, *Langston University: A History* (Norman, OK: University of Oklahoma Press, 1979), pp. 131–140.
34. John P. Davis, "Unrest at the Negro Colleges," *The New Student* 8 (January 1929), p. 14; "8 Strikes Show Revolt Among Race Colleges," *AA*, January 26, 1929.
35. "Strike Looms After 'Coed' Is Expelled," *PT*, February 7, 1929 (womanhood quote); "Nine Youth Ousted From Langston U," *CD*,

February 16, 1929; "The Week," *CD*, February 16, 1929 (unrest quote); "Students Seek Ousting of S.C. College Dean," *AA*, March 23, 1929; "Fifty N.C. College Students on Strike," *AA*, May 4, 1929; "Another North Carolina College Erupts," *AA*, May 11, 1929; "Students Win African Riotous Strike at Brick College," *AA*, May 18, 1929; Wolters, *The New Negro on Campus*, p. 277.

36. "God Help Shaw, Says Alumnus After Strike," *AA*, January 25, 1930; "Situation at Paine Caused Student Row," *CD*, April 19, 1930; "Columbia, S.C.," *PC*, April 26, 1930; "A. & T. College Students Return to Classrooms," *AA*, May 10, 1930.

37. Howard students did threaten a protest in 1931. See "Students Threatened a Strike Unless Dr. Johnson Was Retained," *AA*, April 18, 1931. For the citations of protests in 1932, see "Union Prof.," *AA*, January 23, 1932; "Knoxville, Tenn. College Strike Ended Friday," *AA*, January 30, 1932; "Union Prof.," *AA*, January 23, 1932; "Gammon Theologs Declined Prexy's Bid to 'Pray' During Strike," *AA*, March 12, 1932; "Langston Univ. Students in Upheaval," *AA*, May 7, 1932; "Storer President Fears Student Strike," *ADW*, June 11, 1932.

38. "Howard Students Stage One-Day-Class Strike," *PT*, May 11, 1933; "300 Students Strike Because of Food," *PC*, October 28, 1933; "They Chose Between Closing School and Having President Resign," *AA*, December 16, 1933; "Lincoln U. Head Says Strikes Has Ended," *AA*, December 30, 1933; Jervis Anderson, *Bayard Rustin: Troubles I've Seen: A Biography* (Berkeley, CA: University of California Press, 1997), p. 35; "Threat of Student Strike Stirs Wilberforce," *PC*, May 19, 1934; "Cossacks Rule Virginia Campus," *AA*, June 2, 1934; "Strike at Howard Law School Is Called Off," *AA*, December 22, 1934.

39. "Dismiss 1 Prof. 31 Students in Alcorn Strike," *CD*, December 21, 1935; "Howard University Co-Eds Strike Over Board Raise," *ADW*, January 20, 1936; "Students Picket for 'Hungry' H.U. Football Team," *AA*, November 21, 1936; "Students at Morgan Strike After Insult," *AA*, February 29, 1936; "4 Days of Riot End at A&T," *AA*, November 28, 1936; "St. Augustine, Shaw Hunger Strikes Ended," *AA*, November 28, 1936; "Langston University Students in Quiet Strike," *ADW*, December 7, 1936; "Student Strike at Prairie View Denied," *PC*, December 26, 1936; "Another Student Strike Flares, It's W. KY. This Time," *PC*, December 12, 1936.

5. "Strike While the Iron Is Hot": Civil Rights in the Long Black Student Movement

1. Jacquelyn Down Hall, "The Long Civil Rights Movement and the Political Use of the Past," *Journal of American History* 91 (August 1935), p. 1235.
2. Johnetta Richards, "Fundamentally Determined: James E. Jackson and Ester Cooper Jackson and the Southern Negro Youth Congress—1937–1946," *American Communist History* 7 (2008), p. 192 (CIM quote); Maurice Gates, "Negro Students Challenge Social Forces," *TC*, August 1935; John Hope Franklin, *Mirror to America: The Autobiography of John Hope Franklin* (New York: Farrar, Straus and Giroux, 2005), pp. 52–55.
3. "Negro Students Rush Congress Restaurant in Vain Effort to Test Rule Barring Race," *NYT*, March 18, 1934; "Protest March of H. U. Students, Who Hope to 'Crash' Headlines, May Defeat DePriest Petition," *PC*, March 24, 1934.
4. For example, see Robert Cohen, *When the Old Left Was Young: Student Radicals and America's First Mass Student Movement, 1929–1941* (New York: Oxford University Press, 1997).
5. "'Too Pacific,' Youth Leader Says of Negro," *PT*, July 18, 1935; "'Town Meeting of Youth' Set for Feb. 7, 8, 9," *CD*, February 1, 1941.
6. Julie S. Doar, "National Council of Negro Youth," in *Organizing Black America: An Encyclopedia of African American Associations*, ed. Nina Mjagkij (New York: Taylor & Francis, 2001), p. 392; "Youth Urge Passage of Anti-Poll Tax Law," *ADW*, October 3, 1942 (Norman quote).
7. Robert Cohen, "Student Movements, 1930s," in *Encyclopedia of the American Left*, eds. Mari Jo Buhle, Paul Buhle, and Dan Georgakas (New York: Oxford University Press, 1998), pp. 799–802; "H. U. Students Join National Antiwar Strike," *AA*, May 2, 1936; John H. Johnson, "Along the Youth Front," *CD*, May 1, 1937.
8. Gates, "Negro Students Challenge Social Force," p. 251; "Ex-Richmonder, 5 Others to Appeal Red Convictions," *AA*, August 11, 1956; "Anti-Lynch Speaks," *AA*, March 23, 1940; "Boy Appointed to Wesleyan U. Staff," *CD*, October 15, 1938; "Students Fight Discrimination," *NYAN*, January 4, 1936; "Student Union Takes

Rap at Restaurant Discrimination," *PC*, September 14, 1940; "Student Union OK's Antilynching Bill," *AA*, January 8, 1938; "Report on American Student Union," *CD*, January 22, 1938; "Is Elected Delegate to Students Conference," *PT*, December 23, 1937; "Student Union Hears a Plea for Tolerance," *CD*, January 14, 1939 (Davis quote); "4 Plan Appeal in Café Suit," *AA*, March 12, 1938; "Refuses to Serve Columbia Student," *NYAN*, April 11, 1936; "White Students Aid Boycott of Theaters," *AA*, January 29, 1938; "Anti-Lynch Speaks," *AA*, March 23, 1940; "Club Victory Spurs Move," *AA*, May 11, 1940; "'Red' Changes Give Campus Jitters," *NYT*, December 6, 1940; Cohen, "Student Movements, 1930s."

9. For works on CORE, see August Meier, *CORE: A Study in the Civil Rights Movement* (Urbana, IL: University of Illinois Press, 1973).

10. Hall, "The Long Civil Rights Movement," p. 1245.

11. "Youth Conference Marks Start of New Epoch in Race Equality Struggle," *PT*, February 18, 1937; Robin D. G. Kelley, *Hammer and Hoe: Alabama Communists During the Great Depression* (Chapel Hill, NC: University of North Carolina Press, 1990), p. 200, 207, 212.

12. Ibid.

13. See Johnetta Gladys Richards, "The Southern Negro Youth Congress: A History, 1937–1949" (Ph.D. dissertation, University of Cincinnati, 1987); Johnetta Richards, "Southern Negro Youth Congress (1937–1949)," Blackpast.org, http://www.blackpast.org/?q=aah/southern-negro-youth-congress-1937-1949, accessed November 3, 2011; "Progress Seen in Activity of Youth Groups," *CD*, December 14, 1940; "Robeson Is Greeted with Enthusiasm at Tuskegee," *CD*, May 2, 1942; "New World Order Coming, Says Dr. Bethune," *ADW*, December 2, 1944; "Negro Youth Told Future Is in South," *NYT*, October 21, 1946 (Du Bois quote).

14. "Ask Dies to Investigate Ku Klux Klan," *CD*, November 11, 1939; Richards, "Fundamentally Determined," pp. 193–199, 201; "Youth Congress Launches Vote Crusade," *CD*, July 22, 1939; Kelley, *Hammer and Hoe*, p. 201–202, 212–219, Patricia Sullivan, "Five Decades of Activism," *The Journal of the Southern Regional Council* 12 (1990), pp. 5–6; Richards, "Fundamentally Determined," p. 202.

15. Unless otherwise cited, the following section on the NAACP youth councils and college chapters is from Thomas L. Bynum, "'We Must March Forward!': Juanita Jackson and the Origins of the NAACP Youth Movement," *Journal of African American History* 94 (Fall

2009), pp. 487–508 and "'Our Fight is For Right': The NAACP Youth Councils and College Chapters' Crusade for Civil Rights, 1936–1965" (Ph.D. diss., Georgia State University, 2007).

16. Ibid.

17. Ibid.; "Hampton Institute Students Form Chapter," *AA*, December 21, 1940; "LeMoyne N.A.A.C.P. Branch Sponsors Negro History Group," *PT*, February 6, 1941.

18. "NAACP, with 160,000 Members Says 1942 Was Banner Year," *AA*, January 2, 1943; Pauli Murray, interview by Genna Rae McNeil, February 13, 1976, interview G-0044, transcript, Southern Oral History Program Collection (#4007), series G.1. Southern Women: Individual Biographies, SHC.

19. Tommy L. Bynum, "'Our Fight Is For Right': The NAACP Youth Councils and College Chapters' Crusade for Civil Rights, 1936–1965" (Ph.D. diss., Georgia State University, 2007), pp. 65, 76–79; Arthur L. Johnson, *Race and Remembrance: A Memoir* (Detroit: Wayne University Press, 2008), pp. 22–25; Laura T. McCarty, *Coretta Scott King: A Biography* (Westport, CT: Greenwood Press, 2009), p. 12.

20. "Council on Minority Equality to Meet Thursday in Union," *TDP*, October 10, 1951; "Minority Equality Committee Visits Local Negro Church to Discuss Racial Problems," *TDP*, November 5, 1951, DEPW Archives; "Pa. Students Picket Barbers on Negro Bar," *WP*, December 11, 1948. For a few examples of the turmoil, see "Negroes Cautioned on Resistance Idea," *NYT*, November 23, 1946; "Boston Youth NAACP Suspended for Backing 'Red' Candidate," *ADW*, November 22, 1946. For a new take on the NAACP in these early years, see Patricia Sullivan, *Lift Every Voice: The NAACP and the Making of the Civil Rights Movement* (New York: The New Press, 2009).

21. There are many examples of this marginalization, starting to a certain extent with the books cited in this section.

22. "North Carolina Has Negro Student Row," *NYT*, April 2, 1933; Kenneth Robert Janken, *White: The Biography of Walter White, Mr. NAACP* (New York: The New Press, 2003), pp. 184–185; "Hocutt Loses Suit against College," *CD*, April 8, 1933.

23. "Negro Court Test Faces University," *NYT*, September 1, 1935; Alice Jackson to the Rector and Board of Visitors, U.Va., September 28, 1935, Papers of the Office of the President (RG 2/1/2.491), subseries II, box 18, folder: Negro Admissions and Scholarship Fund,

UVA SC; J. Douglas Smith, *Managing White Supremacy: Race, Politics, and Citizenship in Jim Crow Virginia* (Chapel Hill, NC: University of North Carolina Press, 2002), p. 248.

24. Rawn James Jr., *Root and Branch: Charles Hamilton Houston, Thurgood Marshall, and the Struggle to End Segregation* (New York: Bloomsbury, 2010), pp. 67–75.

25. Joy Ann Williamson, *Black Power on Campus: The University of Illinois, 1965–1975* (Champaign, IL: University of Illinois Press, 2003) p. 11; Christina Asquith, "For Missing Civil Rights Hero, a Degree at Last," *Diverse: Issues in Higher Education*, May 4, 2006, http://diverseeducation.com/article/5827/, accessed November 3, 2011.

26. "Negro Enrolls in University Law School," *AT*, February 3, 1948; "Students Voice Opinions on Admittance of Negro Students," *AT*, February 3, 1948, UAF Archives; Guerdon D. Nichols, "Breaking the Color Barrier at the University of Arkansas," *Arkansas Historical Quarterly* 27 (Spring 1968), pp. 3–21.

27. Williamson, *Black Power on Campus*, pp. 11–12; George Henderson, *Race and the University: A Memoir* (Norman, OK: University of Oklahoma Press, 2010), p. 75.

6. "Justice Is All We Want": Black Students and Desegregation

1. "City College Lists Course by M. Yergan," *NYAN*, September 25, 1937; "James Weldon Johnson, Max Yergan on Faculties of New York University and City College of New York," *ADW*, October 14, 1937; "Nine Wilberforce Student Strikers Expelled," *ADW*, May 4, 1938; "Turmoil Grips Campus as Students Strike," *ADW*, March 26, 1939; "Trustees to Probe Strike of Students at A. And T.," *ADW*, May 21, 1939; "Hampton Goes 'Radical'—Students Strike," *PC*, June 3, 1939.

2. "Jim Crow At N.Y.U. Fought," *CD*, March 22, 1941; "Walsh Joins Race Protest at Harvard," *BG*, April 15, 1941; "H.U. Women Strike; Dean Called Hitler," *AA*, May 31, 1941; "Tuskegee Students Tell 'Inside' Story of Strike," *NYAN*, January 25, 1941; "Tuskegee Students Strike Over Cafeteria Conditions," *ADW*, January 16, 1941; "Spelman Students Strike for Better Food, Socials," *ADW*, February 27, 1942; "Livingston Student Strike Upheld by Court Decision,"

PT, February 9, 1946; "Benedict Students Stage Strike," *ADW*, February 3, 1944; "Food Strike Ended at Benedict," *PT*, November 29, 1947; "More Food Strike Won by Alabama A. & M. Students," *PT*, November 4, 1947; "800 Alabama State College Students Strike Over Food," *AA*, March 13, 1948; "Clark Students Strike Over Food," *PC*, January 22, 1944; "Students Strike at J. C. Smith U.," *AA*, November 20, 1943; "No Action Against Morgan Strikers Yet," *AA*, November 27, 1943; "A. and T. College Strike Ended," *AA*, March 17, 1945; "Lincoln (Mo.) Students Go on Strike over Dismissal," *PT*, June 8, 1948; "51 Striking Co-eds Out at Fort Valley State College," *ADW*, April 19, 1949; "Students Strike at Kentucky State," *AA*, May 23, 1953; "Eggs Cause Bowie Strike," *AA*, November 22, 1941; "Striking Del. Students Defiantly Return to Class," *PT*, April 4, 1942; "St. Augustine Students Back in Class After 8-Day Strike," *PT*, May 1, 1943; "Students of Morris College on 'Strike,'" *ADW*, December 18, 1943; "New Instructor Charged with Fomenting Del. State Riot," *AA*, April 23, 1949; "Students, College Head Clash over Bans," *CD*, November 14, 1942; "One-Day Strike Ends at Va. Union; 1st in History," *AA*, April 8, 1944.

3. "Should College Students Have the Right to Strike," *AA*, February 12, 1944; "U. of C. Students Strike Hits Faculty Jim Crow," *CD*, June 23, 1945; Joy Ann Williamson, *Black Power on Campus: The University of Illinois, 1965–75* (Urbana, IL: University of Illinois Press, 2003), pp. 17–18.

4. Charles Evers and Andrew Szanton, *Have No Fear: The Charles Evers Story* (New York: John Wiley & Sons, 1997), pp. 55–64.

5. "Oust Three in Wiley U. Strike," *CD*, October 18, 1947; "Wiley Students Strike; Protest Social Curbs," *CD*, October 11, 1947; "J. C. Smith Professors Get 1-Year Contracts after Student Strike," *AA*, May 23, 1942; "Instructor Fired, Students Strike," *PC*, May 28, 1949; "Langston Students in Protest Strike," *ADW*, February 2, 1949.

6. "Students Resume Strike on Professors Charged with Bias," *CD*, April 30, 1949; Bynum, "'Our Fight Is for Right,'" pp. 96–97, 99–100.

7. "Decision a Challenge, Say 2 N.C. Students," *CD*, June 12, 1954.

8. Christine Harold and Kevin Michael DeLuca, "Behold the Corpse: Violent Images and the Case of Emmett Till," *Rhetoric & Public Affairs* 8 (Summer 2005), pp. 263–265, 273–276; "Student Strike Ends at Ala. State as Investigation Starts," *ADW*, October 23, 1954; Russell Freedman, *Freedom Walkers: The Story of the Montgomery Bus*

Boycott (New York: Holiday House, 2006) pp. 33–34; Jo Ann Gibson Robinson, *The Montgomery Bus Boycott and the Women Who Started It* (Knoxville, TN: University of Tennessee Press, 1987), pp. 45–46.

9. E. Culpepper Clark, *The Schoolhouse Door: Segregation's Last Stand at the University of Alabama* (New York: Oxford University Press, 1995), p. xvii; Also, for White student reaction, see "College Editors Look at Alabama University," *XUN*, March 9, 1956, XUO Archives.

10. "New Dining Room and Kitchen to Be Constructed at Cheyney," *PT*, November 27, 1956; Jeffrey A. Turner, *Sitting In and Speaking Out: Student Movements in the American South: 1960–1970* (Athens, GA: University of Georgia Press, 2010), pp. 67–68.

11. Ana Maria Spagna, *Test Ride on the Sunnyland Bus: A Daughter's Civil Rights Journey* (Lincoln, NE: University of Nebraska Press, 2010), pp. 27–28; Gregory B. Padgett, "The Tallahassee Bus Boycott," in *Sunbelt Revolution: The Historical Progression of the Civil Rights Struggle in the Gulf South, 1866–2000*, ed. Samuel C. Hyde Jr. (Gainesville, FL: University Press of Florida, 2003), pp. 190–208.

12. Joy Ann Williamson, *Radicalizing the Ebony Tower: Black Colleges and the Black Freedom Struggle in Mississippi* (New York: Teachers College Press, 2008), pp. 39–40.

13. Ibid., pp. 40–42.

14. "Impact of Alcorn Students' Strike," *CD*, March 12, 1957; "Allen Students Upset State!" *PC*, January 25, 1958.

15. Bynum, "'Our Fight Is for Right,'" p. 127.

16. John Lewis and Michael D'Orso, *Walking with the Wind: A Memoir of the Movement* (New York: Harcourt, Brace and Company, 1998), pp. 74–75.

17. "FAMU Students Get Action; Call Off Class Strike," *CD*, May 5, 1959; "FAMU Students Vow to Press Fight for Justice," *CD*, May 6, 1959; "Negro Students Go on Strike," *MG*, May 5, 1959; James Max Fendrich, *Ideal Citizens: The Legacy of the Civil Rights Movement* (Albany, NY: State University of New York Press, 1993), pp. 13–14.

18. Fendrich, *Ideal Citizens*, pp. 14–15.

19. Harvard Sitkoff, *The Struggle for Black Equality: 1954–1992* (New York: Hill and Wang, 1993), p. 59.

20. Lewis and D'Orso, *Walking with the Wind*, pp. 75–87.

21. Bynum, "'Our Fight Is for Right,'" pp. 136–137 (McNeill quote); Darlene Clark Hine, William C. Hine, and Stanley Harrold, *The African American Odyssey: Combined Volume, Fourth Edition* (Upper

Saddle River, NJ: Pearson Education, 2008), pp. 584–585; Sitkoff, *The Struggle for Black Equality*, p. 63; Cleveland Sellers and Robert Terrell, *The River of No Return: The Autobiography of a Black Militant* (Jackson, MS: University of Mississippi Press, 1990), pp. 18–19 (rat quote).

22. Hine, Hine, and Harrold, *The African American Odyssey*, pp. 584–586; Sitkoff, *The Struggle for Black Equality*, pp. 64–69, 74–75.

23. Williamson, *Radicalizing the Ebony Tower*, pp. 44–45; Sellers and Terrell, *The River of No Return*, pp. 23–24; Sitkoff, *The Struggle for Black Equality*, p. 69; John A. Hardin, *Onward And Upward: A Centennial History of Kentucky State University 1886–1986* (Frankfort, KY: Kentucky State University, 1987), p. 50, CESKAA; "Trial Delayed in Suit of 13 against K.S.C.," *CJ*, April 30, 1963

24. Hine, Hine, and Harrold, *The African American Odyssey*, p. 586; Sellers, *The River of No Return*, pp. 33–38; Sitkoff, *The Struggle for Black Equality*, p. 83.

25. Turner, *Sitting In and Speaking Out*, pp. 105–107.

26. Williamson, *Radicalizing the Ebony Tower*, pp. 53–54

27. Sitkoff, *The Struggle for Black Equality*, pp. 103–106.

28. Turner, *Sitting In and Speaking Out*, pp. 107–110; Sitkoff, *The Struggle for Black Equality*, pp. 114–115; Frank Lambert, *The Battle of Ole Miss: Civil Rights v. States' Rights* (New York: Oxford University Press, 2010), pp. 116–138.

7. "March That Won't Turn Around": Formation and Development of the Black Campus Movement

1. "Militant Stand Taken by New All-Black Youth Group," *Young Socialist*, September 1963; Donna Jean Murch, *Living for the City: Migration, Education, and the Rise of the Black Panther Party in Oakland, California* (Chapel Hill, NC: The University of North Carolina Press, 2010), pp. 71, 73; H. Lawrence Ross to Malcolm X, February 8, 1962, box 4, folder 3; Audrey Johnson to Malcolm X, August 31, 1962, box 3, folder 17, Malcolm X Collection: Papers, 1948–1965, SCHBG; Muhammad Ahmad, *We Will Return in the Whirlwind: Black Radical Organizations, 1960–1975* (Chicago: Charles H. Kerr Publishing Company, 2007), pp. 95–99.

2. "A Few Beers with Herman Carter at the Cock n' Bull," *FPM*, 2000, https://web.archive.org/web/20060816070213/http://www. fishpiss.com/archives/148, accessed January 9, 2023; "Interview with Herman Carter by Gabriel Tordjman," Dawson College Humanities/Philosophy Department Newsletter, March 10, 2005; Edward Leroy Whitfield, interview by Bridgette Burge, February 26, 2006, transcript, Heirs to a Fighting Tradition: Oral Histories of North Carolina Social Justice Activists, Heirs Project, Knightdale, North Carolina; Henry N. Drewry and Humphrey Doermann, *Stand and Prosper: Private Black Colleges and Their Students* (Princeton, NJ: Princeton University Press, 2001) p. 32; Bridgette Sanders and Lois Stickell, "Black Student Activism at UNC Charlotte in the Late 1960s" (paper presented at the 90th annual convention of the Association for the Study of African American Life and History, Buffalo, New York, October 20–23, 2005), paper in author's possession, courtesy of UNCC Archives; Chester Grundy, interview by Betsy Brinson, June 23, 1999, interview 20 B 24, Civil Rights Movement in Kentucky Oral History Project, The Kentucky Oral History Commission, KHS.

3. Ahmad, *We Will Return in the Whirlwind*, p. 105.

4. Harvard Sitkoff, *The Struggle for Black Equality: 1954–1992* (New York: Hill and Wang, 1993), pp. 130–132 (Connor quote).

5. "Afro-American Club," *HC*, May 10, 1963; "Past Officers Discuss History of Afro," *HC*, April 29, 1974; "College Negro Club Adopts Constitution," *HC*, April 29, 1963; "Negro Students' Challenge to Liberalism," *HC*, May 31, 1967, HARU Archives.

6. Thomas J. Sugrue, *Sweet Land of Liberty: The Forgotten Struggle for Civil Rights in the North* (New York: Random House, 2008), p. 302; Martin Luther King, "Letter from Birmingham City Jail," in *A Testament of Hope: The Essential Writings and Speeches of Martin Luther King Jr.*, ed. James M. Washington (San Francisco: Harper, 1986), p. 292; Sitkoff, *The Struggle for Black Equality*, pp. 145–146 (Kennedy quote); Jelani Favors, "Shelter in a Time of the Storm: Black Colleges and the Rise of Student Activism in Jackson, Mississippi" (PhD diss., The Ohio State University, 2006), pp. 215–216.

7. Sitkoff, *The Struggle for Black Equality*, pp. 144–145

8. Kareem Abdul-Jabbar and Peter Knobler, *Giant Steps* (New York: Bantam Books, 1983), pp. 60–61.

9. Ann Grundy, interview by Betsy Brinson, February 7, 1999, transcript, Civil Rights Movement in Kentucky Oral History Project, The Kentucky Oral History Commission, KHS.

10. William H. Orrick Jr., *SHUT IT DOWN! A College in Crisis, San Francisco State College October, 1968–April, 1969: A Report to the National Commission on the Causes and Prevention of Violence* (Washington, DC: US Government Printing Office, 1969), pp. 77–78; "Black Student Association," Office of Multicultural Affairs, The University of Memphis, accessed December 13, 2022, https://web.archive.org/web/20111124143405/http://www.memphis.edu/multiculturalaffairs/organizations.htm; Ahmad, *We Will Return in the Whirlwind*, p. 104; Payson S. Wild to Faculty Member, May 8, 1968, General Files, folder: Black Student Protest—I, April–May 1968, NOWU Archives.

11. "Police in Jackson Break Up Protest," *NYT*, February 4, 1964; "College Students Shot Down by Miss. Police," *CD*, February 5, 1964; "Alcorn 1966: An Incident," Pamphlet of the Southern Student Organizing Commission, Nashville, Tennessee, Delos P. Culp Records, 1924–1974, box 124, folder 9, ETSU Archives; "Student Strike Threat at Norfolk State," *JG*, May 23, 1964; Jeffrey A. Turner, *Sitting In and Speaking Out: Student Movements in the American South: 1960–1970* (Athens, GA: University of Georgia Press, 2010), p. 181; Ahmad, *We Will Return in the Whirlwind*, pp. 115–118; Maxwell C. Stanford, "Revolutionary Action Movement (RAM): A Case Study of an Urban Revolutionary Movement in Western Capitalist Society" (M.A. Thesis, Atlanta University, 1986), p. 91.

12. Abdul-Jabbar and Knobler, *Giant Steps*, pp. 71–76; Joseph Boskin, "The Revolt of the Urban Ghettos, 1964–1967," *Annals of the American Academy of Political and Social Science* 382 (March 1969), p. 7.

13. Darlene Clark Hine, William C. Hine, and Stanley Harrold, *The African-American Odyssey, Combined Volume* (Upper Saddle River, NJ: Prentice Hall, 2008), p. 594; Cleveland Sellers and Robert Terrell, *The River of No Return: The Autobiography of a Black Militant* (Jackson, MS: University of Mississippi Press, 1990), p. 94; Kay Mills, *This Little Light of Mine: The Life of Fannie Lou Hamer* (New York: Dutton, 1993), p. 132.

14. Sellers, *River of No Return*, p. 111.

15. Robin Gregory, "Howard University, 1967–1968: 'You Saw the Silhouette of Her Afro,'" in *Voices of Freedom: An Oral History of the*

Civil Rights Movement from the 1950s Through the 1980s, eds. Henry Hampton, Steve Fayer, and Sarah Flynn (New York: Bantam Books, 1990), pp. 427–429, 433–436.

16. Bettina Aptheker, *The Academic Rebellion in the United States* (Secacus, NJ: The Citadel Press, 1972), pp. 21–23, 156–158; Roger A. Fischer, "Ghetto and Gown: The Birth of Black Studies," *Current History* 57 (November 1969), p. 291.

17. "Negro Students Fighting Apathy," *NYT*, December 20, 1964; "New College Magazine Aimed at Ending Negro Indifference," *NYT*, April 16, 1966.

18. The following section on Malcolm's ideological influence on black students is taken from Ibram X. Kendi, "'People All Over the World Are Supporting You': Malcolm X, Ideological Formations, and Black Student Activism, 1960–1972," *The Journal of African American History* 96 (Winter 2011), pp. 14–38; Malcolm X, "The Harvard Law School Forum of December 16, 1964," in *Malcolm X Speeches at Harvard*, ed. Archie Epps (New York: Paragon House, 1991), p. 161.

19. Stokely Carmichael and Ekwueme Michael Thelwell, *Ready for Revolution: The Life and Struggles of STOKELY CARMICHAEL (KWAME TURE)* (New York: Scribner, 2003), pp. 253, 259–260; "1500 Hear Integration—Non-Segregation Debate," *TSD*, November 18, 1961; For the letter of thanks from the Howard student body, see Michael Winston to Malcolm X, November 7, 1961, box 3, folder 17, Malcolm X Collection: Papers, 1948–1965, SCHBG.

20. Bobby Seale, *Seize the Time: The Story of the Black Panther Party and Huey P. Newton* (New York: Vintage, 1970), pp. 5–6.

21. Martin Kilson, "Open Letter to a Negro Student at Harvard," *THC*, March 17, 1965, HARU Archives; "The Murder of Malcolm X," February 1967, Student Nonviolent Coordinating Committee Papers, 1959–1972, Microfilm Reel 22, No. 253, PALL.

22. Photo to the right of "Purpose of Demands Told at AABL Meeting," *TDT*, March 6, 1969, UTXA Archives.

23. Vincent Harding, Robin D. G. Kelley, and Earl Lewis, "We Changed the World, 1945–1970," in *To Make the World Anew: A History of African Americans from 1880*, eds. Robin D. G. Kelley and Earl Lewis (New York: Oxford University Press, 2000), pp. 238–239.

24. For a firsthand account of "Bloody Sunday," see John Lewis and Michael D'Orso, *Walking with the Wind: A Memoir of the Movement* (New York: Harcourt, Brace and Company, 1998), pp. 335–362.
25. "Howard University Student Body Petition," March 9, 1965, WHCF: Human Rights, box 27, folder: GEN HU 2/ST 1 3/9/65, LBJL; James Forman, *Sammy Younge, Jr.: The First Black College Student to Die in the Black Liberation Movement* (New York: Grove Press, 1968), pp. 79–80; Harding, Kelley, and Lewis, "We Changed the World," p. 239.
26. Biographical information on Gwen Patton is from the biography in the Gwendolyn M. Patton Papers, 1955–, TSTC Archives, https://www.trenholmstate.edu/future-students/student-resources/library/collections/gwen-patton-collection, accessed January 10, 2023.
27. Robert J. Norrell, *Reaping the Whirlwind: The Civil Rights Movement in Tuskegee* (New York: Alfred A. Knopf, 1985), p. 173.
28. Forman, *Sammy Younge, Jr.*, p. 110.
29. Norrell, *Reaping the Whirlwind*, p. 173 (first quote); Gwen Patton, "The Student Movement in Introspective Retrospective (The National Association of Black Students, NABS—1969–1972)," in *Black Liberation Movement: Papers Presented at 6th National Council for Black Studies Conference 1982*, ed. Gerald A. McWorter (Urbana, IL: Afro-American Studies and Research Program, University of Illinois, 1982), p. 3 (second quote); Gwendolyn M. Patton, "Insurgent Memories," *Southern Exposure* 9 (Spring 1981), pp. 58–63.
30. Jimmy Garrett, "Watts Thoughts on a Rebellion," *Students for a Democratic Society Bulletin*, 1965, http://content.cdlib.org/view?docId=kt4w1003tt&brand=calisphere &doc.view=entire_text, accessed November 11, 2011; Gerald Horne, *Fire this Time: The Watts Uprising and the 1960s* (Charlottesville, VA: University Press of Virginia, 1995), pp. 3, 239–240.
31. Garrett, "Watts Thoughts on a Rebellion."
32. "The Black Student Union at SFSU Started It All," *SFC*, February 1, 2010.

8. "A New Awareness": Movement Speakers, Conferences, and Periodicals

1. Scot Brown, *Fighting for US: Maulana Karenga, the US Organization, and Black Cultural Nationalism* (New York: New York University Press, 2003), pp. 38–39; William L. Van Deburg, *New Day in Babylon: The Black Power Movement and American Culture, 1965–1975* (Chicago: University of Chicago Press, 1992), p. 31; Earl Anthony, *The Time of the Furnaces: A Case Study of Black Student Revolt* (New York: Dial Press, 1971), pp. 23–25 (Lewis quote); see Maulana Karenga, *The Quotable Karenga* (Los Angeles: US Organization, 1967).

2. "White People Are Deciding Blacks' Fate, Karenga Tells Experimental College," *DB*, October 18, 1967; "Column Directed to Black Students," *DB*, October 24, 1967, UCLA Archives; George Henderson, *Race and the University: A Memoir* (Norman, OK: University of Oklahoma Press, 2010), p. 81.

3. James Forman, *Sammy Younge, Jr.: The First Black College Student to Die in the Black Liberation Movement* (New York: Grove Press, 1968), pp. 185–196; Nancy Regina Hooten to President Lyndon B. Johnson, January 4, 1966, WHCF Name File: Sammy Younge Jr., LBJL.

4. Cleveland Sellers and Robert Terrell, *The River of No Return: The Autobiography of a Black Militant* (Jackson, MS: University of Mississippi Press, 1990), pp. 149–151. For a study of the movement in Lowndes County, see Hasan Kwame Jeffries, *Bloody Lowndes: Civil Rights and Black Power in Alabama's Black Belt* (New York: New York University Press, 2009).

5. Peniel E. Joseph, *Waiting 'Til the Midnight Hour: A Narrative History of Black Power in America* (New York: Henry Holt and Company, 2006), p. 141–142; Sellers, *River of No Return*, pp. 164–167; Stokely Carmichael and Charles Hamilton, *Black Power: The Politics of Liberation in America* (New York: Vintage Books, 1967), p. 44.

6. "Carmichael Urges Negro Unity: 'We're going to turn our ghettoes into communities of love for each other," *BSB*, August 27, 1966; Adrienne Manns, "Howard University, 1967–1968,'" pp. 429–431.

7. Manns, "Howard University, 1967–1968," pp. 429–431.

8. "Appearance of Stokely Carmichael at Morgan State College, Baltimore, Maryland," United States Department of Justice, Federal

Bureau of Investigation, January 24, 1967, Papers of Lyndon B. Johnson: Presidential Papers, Office Files of Mildred Stegall, box 73B, folder: Student Nonviolent Coordinating Committee (Stokely Carmichael) Aug.–Dec. 1966, LBJL. See also Joel Rosenthal, "Southern Black Student Activism: Assimilation vs. Nationalism," *The Journal of Negro Education* 44 (Spring 1975), p. 124 (Howard speech). A transcript of the UC Berkeley speech can be found in Joanne Grant, ed., *Black Protest: History, Documents, and Analyses: 1619 to the Present* (New York: Faucet Publications, 1968), pp. 459–466; "How Did Stokely Carmichael Affect Us?" *TC*, April 1967, TOGC Archives (Tougaloo quote); "Appearance of Stokely Carmichael in Texas," United States Department of Justice, Federal Bureau of Investigation, April 21, 1967 (Houston quote); Jeffrey A. Turner, *Sitting In and Speaking Out: Student Movements in the American South: 1960–1970* (Athens, GA: University of Georgia Press, 2010), p. 177 (Fisk quote); "The Times They Have A-changed," *ST*, January 22, 2002 (Seattle quote). For an inventory of FBI reports on some of his speeches during the spring of 1967, see the above folder at the LBJL.

9. Huey P. Newton and J. Herman Blake, *Revolutionary Suicide* (New York: Harcourt Brace Jovanovich, 1973), pp. 110–113.

10. Mike Floyd, interview by Arthur Murphy, *DCK*, March 7, 1969, DICC Archives (Dickinson quote); "Radicals on Campus," *ST*, November 5, 1968; "Duke University Afro-American Society Ten-Point Program: What We Want and Why We Want It," *HARD*, February 5, 1969, in Black History at Duke Reference Collection, box 1, folder 15, DKU Archives; "B.S.A. & S.Q.E to All Teachers, Administrators & Staff," April 28, 1969, Student Activities Collection, box: NB-STUD-V-BSP, folder: R.U.-N&B-News Releases-General-Black Studies Protest-1969 I, ROSU Archives; "Black Renew Demands, Rap Campus' 'Racism,'" *RB*, May 6, 1969, UGA Archives; "Organization Seeks Black Studies," *COR*, April 15, 1969, F&MC Archives (F&M quote); Franz Schulze, Rosemary Cowler, and Arthur Miller, *30 Miles North: A History of Lake Forest College, Its Town, and Its City of Chicago* (Chicago: Lake Forest College, 2000), p. 158; Jeffrey O. G. Ogbar, *Black Power: Radical Politics and African American Identity* (Baltimore: The John Hopkins University Press, 2004), p. 140.

11. "King in Plea for Rights, Peace," *TO*, April 14, 1967, OC Archives; Jerry Avon, *Up Against the Ivy Wall: A History of the Columbia Crisis* (New York: Atheneum, 1968), p. 20; H. Rap Brown, *Die Nigger Die! A Political Autobiography* (Chicago: Lawrence Hill Books, 2002), p. 99.

12. "Mrs. King Speaks at Harvard," *BSB*, June 20, 1968.

13. "Rep. Chisholm Is Cheered by Howard Grads," *CD*, June 9, 1969; "Negro Leaders and Opponents of War Play Major Role as Graduate Speakers," *NYT*, June 9, 1969; "Militant Jones Coddles Carthage," *TAR*, March 6, 1969 (Jones quote 2); "The Black Movement: A World of Black Change," *TAR*, March 6, 1969 (Trotter quote), CARC Archives.

14. "9 Hours in February: The Takeover," *DC*, February 23, 1999, DKU Archives; Joy Ann Williamson, *Radicalizing the Ebony Tower: Black Colleges and the Black Freedom Struggle in Mississippi* (New York: Teachers College Press, 2008), pp. 140–141 (White quote).

15. "Muhammad Ali at Fairleigh Dickinson," *NYAN*, April 20, 1968.

16. "Presidential Candidate Speaks on Pitt Campus," *TCOL*, September 27, 1968, PSU Archives.

17. "Barbour Prognosticates Bloodshed," *TT*, October 6, 1967, TRIC Archives; "Groppi: 'Black Is Beautiful; Black Power is Christian,'" *TCOR*, January 19, 1968, CLAU Archives; "Fr. Groppi Speaks at Tech on Protest and Racial Revolution," *Michigan Tech Lode*, January 25, 1968, MITU Archives; "Black Students at NCC Accused of Betrayal," *CD*, October 21, 1967.

18. "College Observes 'Black Week,'" *TV*, January 26, 1969, FASU Archives.

19. "Black Cats Working Here; Desperation Spurs Action," *TL*, February 27, 1969, SAPC Archives.

20. "Black America Does Exist," *TTH*, December 13, 1968, THIC Archives; "Black Cats Working Here; Desperation Spurs Action," *TL*, February 27, 1969, SAPC Archives; "Black Coalition Joins CU Blacks, Whites," *TCE*, April 26, 1968, CU Archives; Robert Johnson Jr., "The African-American Legacy at Bowdoin" (unpublished manuscript, February 26, 1997), African American Society Records, box 1, folder 12, BOWU Archives.

21. Richard P. McCormick, *The Black Student Protest Movement at Rutgers* (New Brunswick, NJ: Rutgers University Press, 1990) pp. 17–18; "The Basis of Our Ethos," *WEL*, Spring 2008, WC Archives.

22. "A Dream Defended: The African-American Institute Reaches Ahead as It Looks Back on Thirty Years," *N.U. Magazine Online*, May 1998, http://web.archive.org/web/20050413021104/http:/www.numag.neu.edu/9805/9805page&images/aai.html, accessed December 6, 2022; "Youth Conference Manifesto," *DB*, November 21, 1967, UCLA Archives.

23. "Negro College Students Discuss Ghetto Needs," *NYT*, April 12, 1968; "Negro Students Plan Aid Project," *NYT*, April 13, 1968; "Princeton Talk Exhorts Negroes," *NYT*, April 11, 1968; James E. Cheek to Presidents of Predominantly Negro Colleges, April 16, 1968, George Owen Papers, box 4, folder 15, TOGC Archives.

24. "Negro Students Seek Relevance," *NYT*, November 18, 1968; "Howard Students Discuss Reforms," *NYT*, November 15, 1968; Jerrold Wimbish Roy, "Student Activism and the Historically Black University: Hampton Institute and Howard University, 1960–1972" (PhD. diss., Harvard University, 2000), pp. 125–129; "FSC Students Attend Black Conference," *TV*, February 26, 1969, FASU Archives.

25. David Bishop, "Civil Rights and Race Relations in Durham and in the State: The Shepard, Elder, Massie and Whiting Models," in *A History of N.C. Central University; A Town and Gown Analysis*, ed. George W. Reid (North Carolina: George W. Reid, 1985), p. 78, General Files, NCCU Archives.

26. Lynne Anderson to the editors of *Harambee*, no date, circa 1969, Black Student Alliance Records, 1969–2005, box 1, folder: Afro-American Society materials, 1969–1971, DUKU Archives.

27. John A. Centra, "Black Students at Predominantly White Colleges: A Research Description," *Sociology of Education* 43 (Summer 1970)," pp. 328–334; Patricia Gurin and Edgar Epps, *Black Consciousness, Identity, and Achievement: A Study of Students in Historically Black Colleges* (New York: John Wiley & Sons, 1975), pp. 197–233; *The Report of the President's Commission on Campus Unrest* (New York: Arno Press, 1970), pp. 94–96; Allen B. Ballard, *The Education of Black Folk: The Afro-American Struggle for Knowledge of White America* (New York: Harper & Row, 1973), pp. 90–95; Harry Edwards, *Black Students* (New York: The Free Press, 1970), p. 92.

28. "28% of Students in Poll Protested," *NYT*, May 25, 1969; Gurin and Epps, *Black Consciousness, Identity, and Achievement*; John S. Jackson, "The Political Behavior and Socio-Economic Backgrounds of Black Students: The Antecedents of Protest," *Midwest Journal of Political*

Science 15 (November 1971), pp. 661–686; Frank L. Ellsworth and Martha A. Burns, *Student Activism in American Higher Education* (Washington, DC: American College Personnel Association, 1970), p. 21.; "The Negro Wants to Belong," *NYT*, March 17, 1968; "The Student Scene: Angry Militants," *NYT*, November 20, 1967; Rodney T. Harnett, "Differences in Selected Attitudes and College Orientations Between Black Students Attending Traditionally Negro and Traditionally White Institutions," *Sociology of Education* 43 (Fall 1970), pp. 419–436; "The Negro at Integrated College: Now He's Proud of His Color," NYT, June 3, 1968.

29. For a few examples, see "Black Womanhood Conference," *STY*, March 28, 1969, SUNYB Archives; "Who Is She," *TBC*, February 19, 1971, Thomas H. Eliot Chancellor Papers, series 8, box 1, folder: Association of Black Collegians, 1969–1970, WU Archives.

30. "To Be Young, Black and Female: A Predicament," *CE*, May 10, 1971, NCCU Archives; "The Basis of Our Ethos," WC Archives.

9. "The Black Student Is Demanding": The Black Campus Movement, 1965–1968

1. "A.B.C. List Goals, Objectives," *GK*, November 8, 1968, GAU Archives; "Blacks, Whites Air Views at Forum," *TL*, December 5, 1968, SAPC Archives; "Lawrence Blacks Live One Life Two Ways," *LA*, May-June 1969, LAWU Archives; "Afro-Americans Explain Grievances to University," *DI*, May 30, 1968, UIA Archives; "Night and Day," *FLU*, no date, circa late 1960s, MITU Archives.

2. "BCC Celebrates Its 30th Anniversary," *Polytechnic Online*, November 14, 2001, http://poly.rpi.edu/old/article_view.php3?view=1026&part=1, accessed November 4, 2011; "Blacks Cite Racist Campus Incidents," *CR*, February 12, 1970, MORC Archives; "14 Related Racial Incidents," *TPAR*, May 8, 1969, MARSU Archives; "Black Student's Car Set Ablaze," *TDS*, September 20, 1968; "Why Black Reference?" *TDS*, October 4, 1968, UND Archives; *OGB*, October 31, 1966; "First Fall Carnival Brings in $1300," *OGB*, October 31, 1966; *The Howler* 65 (1967), pp. 14–15, WFU Archives; "Pep Rally Draws 2000; Bonfire, Spirits High," *TECH*, September 27, 1966, NCSU Archives; "The Negro at Integrated College: Now He's Proud of His Color," *NYT*, June 3, 1968; "Negroes in Siege of

Cornell Office," *NYT,* April 5, 1968; "Negroes, Resenting Satire Burn Copies of Magazine at Columbia," *NYT,* May 21, 1967; "Columbia Acting on Race Tension," *NYT,* May 28, 1967. For examples, see "Charges Fly at Meeting," *SNS,* February 26, 1970; Jackie Butler Blackwell, interviewed by Tamara Kennelly, April 29, 1995, transcript, Black Women at Virginia Tech History Project, http://spec. lib.vt.edu/archives/blackwomen/butlerhp.htm, accessed November 4, 2011, VTU Archives; "Discrimination Now Subtle, but Still Seen at Ole Miss," *DB,* March 28, 1968, UCLA Archives; "Apathy Leads to Iowa State Negro Unrest," *ISD,* May 3, 1968, ISU Archives; "Cornell Cautioned on Punishing Sit-ins," *The New York Times,* May 2, 1968.

3. "Black Reflections," *TRI,* April 24, 1970, TRIU Archives; "The Negro at Integrated College: Now He's Proud of His Color," *NYT,* June 3, 1968 (Yale quotes).

4. "Reporter Discovers Unique Black Power at Tougaloo," *TREF,* March 19, 1968, MSSU Archives; Jeffrey A. Turner, *Sitting In and Speaking Out: Student Movements in the American South: 1960–1970* (Athens, GA: University of Georgia Press, 2010), pp. 189–190.

5. Turner, *Sitting in and Speaking Out,* pp. 178–179.

6. Jerrold Wimbish Roy, "Student Activism and the Historically Black University: Hampton Institute and Howard University, 1960–1972" (PhD. diss., Harvard University, 2000), pp. 60–67.

7. "KU Civil Rights Council Protests Discrimination," *TCOL,* March 12, 1965, PSU Archives; "Rules Announced for Campus Students," *TNA,* June 1, 1965, WSSU Archives; "Students' Revolts March 19 Shakes Campus," *CE,* March 31, 1965, NCCU Archives.

8. Lyndon Baines Johnson, "To Fulfill These Rights: Commencement Address at Howard University," in *Affirmative Action: Social Justice or Reverse Discrimination?,* eds. Francis J. Beckwith and Todd E. Jones (Amherst, New York: Prometheus Books, 1997), p. 57; Lawrence B. de Graaf, "Howard: The Evolution of a Black Student Revolt," in *PROTEST! Student Activism in America,* eds. Julian Foster and Durward Long (New York: William & Morrow & Company, 1970), pp. 323–324.

9. Gerald D. Saxon, *Transitions: A Centennial History of the University of Texas at Arlington, 1895–1995* (Arlington, TX: The UTA Press, 1995), p. 113; Jeffrey Alan Turner, "Conscious and Conflict: Patterns in the History of Student Activism on Southern College Campuses,

1960–1970" (Phd. diss., Tulane University, 2000), pp. 269–271 (Carter quote); Robert J. Norrell, *Reaping the Whirlwind: The Civil Rights Movement in Tuskegee* (New York: Alfred A. Knopf, 1985), pp. 173, 178; "Diverse Campuses," *WSJ*, December 22, 1965.

10. William Barlow and Peter Shapiro, *An End to Silence: The San Francisco State College Student movement in the '60s* (New York: Pegasus, 1971), p. 87; "SOUL Seeks Action on Food Discrepancies," *AJR*, March 4, 1966, NATU Archives; "Evers Seeks Ouster of Boyd," *NYT*, April 6, 1966.

11. "Sit-in Is Staged at Marquette," *WT*, December 3, 1966, General Information File: Students United for Racial Equality, MARU Archives; "Senior Women of Jamerson Hall Demand Extension of Closing Hour," *TC*, December 1966, TOGC Archives; William H. Orrick Jr., *SHUT IT DOWN! A College in Crisis, San Francisco State College October, 1968–April, 1969: A Report to the National Commission on the Causes and Prevention of Violence* (Washington, DC: US Government Printing Office, 1969), pp. 114–115.

12. William H. Exum, *Paradoxes of Protest: Black Student Activism in a White University* (Philadelphia: Temple University Press, 1985), pp. 44–45; Alford A. Young, *Revolt of the Privileged: The Coming Together of the Black Community at Wesleyan University, 1965–1976* (Middletown, CT: Wesleyan University, 1988), pp. 21–22.

13. "What's New on Campus," *NYT*, February 26, 1967.

14. Barlow and Shapiro, *An End to Silence*, pp. 125–128.

15. "We, the Undersigned, Register Our Grievances," April 18, 1967, Records Group 11: Student Organizations, 11-8: Black Student's Association, 11-8/1/2: Black Student's Association: Black Issues 1965–1969: Petitions and Committees, IWESU Archives; *The Black Student at Vanderbilt* (Nashville, TN: Office of Undergraduate Admissions, 1970), p. 23, VU Archives; Gretchen Cassel Eick, *Dissent in Wichita: The Civil Rights Movement in the Midwest, 1954–1972* (Urbana, IL: University of Illinois Press, 2001), pp. 121–123. For examples of traditional routes to courses, see "Students Get Black History at Northeastern," *BSB*, October 12, 1967; "Northeastern Students Ask for Black History," *BSB*, May 20, 1967.

16. "Behind the Student Black College Revolt," *EB*, August 1967.

17. "New Black Consciousness Takes Over College Campus," *CD*, December 4, 1967; "The Black Revolt Hits the White Campus," *LK*, October 31, 1967 (Dunbar quote); Joe Palermo, "Black Power on

Campus; The Beginnings," *San Jose Studies* 14 (1988), pp. 34–37; "Negro Students Protest at Berea," *The New York Times*, December 10, 1967; Barlow and Shapiro, *An End to Silence*, p. 119–120; Turner, "Conscious and Conflict," pp. 275–276; "Ohio School Reopens Despite Death Plot Report," *NYT*, November 28, 1967.

18. "Orangeburg Events Cause Outrage," *BSP*, February 29, 1968 (Brown quote); de Graaf, "Howard University," pp. 439–440.

19. Antoinette Frederick, *Northeastern University: An Emerging Giant: 1959–1975* (Boston: Northeastern University, 1982), pp. 402–403; "300 See Black-White Confrontation," *TO*, 26 January 1968, 1; "Begin to Open: Decade of Desegregation," *University of Mary Washington Today* 29 (Winter 2005), pp. 17–18, UMW Archives; "CRAC Hits NMS on Discrimination Charges," *RU*, February 17, 1968; "SLC Hears, Approves BSU Goals," *DB*, February 19, 1968, UCLA Archives; Jaribu Hill, "Excerpts from a Life Standing at the Well," *The Black Scholar* 36 (Spring 2006), pp. 31–32.

20. James L. Palcic, "The History of the Black Student Union at Florida State University, 1968–1978" (PhD. diss., Florida State University, 1979), p. 78; *The Report of the President's Commission on Campus Unrest* (New York: Arno Press, 1970), p. 137; "Colleges' Negro-aid Activities Spurred by Dr. King's Death," *CHE*, April 22, 1968; "Peace Again Reigns at Tennessee State," *CD*, April 27, 1968; "Outbreak in Missouri," *NYT*, April 6, 1968; Robert H. Brisbane, *Black Activism: Racial Revolution in the United States 1954–1970* (Valley Forge, PA: Judson Press, 1974), pp. 230–231; Lawrence E. Eichel, "The Founding of the Afro-American Studies Department: The Crisis of 1969," in *Blacks at Harvard: A Documentary History of African-American Experience at Harvard and Radcliffe*, eds. Werner Sollors, Caldwell Titcomb, and Thomas A. Underwood (New York: New York University Press, 1993), pp. 230–231; "The Negro at Integrated College: Now He's Proud of His Color," *NYT*, June 3, 1968 (Vassar quote).

21. See Stefan Bradley, *Harlem vs. Columbia University: Black Student Power in the Late 1960s* (Urbana, IL: University of Illinois Press, 2009); Ibram X. Kendi, "The Black Campus Movement: An Afrocentric Narrative History of the Struggle to Diversify Higher Education, 1965–1972" (PhD. diss., Temple University, 2009), pp. 100–133.

22. "Colleges' Negro-aid Activities Spurred by Dr. King's Death," *CHE*, April 22, 1968.

23. "Tuskegee Students Lock In Trustees," *NYT*, April 8, 1968; "Black Students Win Many Demands After 38-Hour Bursar's Office Sit-in," *DN*, May 6, 1968, NOWU Archives.

24. "Columbia's Black Students Showed Maturity," *NYAN*, May 11, 1968; Daniel Bell, "Columbia and the New Left," in *Black Power and Student Rebellion: Conflict on the American University*, eds. James McEvoy and Abraham Miller (Belmont, CA: Wadsworth Publishing Company, 1969), pp. 52–55; Jack D. Douglas, *Youth in Turmoil: America's Changing Youth Cultures and Student Protest Movements* (Chevy Chase, MD: National Institute of Mental Health, 1970), p. 226 (restructure quote); "The End of a Siege—and an Era," *Newsweek*, May 13, 1968 (Hayden quote). For the most thorough study of the BCM at Columbia, see Bradley, *Harlem vs. Columbia*.

25. William R. Corson, *Promise or Peril: The Black College Student in America* (New York: W. W. Norton & Company, 1970), p. 65 (Howard militants citation); "BOSA-CUA Seeks Black Awareness," *TOW*, October 18, 1968, CATU Archives; "Black Group Causes Varied Feelings," *OGB*, November 26, 1968, WFU Archives; "The Negro at Integrated College: Now He's Proud of His Color," *NYT*, June 3, 1968 (Yale quote).

26. "Northeastern Teachers 'Afro,'" *BSB*, December 19, 1968; "Predict Many College Outbreaks This Fall," *CD*, August 20, 1968; "War, Political Frustration, Race Issues Presage Deeper Student Unrest," *CHE*, July 22, 1968.

27. Joy Ann Williamson, *Black Power on Campus: The University of Illinois, 1965–1975* (Urbana, IL: University of Illinois, 2003), pp. 81–86; Cecil Brown, *Dude, Where's My Black Studies Department? The Disappearance of Black Americans from Our Universities* (Berkeley, CA: North Atlantic Books, 2007), pp. 73–74; Jan Stradling, *More Than a Game: When Sport and History Collide* (Millers Point, NSW: Pier 9, 2009), p. 175.

28. For an example at Ottawa University, see "Black Concerns," *OTTC*, January 10, 1969, OTTU Archives. For the SF State protest, see Barlow and Shapiro, *An End to Silence* and Dikran Karagueuzian, *Blow It Up! The Black Student Revolt at San Francisco State College and the Emergence of Dr. Hayakawa* (Boston: Gambit, 1971).

29. "Black Thursday at Oshkosh," *TC*, November 1969; President Morse to Members of the Afro-American Society of Case Western Reserve University, December 13, 1968, Records of Afro-American Studies Program, box 1, folder 6, CWRU Archives; "Black Student Union Issues Demands," *TFOG*, November 8, 1968, USF Archives; "Their Crowning Glory," TDC, February 26, 2002, UHOU Archives; Robinson Block, "Afro-Americans for Black Liberation and the Fight for Civil Rights at the University of Houston," *Houston History* 8 (Fall 2010), p. 25.

10. "WE'RE GOING TO GET WHAT WE WANT NOW": THE BLACK CAMPUS MOVEMENT, 1969–1972

1. "Violence Plagues S.F. State; Race Issues Flare Elsewhere," *CHE*, December 9, 1968 (Smith quote); "The Eleven Days at Brandeis—As Seen from the President's Chair," *NYT*, February 16, 1969; "Queens Students Ransack Office," *The New York Times*, January 14, 1969; Daniel Harris and Joseph Honcharik, *Staff Study of Campus Riots and Disorders, October 1967–May 1969* (Washington, DC: US Government Printing Office, 1969), p. 21; "Racial Tensions Still Trouble Ohio Colleges," *CD*, January 21, 1969; "Militants Eliminated From Campus," *WEB*, February 14, 1969, WEBU Archives (Shaw citation); "Protest at Wittenberg University, Documentation," in *Themes and Events of Campus Unrest in Twenty-Two Colleges and University*, Helen S. Austin, Ann S. Bisconti, Michele Herman, and Richard Hofrichter (Washington, DC: Bureau of Social Science Research, 1969), pp. C-138–C-166; Rodney Stark, "Protest + Police = Riot," in *Black Power and Student Rebellion*, pp. 167–185; "Swarthmore College Prexy Dies Amid Dissension," *CD*, January 18, 1969.
2. Scot Brown, *Fighting for Us: Maulana Karenga, the US Organization, and Black Cultural Nationalism* (New York: New York University Press, 2003); "Two Negroes Slain at UCLA Meeting of Black Students," *NYT*, January 18, 1969.
3. "Reform Needed at Universities," *BW*, February 7, 1969, LEHIU SC; Claudrena N. Harold, "'Of the Wings of Atalanta': The Struggle for African American Studies at the University of Virginia, 1969–1995," *Journal of African American Studies*, online first, accessed July 28,

2011, https://doi.org/10.1007/s12111-011-9172-3; "SGA Stages Sit-in," *AJR*, February 14, 1968, NATU Archives; "BATU Issues List of Demands," *FN*, February 11, 1969, UDAY Archives; "Protesters Draw Up Demands in Austin," *TDT*, February 16, 1969, UTXA Archives (Huston-Tillotson citation); "Purpose of Demands Told at AABL Meeting," *TDT*, March 6, 1969; "Protest at Mills College," *NYT*, March 22, 1969; Richard P. McCormick, *The Black Student Protest Movement at Rutgers* (New Brunswick, NJ: Rutgers University Press, 1990), pp. 39–64; Cathy Meeks, *I Want Somebody to Know My Name* (Nashville: Thomas Nelson Publishers, 1978), pp. 68–81; Winston A. Grady-Willis, *Challenging U.S. Apartheid: Atlanta and Black Struggles for Human Rights, 1960–1977* (Durham, NC: Duke University Press, 2006), pp. 144–168; "Students: The New 'Feel' on Campus," *WSJ*, March 20, 1969.

4. Donald Alexander Downs, *Cornell '69: Liberalism and the Crisis of the American University* (Ithaca, NY: Cornell University Press); Harvard Negroes Get Faculty Vote," *NYT*, April 23, 1969; Conrad M. Dyer, "Protest and the Politics of Open Admissions: The Impact of the Black and Puerto Rican Students' Community (of City College)," (PhD. diss., City University of New York, 1990), pp. 114–126; Roy, "Student Activism and the Historically Black University," pp. 69–85; "Armed Students Takeover Voorhees College Building," *CD*, April 29, 1969; "Student Protests Interrupt Spring Semester," *HT*, May 1969, ALSU Archives; "The Siege of Greensboro," *NE*, June 2, 1969.

5. "Student Secessionists," *NYT*, August 28, 1969; "Black Walk Out at NSA Convention," *SO*, August 28, 1969.

6. "The Negro Colleges: Victims of Progress," *NYT*, October 6, 1969.

7. "Unrest Is Found to Be Widespread among Faculty Members as well as Students; Many Groups Are Split," *CHE*, September 15, 1969.

8. For the trials at San Francisco State, for example, see DeVere Pentony, Robert Smith, and Richard Axen, *Unfinished Rebellions* (San Francisco: Jossey-Bass, 1971), pp. 172–176; "S.F. State Strike Trials—A Mixed Bag of Repression," *SR*, November 29, 1969. "Blacks Make Own School in Calif. Area," *CD*, March 20, 1971; "Malcolm X University to Open in Durham as Militants' School," *NYT*, October 28, 1969.

9. Clifford A. Bullock, "Fired by Conscience: The 'Black 14' Incident at the University of Wyoming and Black Protest in the Western Athletic Conference," *Annals of Wyoming: The Wyoming History Journal* 68

(1996), pp. 4–13; "ROTC Is Primary Issue in Unrest during October," *CHE*, November 3, 1969; "Students Interrupt Convocation Speech," *TPAR*, October 3, 1969, MARSU Archives; "S.G.A. Appropriates $1,000 to Blacks," *PSAC*, October 30, 1969, STAU Archives; George W. McDaniel, *A Great and Lasting Beginning, The First 125 Years of St. Ambrose University* (Helena, MT: Sweetgrass Books, 2006), p. 202; "Chronology of Events Friday November 21st," *STA*, December 10, 1969, FARU Archives; "35 Negro Girls Seize Part of a Building at Vassar and Sit In," *NYT*, October 31, 1969; "Fisk Students Want Black University," *CD*, December 15, 1969 (Fisk quote).

10. "Sympathy for Workers and Strikes Spur Students Protests," *CHE*, December 15, 1969; "Harvard Sit-in over Black Painters' Pay," *BSB*, November 27, 1969; "Building Campus Integration," *NYT*, November 8, 1969 (quote); "Black Leaders Speak at Boston College," *BSB*, December 11, 1969; Yohuru Williams, 'A Red, Black and Green Liberation Jumpsuit,'" in *The Black Power Movement: Rethinking the Civil Rights—Black Power Era*, ed. Peniel Joseph (New York: Routledge, 2006), pp. 181, 183–184, 190–191. On the Hampton/Clark murder, see Jeffrey Haas, *The Assassination of Fred Hampton: How the FBI and the Police Murdered a Black Panther* (Chicago: Lawrence Hill Books, 2010).

11. "About the Issue," "Some Words from Black Alumni," *LAFA*, Winter 1970, LAFC Archives.

12. Robert Johnson Jr., "The African-American Legacy at Bowdoin" (unpublished manuscript, February 26, 1997), African American Society Records, box 1, folder 12, BOWU Archives; "Black in the Chapel," *COE*, March 6, 1970, COC Archives; Tiffany McClain, "The Integration Experiment: Black Women at Mount Holyoke College, 1964–1974" (unpublished manuscript, May 1, 2001), pp. 1, 6–8, MHC Archives; Leon Glaster to President James K. Sours, March 12, 1970, James Sours Collection, box 4, folder: Black Student Union, SORU Archives; "Black Student Union Proposals," "The President's Response to the Black Student Union Proposals," *HEIA*, Spring 1970, HEIU Archives; "Black Students Leave: Demands Under Study by Mount Union Officials," *AR*, March 7, 1970; "CCC Has Sit-in, No Bomb," *BW*, March 17, 1970, LEHIU SC; "'It Couldn't Happen Here': Blacks Give Stratton 11 Demands," *KEY*, April 22, 1970, KUP Archives; Ralph W. Schlosser, *History of*

Elizabethtown College, 1899–1970 (Elizabethtown, PA: Elizabethtown College, 1971), pp. 319–321; "Black Students Suggest Positive Improvements," *TRAM*, April 1970, ROSC Archives; Luther J. Carter, "U. of Michigan: Black Activists Win a Change in Priorities," *Science* 168 (April 10, 1970), pp. 229–231; "Negroes Pleased With Talks at TU," *TB*, May 9, 1970; Palcic, "The History of the Black Student Union at Florida State University," pp. 110–118; "Black Want Own College, 5 Student Board Members," *TCE*, February 27, 1970, CU Archives; "Black Students Sit-in At Maucker Home," *NIA*, March 20, 1970, NIAU Archives; "Dallas Students Ousted by Police," *NYT*, February 13, 1970; "Mississippi Students Rebel at Itta Bena," *ADW*, February 27, 1970.

13. "Black Studies Out at San Fran College," *NYAN*, April 4, 1970; "More Trouble at S.F. State," *SR*, March 7, 1970; "Emergency Declared at College," *SO*, May 21, 1970; "Stanford Confab: Black Students Call for Unity," *SR*, May 9, 1970.

14. "A Week of Tragedy: Disorders Flare, 4 Students Die as U.S. Action in Cambodia Inflames Many Campuses," *CHE*, May 11, 1970; "Are College Protests Racist?" *PC*, May 23, 1970; "Will Blacks also Revolt?" *PC*, May 16, 1970; Seymour Martin Lipset, *Rebellion in the University* (Boston: Little and Brown, 1972), pp. 91–92.

15. Tim Spofford, *Lynch Street: The May 1970 Slayings at Jackson State College* (Kent, OH: Kent State University Press, 1988), pp. 29, 56–79; "F.B.I. Investigating the Killing of 2 Negroes in Jackson," *NYT*, May 16, 1970.

16. Ibid.

17. "Jackson State Shootings Stir New Wave of Unrest," *CHE*, May 25, 1970.

18. "Black Presidents Assail Nixon Policies," *CHE*, June 1, 1970; "Evers Blasts College Killings," *PC*, July 11, 1970; "Kent, Jackson and Augusta," *NYAN*, June 13, 1970 (McKissick quote); "Jackson State Travesty," *NYAN*, April 15, 1972; see *The Report of the President's Commission on Campus Unrest* (New York: Arno Press, 1970).

19. "Campuses Quiet but not Content," *NYT*, December 20, 1970.

20. "Jim Brown Meets Syracuse," *BSB*, September 10, 1970; "Syracuse U. Sets Query," *CD*, September 22, 1970; Jane Kehoe Hassett, *As Strong as the Granite: Vitality and Vision: Fontbonne at 75* (St. Louis: Fontbonne College, 2000), pp. 76–78; "We the Members of the Organization of Afro-American Students Demand," no date, circa

October 1970, The Student Government Association Records, box 1, folder 34, WCSU Archives; John Craig Stewart, "The University of South Alabama: The First Thirteen Years," p. 446–448, John Craig Stewart Papers, box 1, file 9, USA Archives; "Riot Flares in Norfolk St. College," *New Pittsburg Courier*, November 21, 1970; "St. Mary's OK's Black Coach," *CD*, February 2, 1971; "Prairie View College Closed Down," *Chicago Daily Defender*, March 1, 1971; Janet Lynn Brewer, 'Keep the Lights Burning': Leadership in Church-Related Institutions" (PhD. diss., University of Kentucky, 2008), pp. 126–135; "Walkout Spurs Black Outcry," *SFF*, February 5, 1971, TCU Archives; "Black Action Association Presents 17 Demands," *ARR*, March 5, 1971; "A Time for Action," *TCO*, April 28, 1971, PC Archives; "Students at University of Ga. Give 3 Point Demands," *ADW*, May 9, 1971; "Florida U. Students Mod Home of President After Police Battle," *NYT*, April 16, 1971; "Florida U Head Disavows Racism," *NYT*, April 18, 1971; "Six Students Resume Classes on Probation," *ADW*, April 27, 1971; "Campus Protests Follow D.C. Activities; Many Involve Blacks," *CHE*, May 17, 1971.

21. For what happened to these voices, see Alphonso Pinkney, *Red, Black, and Green: Black Nationalism in the United States* (New York: Cambridge University Press, 1976), pp. 103–104, 116–117, 142–146. Ralph D. Gray, *IUPUI—The Making of an Urban University* (Bloomington, IN: Indiana University Press, 203); "Rebuttal To President's Speech," October 6, 1971, George A. Owens Papers, box 4, folder 16, TOGC Archives; "Special Committee to Study Human Relations," *WT*, October 22, 1971, WARC Archives; Stephanie Kadel Taras, *On Solid Rock: The Founding Vision of Florida Presbyterian/Eckerd College* (St. Petersburg, FL: Eckerd College, 2008), p. 180; "Classes Canceled at Wilberforce," *CHE*, October 26, 1971; "U of H Blacks Hold Building During Night," *NBH*, November 10, 1971; Warren L. D'Azevedo, "The Ethnic Minority Experience at the University of Nevada, 1874–1974," *Nevada Historical Society Quarterly* 41 (Winter 1998), pp. 225–292; "An Underground Message: Help Liberate The Rambler," Inserted in the 1971–1972 volume of TRA, TRAN Archives.

22. "72 Sees Calmer Days on College Campuses," *CD*, June 3, 1972; "The Traditionally White Institutions: For Most, Still a Long Way to Go," *CHE*, May 20, 1972; "Higher Education and the Black American: Phase 2," *CHE*, May 30, 1972.

23. "BSU Demands Are Viewed by Dean Park," *TF*, October 5, 1972, FC Archives; "ASU Officials Hear Requests of Minorities," *RP*, December 8, 1972, WTXC; "Too Few Blacks on Faculty," *TFA*, October 23, 1972, UNAL SC; Tae Y. Nam, "A Manifesto of the Black Student Activists in a Southern Black College Under the Integration Order," *The Journal of Negro Education* 46 (Spring 1977), pp. 168–185.

24. Tim Thomas, "The Student Movement at Southern University," *Freedomways* 13 (Winter 1973), pp. 17–27; "Southern U.—Tragedy on a Toured Campus," *CHE*, November 27, 1972; "Black Student Unity in New Orleans," *SR*, November 18, 1972; "Disturbance at S.U. Continues," *CD*, November 16, 1972; "'Cops Fired into Crowd,'" *CD*, November 22, 1972; "Student Group Calls Shooting 'Premeditated... Murder,'" *CHE*, November 27, 1972; "Racial Commission Blames Governor, Sheriff for Southern U. Slayings," *PC*, December 2, 1972; "Police 'Possibly' Shot Pair, Admits Governor Edwards," *OP*, November 22, 1972; "Southern U.—Tragedy on a Toured Campus," *CHE*, November 27, 1972; "Panel Says One Blast Killed Two," *OP*, December 20, 1972.

25. Ibid.

26. Ibid.

27. Ibid.

28. "Students Protest Southern Killings," *SR*, November 25, 1972; "Black-College Heads Urged to Confer on Southern U.," *CHE*, November 27, 1972; "Rally Protests Southern U Deaths," *SR*, December 2, 1972.

29. "Black Unity," *LUG*, May 1972, LGU Archives; "Toward Black Unity at MSU," *AFT*, September 30, 1972 (quote one); "Open Letter to Black Students," *AFT*, November-December 1972 (quote two), Presidents Papers: President William L. Giles, accession A81-25, box 49, folder: Student Affairs—Black Students, MSSU Archives; "Harris Discusses Black Milieu," *BW*, December 8, 1972, LEHIU SC; J. K. Obatala, "Black Students: Where Did Their Revolution Go?" *TN*, October 2, 1972.

30. "Black Students Honored With Apathy Award," *TCOL*, January 19, 1973, PSU Archives.

11. "A FLY IN BUTTERMILK": ORGANIZATIONS AND DEMANDS

1. "OASATAU: Black Men Lost," *TE*, March 1, 1968, AU Archives; "Orientation '69," Collection of the Black Students Union Orientation Handbook, 1969, box 1, folder 1, UTNK Archives.
2. See James Baldwin, *Nobody Knows My Name: More Notes of a Native Son* (New York: Dial Press, 1961).
3. Lawrence B. de Graaf, "Howard: The Evolution of a Black Student Revolt," in *PROTEST! Student Activism in America*, eds. Julian Foster and Durward Long (New York: William & Morrow & Company, 1970), p. 331.
4. Nelson Johnson, interviewed by William Chafe, October 24, 1978, interview 4.23.654, transcript, William Henry Chafe Oral History Collection, 1933–1988 and undated, box 2, file: Johnson, Nelson, 1978, Oct. 24, DKU SC; "Hart Runs for President," *TNA*, March-April 1970, WSSU Archives.
5. "Black Student Union," *TNA*, October 1969, WSSU Archives.
6. Frank Morral and Arthur Gropen, "Memorandum on Negro-White Education at Carleton," December 1, 1967, Willis D. Weatherford Papers, box 40, folder 12, BERC Archives; "Afro-American's Seeking More Campus Involvement," *CRW*, May 9, 1968, UA Archives.
7. "Black Action Affairs Council: A Historical Perspective," Monmouth College Oral Histories Collection, box 2, folder: History of Blacks in Monmouth II, MONC Archive; "Black Student Union Promotes Black Pride," *KT*, February 1972, KSU Archives.
8. "BSU," *TF*, November 20, 1970, FC Archives; "President Peters Breaks It Down," *Ra*, October 8, 1969, CLAC Archives
9. "Explains Philosophy of Afro-American Society," *NIA*, December 16, 1969, NIAU Archives; "OASATAU: Black Men Lost," AU Archives.
10. Gary S. Gaston, "Crisis of Affiliation: The Merger of Arkansas Agricultural and Mechanical College with the University of Arkansas" (PhD. diss., University of Arkansas at Little Rock, 1997), p. 97; "Negroes Create Group for Political Purposes," *COR*, May 5, 1967, F&MC Archives; "Black Student Union Forms at MC," *TMAR*, March 7, 1969, MAC Archives.

11. "Black Union Goal; Get Blacks Involved," *TAN*, November 13, 1970, UTC Archives; "Statement of Purpose of the Afro-American Society," *COR*, March 28, 1968, MORC Archives; "The New Black Generation," *PP*, November 22, 1968, CWPLIU Archives; "Black Power Talk in Action," *TCOR*, October 4, 1968, CLAU Archives; "Black American Does Exist," *TTH*, December 13, 1968, THIC Archives; "BASIB," *GUI*, November 8, 1968, GC Archives; "Constitution, Afro-American Society, Case Western Reserve University," no date, circa late 1960s, Records of Afro-American Society, box 1, folder 5, CWRU Archives.

12. "Objectives and Goals Listed by Black United Students," *TPAR*, March 7, 1969, MARSU Archives; Gwen Patton to Brothers and Sisters, September 1969, Student Organizations Records, 67/13 Black Student Union, box 1, folder 2, UKS Archives.

13. "Rallies Demand Action," *TO*, May 28, 1968, OC Archives; "It's Oliver, Shabino, Ylitalo and Jorgensen!" *MM*, April 19, 1968; "Panel Recommends Handbook, Course in Negro Politics," *MM*, May 3, 1968, STOC Archives; "Renee Jones Wins Top Office," *TQ*, April 2, 1969, UC Archives; "Big Man on Campus," *EB*, August 1971.

14. Clifford Hand to Jack, December 12, 1969, Miscellaneous Student Organizations A-L Series: Bodies Affiliated with University Collection, Sub-Series: Small Collections, box: 5.4.1.2.1, folder: Black Student Union, UP Archives; "The Black Demands," February 13, 1969, Allen Building Takeover Collection, 1969–2002, box 1, folder 3, DKU Archives; AABL Statement Presented to Dr. Hoffman, February 7, 1969, President's Office Records, 1927–1981, series 1, sub-series 17, box 44, folder 22, UHOU Archives; "Protest at Mills College," *NYT*, March 22, 1969.

15. "Black Students, SIE Deliver Demands to Administration," *RU*, May 2, 1969, NMSU Archives; Ronald G. Weber to the Parents of Union College Students, Alumni, and Other Friends of the College, 26 March 1970, Historical Collection, Envelope: Black Student Union, UMU Archives.

16. Ernest Stephens, "The Black University in America today: A Student Viewpoint," *Freedomways 7* (Spring 1967), p. 131; de Graaf, "Howard University," p. 326.

17. John Hope Franklin, *Mirror to America: An Autobiography of John Hope Franklin* (New York: Farrar, Straus and Giroux, 2005), pp. 247–248.

18. "Attention!!," no date, circa spring 1971, Vertical Files: Multiculturalism/Multicultural Affairs, 1954–1997, SKIC Archives; "Blacks Walkout Draws Response," *BDH*, December 6, 1968, BRWU Archives.

19. "The Following Demands Are Being Presented," September 29, 1969, Records Group 11: Student Organizations, 11-8: Black Student's Association, 11-8/1/2: Black Student's Association: Black Issues 1965–1969: Petitions and Committees, IWESU Archives; "Black Student Union Issues Demands," *TFOG*, November 8, 1968, USF Archives; "Statement of Demands," 1970, Office of the Dean of Students—Student Life Collection, box 12, folder: Integration—Racial, 1923–1965, GOC Archives; Claudrena N. Harold, "Of the Wings of Atalanta: The Struggle for African American Studies at the University of Virginia, 1969–1995," *Journal of African American Studies*, Online First, accessed November 21, 2011, https://doi. org/10.1007/s12111-011-9172-3; "A Time for Action," *TCO*, April 28, 1971, PC Archives; "Concerned Black Students' Demands," *WIT*, April 23, 1971, WIC Archives; "The Black Demands," DKU Archives; Black Student Association to Paul Hardin, March 13, 1970, Administrative Records, Series—Office of the Dean (Dr. Harold Jacoby), box 3, folder: Black Studies, MILLC Archives; "Statement to Members of the Black Student Organization of The John Hopkins University," May 17, 1968, Records of the Office of the President, series 9, box 40, folder: Students Affairs—Black Students' Organization, 1968, JHU Archives; Dale W. Patton, "Memo on Meeting with Negro Students—May 28, 1968, June 4, 1968," Records of the President, 1965–1970, box 12 (6F.7b), folder 10, STCST Archives.

20. "Afro Center Establishes Cultural Identity," *TDP*, February 3, 1970, DEPW Archives; "Black Cultural Centers," *MNL*, Summer 1972, MIDC Archives; Eugene R. McPhee to Each Regent and President Guiles, November 27, 1968, "November 21, 1968 Incident" Records, 1968–1971, series 1, box 1, folder 7, UWOSH Archives.

21. "Text of Demands Presented by BSA," April 7, 1969, Records of Student Unrest, box 1, folder 7, CSU Archives; "Commentary: Black Studies—The Things We Need to Know," *CHO*, November 14, 1968, MHC Archives.

22. Black Students Association to Dean of Instruction, no date, circa February 1969, Student Activities Collection, NB-STUD-V-BSP,

folder: R.U.-N&B—News Releases—General—Black Studies Protest—1969, I, ROSU Archives; "Demands and Recommendations from the Maryland State College Student Body," April 19, 1970, Student Government Association Records (RG #132), box 1, folder: 1970, UMES Archives; AABL Statement, UHOU Archives.

23. "Reed College Bars Autonomous Center for Negro Studies," *NYT*, January 27, 1969; "Blacks Want Own College 5 Student Board Members," *TCE*, February 27, 1970, CU Archives; "Demands," no date, circa 1969, Vice President for Business and Finance Series (5B/3/356), box: Black United Students, folder: Injunction File, UAK Archives; "Negro Students Press Demands," *NYT*, February 8, 1969 (Stony Brook quote); "The May Demands: A Restatement of Intentions," *TMN*, November 7, 1969, VC Archives; Rollin S. Armour to Joe Adams, May 25, 1970, General Files: Integration, STU Archives; *The Bulletin of Beloit College*, March 1969, Willis D. Weatherford Papers, box 40, folder 12, BERC Archives; John Coffee, *A Century of Eloquence: The History of Emerson College, 1880–1980* (Boston: Alternative, 1982), p. 385.

24. Robert McCray to Daniel Walker, March 16, 1973, Chancellor's Central Files (RG # 3-1-2), series 3, box 51, folder 725, UIC Archives.

25. "In Recent Years Saint Peter's College," early February 1969, RG-15 Student Activities and Campus Life, 15.7 Black Action Committee, Accession 015—XX-0002, SPC Archives; "On Niggers and Honkies," *TDS*, February 21, 1969, UND Archives; "Stanford Fails to Win Approval of Militants With Pioneer Program," *WSF*, June 11, 1969; "Racism at Howard," *The Spear and Shield*, February 3, 1970, Student Movement Records, Liberal/Left Archival Studies Papers, MS2096 series 2, box 4, folder 7, GWU SC.

26. "Documents on Demands," *XUN*, November 19, 1969, XUO Archives; Black Student Demands at Providence College, March 16, 1971, General Files: Afro-American Society of Providence College, PC Archives; Demands of Roosevelt Black Students Association, no date, circa May 1968, Student Activities Collection, NB-STUD-V-BSP, folder: R.U.-N&B—News Releases—General—Black Studies Protest—1969, I, ROSU Archives

27. "Concerned Black Students' Demands," WIC Archives; "Black Students Demands," February 20, 1969, Student Demonstrations, 1960–Present Collection, box 001, folder 3, EMU Archives; Demands of the Organization of Afro-American Students, no date, circa early

1970s, The Student Government Association Records, box 1, folder 34, WCSU Archives; "Demonstration at Coe in Support for Negro Demands," *CRP*, May 20, 1968; "What the B.S.A. Wants," no date, circa late 1960s, Student Life Collection, box 20, folder: Black Student Alliance, 1968–1977, RPI Archives.

28. The Black Student Union Demands to Administration, November 21, 1969, Black Student Union Scrapbook 1969–1991, University Records Collection—UR 38, box 1, folder 1, UMAD Archives; "ASU Officials Hear Requests of Minorities," *RP*, December 8, 1972, WTXC; Frank McClellan to McCloskey, May 7, 1969, Unprocessed Student Affairs Records, DQU Archives; "Text of the Statement Presented to President Umbeck, Dean Salter and Dean Harlan by Allied Blacks for Liberty and Equality on February 11, 1969," Organization Series: A.B.L.E., "10 Demands," 1969, KC Archives.

29. "Demands," UAK Archives; Edward D. Eddy to Members of the Faculty and Staff and the Students of Chatham College, March 3, 1970, Alphabetical Files: Black Student Union, CHU Archives; Warren L. D'Azevedo, "The Ethnic Minority Experience at the University of Nevada, 1874–1974," *Nevada Historical Society Quarterly* 41 (Winter 1998), pp. 225–292.

30. David Simons, "Perspectives: A Brief History of CBS's roots," Concerned Black Students of Grinnell College, https://web.archive.org/web/20080123100510/http://www.grinnell.edu/student/groups/cbs/history/manifesto, accessed December 13, 2022; "Students Tell Demands," *DCN*, April 9, 1970, DEC Archives; "In Recent Years Saint Peter's College," SPC Archives; "Black Student Problems Given Top Priority," *BQ*, April 3, 1972, RWU Archives; Press Release on Black Students Demands, no date, circa 1971, Records of the Affirmative Action/Equal Opportunity Office, box 5, folder 2, SRU Archives; "Black Students Present Demands," *TIN*, April 2, 1969, TRSU Archives.

31. John Craig Stewart, "The University of South Alabama: The First Thirteen Years," p. 446–448, John Craig Stewart Papers, box 1, file 9; USA Archives; AABL Statement, UHOU Archives; Memo from the Black Student Organization Regarding their Demands, May 6, 1968, Records of the President (R 3/13), box 1, folder 7, KAC Archives; "Text of Demands Presented by BSA," April 7, 1969, Records of Student Unrest, box 1, folder 7, CSU Archives.

32. President Morse to Members of The Afro-American Society of Case Western Reserve University, December 13, 1968, Records of the Afro-American Studies Program, box 1, folder 6, CWRU Archives; Urban Institute, "Student Unrest A Chronology, 1964–June 1969," Martin K. Gordon Collection, box 1, folder 6, GWU SC; Demands to President Jerome Sachs Northeastern Illinois State College, May 27, 1968, General Files: Student Life and Customs—Clubs and Organizations M3/46 to M3/51, folder: Student Life and Customs—Clubs and Organizations—Memos M3/51, re: Student Black Caucus Demonstration in History Department, NEIU Archives; "CCC Has Sit-in, No Bomb," *BW*, March 17, 1970, LEHIU SC; Black Student Demands at East Tennessee State University, no date, circa May 1972, D. P. Culp Papers, box 60, folder 5, ETSU Archives; John Egerton, *State Universities and Black Americans: An Inquiry into Desegregation and Equity for Negroes in 100 Public Universities* (Atlanta: Southern Education Reporting Service, 1969), p. 82.

33. Harry Edwards, *Black Students* (New York: Free Press, 1970) pp. 144–155; Earl Anthony, *The Time of the Furnaces: A Case Study of Black Student Revolt* (New York: Dial Press, 1971), pp. 50–51; "Racism Uproots Murphy," *PC*, March 30, 1968; "The Angry Black Athlete," *NE*, July 15, 1968.

34. John Matthew Smith, "'Breaking the Plan': Integration and Black Protest in Michigan State University Football during the 1960s," *The Michigan Historical Review* 33 (Fall 2007), pp. 50–55.

35. Gayraud S. Wilmore, *Black Religion and Black Radicalism* (Garden City, NY: Doubleday, 1972), p. 281; "Black Militants' Demands Are Changing Churches," *NYT*, May 25, 1969; "Union Seminary Back to Normal," *NYT*, May 14, 1969; "Protest Delays Exams at Seminary," *CD*, May 13, 1969; "Social Welfare Accepts BSU Demands," *DB*, April 16, 1969, UCLA Archives; The Black Graduate Student Union to Milton Eisenhow, May 5, 1971, Records of the Office of the Presidents, series 13, box 4, folder: "Black Students," JHU Archives; Harry Alpert to R. D. Clark, May 15, 1972, Office of the President Records, Robert D. Clark (UA 16), box 68, folder: Black Graduate Student Council, UO Archives. Cone's major text was *Black Theology and Black Power* (New York: Seabury Press, 1969).

36. "Protest at Wittenberg University," pp. C-138–C-166; Winston A. Grady-Willis, *Challenging U.S. Apartheid: Atlanta and Black Struggles for Human Rights, 1960–1977* (Durham, NC: Duke

University Press, 2006), pp. 146–148; Jeffrey Alan Turner, "Conscious and Conflict: Patterns in the History of Student Activism on Southern College Campuses, 1960–1970" (PhD. diss., Tulane University, 2000), pp. 356–363; Payson S. Wild to Faculty Member, May 8, 1968, General Files, folder: Black Student Protest—I, April-May 1968, NOWU Archives.

37. "A Position Concerning Black Survival, Part I," November 11, 1970, General Folders: Black Student Union Minority Issues, 1969–1970, SJU Archives.

38. "Strider," "Blacks," *COE*, March 6, 1970, COC Archives.

12. "A New Sense of My Black Self": Protests and Support

1. *Staff Study of Campus Riots and Disorders, October 1967–May 1969* (Washington, DC: US Government Printing Office, 1969) p. 16. Howard and City College protests are cited in previous chapter.

2. "When Black Students Take Over a Campus," *TNR*, April 13, 1968; Jerrold Wimbish Roy, "Student Activism and the Historically Black University: Hampton Institute and Howard University, 1960–1972" (PhD. diss., Harvard University, 2000) pp. 73–85.

3. Zira DeFries and Lilo Grothe, "'Les Jours De Mai' 1968—Barnard College," *Adolescence* 4 (Summer 1969), pp. 158–160; Lawrence B. de Graaf, "Howard: The Evolution of a Black Student Revolt," in *PROTEST! Student Activism in America*, eds. Julian Foster and Durward Long (New York: William & Morrow & Company, 1970), p. 447.

4. "Negroes Stage Radcliffe Sit-in; Colleges Act on Their Demands," *NYT*, December 11, 1968.

5. "Blacks Walkout Draws Response," BRWU Archives.

6. "Presidents Speaks With Blacks About Student Relations Center," *TPAR*, October 2, 1969, MARSU Archives; "200 Students March Quietly to Rice Hall," *THAT*, April 30, 1968, GWU SC; Adam Gray, "African American Activism at Northern Michigan University: 1968–1970" (unpublished manuscript, no date), Student Papers, box 1, folder 30, NMU Archives; Steven C. Phillips, *Justice and Hope: Past Reflections and Future Visions of the Stanford Black Student*

Union, 1967–1989 (Stanford, CA: Stanford Black Student Union, 1990), pp. 15–18.

7. Alford A. Young, *Revolt of the Privileged: The Coming Together of the Black Community at Wesleyan University, 1965–1976* (Middletown, CT: Center for Afro-American Studies, Wesleyan University, 1988) pp. 33–34; Alexander W. Astin, Helen S. Astin, Alan E. Bayer, and Ann S. Bisconti, *The Power of Protest: A National Study of Student and Faculty Disruptions with Implications for the Future* (San Francisco: Jossey-Bass, 1975), pp. 98–105; Franklin, *Mirror to America*, pp. 247–248; "Fisk Students Want Black University," *CD*, December 15, 1969.

8. *Staff Study of Campus Riots and Disorders*, p. 34; "Armed Troopers Patrol Lane College," *CD*, March 25, 1969; "Fear More Violence at Lane College," *CD*, March 24, 1969; "Rebellion, Fires Hit Quinn Campus," *CD*, July 30, 1970; "Negro Student Is Charged in Bluefield College Bombing," *NYT*, November 25, 1968; Roy, "Student Activism and the Historically Black University," p. 85–90; "Prairie View College Closed Down," *CD*, March 1, 1971; "Queens Students Ransack Office," *NYT*, January 14, 1969.

9. Fabio Rojas, *From Black Power to Black Studies: How a Radical Social Movement Became an Academic Discipline* (Baltimore: The John Hopkins University Press, 2007), p. 55; "The Eleven Days at Brandeis—As Seen from the President's chair," *NYT*, February 16, 1969; Ione D. Vargus, *Revival of Ideology: The Afro-American Society Movement* (San Francisco: R & E Research Associates, 1977), pp. 118–119; Richard P. McCormick, *The Black Student Protest Movement at Rutgers* (New Brunswick, NJ: Rutgers University Press, 1990) pp. 3–4, 50–60; "Negroes at Rutgers Main Campus Stage Protest," *NYT*, February 26, 1969. See also Ernesto "Che" Guevara, *Guerilla Warfare* (New York: Ocean Press, 2006); Robert Taber, *The War of the Flea: Guerrilla Warfare Theory and Practice* (London: Paladin, 1970).

10. Richard E. Peterson, *The Scope of Organized Student Protest in 1967–1968* (Princeton, NJ: Institutional Research Program for Higher Education, Educational Testing Service, 1968), pp. 11, 13; Alan Bayer and Alexander Astin, "Violence and Disruption on the U.S. Campus, 1968–1969," *Educational Record* 50 (Fall 1969), pp. 337–350; *Student Protests, 1969* (Chicago: Urban Research Corporation, 1969); "Student Strikes: 1968–1969," *Black Scholar* 1

(January-February 1970), pp. 65–75; Alexander Astin, "New Evidence on Campus Unrest, 1969–70," *Educational Record* 52 (Winter 1971), pp. 41–46; Dale Gaddy, *The Scope of Organized Student Protest in Junior Colleges* (Washington, DC: American Association of Junior Colleges, 1970); "Demonstrations Occur at Rate of One a Day in 1970; Major Protests Hit Michigan, Washington U," *CHE*, April 6, 1970.

11. "Brooklyn College Resumes Class after Arrest of 42," *NYT*, May 22, 1968; "Police Break Up Sit-in in Brooklyn College at College Office," *NYT*, May 21, 1968; "Sit-in a Fraud Dean Declares," *NYT*, May 21, 1968.

12. "Minority Students Present Ultimatum to Regents," *TMIR*, November 14, 1969, ACSD Archives; See Jeffrey O. G. Ogbar, "Rainbow Radicalism: The Rise of the Radical Ethnic Nationalism," in *The Black Power Movement: Rethinking the Civil Rights—Black Power Era*, ed. Peniel E. Joseph (New York: Routledge, 2006), pp. 193–228.

13. Statement by Forty Faculty Members Who Actively Supported the Association of Black Collegians, April 14, 1968, Box: Colgate—Vietnam Era, COLU Archives; "Alumni Request Ghetto Recruitment," *TMAR*, May 10, 1968, MAC Archives.

14. "Negro Students Continue Their Protest at Brandeis," *NYT*, January 16, 1969; "Black Students Alive and Well at Malcolm X U.," *BSB*, January 16, 1969; Tuskegee—Students Take Care of Business!!, George Owens Papers, box 4, folder 15, TOGC Archives; Attached FBI Bulletin on University of Hawaii, December 11, 1968, Papers of Lyndon B. Johnson: Presidential Papers, Office Files of Mildred Stegall, box 73B, folder: Students for a Democratic Society [1968], LBJL; Loretta Johnson to President Harrison, February 22, 1969; Willie J. Wiley to Sir, February 26, 1969; Sammy Roberts to Mr. Harrison, no date, circa February 1969; Mary Dixon to President Harrison, February 24, 1969; Afro-American Student Union to President Harrison, February 27, 1969; David L. Uhuru to Mr. Harrison, March 3, 1969, Franklin Harrison Papers, box 4, folder 8, UTA Archives.

13. "AMERICAN VERSION OF STORM TROOPERS":
OPPOSITION AND REPRESSION, 1965–1968

1. "Mississippi Police Rout 1,000 Negroes with Gas and Clubs," *NYT,* April 6, 1966.
2. "Rioting Nashville Negroes Fire on Cars, Stone Police," *NYT,* April 10, 1967; *The Report of the President's Commission on Campus Unrest* (New York: Arno Press, 1970), pp. 414–416; Joy Ann Williamson, *Radicalizing the Ebony Tower: Black Colleges and the Black Freedom Struggle in Mississippi* (New York: Teachers College Press, 2008), p. 137; "University in Ohio Closes Doors to Avert a Renewal of Violence," *NYT,* November 15, 1967; "Central State College Closes over Campus Black Power," *NYAN,* November 25, 1967; "Texas Cops Beat Students," *BSB,* May 27, 1967; "Bricks without Straw," *TH,* August 31, 2007; "Texas Indicts 5 in Police Killing," *NYT,* June 3, 1967; "Shot Kills Texas Policeman in Riot at a Negro College," *NYT,* May 18, 1967; "Texas Student Charged with Murder," *BSB,* August 3, 1967; "NAACP Protests: Reinstate Students," *NYAN,* November 11, 1967.
3. "ACLU Statement on Demonstrations," *CHE,* May 17, 1967; "Unrest Campus Style," *PC,* June 10, 1967; "One Method Versus Another," *NYAN,* May 13, 1967.
4. "Afro-American Society Pushes for Administrative Approval in Council," *CR,* March 21, 1968, Unprocessed Files of Tim Orwig, MORC Archives; "Action Gets Heavy During Senate Passage of Black Student Union Constitution," *TA,* February 26, 1971, BSU Archives; "'Segregation,'" "Acknowledgement," *TT,* May 2, 1967, TRIC Archives; Downs, *Cornell '69,* p. 62; Wayne Glasker, *Black Students in the Ivory Tower: African American Student Activism at the University of Pennsylvania, 1967–1990* (Amherst, MA: University of Massachusetts, 2002), p. 31.
5. Clarence L. Mohr and Joseph E. Gordon, *Tulane: The Emergence of a Modern University, 1945–1980* (Baton Rouge, LA: Louisiana State University Press, 2001), pp. 357–358.
6. "We Are Afro-Americans," *TEM,* February 21, 1968; "Rebuttal: Being Black a State of Mind," *TEM,* February 28, 1968, CSTU Archives; "Student Speaks Out against Wilson's Negro Non-Acceptance," *TB,* November 10, 1967; "An Open Letter to Madelyn,"

TB, November 17, 1967, WILC Archives; Jeffrey Alan Turner, *Sitting In and Speaking Out: Student Movements in the American South, 1960–1970* (Athens, GA: University of Georgia Press, 2010), p. 190.

7. Jeffrey Alan Turner, "Conscious and Conflict: Patterns in the History of Student Activism on Southern College Campuses, 1960–1970" (PhD. diss., Tulane University, 2000), p. 276; "National Guardsmen Sent to 3 Troubled Campuses," *CHE*, June 16, 1969; Cleveland Sellers and Robert Terrell, *The River of No Return: The Autobiography of a Black Militant* (Jackson, MS: University of Mississippi Press, 1990), pp. 210–212, 218.

8. "Overuse of Force on Negroes Found," *NYT*, February 25, 1968; "My View," *PC*, March 16, 1968; "Police Slayings of 3 Students Arouse South," *CHE*, March 11, 1968; "6 Hurt in Clashes at Negro College," *NYT*, February 22, 1968; Williamson, *Radicalizing the Ebony Tower*, pp. 154–155; "South Carolina Verdict," *CD*, June 12, 1969; "Carolina Patrolmen Cleared of Liability in Orangeburg Suit," *NYT*, November 14, 1970.

9. "Negro Students Seize Colgate Fraternity House," *NYT*, April 8, 1968; "Colgate Students Fraternity Bias," *NYT*, April 10, 1968; "Colgate Bans 2 Biased Frats after Shooting," *PC*, April 27, 1968; "Two Bias Incidents Hit Students after 'Black Week,'" *CD*, May 10, 1969.

10. "OSU Indictments Likened to Lynching," *CD*, April 2, 1969; Durward Long, "Black Protest," in *PROTEST! Student Activism in America*, eds. Julian Foster and Durward Long (New York: William Morrow and Company, 1970), p. 473; "Patrolmen Guard Ohio State Campus," *NYT*, May 1, 1968; "34 at Ohio State Gain Settlement," *NYT*, July 29, 1969.

11. "My View," *PC*, August 10, 1968; "Surveillance on Campus: Some Administrators Are Shocked, Others Cooperate," *CHE*, May 3, 1971 (first quote); "FBI Approved Hiring Student Informers, Sen. Weicker Says," *CHE*, June 18, 1973 (second quote); Interdepartmental correspondence to Robert E. Smith, September 30, 1968, Chancellor James Bugg's Papers, box 1, folder 29, UMSTL Archives; "Chicano and Black Student Demands and Rationale," no date, circa 1969, Campus Unrest Collection, box 2, folder: Ethnic Minorities; African American students, 1968–1971 and undated, CSUFRES Archives. Also see "How the FBI Tried to Subvert Campus Rebellion," *CHE*, September 15, 1975; "FBI is Reported Active on Campuses since

1968," *CHE*, April 12, 1971; "FBI, under Hoover, Sought to Discredit Texas U., Antioch," *CHE*, December 1, 1975; "F.B.I. Planned to Neutralize Key Activists," *CHE*, December 17, 1973; Kenneth O'Reilly, *Racial Matters: The FBI's Secret File on Black America, 1960–1972* (New York: Free Press, 1989).

12. "Incidents Urge Respect of Blacks," *CC*, March 14, 1969, LUTC Archives; "Rights for the Whites, Inc." to University of Utah, October 28, 1971; "A Loyal Tennessee Fan" to President, October 29, 1971, Student Affairs Office Records, 1970–1977, Box 4, Folder 14, UUTAH Archives.

13. "Silent Majority" to "NIGGERS," no date, circa late 1960s, Center for African American Studies, Administrative Subject Files, 1969–, box 16, folder (Black Faculty/Staff of So. Calif 1968–1969), UCLA Archives; Block, "Afro-Americans for Black Liberation," p. 26; "Blacks Take Credit for DeKalb Rioting," *CD*, March 24, 1969; "Riot Hits NIU Campus," *CD*, March 24, 1969.

14. John Craig Stewart, "The University of South Alabama: The First Thirteen Years," p. 449, John Craig Stewart Papers, box 1, file 9; "Whiteurs Discusses Shooting," *VA*, March 12, 1971, USA Archives; "Events of Yesterday," no date, circa late 1960s, Jose Joel Garcia Collection CEMA 73, series 3, box 1, folder 18, CEMA.

15. Rusty L. Monhollon, *This is America?: The Sixties in Lawrence, Kansas* (New York: Palgrave Macmillan, 2002), pp. 100–106; Beryl Ann New, "A Fire in the Sky: Student Activism in Topeka, Kansas and Lawrence, Kansas High School in 1969 and 1970" (Masters Ed., Washburn University, 2002), pp. 52–54; Judith Jackson Fossett, *Race Consciousness: African-American Studies For the New Century* (New York: New York University Press, 1997), pp. 248 (Garrett and BSU quotes); Bryce Nelson, "Kansas: Police-Student Violence Imperils University," *Science* 169 (August 7, 1970), pp. 567–569.

16. "Black Thursday at Oshkosh," *TC*, November 1969; "100 Negro Students Seized in Wisconsin Protest," *NYT*, November 22, 1968; "Black Students Ransack Oshkosh Prexy's Office," *PC*, November 30, 1968; "200 Students Storm Wisconsin Regents to Press Demands," *NYT*, December 7, 1968; "Negro Student Is Charged in Bluefield College Bombing," *NYT*, November 25, 1968.

17. Anonymous to Thomas H. Eliot, December 11, 1968 (first quote); C. L. Husbands to Thomas H. Eliot, December 16, 1968 (second quote); Ex-Student to Thomas H. Eliot, December 12, 1968 (third

quote), series 11, box 1, folder: Student Demonstrations WU, Correspondence A–K, 1968–1969, WU Archives.

18. Dikran Karagueuzian, *Blow It Up!: The Black Student Revolt at San Francisco State and the Emergence of Dr. Hayakawa* (Boston: Gambit, 1971), pp. 168–169; William Barlow and Peter Shapiro, *An End to Silence: The San Francisco State College Student Movement in the '60s* (New York: Pegasus, 1971), pp. 236–264; "Police Repel Students at College in San Francisco," *NYT*, December 4, 1968.

19. Ibid.

14. "Black Jim Crow Studies": Opposition and Repression, 1969–1972

1. "Incident in Minneapolis," *NYT*, January 15, 1969; "Students End Siege on U. of Minnesota Campus," *NYT*, January 16, 1969; Calvin B. T. Lee, *The Campus Scene, 1900–1970: Changing Styles in Undergraduate Life* (New York: McKay, 1970), pp. 147–148 (bath quote); "Black Culture at SSC," *TS*, March 31, 1970, CSUSTAN Archives; "Marquette Head Criticized, Kenosha News, May 22, 1968, Office of Student Affairs Records, series 3, box 3, folder: Institutional Racism Protest Newspaper Clippings, May 21–26, 1969, MARU Archives; "UCSB Black Studies Dept. Built From 1968 Black Student Union Protest," *DN*, February 12, 2001, UC SAN Archives; "Coast Negroes Seize University Center," *NYT*, October 14, 1968; Richard D. Strahan to Hugh C. Smith, March 11, 1969, 1969 Demonstrations Collection, DSU Archives.

2. William Barlow and Peter Shapiro, *An End to Silence: The San Francisco State College Student Movement in the '60s* (New York: Pegasus, 1971), pp. 299–301 Dikran Karagueuzian, *Blow It Up!: The Black Student Revolt at San Francisco State and the Emergence of Dr. Hayakawa* (Boston: Gambit, 1971), pp. 183–184; "House Committee Opens Hearings on Impact of Student Protests," *CHE*, February 10, 1969; "Negro Students Push Demands; Reaction Grows," *CHE*, January 27, 1969; "CORE's Chief Assails Wilkins Stand," *NYT*, January 22, 1969; "NAACP Opposes Student Control of Black Studies," *SR*, February 1, 1969.

3. "The Case for Separatism: 'Black Perspective'"; "The Case Against Separatism: 'Black Jim Crow,'" *NE*, February 10, 1969.
4. Allan Kornberg and Joel Smith, "'It Ain't Over Yet': Activism in a Southern University," in *Black Power and Student Rebellion: Conflict on the American University*, eds. James McEvoy and Abraham Miller (Belmont, CA: Wadsworth Publishing Company, 1969), pp. 107–109; Alan Kornberg and Mary L. Brehm, "Ideology, Institutional Identification, and Campus Activism," *Social Forces* 49 (March 1971), pp. 445–446; Rodney Stark, "Protest + Police = Riot," in *Black Power and Student Rebellion*, pp. 186–190.
5. "Silbert Attacks Afro Demands As 'Unrealistic, Vague, Racist,'" *TDT*, February 28, 1969, UTXA Archives; "United We Welsh," no date, circa early 1969, Student Demonstrations, 1960–Present Collection, box 001, folder 3, EMU Archives; Bill Kost, "Minority Groups," *TPC*, December 6, 1968, WPU Archives; Eugene G. Williams to the Editors, November 22, 1968, "November 21, 1968 Incident" Records, 1968–1971, series 1, box 1, folder 7, UWOSH Archives; "Campus Backlash: Students Protest Protests," *NYT*, February 26, 1969; "'Black Studies Furora Fad,' says Brinley," *OP*, February 27, 1969 (Huntley quote); "Separate Is Not Equal," *NYAN*, February 22, 1969 (Rustin quote); "Reactions to Disorders Gains in Intensity," *CHE*, March 10, 1969; "Tough Responses to Dissent Seen Stifling Reforms," *CHE*, March 10, 1969; "Governors Reject Hard Line on Colleges," *CHE*, March 10, 1969; "Poll Shows Adult Public Favors Hard Line as Campus Protests Continue to Spread," *CHE*, March 29, 1969.
6. "A.C.E. Special Report: Text of the Memorandum from the Office for Civil Rights, Dated March, 1969," Willis D. Weatherford Papers, box 40, folder 12, BERC Archives; "Black Students Blamed in New Jim Crow," *CD*, March 1, 1969; "Dozen Colleges Warned on Excluding Whites," *CHE*, March 10, 1969; "Is Crow-Jim Democratic," *CD*, March 8, 1969 (first quote); "Clark Scores Separatism at Antioch," *NYT*, May 23, 1969 (second quote)
7. Jeffrey Alan Turner, "Conscious and Conflict: Patterns in the History of Student Activism on Southern College Campuses, 1960–1970" (PhD. diss., Tulane University, 2000), pp. 311–314; "Fly 'Black Flag' at Southern," *CD*, April 16, 1969; "Cops Nab 109 MSU Students," *CD*, April 30, 1969; "Armed Students Takeover Voorhees College Building," *CD*, April 29, 1969; "Voorhees College Students on Trial

for Rioting," *SR*, July 25, 1970; "Negro Students Reach Accord with Pratt Institute President," *NYT*, May 11, 1969; "20 Arrested at Howard as Campus Siege Ends," *NYT*, May 10, 1969; "365 Held in Alabama," *NYT*, May 6, 1969.

8. This opening narrative about the Cornell protest comes from Donald Alexander Downs, *Cornell '69: Liberalism and the Crisis of the American University* (Ithaca, NY: Cornell University Press, 1999); William H. Friedland and Harry Edwards, "Confrontation at Cornell," *Trans-action* 6 (June 1969), pp. 29–36, 76.

9. Ibid.

10. Ibid.

11. Ibid.

12. Ibid.

13. Ibid.

14. "Cornell Faculty Votes Down Pact Ending Take-over," *NYT*, April 22, 1969; "Peaceful Sit-in at Cornell Ends New Seizure Threat," *NYT*, April 23, 1969; Friedland and Edwards, "Confrontation at Cornell," p. 34; "Cornell Faculty Reverses Itself on Negroes," *NYT*, April 24, 1969.

15. "What People Are Saying about Campus Disorders: A Sampler," *CHE*, May 5, 1969; "Backlash Grows in Congress as Campus Protests Intensify," *CHE*, May 5, 1969; "Negro Professor Quits Cornell, Charges Leniency Hurts Blacks," *NYT*, June 2, 1969; "Response to Armed Negroes Divides Cornell Community," *CHE*, May 5, 1969; "Cornell Blacks," *CD*, April 29, 1969; "Guns on Campus," *NYT*, April 22, 1969.

16. Conrad M. Dyer, "Protest and the Politics of Open Admissions: The Impact of the Black and Puerto Rican Students' Community (of City College)," (PhD. diss., City University of New York, 1990)," pp. 127–129; "Rash of Vandalism at QC Brings 500 Cops," *NYAN*, May 10, 1969; "2 More Campuses of City U. Closed after Disorders," *NYT*, May 3, 1969.

17. "Negro Students Criticized by Rustin," *NYT*, April 28, 1969; "Negro Students Reply to Critics," *NYT*, May 17, 1969; "Allen Comments on Protests," *NYT*, June 1, 1969.

18. "U. of Louisville Expels 8," *NYT*, May 3, 1969; "Student Revolutionaries Condemned by President," *CD*, April 30, 1969.

19. "The Siege of Greensboro," *NE*, June 2, 1969; "Greensboro Calm as Guard Leaves," *NYT*, May 25, 1969.

20. Ibid.

21. "Thurgood Marshall Denounces Militants," *SR*, May 17, 1969; "Negro Leaders and Opponents of War Play Major Role as Graduate Speakers," *NYT*, June 9, 1969; "Negro Extremists Scored at Parley," *NYT*, July 3, 1969 (Kilson quote one); "Professor Scores Black Separatism," *NYT*, September 7, 1969 (Kilson quote two); "The Case against Black Studies," *PC*, August 2, 1969 (Lewis quote).

22. "Black Problem Unsolved," BW, September 23, 1969, LEHIU SC (Mills quote); Glen R. Driscoll to Robert, June 11, 1970, Papers of the Chancellors, Glen Driscoll (1969–1972), box 4, folder 205, UMSTL Archives.

23. "Initiators Withdraw Referendum Petition," *CR*, February 26, 1970, MORC Archives; "Why Put a Color on the Center," *TCC*, November 22, 1968, STCST Archives; "Olaf Black Population Alienates Most Whites," *MM*, November 17, 1969; "Olaf Black Say Union Open to All," *MM*, November 25, 1969, STOC Archives

24. "House Action on Disorders Appears Near," *CHE*, June 16, 1969; "Campus Disorder Brings Demands for States to Act," *NYT*, May 4, 1969; Janet Harris, *Students in Revolt* (New York: McGraw-Hill Book Company, 1970), p. 165–167; "Campus Gun Ban Is Voted in Albany," *NYT*, May 1, 1969; "Assembly Votes Campus Gun Ban," *NYT*, April 29, 1969; "Many State Legislatures Act against Campus Disrupters," *CHE*, June 16, 1969; "Disorders Puzzle Legislators," *CHE*, August 11, 1969; "Police Seeking to Avoid Clashes with Students," *CHE*, July 14, 1969; "Confrontations Alter Role of Campus Officers," *CHE*, July 14, 1969.

25. "Stern Anti-Disruption Warnings Greet Returning Students, but so Do Conciliatory Moves Giving Them More Say," *CHE*, September 29, 1969 (Ohio quote); "Colleges Strengthen Security and Rules; Students Warned on Disruptions," *CHE*, September 28, 1970.

26. "68 Colleges Cut Off Funds to Disrupters," *CHE*, October 20, 1969; DeVere Pentony, Robert Smith, and Richard Axen, *Unfinished Rebellions* (San Francisco: Jossey-Bass, 1971), pp.172–176; "S.F. State Strike Trials—Mixed Bag of Repression," *SR*, November 29, 1969; "2 at Minnesota U. Guilty in Protest," *NYT*, November 8, 1969; "Students Trial Is Seen as Vital," *NYT*, September 21, 1969; "Valley State Students Face New Troubles," *SR*, December 13, 1969; "NAACP Defends College Students," *TC*, November 1969; "2

Decisions Set Precedents in Curbing Campus Disorders," *CHE*, December 8, 1969.

27. "Campus Militants Given 1–25 Years," *NYT*, February 1, 1970; "Judicial Lynching of Calif. Students," *CD*, February 21, 1970; Earl Anthony, *The Time of the Furnaces: A Case Study of Black Student Revolt* (New York: The Dial Press, 1971) pp. 87–100.

28. Clifford A. Bullock, "Fired by Conscience: The 'Black 14' Incident at the University of Wyoming and Black Protest in the Western Athletic Conference," *Annals of Wyoming: The Wyoming History Journal* 68 (1996), pp. 4–13; "Wyoming U Still Tense," *CD*, October 25, 1969; "Black Athletes Having Their Day in Court," *CD*, November 11, 1969; "Court Disclaims Black-14s Petition," *CD*, October 19, 1971.

29. "Rule of Law at Harvard," *NYT*, December 13, 1969; "Negroes Skip Harvard Classes," *NYT*, December 17, 1969; "Students Suspended: Blacks Press Harvard for Jobs," *BSB*, December 18, 1969; "Dean at Harvard Charges 40 Students in Take-over," *NYT*, December 20, 1969; "Harvard Acts against Blacks," *CD*, January 3, 1970; "Harvard Hearings Boycott," *NYT*, January 10, 1970; "Black Students Judge Harvard," *BSB*, January 22, 1970.

30. Joy Ann Williamson, *Radicalizing the Ebony Tower: Black Colleges and the Black Freedom Struggle in Mississippi* (New York: Teachers College Press, 2008), pp. 140–141; "Mississippi Students Rebel at Itta Bena," *ADW*, February 27, 1970; "894 Students Are Arrested at a Mississippi College," *CHE*, March 2, 1970; "Dallas Students Ousted by Police," *NYT*, February 13, 1970; Turner, "Conscious and Conflict," pp. 294–296; James Forman, *Sammy Younge, Jr.: The First Black College Student to Die in the Black Liberation Movement* (New York: Grove Press, 1968), pp. 262–282.

31. "OBC Protest Dean's Letter," *TTH*, March 6, 1970, THIC Archives; "Brandeis Quiet Despite Student Sit-in," *NYT*, January 15, 1969.

32. "Campus Protests Follow D.C. Activities; Many Involve Blacks," *CHE*, May 17, 1971; Jerrold Wimbish Roy, "Student Activism and the Historically Black University: Hampton Institute and Howard University, 1960–1972" (PhD. diss., Harvard University, 2000), pp. 90–93.

33. "A Settlement—And Why We Signed It," *Black Fire*, May 3, 1969, Author's Personal Collection, Supplied by Bernard Stringer.

15. "Black Students Refuse to Pass the Buck": The Racial Reconstitution of Higher Education

1. "Black Scholarship," *NYT*, January 23, 1969; "Harvard Report Calls for Degree in Negro Studies," *NYT*, January 22, 1969; Henry Rosovsky, "Black Studies at Harvard: Personal Reflections Concerning Recent Events," *The American Scholar* 38 (Autumn 1969), pp. 562–572; Roger Rosenblatt, *Coming Apart: A Memoir of the Harvard Wards of 1969* (Boston: Little, Brown and Company, 1997), p. 141.

2. Ibid.; "Among the Harvard Faculty, an Intense Feeling of Uncertainty," *NYT*, April 24, 1969; "Harvard Negroes Get Faculty Voice," *NYT*, April 23, 1969; Lawrence E. Eichel, Kenneth W. Jost, Robert D. Luskin, and Richard M. Neustadt, *The Harvard Strike* (Boston: Hougton Mifflin Company, 1970), pp. 268–269, 284–286.

3. Ibid.

4. Ibid.

5. "Boycotting Students at Howard Threaten an Injunction," *NYT*, May 13, 1969; "Nkrumah for Howard U.," *CD*, June 3, 1969; "20 Arrested at Howard as Campus Siege Ends," *NYT*, May 10, 1969; "Howard Prexy Maps Plans for 'Black Education,'" *CD*, September 24, 1969; Jerrold Wimbish Roy, "Student Activism and the Historically Black University: Hampton Institute and Howard University, 1960–1972" (PhD. diss., Harvard University, 2000), pp. 138–147.

6. Ibid.

7. Ibid.

8. "Colleges Step Up Changes in Bid to Avert Disruption," *NYT*, May 11, 1969 (Roose quote); "'Education Authority Crisis' Discussed by Ford Fund," *CHE*, March 10, 1969 (Ward quote); "Black Collegians," *WSJ*, July 28, 1969; W. Todd Furniss, "Racial Minorities and Curriculum Change," *Educational Record* 50 (Fall 1969), p. 360–370; "Vast Changes on Campuses Seen in 70s," *CHE*, December 8, 1969; "More Negroes, Women Joining Trustee Ranks," *CHE*, April 6, 1970.

9. "C. E. Daye Delivers 'State of Campus,'" *CE*, February 28, 1966, NCCU Archives; Joy Ann Williamson, *Radicalizing the Ebony Tower: Black Colleges and the Black Freedom Struggle in Mississippi* (New York: Teachers College Press, 2008). p. 39.

10. "Disruptive Tactics May Not Be Used Again," *AJR*, March 7, 1969, NATU Archives; "Demands and Recommendations from the Maryland State College Student Body," UMES Archives.

11. "Temporary Accord Ends Bowie Demonstration," *THAT*, April 2, 1968, GWU SC; "Alcorn 1966: An Incident," ETSU Archives; George Henderson, *Race and the University: A Memoir* (Norman, OK: University of Oklahoma Press, 2010), p. 26.

12. *Special Financial Needs of Traditional Negro Colleges: A Task Force Report* (Atlanta: Southern Regional Education Board, 1969).

13. "46 Black College Heads Appeal for U.S. Funds," *CD*, May 29, 1971.

14. Vivian W. Henderson, "Blacks and Change in Higher Education," *Daedalus* 104 (Fall 1974), p. 74; "A Professor's Point of View," *NI*, June 1969; "Board of Trustees Gets First Black Chairman," *AJR*, November 7, 1969, NATU Archives.

15. Robert W. Morse to Raymond A. Henry, December 1, 1969, Records of the Afro-American Society, box 1, folder 4, CWRU Archives.

16. Ronald Walters and Robert Smith, "The Black Education Strategy in the 1970s," *The Journal of Negro Education* 48 (Spring 1979), pp. 158, 165–166; "Black Youths' Share of Enrollment Grows," *CHE*, December 15, 1975; 12% of College Frosh in '74 Were Blacks," *CD*, December 10, 1975; "Enrollment of Black Freshmen Slowed This Year, Study Indicates," *CHE*, February 11, 1974; "Black Enrollment Rising Again," *CHE*, March 17, 1975; See Susan T. Hill, *Participation of Black Students in Higher Education: A Statistical Profile from 1970–71 to 1980–81* (Washington, DC: National Center for Education Statistics, 1983).

17. Alexander W. Astin, Helen S. Astin, Alan E. Bayer, and Ann S. Bisconti, *The Power of Protest: A National Study of Student and Faculty Disruptions with Implications for the Future* (San Francisco: Jossey-Bass, 1975), pp. 148–149; See Reuben R. McDaniel Jr. and James W. McKee, *An Evaluation of Higher Education's Response to Black Students* (Bloomington, IN: Student Association of Higher Education, 1971).

18. Ama Mazama, ed., *The Afrocentric Paradigm* (Trenton, NJ: Africa World Press, 2003), pp. 4–5.

19. AABL Statement Presented to Dr. Hoffman, UHOU Archives; "Educational Reform Discussion Target," *RU*, October 9, 1970, NMSU Archives; "Racism at Howard," GWU SC; Roy, "Student Activism and the Historically Black University," pp. 69–73 (Masingale

quote); "BSU News Release," *RB*, April 8, 1969, UGA Archives; Students for a Black University, "Week of Reckoning, Toward a Black University" Pamphlet, no date, circa late 1969, FU SC; Paul E. Wisdom and Kenneth A. Shaw, "Black Challenge to Higher Education," *Educational Record* 50 (Fall 1969), pp. 352–353.

20. "No More Inferior Education," *TNA*, March 1969; "Black Student Union," *TNA*, October 1969, WSSU Archives; Jeffrey A. Turner, *Sitting In and Speaking Out: Student Movements in the American South: 1960–1970* (Athens, GA: University of Georgia Press, 2010), pp. 165, 180 (Morehouse and graduate dean quotes).

21. "Student Strikes: 1968–69," *The Black Scholar* 1 (January-February 1970), p. 65.

22. Genna Rae McNeil to the Faculty and Administration of Kalamazoo College, May 19, 1969, Records of the President (R 3/13), box 1, folder 8, KAC Archives.

23. Astin, Astin, Bayer, and Bisconti, *The Power of Protest*, pp. 148–149; McDaniel Jr. and McKee, *An Evaluation of Higher Education's Response to Black Students*; "Education Find Black Studies Are Changing Higher Education," *NYT*, June 4, 1972; "Black Studies on the Rise," *CD*, March 12, 1974; "The State of Black Studies," *CHE*, December 8, 1975; Nick Aaron Ford, *Black Studies: Threat or Challenge* (Port Washington, NY: Kennikat Press, 1973).

24. "Anguish over Relevance Strains Three Social Sciences, Psychologists: One Session Taken Over, Five Dissident Groups Seek Changes," *CHE*, September 15, 1969; "*Disciplines Experiencing Rifts Between Old Guard and Proponents of Change*," *CHE*, September 15, 1969; "Many Geographers Urge Focus on Urban Problems," *CHE*, September 15, 1969.

25. "Two Types of Instructors in Negro Colleges—Daye," *CE*, May 18, 1966; "Prairie View A&M Re-Opens," *SOBU Newsletter*, March 20, 1971, ECSU Archives.

26. "'The New Alcorn,'" *AH*, October 1969, ASU Archives.

27. "Demands Made by Black Caucus," *NS*, May 2, 1969, IUN Archives; "Proposal for Establishing a Black Studies Program," no date, circa late 1960s, Chancellor James Bugg's Papers, 1940–1978, box 1, folder 29, UMSTL Archives; "Education or Indoctrination," *AFT*, October 31, 1972, Presidents Papers: President William L. Giles, accession A81-25, box 49, folder: Student Affairs—Black Students, MSSU Archives; "Statement of the Black Student Alliance," no date,

circa 1968, Student Protest Files of the Vice President for Student Affairs, 1965–1971, box 1050H, folder 11, MSU Archives; Gregory, "'Howard University, 1967–1968,'" p. 428; Barbara Garrison, Statement of the Alliance of Black Students, February 13, 1969, Communication & Media Relations Records (AR 134), box 11, folder 35, UWM Archives.

28. Gilbert L. Lycan, *Stetson University: The First 100 Years* (DeLand, FL: Stetson University Press, 1983), pp. 462–463; "Proposal for Establishing a Black Studies Program," no date, circa late 1960s, Chancellor James Bugg's Papers, 1940–1978, box 1, folder 29, UMSTL Archives.

29. "Black Students Speak Out," *TELB*, 1970, UAK Archives; Black Students Association to Dean of Instruction, "A Minority Report," no date, early 1969, Student Activities Collection, box: NB-STUD-V-BSP, folder: R.U.-N&B-News Releases-General-Black Studies Protest-1969 I, ROSU Archives; The Black Students Alliance of the University of Chicago to Lyndon B. Johnson, March 1, 1968, WHCF Name File: Black, S, LBJL; "Blackwell Calls for End To 'Whitewashing' of Blacks," *XUN*, March 11, 1970, XUO Archives; Gwen Patton to Brothers and Sisters, UKS Archives.

30. "Black Student Union Demands," May 1, 1968, Vertical Files: Black Student Union, 1968–1975, CLAC Archives; "Campus Dis-unity," *Harambee*, February 14, 1969, TOGC Archives.

31. Gregory D. Stanford to John P. Raynor, S.J., November 23, 1967, Office of Student Affairs Records, series 3, box 3, folder: Institutional Racism Protest—Students United for Racial Equality (SURE) Correspondence, 1967–1968, MARU Archives. Two examples of the AP story's publication are "Marquette May Never Be Same," *The Rhinelander Daily News*, May 24, 1968; "Crisis Over, but Marquette May Never Be Same," *Beloit Daily News*, May 24, 1968, All-University Faculty Committee Records, series 3, box 2, folder: Association for Interracial Justice—Students United for Racial Equality (SURE) General Correspondence n.d., MARU Archives.

32. "Tough Responses to Dissent Seen Stifling Reforms," *CHE*, March 10, 1969 (Birenbaum quote); "Gould Foresees Hope and Accomplishment Arising from Today's Agony of Nation's Universities," *CHE*, October 6, 1969 (Gould quote); Harold L. Enarson, "Higher Education and Community Services," in *The Campus and the Racial Crisis*, eds. David C. Nichols and Olive Mills

(Washington, DC: American Council of Education, 1970), p. 241; Robert H. Finch, "Challenge and Response in the American Educational Environment," in *The Campus and the Racial Crisis*, p. 302.

33. "The Negro Colleges: Victims of Progress," *NYT*, October 6, 1969 (Pitts quote); "Black Colleges Offer Negro Youths Road Out of the Ghetto," *CT*, May 24, 1970 (Gates quote).

34. "Black Colleges Starved of Funds," *BG*, December 28, 1969; Henderson, "Blacks and Change in Higher Education," p. 74; "Dowdy Says Leaders Needed," *AJR*, October 3, 1969.

EPILOGUE: BACKLASH AND FORWARD LASHES

1. Peter Louis Goldman, *The Death and Life of Malcolm X* (Urbana, IL: University of Illinois Press, 1979), p. 16.

2. Devin Dwyer and Alexandra Hutzler, "Supreme Court effectively ends affirmative action at colleges in landmark ruling," ABC News, June 29, 2023, https://abcnews.go.com/Politics/supreme-court-sets-new-limits-affirmative-action-programs/story?id=99230954, accessed July 11, 2023; "The SAT's Growing Gaps," *Inside Higher Ed*, August 27, 2008, https://web.archive.org/web/20111106122638/https://www.insidehighered.com/news/2008/08/27/sat, accessed December 14, 2022; Abigail Johnson Hess, "Rich students get better SAT scores—here's why," CNBC, October 3, 2019, https://www.cnbc.com/2019/10/03/rich-students-get-better-sat-scores-heres-why.html, accessed July 11, 2023.

3. I am defining egalitarian exclusion as exclusion utilizing principles of equality, while inclusive exclusion is slightly different—the mutual inclusion and exclusion of African Americans. Amy S. Blodgett, "The Fight for Racial Equality at Dickinson College During the Sixties," pp. 5–6 (unpublished manuscript, May 5, 1982), DICC Archives.

4. "Black Monday," *TNA*, November 1971, WSSU Archives; Student Organization for Black Unity, "Save Black Schools: What Is the Future of Black Higher Education in North Carolina, A Report on the Crisis in Black Higher Education in North Carolina," April 1971,

SOBU Publications, box 2, folder: reports, ECSU Archive; "July Merger Threatens AM&N," *SOBUN*, March 20, 1971.

5. "A.C.E. Special Report," BERC Archives; Reply by Chancellor J. Carlyle Sitterson to Demands Presented by Black Student Movement, January 24, 1969; New University Conference at Chapel Hill, Statement on Chancellor Sittersen's reply to Black Student Movement's demands, February 1, 1969, Office of the Chancellor of North Carolina Chapel Hill: Joseph Carlyle Sitterson Records, 1966–1972 (#40022), box 1, folder: Black Student Movement: Statements, 1968–1969, UNC Archives; Jeffrey Alan Turner, "Conscious and Conflict: Patterns in the History of Activism on Southern College Campuses, 1960–1970" (PhD. diss., Tulane University, 2000), pp. 345–354; "35 Negroes March in Student Protest at North Carolina," *NYT*, February 22, 1969.

6. "Black Protests Air Problems," *CD*, May 25, 1974; Roderick Kieth Linzie, "Analysis of the Anti-Racist Student Movement at the University of Michigan—Ann Arbor" (PhD. diss., University of Michigan, 1993); "Campus Cops End Student Takeover," *CD*, May 6, 1975; "25 Protesters Arrested at Santa Barbara," *CHE*, May 12, 1975; "Student Protest, 1975: Stress on Economic Issues," *CHE*, June 9, 1975.

7. "The Bakke Decision: Attack on Your Civil Rights!" no date, circa 1978, Student Activities Collection, box: NB-STUD-V-BSP, folder: R.U.-N&B-News ReleasesGeneral-Black Studies Protest-1969 I, ROSU Archives; "Demonstration on Bakke Suit," *TWP*, April 16, 1978; "30,000 Join March Against Bakke," *NYAN*, April 22, 1978.

8. Mary Frances Berry, "Atlanta and Affirmative Action, 1973–1980,'" in *Voices of Freedom: An Oral History of the Civil Rights Movement from the 1950s Through the 1980s*, eds. Henry Hampton, Steve Fayer, and Sarah Flynn (New York: Bantam Books, 1990), pp. 644–645.

9. Hampton University Dress Code, accessed August 10, 2011, http://www.hamptonu.edu/student_life/dresscode.cfm.

10. I choose not to define "real diversity," because it differs at every college in America, depending on its location, whether it is private or public, its mission, its local, regional, and national drawing power, and so forth. I think the communities of each institution can define real diversity.

11. *Status and Trends in the Education of Racial and Ethnic Minorities*, National Center for Education Statistics Publication # 2010-015,

July 2010, https://nces.ed.gov/pubs2010/2010015/indicator6_24.asp, accessed July 10, 2023; "Undergraduate Enrollment," *Condition of Education*, National Center for Education Statistics, May 2023, https://nces.ed.gov/programs/coe/indicator/cha, accessed July 10, 2023; "Black Enrollments in Post-Pandemic Higher Education," *Journal of Blacks in Higher Education*, January 2, 2023, https://www.jbhe.com/2023/01/black-enrollments-in-post-pandemic-higher-education/#:~:text=Blacks%20were%2013%20percent%20of,2021%20and%201%2C772.000%20Black%20women, accessed July 10, 2023; Christine Tamir and Monica Anderson, "3. A growing share of Black immigrants have a college degree or higher," Pew Research Center, January 20, 2022, https://www.pewresearch.org/race-ethnicity/2022/01/20/a-growing-share-of-black-immigrants-have-a-college-degree-or-higher/, accessed July 11, 2023; "Table 318.45. Number and percentage distribution of science, technology, engineering, and mathematics (STEM) degrees/certificates conferred by postsecondary institutions, by race/ethnicity, level of degree/certificate, and sex of student: Academic years 2011–12 through 2020–21," *Digest of Education Statistics*, National Center for Education Statistics, September 2022, https://nces.ed.gov/programs/digest/d22/tables/dt22_318.45.asp, accessed July 11, 2023; Catherine Riegle-Crumb, Barbara King, and Yasmiyn Irizarry, "Does STEM Stand Out? Examining Racial/Ethnic Gaps in Persistence Across Postsecondary Fields," *Educational Researcher* 48 (2019), https://doi.org/10.3102/0013189X19831006; "College Enrollment Rates," *Condition of Education*, National Center for Education Statistics, May 2023, https://nces.ed.gov/programs/coe/indicator/cpb/college-enrollment-rate#:~:text=The%20college%20enrollment%20rate%20in,Alaska%20Native%20(28%20percent); E. Ann Carson, "Prisoners in 2021—Statistical Tables," U.S. Bureau of Justice Statistics, Statistical Tables, NCJ 305125, December 2022, https://bjs.ojp.gov/sites/g/files/xyckuh236/files/media/document/p21st.pdf, p. 10; Michelle Alexander, *The New Jim Crow: Mass Incarceration in the Age of Colorblindness* (New York: The New Press, 2010); Noliwe Rooks, *White Money/Black Power: The History of African American Studies and the Crisis of Race in Higher Education* (Boston: Beacon Press, 2006).
12. Emma Whitford, "'There Are So Few That Have Made Their Way,'" *Insider Higher Ed*, October 27, 2020, https://www.insidehighered.com/news/2020/10/28/black-administrators-are-too-rare-top-

ranks-higher-education-it's-not-just-pipeline, accessed July 10, 2023; "Characteristics of Postsecondary Faculty," *Condition of Education*, National Center for Education Statistics, May 31, 2022, https:// nces.ed.gov/fastfacts/display.asp?id=61, accessed July 10, 2023; Richard Chait and Cathy Tower, "Professors at the Color Line," *NYT*, September 11, 2001, https://www.nytimes.com/2001/09/11/ opinion/professors-at-the-color-line.html, accessed July 10, 2023; Colleen Flaherty, "Faculty Diversification Must Accelerate, Report Says," *Inside Higher Ed*, December 5, 2022, https://www.insidehigh-ered.com/news/2022/12/06/study-finds-true-faculty-diversity-possible-2050, accessed July 11, 2023; "Table 1-11: U.S. citizen and permanent resident research doctorate recipients, by historical broad field of doctorate, ethnicity, and race: Selected years, 1976–2021," *Survey of Earned Doctorates*, National Science Foundation, National Center for Science and Engineering Statistics, 2022, https://ncses.nsf.gov/pubs/nsf23300/table/1-11, accessed July 10, 2023.

13. Rooks, *White Money/Black Power*, p. 78 (Bundy quote); Robert Allen, "Politics of the Attack on Black Studies," *Black Scholar* 6 (September 1974), pp. 2, 5.

14. Robert McCray to Daniel Walker, March 16, 1973, Chancellor's Central Files (RG # 3-1-2), series 3, box 51, folder 725, UIC Archives.

15. Fabio Rojas, *From Black Power to Black Studies: How a Radical Social Movement Became an Academic Discipline* (Baltimore: The John Hopkins University Press, 2007), p. 21; "Africana Studies Graduate Programs," National Council for Black Studies, https://ncbsonline.org/students/as-grad-programs/, accessed July 11, 2023; "Emory established first African American studies PhD program in the Southeast," Emory News Center, Emory University, October 24, 2022, https://news.emory.edu/stories/2022/10/er_african_amer-ican_phd_24-10-2022/story.html, accessed July 11, 2023; Ashley Quincin, "AAAD department compiling graduate curriculum, hiring faculty," *The Daily Tar Heel*, February 21, 2023, https://www.daily-tarheel.com/article/2023/02/university-aaad-graduate-program-coming, accessed July 11, 2023.

16. Nathan Hare, "Appendix 4: A Conceptual Proposal for a Department of Black Studies," in William H. Orrick, *Shut It Down! A College in Crisis: San Francisco State College October, 1968–April 1969* (Washington, DC: US Government Printing Office, 1969), pp. 160–161.

Index

© The Author(s), under exclusive license to Springer Nature Switzerland AG 2025
I. X. Kendi, *The Black Campus Movement*, Contemporary Black History, https://doi.org/10.1007/978-3-031-37394-7